Global Business and the Terrorist Threat

Global Business and the Terrorist Threat

Edited by

Harry W. Richardson
University of Southern California, USA

Peter Gordon
University of Southern California, USA

and

James E. Moore II
University of Southern California, USA

Edward Elgar
Cheltenham, UK • Northampton, MA, USA

© Harry W. Richardson, Peter Gordon and James E. Moore II 2009

All rights reserved. No part of this publication may be reproduced, stored in a retrieval system or transmitted in any form or by any means, electronic, mechanical or photocopying, recording, or otherwise without the prior permission of the publisher.

Published by
Edward Elgar Publishing Limited
The Lypiatts
15 Lansdown Road
Cheltenham
Glos GL50 2JA
UK

Edward Elgar Publishing, Inc.
William Pratt House
9 Dewey Court
Northampton
Massachusetts 01060
USA

A catalogue record for this book
is available from the British Library

Library of Congress Control Number: 2009922763

PEFC
PEFC/16-33-111
CATG-PEFC-052
www.pefc.org

ISBN 978 1 84720 850 7 (cased)

Printed and bound by MPG Books Group, UK

Contents

List of contributors		vii
Preface and acknowledgements		ix
1.	Introduction	1
	Harry W. Richardson, Peter Gordon and James E. Moore II	
2.	Globalization, global business and global terrorism: the value of mutual support	10
	Michael D. Intriligator	
3.	Business continuity: a systematic approach	23
	Yossi Sheffi	
4.	Assessing, managing and benefiting from global interdependent risks: the case of terrorism and natural disasters	42
	Howard C. Kunreuther and Erwann O. Michel-Kerjan	
5.	NBCR terrorism: who should bear the risk?	74
	Dwight Jaffee and Thomas Russell	
6.	The resilient response to economic terrorist targeting in the UK	92
	Jon Coaffee	
7.	Terrorism, news flows and stock markets	119
	Thomas Baumert	
8.	Dancing with wolves: avoiding transnational corporation interactions with terrorist groups	136
	Dean C. Alexander	
9.	The impact of 9/11 on airport passenger density and regional travel	148
	Garrett R. Beeler Asay and Jeffrey Clemens	
10.	The effect of transnational terrorism on bilateral trade	169
	Quan Li	
11.	A global business strategy for North Korea	187
	Harry W. Richardson and Chang-Hee Christine Bae	
12.	The economic impacts of international border closure: a state-by-state analysis	201
	Peter Gordon, James E. Moore II, Jiyoung Park and Harry W. Richardson	

13. Macroeconomic impacts of shutting down the US borders in response to a security or health threat 228
    Adam Z. Rose, Garrett R. Beeler Asay, Dan Wei and Billy Leung
14. Challenges of benefit–cost analyses for terrorism security regulations: observations from regulatory analysis of the Western Hemisphere Travel Initiative 271
    Henry H. Willis and Tom LaTourrette

Index 289

Contributors

Dean C. Alexander, Director of the Homeland Security Research Program, Department of Law Enforcement and Justice Administration, Western Illinois University, USA.

Chang-Hee Christine Bae, Associate Professor, Department of Urban Design and Planning, University of Washington, Seattle, USA.

Thomas Baumert, Professor of Applied Economics, Universidad Catolica de Valencia and Fellow, Universidad Complutense de Madrid – CET, Spain.

Garrett R. Beeler Asay, Research Scientist, Center for Disease Control, Atlanta, USA.

Jeffrey Clemens, Department of Economics, Harvard University, USA.

Jon Coaffee, Senior Lecturer in Spatial Planning (Urban Regeneration), School of Environment and Development, University of Manchester, UK.

Peter Gordon, Professor of Planning, School of Policy, Planning and Development, University of Southern California, Los Angeles, USA.

Michael D. Intriligator, Professor of Economics, Political Science and Public Policy, University of California, Los Angeles, USA.

Dwight Jaffee, Willis Booth Professor, Banking and Finance, Haas School of Business, University of California, Berkeley, USA.

Howard C. Kunreuther, Cecilia Yen Koo Professor of Decision Sciences and Public Policy, Wharton School of Business, University of Pennsylvania, USA.

Tom LaTourrette, Senior Physical Scientist, RAND Corporation, Santa Monica, California, USA.

Billy Leung, Regional Econometric Models, Inc., Amherst, MA, USA.

Quan Li, Professor of Political Science, Department of Political Science, Texas A & M University, USA.

Erwann O. Michel-Kerjan, Managing Director, Wharton Risk Management and Decision Processes Center, Wharton School of Business, University of Pennsylvania, USA.

James E. Moore II, Chair, Department of Industrial and Systems Engineering, Viterbi School of Engineering, and Professor of Policy, Planning and Development, University of Southern California, Los Angeles, USA.

Jiyoung Park, Assistant Professor, Department of Urban and Regional Planning, State University of New York, Buffalo, USA.

Harry W. Richardson, The James Irvine Chair of Urban and Regional Planning, School of Policy, Planning and Development, and Professor of Economics, University of Southern California, Los Angeles, USA.

Adam Z. Rose, Research Professor, School of Policy, Planning and Development, University of Southern California, Los Angeles.

Thomas Russell, Associate Professor of Economics, Leavey School of Business, Santa Clara University, California, USA.

Yossi Sheffi, Professor of Civil and Environmental Engineering and Director of the Center for Transportation Studies, Massachusetts Institute of Technology, Cambridge, MA, USA.

Dan Wei, Pennsylvania State University, USA.

Henry H. Willis, Policy Researcher, RAND Corporation, Pittsburgh, PA, USA.

Preface and acknowledgements

This book had its origins in a two-day symposium held at the University of Southern California in August 2007. This is the fourth and last in a series organized by the current editorial team. Other symposia and books will take place at CREATE (Center for Risk and Economic Analysis of Terrorism Events) but under different editors. This research was supported by the United States Department of Homeland Security through CREATE under grant number 2007-ST-061-000001. However, any opinions, findings, and conclusions or recommendations in this document are those of the authors and do not necessarily reflect views of the United States Department of Homeland Security. The research was also supported by the United States Department of Education under its CIBER (Centers for International Business Education Research) program. We are grateful to our University of Southern California colleagues, Detlof Von Winterfeldt (CREATE) and Richard Drobnick (CIBER), for their continuous support for this project.

1. Introduction
Harry W. Richardson, Peter Gordon and James E. Moore II

This book is an eclectic collection of chapters that explores the relationships between global business and terrorism. The rationale for the book is clear. One of the sponsors of this research, the Department of Homeland Security, has spent large sums of money inside the United States to protect the homeland, but has devoted little attention, at least openly, to the international aspects of terrorism and how its threats can affect the global economy.

There are many examples of the potential links between global business and terrorism, some of which (but not all) are discussed in this book. One important example is how a major terrorist attack in a Western country might affect the global economy, typically by a crash in world stock markets. Baumert's chapter (Chapter 7) sheds some light on this by showing that the Madrid train bombing had a modest and short-term impact on stock markets. However, we should not generalize from a single case.

Another example is what might be the consequences of an attack on a multinational corporation. There have been a few individual abductions and assassinations, but no massive attack. Alexander's chapter (Chapter 8) shows how a multinational corporation caved in to threats by paying protection money, but this was not in response to a direct major attack. There have been several attacks in the Nigerian oil sector, for instance, but they have not received much attention and appear to be more locally inspired than related to international terrorism. If there were attacks on major corporations, this could have significant repercussions by raising operating costs in the form of protection or by resulting in a pull-out from a region or even a country.

An especially vulnerable aspect of global business that is vulnerable to terrorist attacks is oil and natural gas pipelines, especially outside the United States (70 percent of US oil consumption is from overseas and transferred locally via pipelines). Some pipelines have been attacked many times, but with minimal long-term disruptions probably because the pipelines are relatively easy to repair. Nevertheless, because of their isolation and long distances, pipelines are very difficult to protect so there is a possibility that a small number of simultaneous attacks at a few strategic locations could be much more damaging.

An interesting idea suggested by Napoleoni (2003) is that international terrorism is itself a global business in the sense that terrorist organizations have raised funds for terrorist activities by investing in profitable businesses. A widely quoted example is that while in Sudan in 1997, Bin Laden invested heavily in the Gum Arabic Co., of which 80 percent of its output was exported to the United States. One estimate, quoted by Napoleoni but not clearly substantiated, is that the global terrorism business is worth $1.5 trillion. A related but unsupported argument is that terrorists, being aware of 9/11 in advance, indulged in insider trading to take advantage of post-9/11 stock market changes. There is no firm evidence for these arguments, although it is clear that international terrorism has derived some funding from direct or indirect business activities.

Yet another possibility, hinted at by Intriligator (Chapter 2), is the opportunities for global businesses to counter terrorism via a range of activities from consultancy services to developing new technologies for protective devices and systems. There are again no hard data on the scale of this business, but judging by the number and size of business shows and conventions as proxy variables, this appears to be a rapidly growing business.

In his chapter (Chapter 3), Sheffi discusses the importance of 'business continuity'; a more general term might be 'business resilience'. One of the surprising immediate consequences of 9/11 was the speed of adjustment by downtown Manhattan firms impacted by the attack to continue their businesses at satellite locations in New Jersey and elsewhere. As a result, many large corporations have now developed contingency plans to open up offices elsewhere away from their headquarters; some have even decentralized completely to locations less at risk.

The second part of this Introduction is a brief review of the chapters in this book. As pointed out by Intriligator (Chapter 2), globalization is a powerful real aspect of the new world system, and it represents one of the most influential forces in determining the future course of the planet. It has manifold dimensions: economic, security, political and others. Two important aspects of globalization are global business and global terrorism, with the two linked. This chapter discusses these links and evaluates how the two influence each other, including how global terrorism makes use of global business and how global business could play a major role in reducing the dangers of global terrorism. Global business could have an important role as a major player in the development of new global institutions that would combine public and private interests on a multinational basis to counter global terrorism, challenging the acquisition of various resources by global terrorists.

Sheffi's chapter (Chapter 3) suggests a comprehensive framework for thinking about and applying business continuity at the corporate level. It looks at the role of security; the role of planning in creating options for response and resilience; how detection should be integrated into the framework both for 'expected' and 'unexpected' disruptions; the execution of business continuity; and issues of corporate culture beyond planning for bouncing back from disruptions.

Operational planning in every company takes into account several sources of uncertainty. The main one is customer demand, but other sources of uncertainty include manufacturing yield, the quality of parts, late deliveries and other normal fluctuations. The chapter focuses on high-impact, low-probability disruptive events for which the normal recovery means of keeping extra inventory or increasing overtime are not enough. In fact, many of these events can result in the loss of the business.

The chapter also classifies the sources of such events and then outlines an organization's possible responses. During these recovery activities the organization can only adopt options that were prepared and planned ahead of time. The chapter then outlines the planning activities which should be undertaken to generate these options, and describes corporate culture issues that go beyond a narrow definition of business continuity planning.

Kunreuther and Michel-Kerjan (Chapter 4) explain that increasing globalization of economic and social activities worldwide makes catastrophic risks more and more global because of interdependencies across sectors and over time. A hallmark of the twenty-first century is a new era of catastrophic risks, with pressure for the private and public sectors to react very quickly even though they cannot always predict the impact that their actions will have.

Managing global risks under conditions of uncertainty, interdependency and competing interests is not simple. Three years ago, the World Economic Forum (WEF) launched the Global Risks Initiative to address the issues related to these events, under a joint initiative with several large companies and the Wharton Risk Management and Decision Processes Center at the University of Pennsylvania. Building on the WEF Global Risks 2007 report, this chapter applies pathways to mitigation of the risks of terrorism and natural disasters by both the private and public sectors. These pathways include improving insight, enhancing information flow, refocusing incentives and improving investment.

The chapter also explores the decision-making processes of individuals that are critical to developing better strategies and public policies for mitigating global risks. One of the biggest challenges in implementing these strategies is overcoming the tendency to focus only on immediate pay-offs. Because of myopia, individuals and firms require a sufficient return in the short run to justify the upfront costs of protection. We often decide not to invest in risk-reducing measures because we fail to consider that the expected benefits from these options are likely to extend over many years.

Jaffee and Russell (Chapter 5) extend the discussion on similar lines, but to more complicated issues. Terrorists equipped with unconventional weapons (also known as nuclear, biological, chemical and radiological or NBCR weapons) present a real and present threat of creating catastrophic losses for the US, as well as for many other countries in the world. NBCR risks have long been excluded from many insurance policies in the US and other countries, even though the risk-sharing created by insurance would clearly be welfare enhancing. Since the 9/11 terrorist attack, however, the US and other countries have created government programs that backstop at least some of the losses that would be created by terrorist attacks, in some cases including, and other cases excluding, losses created by NBCR attacks.

In the chapter, the authors begin by exploring the reasons why NBCR risks are so often excluded from insurance coverage, starting with the historical context and finishing with the recently created government programs. Not surprisingly, the dominant reason is the magnitude of the possible losses, which could well exceed the resources available to a country's insurance industry. The chapter then focuses on solutions, including the possibility of unifying resources on a worldwide basis through either reinsurance entities or the capital markets directly.

Coaffee (Chapter 6) turns his attention to London. The early 1990s witnessed a noticeable targeting of global cities and in particular their economic infrastructure by terrorist organizations in order to attract global media publicity and cause severe insurance losses and disruptions in trade. In London the Provisional IRA (Irish Republican Army) successfully attacked a number of key economic targets in the 1990s with large bombs exploding within the London financial core. These bombings, and the subsequent reaction of the urban authorities, served to highlight the need for more advanced approaches of counter-terrorism and new forms of terrorism insurance, in order to stop the relocation of international business and to protect the image of the UK economy.

In the chapter, the response of central London authorities both pre- and post-9/11 is used as the lens through which to view attempts to reduce the real and perceived threat of terrorist attacks against economic infrastructure in the UK, including a consideration of the main provincial cities identified as key terrorist targets. Increasingly, such responses are seen in terms of attempts to embed 'resilience' into the managerial and urban design responses of both local and national government in order to reduce risk and give confidence to business communities by enhanced securitization of the public realm and more proactive contingency planning.

Baumert (Chapter 7) explores another European case, the Madrid rail bombings of 11 March 2003, with some comparison with the New York City attack of 9/11 and the London attacks of 7 July 2005, specifically focusing on the impact with respect to international stock markets. The financial markets' reactions to these events are especially relevant, as they reflect immediate investor perceptions about the short- and medium-term economic impact of the attacks *ceteris paribus* (normally no additional information except that referring to the attacks is considered). Thus, financial markets are the first to transform the news of a terrorist attack efficiently into economic information.

As for the determining elements of the stock exchange reaction in the specific case of the March 11 attacks, it can be seen that there were two key factors which influenced market trends: the number of victims (the only objective measurement available to investors when quantifying the magnitude of the attacks), and who was responsible for them (and the probabilities of whether they might spread to the rest of Europe).

Comparing the sequential impacts of 11 March, 11 September and 7 July, both the intensities and durations of the reactions became smaller. On the one hand, this has been because of effective macroeconomic responses (assuring liquidity, suspending electronic trading and controlling the news flow). On the other hand, most large firms with their headquarters in big cities have developed evacuation plans which enable them to transfer their business very quickly from a central location in the City to alternative suburban or other peripheral locations. These plans enable business to continue with minimal interruption.

Alexander (Chapter 8) examines a case study of a very different type. In March 2007 US-headquartered Chiquita Brands International (CBI) admitted to engaging in financial transactions with the right-wing Colombian terrorist group Autodefensas Unidas de Colombia. The case provides an example of how collaboration (almost conspiracy) may arise between transnational companies and terrorist groups based in host countries.

The chapter provides an analysis of the CBI case and sheds light on the challenges such firms face doing business in politically unstable environments. It addresses the disparate steps global firms may pursue should they face similar circumstances. The study then analyzes the multifaceted implications of several alternatives. The study concludes that terrorist activity injects another layer of complexity that companies have to contend with while doing business abroad.

The research in Asay and Clemens (Chapter 9) aims to understand changes in the patterns of air travel within the United States after 9/11, with particular attention paid to two hypotheses. First, it considers the hypothesis that large and high-volume airports were hurt more relative to lower-volume airports. Second, it examines the regional impacts of 9/11 on air travel and large airports. Key ideas are that getting through security is easier in small airports and that the risks of an attack are lower there because of much less visibility. It is also possible, however, that the finding of advantage to smaller airports is explained by pre-existing trends in the market for air travel, for example the emergence of low-cost airlines that concentrated on smaller airports. The chapter was not able to tease out further the extent to which the results can be attributed to 9/11 itself. However, there is no evidence that East Coast airports were more adversely affected than West Coast airports, despite the fact that 9/11 was primarily an East Coast attack. Nevertheless, it is possible that such an impact might be observable in data on international passenger traffic via shifts away from the US to other countries and/or to non-US airlines as a result of changes in travel behavior when individuals have higher perceived risk (or fear). In addition, leisure travel is more susceptible to the fear factor than business travel because the marginal fear factor declines rapidly with the number of trips taken. Similarly, tourist destinations suffer more than other destinations.

Current research on the effects of transnational terrorist attacks on international commerce has found evidence that terrorism reduces bilateral trade flows. One problem with the existing research is that the indicators of terrorism employed are measured at the country level. As a result they reflect country attributes more than the effects of 'directional' terrorist attacks. It is plausible that the country-level terrorism indicators merely reflect the overall risk environment for businesses in a country, not terrorism per se. Furthermore, many terrorist attacks involve an attacker from one particular country and a target in another. To gauge accurately the effect of terrorism on trade between countries, one should directly examine the effect of a terrorist incident involving an attacker from one country against a target in another. The idea is that such bilateral terrorist attacks more closely reflect the affinity and quality of the relationship between citizens in the two relevant countries, and hence better represent the actual risk posed to traders in the two countries.

This effect is empirically evaluated and estimated by Li (Chapter 10) within a gravity model framework using bilateral trade data and transnational terrorist attacks data from 1968 to 2000. The findings provide a better assessment and estimation of the effect of terrorism on international commerce. The study tests for the implications of controlling for unobservables, political ties between governments of country pairs, and subsamples based on development stage. There is no consistent evidence that terrorist incidents within countries reduce bilateral trade flows. Bilateral terrorist attacks only reduce bilateral trade in country pairs that involve at least one advanced economy. Overall, the evidence is too weak to support the view that transnational terrorism reduces bilateral trade flows. The finding suggests caution in estimating the impact of terrorist attacks on commerce.

North Korea has a terrorist past, primarily against South Korea. Today, the threat is more indirect, supplying weapons (possibly even weapons of mass destruction) to terrorists around the world and/or rogue nations. The reunification of the Korean peninsula might resolve these concerns. Would an improvement in the North Korean economy assist in this goal, and can, and should, the rest of the world contribute? Currently, only South Korea and China are investing in the North. If the strategy is justifiable, it would probably require a combination of public investment by governments (primarily in infrastructure projects that have a problematic payback) and private investment by transnational corporations (focusing on job creation in export activities). However, the risks to foreign direct investment prior to reunification are huge, pending resolution of the political instability problem.

Richardson and Bae (Chapter 11) place this discussion in the context of alternative reunification strategies: a sudden R-day (Reunification Day), that is, the German model; and the TP (transition phase) approach that requires actions both before and after reunification. The chapter argues that the TP approach is preferable (in part because of the economic implications for South Korea), but that its success would depend on the participation of global business and international financial institutions. The research illustrates this argument with two case studies, the Kaesong Industrial Complex and the Tumen River Project. The Kaesong project, while perhaps overambitious, is quite promising, while the Tumen River Project is hitherto very problematic.

The possibility of an international avian influenza pandemic has suggested to policy-makers the need to consider the possibility of border closures to interrupt trade, international business travel, tourism and immigration. In an era of significant globalization, the costs of such measures are substantial. On the other hand, the duration of a worst-case outbreak could be as long as a year and hundreds of thousands of Americans could die. In this light, extreme measures may have to be contemplated. Gordon et al. (Chapter 12) apply NIEMO (a 47-sector, 50-state National Interstate Economic Model), the first operational multiregional input–output model, to simulate these possible impacts, their magnitude, and their spatial incidence. The research considers the loss of imports and exports (but allows for exporters and importers to mitigate impacts by trading with each other domestically), an interruption to international travel, the loss of tourism, and the loss of immigrant labor and cross-border interactions. Border closures of different levels of intensity and different durations are analyzed. The results must be assessed carefully in light of the uncertainties involved and the fact that this could be an extreme event (possibly resulting in a 14 percent decline in US gross domestic product, GDP) outside the normal range of the data used to estimate the model. Nevertheless, the estimated costs of border closure and the benefits (the dollar value of lives saved and health expenses minimized) are sufficiently close to each other that closing the border merits serious attention as a mitigation strategy if a pandemic breaks out.

Rose et al. (Chapter 13) analyze the same problem, but use a different type of model (more macro rather than spatial), and examine alternative types of threats and various durations and degrees of border closure. Given that the US economy is highly dependent on international mobility of goods and people, the economic impacts of a partial or total border closure are significant. Major economic impacts would stem from four factors. First, the US imports a significant volume of both intermediate and final goods. Second, its exports are an important source of foreign exchange, and the United States may face retaliation in the form of import bans on its goods if it imposes restrictions on goods coming in from other countries. Third, international visitors are a significant stimulus to the US economy. Fourth, in-migration provides important workers at all skill levels.

The research analyzes the impacts of the curtailment of all of these actions using the REMI (Regional Economic Models Inc.) Economic Forecasting and Simulation Model. The analysis is performed via a set of comparative static simulations to isolate the impact of each aspect of a curtailment as well as a comprehensive simulation to identify interaction effects. In addition, resilience actions are factored in to minimize the potential shock at both the individual business and market levels. These include the use of inventories, excess capacity, conservation, domestic input substitution in response to price changes, redirecting exports to domestic input needs, and rescheduling lost production to a later date.

In the final chapter (Chapter 14), Willis and LaTourrette explore some of the problems involved in applying cost–benefit analysis to terrorism security problems. Under the authority of Executive Order 12866, the White House Office of Management and Budget directs agencies to conduct regulatory impact analyses to evaluate the benefits and costs of proposed regulations. However, conducting cost–benefit analyses of terrorism security efforts is difficult for several reasons, including: uncertainty about terrorism threats; lack of data on the effects of security measures in reducing terrorism risks; and the possible occurrence of catastrophes that experts suggest are low-probability events. The chapter discusses the challenges posed by each of these factors as well as approaches to addressing them within the context of a Department of Homeland Security regulation (the Western Hemisphere Travel Initiative) to be fully implemented by June 2009.

REFERENCE

Napoleoni, L. (2003), *Modern Jihad: Tracing the Dollars Behind the Terror Networks*, New York: Pluto Press.

2. Globalization, global business and global terrorism: the value of mutual support
Michael D. Intriligator

INTRODUCTION: GLOBALIZATION, GLOBAL TERRORISM AND MUTUAL SUPPORT

Global terrorism and global business are two important aspects of the current wave of globalization. This chapter emphasizes the value of mutual support in countering global terrorism, ranging from local law enforcement agencies and first responders, as in the Los Angeles County Sheriff's Department Terrorism Early Warning (TEW) unit, to corporations, states and regions, up to and including nations and international organizations. A historical example of such mutual support is the aid from over a century ago that the citizens of Los Angeles provided San Francisco after its 1906 earthquake and fire, where they sent a train filled with relief supplies of food, medicine, tents, blankets, and so on that arrived just one day after the disaster. Local jurisdictions like Los Angeles have mutual aid agreements with other jurisdictions, but it is not clear how well they will work in a major disaster such as a terrorist strike using weapons of mass destruction, including nuclear weapons, which may happen (see Katona et al. 2006, and especially Intriligator and Toukan, 2006; see also Allison, 2005, 2006). Also illustrative of such mutual support are the examples in the recent Yossi Sheffi book, *The Resilient Enterprise* (Sheffi, 2005), of companies helping each other in emergency situations, whether natural disasters or terrorist strikes. Current anti-terrorism entities, whether at the national level such as the US Department of Homeland Security, or at the international level, could well learn the value of augmenting their use of such mutual support from the experience of local first responders as well as that of business entities. In addition, global business could play an important role in depriving global terrorist organizations, such as al-Qaeda, of resources needed to conduct terrorist acts.

GLOBALIZATION AND PARALLELS BETWEEN TODAY AND 1913

There has been much recent discussion of globalization, which is a reality in the current world system. As discussed in Intriligator (2004), globalization is a powerful real aspect of the new world system, and it represents one of the most influential forces in determining the future evolution of the planet. It has manifold dimensions: economic, political, security, environmental, health, social, cultural, and others. The term was coined in the 1980s, and it was a guiding principle as well as a slogan of the US Clinton administration from 1993 to 2001, as discussed in Brzezinski (2007). The concept, however, is an old one that has different interpretations for different people. Partly as a result of these different interpretations, there are very different reactions to 'globalization', with some policy-makers, scholars and activists seeing it as a force for advancing the world economy, and others seeing it as a serious danger to the world economic system. Intriligator (2004) provides a discussion of the benefits and costs of globalization and a net assessment that concludes that globalization can be a positive force in a world featuring cooperation to solve common problems but, conversely, a negative force in a world without such cooperation.

'Globalization' will be understood here to mean major increases in worldwide trade and exchanges in an increasingly open, integrated and virtually borderless international economy. There has been remarkable growth since 1960 in such trade and exchanges, not only in traditional international trade in goods and services, but also in exchange of currencies, in capital movements, in technology transfer, in people moving through international travel and migration, and in international flows of information and ideas, as well as in other global flows.

Globalization has built on greater openness in the international economy, the integration of markets on a worldwide basis, and a movement toward a borderless world, all of which have led to such increases in global flows. There are several sources of globalization over the last several decades. One such source has been the technological advances and competition that have significantly lowered the costs of transportation and communication, and dramatically lowered the costs of data processing and information storage and retrieval. The latter stems from developments over the last few decades in electronics, especially the microchip and computer revolutions. Electronic mail, the Internet, wireless technology and the World Wide Web are some of the manifestations of this new technology, where today's $2000 laptop computer is many times more powerful than a $10 million mainframe computer of a generation ago.

A second source of globalization has been trade liberalization and other changes in economic policy that have led to reductions in trade protection and to a more open world trading system. The current process of liberalization started after World War II with the most-favored-nation approach to trade liberalization, as embodied in the 1946 General Agreement on Tariffs and Trade (GATT) that evolved into the World Trade Organization (WTO) in 1995. As a result, there have been significant reductions in tariffs and other barriers to trade in goods and services. Other aspects of such liberalization have led to increases in the movement of capital, labor, energy, knowledge and other factors of production.

It should not be forgotten, however, that the current age of globalization is just the latest manifestation of this phenomenon that has recurred throughout history. There have been repeated waves of globalization, going back at least to the Mongol empire and the empires of Alexander the Great and Tamerlane (Timur) as well as the Roman Empire. The last wave of globalization, extending over the century from the end of the Napoleonic Wars in the 1815 Congress of Vienna to the outbreak of World War I in 1914, and embodied in the colonial system, ended with four disastrous blows. The first was World War I, the so-called 'War to End All Wars'; the second was the influenza pandemic of 1918–19, that killed more people than most of the wars ever fought; the third was the Great Depression starting in October 1929; and the fourth was World War II, starting in Europe in 1939 and even earlier in Asia, the greatest war ever fought on the planet. In addition there were rebellions against the colonial system, which included episodes of terrorism. The global system today must be prepared to deal with comparable challenges in the future, including wars, pandemics, economic depression and other threats that could recur. In 1905, just before these four blows materialized, the Harvard philosopher George Santayana wrote: 'Those who cannot remember the past are condemned to repeat it.' We should recognize that the world system of the twenty-first century could possibly go the same disastrous route as that of the twentieth century. We should consider, as Santayana warned, the possible repetition of these earlier disasters and how they could be avoided through effective reforms and, in particular, a revitalization of the global system. Indeed, there are disquieting similarities between what was about to occur in 1913, on the eve of World War I, and now: then the unprecedented threat of extreme nationalism and now that of global Islamist terrorism; then the Spanish flu pandemic and now a potential avian flu pandemic; as well as the possibility of major wars and recessions or depressions. It is therefore vital that organizations at all levels, ranging from local institutions to nations to international institutions, including global businesses, take the initiative in dealing with today's issues and major threats to the international system, including global terrorism.

GLOBAL BUSINESS

The emergence of global business that evolved from transnational business is an important aspect of globalization. Indeed, another major source of today's globalization has been changes in institutions, where organizations, including businesses, have a wider reach. This change has been due, in part, to technological changes and to the more wide-ranging horizons of managers, who have been empowered by advances in communications. Thus, corporations that had in earlier epochs been mainly focused on local markets have extended their range in terms of markets and production facilities to a national, multinational, transnational and, increasingly, global reach. These changes in industrial structure have led to increases in the productivity, profits and power of those firms that can choose among many nations for their sources of materials, production facilities, markets and ideas, quickly adjusting to changing market conditions. Virtually every major national or international enterprise has such a structure or relies on subsidiaries or strategic alliances to obtain a comparable degree of influence and flexibility.

As one measure of this change in industrial structure, almost a third of total international trade now occurs solely within multinational enterprises. As another measure, the number of global businesses has increased from some 7000 in 1968 to 35,000 in 1990 and to 45,000 by the year 2000. Their size has also increased dramatically, with the United Nations Conference on Trade and Development (UNCTAD) finding that, of the largest 100 economic entities in the world in 2000, 29 were global corporations, the remaining 71 being nations. As one example, ExxonMobil, the largest corporation, ranked 45th on this list, at about the same size as Chile and Pakistan. The combined sales of the world's largest 200 corporations are far greater than a quarter of the world's economic activity and are bigger than the combined economies of all countries minus the biggest nine; that is, they surpass the combined economies of 182 countries. Wal-Mart, the number 12 corporation, is bigger than 161 countries, including Israel, Poland and Greece. Mitsubishi is economically larger than the fourth most populous nation on earth, Indonesia; General Motors is bigger than Denmark; Ford is bigger than South Africa; and Toyota is bigger than Norway.

With the advent of such global firms, international conflict has, to some extent, moved from nations to these firms, with the battle no longer among nations over territory but rather among firms over their share of world markets. These global firms are seen by some as a threat to the scope and autonomy of the state, but while these firms are powerful and growing, the nation state still retains its traditional dominant role in the world economic and political system and is likely to remain in this role.

These global firms are also partly a stimulus to terrorism, as many people resent their role and influence in the global economy. Compounding this perception is the fact that these global firms typically have their headquarters in advanced industrialized nations. The vast majority, 186, of the largest 200 firms have their headquarters in just seven countries: Japan, the United States, Germany, France, the United Kingdom, the Netherlands and Switzerland.

GLOBAL TERRORISM

Terrorism is 'the premeditated use or threat to use violence by individuals or subnational groups in order to obtain a political or social objective through the intimidation of a large audience beyond that of the immediate victims' (Enders and Sandler, 2005). Terrorism has also become a global phenomenon in what amounts to yet another manifestation of globalization. What was formerly a phenomenon of nations, such as Ireland, Sri Lanka and Israel, and, earlier, a tactic used in the developing world's struggle for independence from the colonial empires of Britain, France, Holland, Belgium and other great powers, has evolved from a regional to a multinational and even global phenomenon due to the same trends noted earlier. For example, the terrorist organization responsible for the 11 September 2001 attacks on the US in New York and Washington, DC, al-Qaeda ('the base'), which had earlier operated in Sudan, then Afghanistan and Pakistan, is now a global organization with branches in Great Britain, Morocco, Iraq, Indonesia the Philippines and elsewhere. It has, in fact, learned from global business entities such as McDonald's and Starbucks the value of franchising, setting up franchise operations in many nations. Indeed, Osama bin Laden has run his operations in Sudan and Afghanistan and now in Pakistan like a multinational corporation. By contrast, the US after the September 11th attacks set up a hierarchical organization, the Department of Homeland Security (DHS), to counter al-Qaeda and other terrorist organizations, that was shown to be dysfunctional in the aftermath of hurricanes Katrina and Rita. The terrorists have created dispersed and flat organizations, while the DHS, the main US antiterrorist organization, is one that is concentrated and top-heavy, attempting to pull together many prior agencies and operations that do not fit together and cannot work together. Global terrorist organizations, including al-Qaeda, have also borrowed from global business the value of modern technology, making extensive use of the Web, the Internet, cellphones, and so on for purposes of communication, recruitment, training, fund-raising, planning, identification of targets (for example via Google World), and so on.

The phenomenon of global terrorism has made most industrialized countries highly vulnerable to terrorist attacks due to the globalization of communications, the development of international transport (notably air transport), the concentration of populations and resources in urban zones, and so on. For many reasons – including the growth of grievances, particularly those toward the US and Europe; religious fanaticism; the advent of weak or failed transitional states; the diffusion of technology; the composition of the population, with more single young men who may become recruits for the terrorists; extremist ideologies; global funding; the growth of transnational crime organizations; and other factors – there will in all likelihood be a continuation of high levels or even the growth of global terrorism in the foreseeable future. These factors are discussed by a Norwegian expert on terrorism, Brynjar Lia, in his authoritative and comprehensive book, *Globalization and the Future of Terrorism: Patterns and Predictions*, which concludes by stating that there are 'important structural factors in today's world creating more propitious conditions for terrorism . . . [leading to a] sustained, if not higher, level of transnational terrorism'. Lia ends his book by stating that: 'Regrettably, high levels of terrorism are going to be with us for a very long time.' (Lia, 2005).

Because of globalization, a terrorist threat cannot be addressed by one nation, no matter how powerful, acting alone. Rather, it requires international cooperation, with revitalized as well as new international institutions. This threat of global terrorism also demands coordinated measures at the global level, involving governments, United Nations (UN) bodies, other international organizations, non-governmental organizations (NGOs) and the private sector. At the heart of such a coordinated approach is mutual support, with entities that could be damaged by international or global terrorism, whether nations, international organizations or businesses, providing as well as making use of such support.

For a system of global governance to deal effectively with a fundamental threat to security in the form of global terrorism, whether through the UN or other organizations, it will be necessary to approach security from a global perspective rather than a national or regional one. Our world is now so highly connected and interdependent that it is impossible to confine security to arbitrarily defined national frontiers, as in the concept of 'national security'. By contrast, the concept of 'global security' recognizes the need to create a new global system comparable to the creation of a new world system that occurred after World War II, one that would encompass not only security but also economic, political and other issue areas. (See Intriligator, 1994, my 1993 Presidential Address to the Peace Science Society (International), 'Global security after the end of the Cold War'; see also the outstanding work of the Global Governance Group in promoting global security.) This new global system would treat problems of security, both military and non-military, including the threat of global terrorism, through strengthening existing international institutions or the creation of new global institutions. These new institutions could be built, in part, on the UN system and its components. They should ideally involve supranational decision-making and authority, with enforcement capabilities, transparency and accountability, along with global perspectives and responses. Participation in the global decision-making process should be through close international cooperation and mutual support. It would favor collective action over pre-emption by any one nation, no matter how powerful, including by the US, the current hegemonic global power. Such a system of global security should be preferred to the current system of a virtually powerless UN system with no independent ability to raise funds or commit troops. (Tinbergen and Fischer, 1987 note that while the UN has components comparable to those in national governments, such as the World Health Organization as a counterpart to national ministries of health, it has neither a treasury nor a ministry of defense.)

MUTUAL SUPPORT AS THE WAY TO COUNTER GLOBAL TERRORISM

One of the most effective ways to counter global terrorism is that of mutual support at various levels and among different governments and organizations, including international organizations.

As already noted, an example from over a century ago of this mutual support was the aid that the people of Los Angeles provided their fellow Californians in San Francisco after the 1906 earthquake and fire. They sent a train filled with relief supplies of food, medicine, tents, blankets, and so on that arrived just one day after the disaster. Despite great strides in communication, transportation and organization over the last century, it is questionable whether this could be accomplished today, whether through private initiatives as in the 1906 case or through Federal (Federal Emergency Management Agency – FEMA or DHS), state or local governmental action.

A long-established principle of mutual support exists among fire departments, which regularly support one another. The same principle also applies in police departments and hospitals, which regularly rely on one another for support in extreme situations.

Mutual support can magnify the ability of any one entity to deal with terrorism, whether at the local, national or global level. Indeed, entities at the national and global levels can learn from the experience of both local entities and businesses in coping with such challenges through mutual support. Unfortunately, however, many national and global agencies dealing with terrorism typically tend to believe that they can only teach local agencies and businesses and cannot learn from them. In fact, cooperation and mutual support between business and the government as well as between governments and international organizations is needed to reduce the vulnerability of critical infrastructure to terrorism (Auerswald et al., 2006).

MUTUAL SUPPORT AT THE LOCAL LEVEL: THE TEW EXAMPLE IN LOS ANGELES COUNTY THAT HAS BEEN COPIED ACROSS THE NATION

The Terrorism Early Warning (TEW) unit of the Los Angeles County Sheriff's Department provides an excellent example and model of mutual support at the local level to combat terrorist threats. Since its founding in 1996 it has brought together first responders, including police, fire, hospital, public health and emergency services, as well as federal, state and local agencies, to review current threats and conduct exercises to prepare for a possible terror attack. At the heart of the organization, as its founder Lieutenant John P. Sullivan of the Los Angeles County Sheriff's Department states, is 'a distributed global network for the co-production of intelligence' rather than simply intelligence sharing (Sullivan, 2005, 2006). As he notes: 'Traditional intelligence and homeland security approaches are insufficient to address these issues [of networked global insurgents that mix political and religious fanaticism with criminal enterprises to exploit the seams between crime and war] without major structural overhaul and an infusion of new approaches, tools, and processes' (Sullivan, 2006). As a result of the TEW approach of a networked approach to intelligence fusion, built on mutual support, its participating organizations that are responsible for security are both informed and prepared to work together in the event of a terrorist strike. Overall, TEW seeks to identify 'emerging threats and provide early warning by integrating inputs and analysis from a multidisciplinary, interagency team' (Sullivan, 2005). It also circulates 'open-source intelligence' (OSINT) to its members on information derived from a variety of open and unclassified sources. The TEW model, based on mutual support, is far ahead of other intelligence initiatives, including those at the national level, and it has been copied in many other cities and counties, with 26 other such units currently in operation across the US. It can also be adopted in other nations to improve responses to terrorism.

MUTUAL SUPPORT AMONG BUSINESSES

Businesses at the national and global level also rely on mutual support to deal with the threat of terrorism and other threats, such as natural disasters. Many examples of such mutual support are discussed in Yossi Sheffi's 2005 book, *The Resilient Enterprise*. He borrowed the term 'resilient' from materials science, referring to the ability of a substance to restore itself to its previous condition after being deformed. He applies this idea to businesses restoring themselves after terrorist attacks as well as natural disasters such as fires, hurricanes, earthquakes and pandemics. Businesses can avoid disaster by working together and planning to help one another in the event of such low-probability but high-impact disruptions. Sheffi's many examples show that companies that work with others, whether suppliers, customers or even competitors, can bounce back after such disruptions. His many examples include enterprises ranging from Toyota and General Motors to Intel, Amazon, the US Navy and UPS. Conversely, he shows that those that did not work with others are often out of business after such disruptions. One important case study was comparing the reaction of two large competitors in the same industry, Nokia and Ericsson, to a disruption in the supply of chips from Philips Electronics. Nokia quickly detected the problem and found alternative supplies, while Ericsson did not and eventually had to exit the market.

Sheffi notes that modern supply chains in companies, which now often involve several nations, can be highly vulnerable to low-probability, high-impact disruptions, including those stemming from terrorist attacks. This threat is compounded by the use of just-in-time inventory and other such operations that make companies highly vulnerable to a terrorist attack. If a group of companies had an agreement or understanding ahead of the time of these disruptions to help one another in an emergency situation, that would significantly reduce this threat. Terrorist strikes are probably the most serious of such emergency situations, since terrorists would likely strike the most vulnerable part of a company in order to cause the most damage, in contrast to a natural disaster. Mutual support in such a situation can involve suppliers and even competitors, who realize that there is much to gain for all parties in avoiding possible disruptions.

MUTUAL SUPPORT AMONG NATIONS

Nations must also rely on mutual support to deal with the threat of global terrorism. There must be joint production of intelligence to combine and collate information about potential terrorist strikes and the capabilities of terrorist organizations.

It should also be recognized that the most effective way to defeat terrorism is not to try to protect vulnerable assets – the approach of the US Department of Homeland Security (DHS) which concentrates on protecting airplanes and airports, ignoring other potential targets. This is like generals fighting the last war, in this case the 9/11 attacks, but many other types of attack are possible, as seen in the Madrid, London, Bali and other al-Qaeda attacks on trains, buses, subways and nightclubs since 2001. In fact, there are an enormous number of potential targets, including seaports, chemical plants, nuclear power plants, bridges, tunnels and high-rise buildings, to name just a few. If certain potential targets are protected, such as airplanes and airports, that does not solve the problem of terrorism since the terrorists will simply substitute other targets, following the path of least resistance. An economist, William Landes, recognized the importance of such substitution 50 years ago in his 1957 article, where he noted that in a period of airplane hijackings, simply improving the safety of the airplanes would lead the terrorists to substitute other targets for airplanes (Landes, 1978). He noted as one possibility terrorist strikes on embassies, which in fact occurred many years later in East Africa in the al-Qaeda strikes on US embassies in Kenya and Tanzania.

A much more effective strategy to deal with terrorism is to deprive terrorist organizations of their resources of funding, recruits, weapons, information, and so on through joint actions of nations in collaboration with international organizations. That would be an appropriate part of President George W. Bush's 'Global War on Terror'. It should also include directly confronting the terrorists in their bases and training camps, such as those of al-Qaeda in the tribal areas of Pakistan.

THE ROLE OF INTERNATIONAL INSTITUTIONS

The international institutions created after World War II shared the ambition of avoiding future international conflicts, and the UN became the main venue for interstate dialogue. Today the UN remains the only international institution allowing for the collective management of the major threats facing humanity. A closer collaboration with representatives of the civil society, in particular NGOs and other associations, could reinforce its role and provide the mutual support needed to deal with various threats, including those of international terrorism.

The UN and its various agencies should cooperate more closely with other major institutions at the global or regional level to provide mutual support.

Many of these institutions did not exist when the UN was created and are thus not part of its Charter, while others play too small a role in 'business as usual' at the UN. Among these institutions are many non-governmental organizations, particularly the international NGOs that are accredited to the UN and its constituent bodies. These international NGOs are action organizations with global constituencies and reach. For example, without the involvement and active participation of NGOs there would be no Landmines Treaty; nor would many of the various environmental conventions and treaties exist.

Other major institutions should also be regularly involved in UN programs, including major global corporations, multinational banks and other financial institutions, workers' associations and other international organizations, so as to deal cooperatively with the common threats that they all face. The last category would include the World Bank, the International Monetary Fund (IMF) and the World Trade Organization, all of which operate largely independently of the UN.

Some connections along these lines already exist, but they are informal and haphazard. These organizations should schedule regular forums where these institutions can meet with appropriate UN agencies and officials both to receive information about their programs and to make suggestions for new initiatives. Attempts towards this kind of collaboration do occur, for instance at the World Economic Forum and World Social Forum meetings, but the UN would be the more natural and better body to lead this cooperative approach to solving global problems. Some steps have already been taken, such as the Disarmament Week held every October in New York sponsored by the UN Under-Secretary-General for Disarmament Affairs, and the meetings in Vienna of the International Atomic Energy Agency (IAEA) and interested NGOs.

In addition to standing institutions, ad hoc groups of organizations and nations can often focus productively on certain issue areas. A current example is the so-called 'Quartet' of the UN, the US, the EU and Russia in the Middle East peace process. Another is the EU-3 of France, Germany and Great Britain, which has been negotiating with Iran to suspend its uranium enrichment activities. Yet another example is the Proliferation Security Initiative (PSI), a practical response to the growing challenge posed by the worldwide spread of weapons of mass destruction (WMD), their delivery systems and related materials. The PSI aims to impede illicit WMD-related trade to and from states of proliferation concern and terrorist groups. President George W. Bush launched the PSI in May 2003, and core participants include Australia, Canada, France, Germany, Italy, Japan, the Netherlands, Norway, Poland, Portugal, Russia, Singapore, Spain, the UK and the US. Under the initiative, countries commit to disrupt illicit trade in WMD by interdicting vessels, aircraft or other modes of transport in their territory or territorial waters that are reasonably suspected of carrying suspicious cargo. For example, in October 2003, the US, the UK, Germany and Italy, acting under the auspices of the PSI, stopped an illegal cargo of centrifuge parts for uranium enrichment destined for Libya, which played an important role in Libya abandoning its nuclear program.

Other examples of combinations of nations to deal with common problems are the G-8, the Asia-Pacific Economic Cooperation (APEC), the Association of South-East Asian Nations (ASEAN), the African Union (AU), the Arab League, the Islamic Conference and similar organizations. The UN should be working closely with these regional organizations and should help establish others.

Overall, the key to UN reform is its cooperation with other major world players, including NGOs, major transnational and global corporations, multinational banks and other international organizations. The UN could also make greater use of ad hoc groups of nations to deal with specific threats, such as a pandemic flu.

A twenty-first-century approach would involve people worldwide, through innovative use of the Internet in a form of e-governance. The UN system extends well beyond its member states and UN reform should incorporate these other world players, including the citizens of every country. The goals and objectives of the United Nations remain as important and relevant today as at the time of its establishment in 1945. Through more than 60 years of evolution, the UN's structures are more streamlined, its working methods more effective and its various programs better coordinated. However, it remains an organization built for a different era. To meet the challenges and priorities of the present, the UN must modify its practices and strengthen its structure.

CONCLUSIONS

Global terrorism is a new phenomenon that clearly represents a serious threat today. Equally clearly, the current US and other national systems to defend against global terrorism, as well as current global institutions, are not prepared to deal with this threat. Both national and international systems can learn how these threats can be addressed through mutual support, following the example of local police, fire and other first responders, as in the case of the Los Angeles County Terrorism Early Warning unit and similar units throughout the US. They can also follow the example of global business, in both cases making much greater use of mutual support. Local safety agencies and global businesses have learned the value of cooperation and mutual support from experience. This experience could be applied at other levels, whether at the national or international level, to address the threat of global terrorism.

REFERENCES

Allison, Graham (2005), *Nuclear Terrorism: The Ultimate Preventable Catastrophe*, New York: Holt Paperbacks.
Allison, Graham (ed.) (2006), 'Confronting the Specter of Nuclear Terrorism', *ANNALS of the American Academy of Political and Social Science Series*, Sage Publications.
Auerswald, Philip E., Lewis M. Branscomb, Todd M. LaPorte and Erwann O. Michel-Kerjan (eds) (2006), *Seeds of Disaster, Roots of Response; How Private Action Can Reduce Public Vulnerability*, New York: Cambridge University Press.
Brzezinski, Zbigniew (2007), *Second Chance*, Ardsley, NY: Basic Books.
Enders, Walter and Todd Sandler (2005), *The Political Economy of Terrorism*, New York: Cambridge University Press.
Intriligator, Michael D. (1994), 'Global security after the end of the Cold War', 1993 Presidential Address to the Peace Science Society (International), *Conflict Management and Peace Science*, **13** (2), 1–11.
Intriligator, Michael D. (2004), 'Globalization of the world economy: potential benefits and costs and a net assessment', Special Issue on Globalization of the *Journal of Policy Modeling*, ed. Dominick Salvatore, **26** (June), 485–98. Also in Partha Gangopadhyay and Manas Chatterji (eds) (2005), *The Economics of Globalisation*, Aldershot: Ashgate Publishing. Forthcoming in Linda Y. Yueh (ed.), *Globalisation in Flux: Legal and Economic Challenges*, Cheltenham, UK and Brookfield, MA, USA: Edward Elgar.
Intriligator, Michael D and Abdullah Toukan (2006), 'Terrorism and weapons of mass destruction', in Katona, Sullivan, and Intriligator (eds).
Katona, Peter, John P. Sullivan and Michael D. Intriligator (eds) (2006), *Countering Terrorism and WMD: Creating a Global Counter-Terrorism Network*, London: Routledge.
Landes, William (1978), 'An economic study of US aircraft hijacking, 1961–1976', *Journal of Law and Economics*, **21** (1), April, 1–31.
Lia, Brynjar (2005), *Globalization and the Future of Terrorism: Patterns and Predictions*, London and New York: Routledge.
Sheffi, Yossi (2005), *The Resilient Enterprise*, Cambridge, MA: MIT Press.
Sullivan, John P. (2005), 'Terrorism early warning and co-production of counter-terrorism intelligence', Paper prepared for the Canadian Association for Security and Intelligence Studies, 20th Anniversary International Conference, Montreal, Quebec, Canada.
Sullivan, John P. (2006), 'Intelligence co-production and transaction analysis for counterterrorism and counter-netwar', Paper prepared for the International Studies Association, Annual Conference, San Diego, CA.
Tinbergen, Jan and Dietrich Fischer (1987), *Warfare and Welfare: Integrating Security Policy into Socio-Economic Policy*, New York: Macmillan.

3. Business continuity: a systematic approach
Yossi Sheffi

Company operations can be disrupted in multiple and unexpected ways. Some disruptions are routine and can easily be overcome with available safety stock, expediting shipments, or well-rehearsed processes. Others, however, can be fatal to an enterprise, leading to tainting of the brand, loss of customers and even unplanned exit from the business, as the examples below demonstrate:

- Following an unsuccessful implementation of SAP's enterprise requirement planning system, coupled with the installation of a flawed automated warehouse management system, Foxmeyer, a $5 billion distributor of drugs, had to file for bankruptcy. Its main operating division was sold to McKesson, its largest rival, for only $80 million.
- As a result of a fire in an Albuquerque Philips plant in 2001, one of the plant's main customers, the Swedish electronic giant Ericsson, was driven out of the cellphone handset business, due to its slow response. This was in contrast to Nokia, also a major customer of the same Philips plant, which reacted quickly and was able to increase its market share.
- In 2002, Arthur Andersen & Co was basically liquidated after two of its partners were convicted of shredding documents related to the company's audit of Enron. In 2005, the US Supreme Court overturned the conviction unanimously but it was too late for Andersen.

Numerous other examples abound.[1]

DICHOTOMY OF DISRUPTIONS

Disruptions can be classified into four categories: natural disasters, accidents, negligence and intentional attacks. These categories differ in the relative roles that human beings and random factors play in their cause.

Natural Disasters

Because many natural disasters are frequent, statistical models can be used to estimate the likelihood of their occurrence and their magnitude. Insurance companies have well-developed models of the likelihood of earthquakes, floods, hurricanes and lightning strikes for various areas of the United States as well as for other countries. Insurance premiums can even serve as a proxy for the likelihood of the relevant risk.

The statistics underlying these models are based on government data. Thus, the US Geological Survey (USGS) estimates that the areas most susceptible to earthquakes in the United States include the western US, the New Madrid zone in Missouri, and a few isolated locations on the United States East Coast. The US National Oceanic and Atmospheric Administration (NOAA) publishes statistics about severe weather. For example, the frequency of tornadoes in Oklahoma City is shown in Figure 3.1. Figure 3.2 depicts the time of day of tornadoes in Oklahoma City, indicating that they take place mostly in the afternoon and early evening hours. By knowing the increased likelihood of tornadoes at these times, organizations can train the right work shift at a plant in emergency evacuation.

Such preparations proved life-saving when a tornado hit the GM plant in Oklahoma on 8 May 2003, at 5.30 p.m. None of the more than 1000 employees who were at the plant was hurt because they all took shelter in the plant's fortified safe room when the tornado sirens sounded at 5 p.m. The tornado hit during the most likely month and at the most likely time of day.

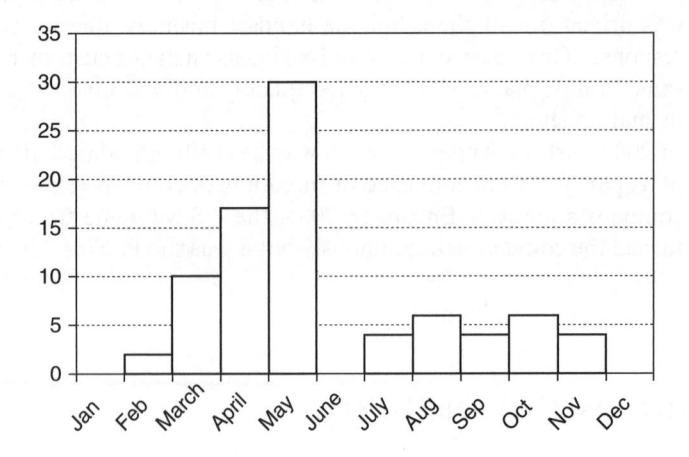

Source: Branick (2000)

Figure 3.1 Tornado frequency in Oklahoma

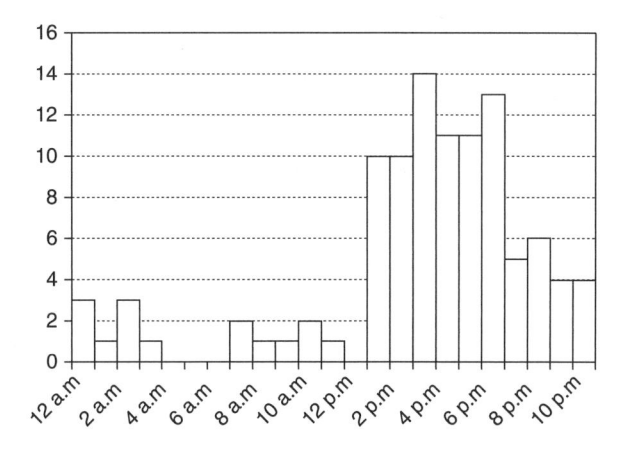

Source: Branick (2000)

Figure 3.2 Time of day for tornados in Oklahoma

Accidents

Accidental disruptions are unexpected detrimental events resulting from human errors. In many cases accidents result in investigations using root cause analyses aimed to improve procedures, designs, organization or some other contributing aspect. Furthermore, as it turns out, safety experts have documented the fact that when a system experiences hundreds of small accidents (with no injury), one can expect dozens of accidents resulting in one or more injuries and one major accident involving loss of life or serious injuries (Heinrich, 1959). Consequently, many safety efforts are focused on the 'Safety Pyramid' shown in Figure 3.3 – working to eliminate unsafe and/or hazardous conditions, reducing the number of small mishaps, leading to a reduced likelihood of more serious accidents.

To this end, air traffic control systems, the nuclear energy industry and the chemical industry have all developed processes of 'near miss'. Such processes involve the reporting, investigation and dissemination of lessons learned from unsafe occurrences, even when no accident took place. In addition, many companies dealing with hazardous conditions have implemented process safety management (PSM)[2] systems aimed at reducing the number of incidents, since that should lead to a reduced accident rate and the elimination of severe accidents. PSM systems include audit programs that verify the compliance with and safe implementation of procedures. For example, Figure 3.4 depicts the marked reduction of incidents as a function of the audit process at Du Pont; a process which is part of the manufacturer's PSM.

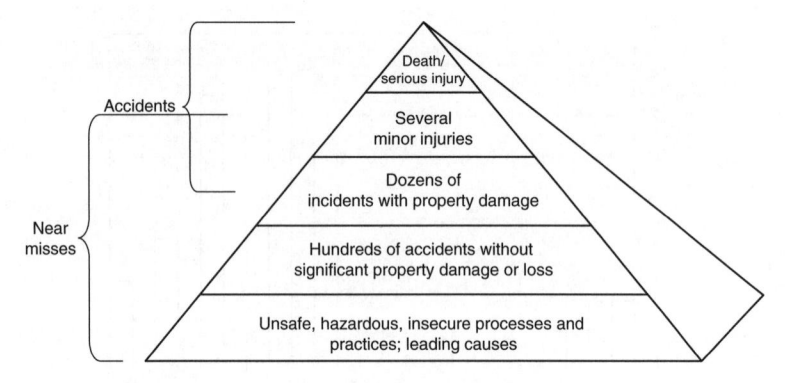

Figure 3.3   The safety pyramid

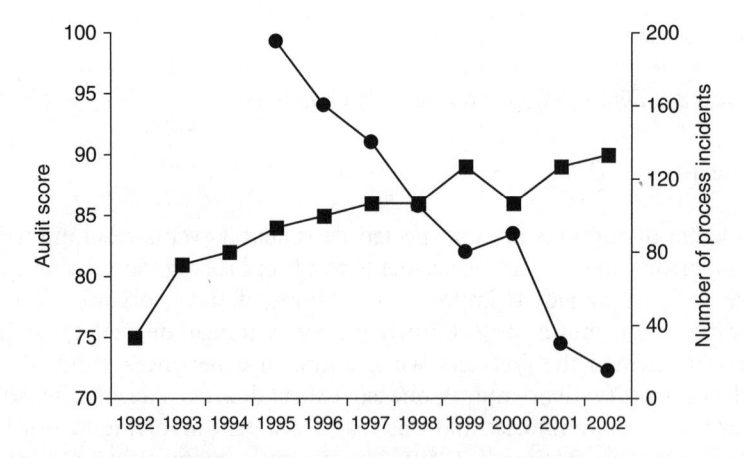

Source: E.I. Du Pont de Nemours & Co. (2004)

Figure 3.4   Incidents versus audit scores at DuPont

Negligence

Disruptions based on negligence are, in some sense, close in nature to disruptions resulting from accidents. The root causes, however, are somewhat different and the avoidance mechanisms are different.

Negligence disruptions are of two main types: (1) non-compliance with regulations; and (2) disconnection from (changing) societal norms and expectations.

Non-compliance with regulations can result in the confiscation of shipments, but also the closure of plants. In 2004 the UK government suspended the license of Chiron Inc. to manufacture Fluvirin, an influenza virus vaccine, at its plant in Liverpool because of contamination at the plant. This suspension took the Liverpool plant offline for five months, resulting in severe shortages of flu vaccine in the US since Chiron was supposed to supply about half of the US's 100 million annual doses. Chiron's non-compliance with the UK government's pharmaceutical manufacturing procedures caused the company to lose a large volume of sales, as well as tainting its brand. It also created significant difficulties for US consumers; during the 2004–05 flu season flu vaccines had to be rationed and the health givers had to manage a priority scheme for consumers. In 2006 Chiron was acquired by Novartis.

But negligence on the part of an enterprise does not result only from non-compliance with regulations. In many cases, companies can suffer significant losses, including tainting of their brand, due to not keeping up with changing consumer and media expectations.

The June 1996 issue of *Life* magazine carried an article about child labor in Pakistan. The article was accompanied by a photograph of 12-year-old Tariq surrounded by parts of Nike soccer balls he was stitching for 60 cents a day. The article generated a public outcry, including demonstrations of activists in front of Nike outlets. In an effort to pre-empt legislation by politicians responding to their constituents, the soccer ball industry came up with a self-monitoring Partnership Agreement, which it co-signed with UNICEF and the International Labour Organization. Nike's brand, however, was tarnished by the episode.

Thus, child labor, environmental protection, global warming, retail diversity, executives' morals, and other causes can make a company the target of well-funded and well-organized consumer groups as well as a media target. Despite the fact that the underlying activities are not illegal, dealing with such incidents can, at the very least, divert management attention from the business; but these incidents can also cause permanent damage to companies in terms of brand equity and actual sales.

Intentional Disruptions

Intentional disruptions constitute 'adaptable threats' in which the perpetrators attempt to maximize their likelihood of success. Consequently, such attacks are likely to take place at the worst time and in the worst place – when the organization is most unprepared and vulnerable.

In the summer of 2002, for example, the International Longshore and Warehouse Union (ILWU) staged a work slowdown in the Pacific coast ports of the USA. To maximize the effect of its action, the union timed it to October, planning to choke the ports just as the volume of shipments from Southeast Asia increased before the holiday shopping season in the United States.

On 28 November 1995, French workers participated in their second nationwide strike in five days to protest against austerity measures proposed by the government of Prime Minister Alain Juppe. In Paris, 85 bus drivers employed by the Parisian transportation authority, the Régie Autonome des Transports Parisiens (RATP), decided to create a disruption in support of the general strike. They knew exactly what to do. The 85 buses blocked the main RATP garage and within hours the entire bus and subway system ground to a halt throughout Paris.[3]

After the United States imposed tariffs on steel imports in March 2002, the World Trade Organization (WTO) ruled that the tariffs were a violation of international trade rules. The WTO decision gave the European Union (EU) and several other countries the right to impose retaliatory tariffs on billions of dollars' worth of American exports. Rather than retaliate by imposing steel tariffs, the EU decided to hit the Bush administration where the tariffs would hurt the most. It published a list of products targeted for tariffs that included citrus fruit, textiles, motorcycles, farm machinery, shoes and other products. The common denominator for these products was that they were all made primarily in political 'battleground states' that the Bush administration would need to win in the November 2004 US presidential elections (Allen, 2003).

These examples demonstrate the non-random, adaptive nature of purposeful disruptions. Terrorism, of course, is the ultimate form of intentional attack. The 11 March 2004 Madrid bombers did not blow up an airliner or attack an airport because, after 9/11, airports around the world had enhanced security measures. Instead, the bombers struck an undefended target – trains in the heart of Madrid. The March 2004 attack took place at the height of the rush hour when the packed trains ensured maximum carnage.

Clearly, labor actions and political maneuvering have nothing to do with terrorism; managers have only to remember that intentional disruptions will strike at the least-defended place at the most inconvenient time. The adaptive nature of intentional disruptions is also the reason that insurance companies find it difficult to calculate premiums in these cases.

Summary of Disruption Types

Since high-impact disruptions make headlines, and in many cases involve court battles, such disruptions are well documented. Examining hundreds of disruptions, one can conclude the following.

Disruptions should be thought of as supply chain issues, rather than company issues. They can be caused by problems with a company's

Business continuity: a systematic approach 29

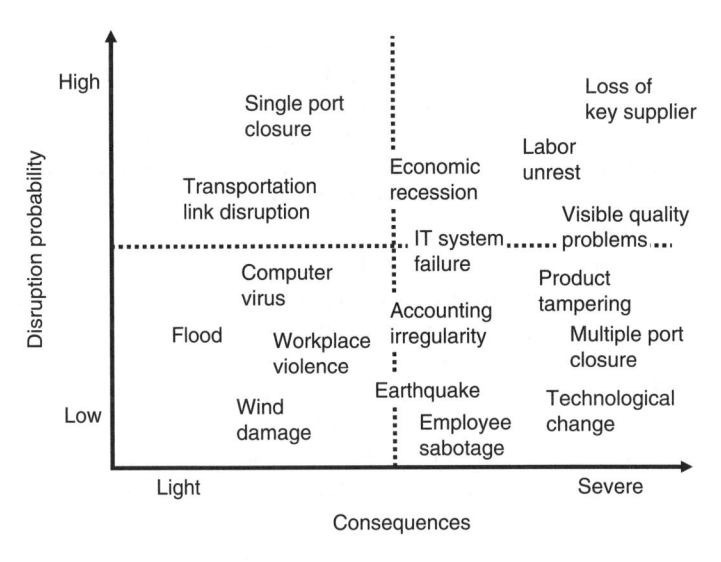

Figure 3.5 Incident priority chart

A chart with Disruption probability (Low to High) on the vertical axis and Consequences (Light to Severe) on the horizontal axis, plotting various incidents:
- Single port closure (high probability, light-moderate consequences)
- Loss of key supplier (high probability, severe consequences)
- Transportation link disruption
- Economic recession
- Labor unrest
- Visible quality problems
- IT system failure
- Computer virus
- Accounting irregularity
- Product tampering
- Flood
- Workplace violence
- Multiple port closure
- Wind damage
- Earthquake
- Employee sabotage
- Technological change

suppliers, transportation routes, distribution network or customers. They can also be caused by the environment (physical, legal or cultural) the company is in. Thus, detection requires a focused and sustained effort throughout an enterprise's ecosystem.

Some disruptions can be specified and measures can be taken to avoid them or minimize their consequences. These include industrial actions, computer viruses, financial irregularities and so on. Many companies plot such disruptions on two axes – disruption likelihood and disruption severity – in order to prioritize avoidance and resilience measures aimed at these disruptions. A stylized example of such a priority map is depicted in Figure 3.5.

In many cases, however, disruptions cannot be reasonably anticipated or their nature is so different from past experience that standard measures are insufficient. Examples include 9/11, SARS (Severe Acute Respiratory Syndrome), Chernobyl, Bhopal, Ford/Firestone and many others. Furthermore, while the probability of a particular disruption hitting at a particular site at a given time is very small, the probability that some disruption will hit somewhere in the company's ecosystem is likely to be significant. This is particularly relevant for large multinationals operating throughout the globe, such as General Motors or Procter & Gamble (P&G). This means that in addition to trying to identify specific risks, companies should build general resilience – the ability to bounce back from any type of disruption, regardless of its nature.

Risk management involves two components: prevention and recovery. The focus of prevention is on avoiding disruption, and the avoidance methods depend on the type of disruption. Recovery and business continuity are concerned with activities after a disruption has taken place. The question at that point is how resilient the business is – how quickly can it recover and get back to the prior level of production, service or any other relevant metric.

Like any other business function, business continuity involves planning and execution. In the context of business continuity, planning is about creating options for the emergency management team which has to respond to an unfolding disruption. (Note that this chapter does not focus on disaster recovery, DR, which in most companies is focused on information technology. Information Technology or IT disaster recovery is based on building in redundancy, including backups and shadow operations. DR is a relatively mature function with many suppliers offering services in this area.)

EMERGENCY MANAGEMENT

In order to understand the options that emergency management planners have to be ready for, one has to examine the process of emergency response. What will the team responding to a disruption need in order to be effective? At the outset, it should be mentioned that this chapter is not concerned with 'small disruptions' for which normal safety stock (of parts or products), expediting items, or overtime at certain facilities will suffice. The focus of this chapter is on those significant yet rare disruptions that pose a danger to the continuation of the business.

Managing such high-impact, low-probability disruptions involves certain elements which are described in this section.

The Emergency Management Center

A central emergency management center (EMC) is essential to a timely and coordinated response to major disruptions. The main functions of the EMC include information dissemination and response coordination.

In order to be able to disseminate accurate information, the EMC should be able to get accurate information, process it and then assess it, and decide which channels of information dissemination to use and how to use them.

The information collected should include both the present and the expected future status of employees, plants, orders, deliveries and any other aspect of the disruption affecting the company's eco-systems. To be able to disseminate such information the EMC needs to have a clear list of priorities and execution levers – to be able to change suppliers, prioritize customers and communicate to Wall Street and shareholders estimates of the extent of the disruption, the ongoing efforts and estimates of future status, including timing to recovery.

Many companies run such centers. For example, Wal-Mart's Emergency Operation Center was instrumental in the company's response to Hurricane Katrina in 2005. Wal-Mart was able to recognize the magnitude of the oncoming storm early, and to prepare the supplies and equipment that would be needed as well as to stage them around Louisiana and Mississippi well before the hurricane hit. Immediately after the hurricane hit, it was instrumental in helping the devastated communities with 1500 truckloads of free merchandise, including food for 100,000 meals.

Most states, cities and towns around the US have some type of emergency management center. For example, the city of New York operates an independent agency, the Office of Emergency Management, whose nerve center is New York's Emergency Operations Center. The center includes representatives from some 130 city, state, federal and non-profit agencies and is staffed around the clock, monitoring emergencies around the city. It serves as a central information and decision-making clearing-house, assessing emergency situations and coordinating the response.[4]

Taking Care of Employees

Most companies understand that their most important assets are their employees. Furthermore, implicitly or explicitly they create the expectation that they will help their employees in case they are in need as a result of a high-impact event. Indeed, Wal-Mart, BP and other large companies operating in the areas hit by Hurricane Katrina made special efforts to locate employees and take care of their needs in the hours and days after the hurricane devastated parts of Louisiana and Mississippi on 28 August 2005.

BP philosophy in their makeshift emergency operation center was to 'overwhelm employees with support'.[5] BP had 1064 employees in the affected areas, with 450 of them in the hardest-hit areas. They also were dealing with employees' families and contractors. In dealing with each case, BP provided salary continuation, supplies and equipment, interest-free loans, temporary housing, car rentals, child, elder and pet care, Federal Emergency Management Agency (FEMA) insurance advice and other assistance. Many of these policies were developed 'on the fly' but were then quickly codified and used immediately in the aftermath of hurricanes Rita on 23 September and Wilma on 21 October of 2005.

Similarly, Wal-Mart not only worked to locate and help all its associates in the devastated communities in the wake of Hurricane Katrina, but also guaranteed a job for every one of its displaced workers.

Taking Care of Business

Naturally, after the initial 'first response' of taking care of employees and helping the devastated communities, businesses have to turn to business. In some cases business can rely on operational redundancies, such as safety stock, redundant capacity, and stand by suppliers and can continue operations relatively quickly. Immediately following the 9/11 attack, Merrill Lynch was able to move its operations and manage its business from backup locations which were complete with backup IT infrastructure in New Jersey (Ballman, 2001). Deutsche Bank was able, on the very same day, to clear more than $300 billion with the Fed (the Federal Reserve System), even though its US operations center was located in the South Tower of the World Trade Center. Redundant ('just in case') IT systems in Ireland took over when the New York systems were destroyed.

In other cases, businesses adjust quickly, using Herculean efforts by employees to get the business going again. Hurricane Katrina left 195,000 Mississippi Power customers without electricity. The company hired nearly 11,000 outside workers to complement its 1250 employees, and within 12 days was able to restore power to all its customers who could safely take electricity. And this feat was accomplished in the harshest conditions, with its corporate headquarters destroyed and its disaster management center flooded.

Within four days of the storm, all but 15 of Wal-Mart's 126 stores in the devastated region were reopened, using field generators and dry ice where power was not available. This quick action helped not only the business, but also employees and the communities where Wal-Mart operates.

Procter & Gamble's Folgers coffee plant in New Orleans is the largest of its kind in the US and it produces more than half of all Folgers coffee. Not only was the plant flooded during Hurricane Katrina, but it lost its water source (the plant requires 300 gallons per second to process the coffee beans) and most employees lost their homes and had to take care of their families. Through preplanning (for generators and emergency processes) and improvisation (digging a special well and housing employees in trailers), P&G was able to restore the plant to full production within a few weeks. By 17 September 2005 the first production batch left the New Orleans plant and by 16 October all plant operations resumed.

PLANNING: CREATING THE OPTIONS

A growing body of legal opinions suggests that courts are likely to hold that most events are foreseeable and that there is a responsibility to undertake reasonable efforts to prepare for and mitigate disruptions. The risks of low-probability events are, however, difficult to assess since there are not 'enough of them' to develop their estimated likelihood.

Any planning effort is about preparing the largest number of options for the team responsible for their execution in the aftermath of a disruption. Having safety stock, secondary supply sources, alternative transportation routes, and other such ready alternatives gives the execution team options for responding to the disruption. It also gives them time to develop new, long term options while the redundant capacity is being utilized.

Planning for disruptions can be divided into two clear categories:

1. preparing for specific disruptions; and
2. preparing for the unknown (and in many cases unknowable) disruptions.

As mentioned above (see also Figure 3.5), preparations for specific disruptions can be prioritized and specific measures can be taken. Preparations for unknown disruptions, especially high-impact ones, require building general resilience throughout the enterprise's supply chain.

The following sections outline several aspects of business continuity planning, from the perspective of creating options for the emergency management team. One should remember, however, the old military adage that no battle plan survives the first shot. This is also true about business continuity plans when significant disruptions take place – especially low-probability disruptions. The corollary is that business continuity plans should be understood only as creating options for the emergency managers, not dictating specific actions. It also means that in some cases emergency managers will have to fall back on corporate values and culture to guide their actions. This is discussed below in the section on 'Beyond Contingency Planning'.

Mitigating Financial Fallout

Naturally, every disruption involves a potential financial loss. The short-term financial impact of any disruption can be protected against with insurance and other financial engineering tools. For example, Southwest Airlines' hedging of fuel prices in 2001 helped it maintain profitability in the aftermath of the airline industry slump following 9/11 and the sharp increases in oil prices following the Iraq War and Hurricane Katrina. Naturally, insurance instruments are designed specifically to compensate enterprises for certain specific disruptions. Typically, insurance covers disruptions rooted either in natural phenomenon, such as earthquakes, or in accidents, such as plant fire.

Some high-impact, low-probability disruptions, however, are difficult to insure against. The reasons are that they either cannot be specified, are rooted in phenomena outside the enterprise (a supplier's failure), or involve terror or war acts. Many insurers exclude such risks from their coverage because the probability of the underlying phenomenon cannot be calculated and therefore there is little basis for setting the premium. In cases such as a terror act or war the damage can be so great that spreading the risk is not sufficient to ensure the viability of the insurance carriers. For example, in Israel, the government is the 'insurer of first resort' for war-related damage. It has a formula for compensating individuals and businesses for war- and terror-related losses of property.

Most of the high-impact, low-probability disruptions, which are the focus of this chapter, are not insurable. They involve business continuity activities which have to be planned well in advance, even though the nature of the disruption is not known. There are several aspects of preparation, however, which are common to all high-impact disruptions. Many aspects of such planning can be gleaned from examining actual disasters and analyzing what was necessary to make the effort succeed.

Building the Emergency Response Infrastructure

As mentioned earlier, an effective emergency management center (EMC) is necessary for effective disruption mitigation and recovery efforts. Thus, one of the first steps in business continuity planning is the organization of such a center. The most important function of the EMC is information collection, analysis and dissemination. To ensure the flow of information, Intel, for example, has a regional EMC in every region of the globe where it does business. These centers are equipped with every conceivable type of communication gear from land lines to cellular to satellite phones, as well as VHF, UHF, SSB[6] and even ham radio. These centers are also tuned to local television, radio and Internet sources of news. All the regional EMCs feed data and information to a central EMC.

Naturally, getting the information is only half the battle. Analyzing what is going on, taking actions and feeding information to executives is the other half. To this end, the EMC has to be staffed by trained professionals who become team leaders for manufacturing, procurement, logistics, human resources, public relations, legal and other relevant functions. The structure of the EMC and the make-up and training of EMC personnel are some of the most important elements of business continuity planning. Just as important is the delegation of authority to the EMC. The EMC may operate in conditions of uncertainty and without constant communication with senior management. Yet decisions may have to be taken quickly. Thus the EMC needs clear guidelines regarding the actions it may (and may not) undertake. Some organizations put in place 'triggers' for delegation of authority, making certain types of decisions conditional on the nature and extent of a disruption.

Planning to Take Care of Employees

As mentioned earlier, most companies are committed to accounting for and helping their employees in the event of a high-impact disruption. In preparation for this, human resources policies have to be developed and communicated – how long can employees expect salary continuation? To what extent can they expect interest-free loans? What type of family assistance can they expect?

Some companies are reluctant to develop and communicate such policies, arguing that such policies will commit them to a level of care they may not be willing or able to provide their employees. However, this may be moot since prior behavior is likely to create a level of expectation which companies will be expected to provide – even if the standard was set by other companies in the same geographical area or the same industry. The level of employee support, as well as community assistance, offered by Wal-Mart in the aftermath of Katrina, the care shown by BP for its employees and their families, and the speed with which Mississippi Power restored electricity to its customers, all create a standard which other companies will be held to.

In addition, publishing certain emergency processes, including emergency phone numbers and information channels, will help the recovery and business continuity efforts themselves by creating a tactical 'playbook' for the recovery teams and a set of behavioral expectations for the employees. For example, the EMC may expect every employee household in the hurricane-prone Southeastern US to have food and water for a few days as part of the two-way expectation. Thus the provision of certain necessities will not be a top priority in the first few days.

But the most important element in preparing to take care of employees and their families is to have the data. To this end, BP developed a geographical information system which charts the location of every employee's home as well as family-related information, so that in a disaster, the EMC knows what it has to deal with.

Building Redundancy

In the immediate aftermath of a disruption, business continuity is based primarily on redundancy: inventory of finished goods can be used to satisfy customer orders, safety stock of parts and materials can be used to keep factories going, manufacturing and other operations can be relocated from disrupted facilities to facilities that have extra capacity, and so on.

Keeping extra inventories or underutilized capacity just in case of a disruption is expensive. In particular, when preparing for high-impact, low-probability events, this approach will require a lot of extra inventory (and/or redundant capacity) held for long periods of time. Today's lean supply chain operations obviate such a business continuity strategy since the extra cost will render the business uncompetitive.

Some level of strategic redundancy is justified, however, since it will give the enterprise some 'breathing room' to plan the recovery.

Building Flexibility

Since redundancy is expensive, the solution for business continuity and speedy recovery is the development of flexibility. Business and supply chains can be designed so that they can move to alternate suppliers, transportation routes or manufacturing sites with relative ease.

Flexibility is a company characteristic which is well beyond the charter of any business continuity planner – but it has the potential to provide most of the benefits for business continuity planning. The reason is that at its core, building flexibility into an enterprise and its supply chain is, in fact, a business continuity planning activity which is all-encompassing.

Flexibility is based on three principles: interchangeability, speed and process design.

Interchangeability is the capability to move from one supplier to another, from one manufacturing facility to another, and from one transportation route to another. Interchangeability requires that equipment be standard, like Southwest Airlines' exclusive use of Boeing 737 aircrafts or Intel's identical design of all its plants. It also requires standardization of parts, as well as use of commodity parts and materials which are commonly available, rather than special-purpose parts. Interchangeability also requires cross-training of employees so that they can perform tasks other than their day-to-day ones.

Speed means efficient internal communications links as well as the ability to work across functions and company 'silos' in order to accomplish tasks. Thus, companies which use cross-functional teams extensively in their day-to-day operations are, in fact, preparing for disruptions already.

Process design involves many aspects. For example, some companies use postponement strategies – adding specific value to certain products at the latest possible time. For example, Hewlett-Packard (HP) separates the manufacturing of its printers for the European market from the activities of putting in the right power supply, cable, decals and user manual which are specific to each country. If there is a disruption in a given country, HP is not stuck with too many printers in that language but can redirect the flow of printers elsewhere. In another example of process design, Helix used demand flow technology to break down its manufacturing process to small, standard subtasks that workers can learn quickly. This allows the company not only to cross-train employees easily but also, in case of a disruption in its plants, to move production to suppliers who can be quickly trained to manufacture its vacuum pumps.

As mentioned above, building in flexibility involves all corporate functions. For example:

- Engineering can specify standard parts.
- Procurement can ensure multiple sources.
- Manufacturing can use simple, standard processes.
- Distribution can use multiple channels.
- Supply chain management can use postponement strategies to push value addition back in time.
- Human resources can build incentives for cross-training.
- Legal management can develop procurement and sales contracts with built-in flexibility.

Having the flexibility gives the EMC many options to redirect products and materials, outsource manufacturing, change suppliers, and so on.

Collaboration

When a disruption hits, speed of communications is paramount. For example, imagine an executive calling the local chief of police at 1 a.m. and having to explain who she is, where she works and what the needs are. Clearly an unfolding disaster is not the time for first introductions.

To prepare for effective disruption management, executives who will be manning the EMC should develop ties with local, state and federal authorities in the regions where they do business. They should also develop contacts with other companies in the same industry and in the same geographical area.

Large-scale disasters will invariably involve government help – which is the reason for developing public–private contacts in preparation. But banding together with other companies who may either have the same problem (and are thereby able to help each other by combining resources) or may just be able to help is also important. Such relationships can be developed through participation in chambers of commerce, professional associations and other industry and/or local groups.

Detection

One of the most important preparations which any organization can take is building early detection mechanisms. Early warning allows organizations to prepare, thereby at best avoiding or mitigating the disruption, or at the very least making a more effective recovery effort.

In some cases, early detection is the most important factor in the response plan; as is the case with pandemic planning. This is why the World Health Organization and national authorities are watching for any sign of human-to-human transmission of the avian flu. Early detection will allow for effective quarantine, identification of specific strains and development of vaccines.

Companies operating in uncertain environments invest in early warning systems. For example, UPS operates its own meteorology department. The department issues detailed forecasts regarding key airports where UPS operates – routinely besting the US meteorological service in its forecast accuracy.

A tsunami detection system has been in place in the Pacific Ocean since 1948. It is based on signals from eight deep-ocean sensors mounted on buoys and about 100 coastal monitors, all tuned to detect wave patterns characteristic of a tsunami. In the United States the National Weather Service operates a program called TsunamiReady, promoting emergency awareness, and coastal communities at risk have installed warning systems and disseminate information about evacuation procedures. The system is credited with saving hundreds of lives when Crescent City in Hawaii was evacuated before the tsunami generated by the 1964 Alaska earthquake reached the island. The lack of a tsunami warning system around the Indian Ocean meant that the December 2004 Sumatra tsunami killed 175,000 people in Indonesia, Thailand, India, Sri Lanka, Bangladesh, the Maldives, Myanmar, and even Somalia on the east coast of Africa.

An early warning system for a company's supply chain requires continuous monitoring of its key suppliers for financial health, quality of parts and ethical treatment of employees. In the near future it may also mean monitoring suppliers for their environmental policies and carbon footprint, since the market may demand that companies not only comply with government regulations but also lead in these areas. A failure may have negative consequences for the brand and sales.

BEYOND CONTINGENCY PLANNING

Building in flexibility and redundancy, building the response infrastructure and revisiting insurance requirements, and building collaborative linkages with public and private organizations, go a long way towards increasing the number and quality of options that will be open to the people who will be executing recovery efforts.

High-impact disruptions, however, can go well beyond the 'normally unexpected' events. Predicting and preparing for the consequences of 9/11, SARS, Chernobyl, hurricanes Katrina, Wilma and Rita, Bhopal, or other past disruptions was difficult. Predicting and preparing effective responses for an avian flu pandemic, a possible Tiananmen Square II, jihadist control of Middle East oil, or 'intifada-like' patterns of suicide bombings in Europe and the US is difficult. In part, the difficulties arise from the fact that effective communications and therefore command and control will not be quickly established.

In any of these situations, organizations will have to rely on their local units, managers and employees, regardless of their level and training and preparation, to lead in the recovery efforts. For this purpose, as well as for dealing with smaller disruptions, companies and other organizations can build a culture of empowering lower levels in the organization to take the initiative. Such an 'asking for forgiveness rather than permission' culture is likely to encourage local units close to the problem to take action in a timely fashion.

Again, this chapter comes back to Katrina as an example in which several organizations did not perform as expected:

- The mayor of New Orleans was hesitant to issue evacuation orders until 36 hours before Katrina hit.
- The government of Louisiana was slow in marshalling its resources and asking for federal help.
- The federal government and its lead agency, the Federal Emergency Management Administration (FEMA), was assessing what was going on and worried about organization charts, while people were drowning.

Other organizations sprung into action. And it was another agency of the Department of Homeland Security (DHS) which demonstrated how disaster recovery should be handled. Anticipating the disaster, the US Coast Guard (USCG) moved assets and personnel into the perimeter of the affected area and sprung into action first. The USCG is credited with saving 33,000 people in the aftermath of Katrina. To appreciate the magnitude of this effort, note that in an average year, the USCG saves about 4500 people around the entire country. Interestingly, the DHS has never issued a specific order for the USCG to deploy. The USCG and its units around the country just did so. Even more telling – several of the media sources and follow-up investigations cited the fact that the Coast Guard's Air Station New Orleans (ASNO) managed the operation despite complete loss of communication with the outside world and its own chain of command for extended periods. This was testament to the value of the USCG's 'Principles of Operations'[7] which include 'On Scene Initiative' among other principles such as flexibility, clear objective, unity of effort and effective presence.

Building such a culture in a commercial organization is not easy, but many resilient companies exhibit such corporate culture. At UPS, 'nobody goes home until all the packages are delivered', and at Toyota any line worker can stop the production line if they notice a defect moving on the production line. Gordon Bethune was able to move Continental Airlines within a short period from last to first in on-time performance among US airlines and from first to last in percentage of lost luggage, by empowering employees to take charge.

SUMMARY

To have effective business continuity efforts, executives and managers facing a high-impact disruption need to have as many options open to them as possible. The development of these options is what business continuity planning is about.

The most important preparation is setting up the appropriate infrastructure for collecting and disseminating information. Such a facility should coincide with the analysis and decision-making function which we referred to as the emergency management center. To ensure the effectiveness of the EMC, a clear delegation of authority to the executive in charge and the team involved should be outlined in advance.

Building the options for effective recovery involves: building redundancy and flexibility into the supply chain of the organization; designing products and processes which have ready substitutes; building collaborative linkages with local, state and federal authorities, as well as with other industry and local organizations; and building an effective detection and warning mechanism in order to allow emergency managers the maximum time to plan and organize specific recovery efforts.

One of the most important aspects of business continuity planning is recognizing that corporate culture, employee loyalty and corporate values are likely to play a very significant role in the success of recovery efforts. This is particularly relevant for extreme disruptions that may involve loss of communication for prolonged periods.

NOTES

1. See, for example, Sheffi (2005). Also see *Supply Chain Digest* (2006).
2. The US Occupational Safety and Health Administration (OHSA) has issued PSM regulations and the Environmental Protection Agency has issued requirements for accident prevention. Many companies, such as Du Pont, go beyond the minimum required in the regulations in their processes and procedures.
3. A general report on the strike was retrieved 5 October 2004 from: http://www.cnn.com/WORLD/9511/france_strike/. The site of the *International Workers Bulletin* (retrieved 5 October 2004) mentions some of the tactics employed, http://www.wsws.org/public_html/prioriss/iwb12-4/france.htm.
4. See http://www.nyc.gov/html/oem/html/home/home.shtml.
5. Presentation by Mark Dice, BP at BP's 'Blue Chalk' Leadership Conference, San Francisco, 13 September 2006.
6. SSB = Single Side Band. It is a form of high frequency (HF) communication mechanism.
7. See, for example, http://www.uscg.mil/top/about/doc/Chapter_Four.pdf.

REFERENCES

Allen, Mike (2003), 'President to drop tariffs on steel', *Washington Post*, 1 December.
Ballman, J. (2001), 'Merrill Lynch Resumes Business Critical Functions within Minutes of Attack', *Disaster Recovery Journal*, **4** (4), http://www.drj.com/special/wtc/1404-04.html, retrieved 12 October 2004.
Branick, Michael L. (2000), 'Tornadoes in the Oklahoma City, Oklahoma area since 1890', National Weather Service Forecast Office, Norman, Oklahoma, February, http://www.nwsnorman.noaa.gov/tornadodata/okc_main.html, downloaded 5 October 2004.
E.I. Du Pont de Nemours & Company (2004)
Heinrich, H.W. (1959), 'Industrial Accident Prevention: A Scientific Approach', New York: McGraw-Hill.
Sheffi, Y. (2005), *The Resilient Enterprise: Overcoming Vulnerability for Competitive Advantage*, Cambridge, MA: MIT Press.

4. Assessing, managing and benefiting from global interdependent risks: the case of terrorism and natural disasters

Howard C. Kunreuther and Erwann O. Michel-Kerjan

INTRODUCTION

With the increasing globalization of economic and social activities, the world has now become so interdependent that actions taken today 5000 miles away could affect you tomorrow. Conventional wisdom holds that one country or one organization has the capacity and expertise to manage future large-scale risks alone. However, in an increasingly global interdependent world, they have neither.

A hallmark of the twenty-first century is that we have entered a new era of catastrophic risks, as illustrated by the evolution of economic and insured losses associated with a series of global events that occurred in just the past few years. The increase in insured losses from man-made (including terrorism) and natural disasters worldwide since 1970 (see Figure 4.1) graphically depicts the new era we have entered. From Table 4.1 we see that the 9/11 terrorist attacks inflicted $35 billion in insured losses.[1] Claims were paid by over 150 insurers and reinsurers worldwide, illustrating how risks are today diversified over global markets. Four major hurricanes hit one of the most populated states in the US (Florida) in 2004, and three major hurricanes hit the Gulf of Mexico the following year. The devastation due to Hurricane Katrina in 2005 was unprecedented both in terms of human and economic losses. It is the most costly catastrophe in the history of insurance worldwide ($46.3 billion in insured losses) as shown in Table 4.1. Of the 20 most costly insured catastrophes that have occurred in the world since 1970, half of them have occurred since 2001.

There are a number of other large-scale risks which have similar features to terrorism and natural disasters. The trigger for the August 2003 power

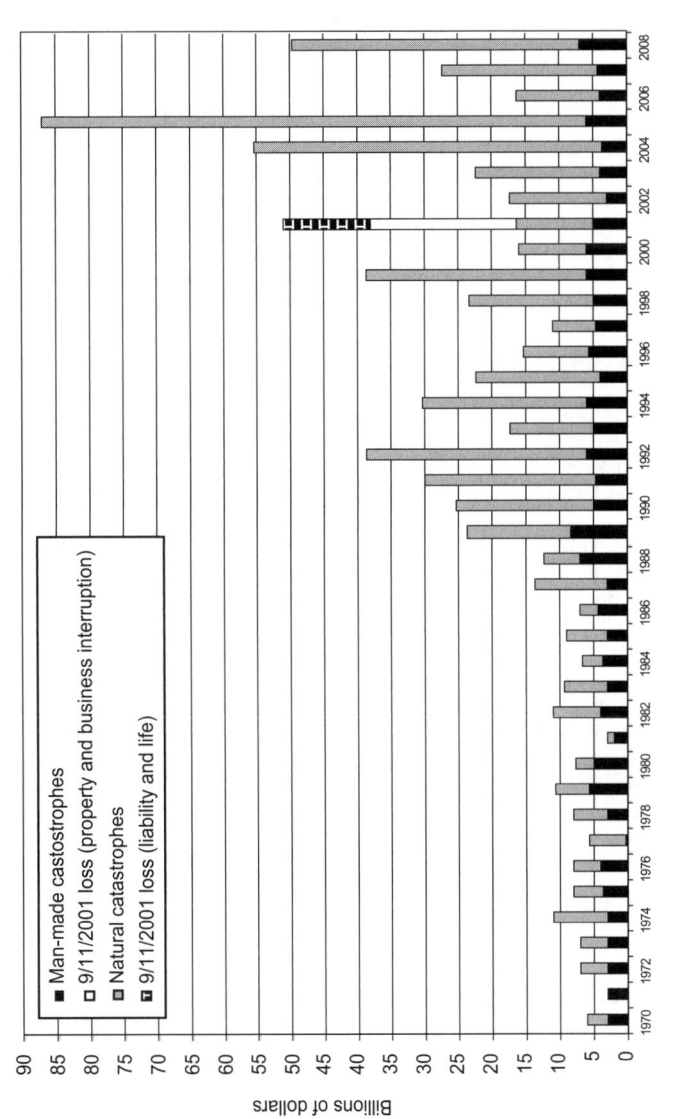

Note: Losses in billions of dollars indexed to 2007, except for 2008 which is in current dollars. 9/11: All lines, including property and business interruption (BI).

Sources: Wharton Risk Center with data from Swiss Re and Insurance Information Institute.

Figure 4.1 Worldwide insured losses from catastrophes, 1970–2008

Table 4.1 The 20 most costly insured catastrophes in the world, 1970–2008

Cost*	Event	Victims (dead or missing)	Year	Area of primary damage
$46.3	Hurricane Katrina	1,836	2005	USA, Gulf of Mexico, et al.
35.5	9/11 Attacks	3,025	2001	United States
23.7	Hurricane Andrew	43	1992	United States, Bahamas
19.6	Northridge Earthquake	61	1994	United States
16.0	Hurricane Ike	358	2008	United States, Caribbean
14.1	Hurricane Ivan	124	2004	United States, Caribbean
13.3	Hurricane Wilma	35	2005	United States, Gulf of Mexico
10.7	Hurricane Rita	34	2005	United States, Gulf of Mexico
8.8	Hurricane Charley	24	2004	United States, Caribbean
8.6	Typhoon Mireille	51	1991	Japan
7.6	Hurricane Hugo	71	1989	Puerto Rico, United States
7.4	Winterstorm Daria	95	1990	France, United Kingdom
7.2	Winterstorm Lothar	110	1999	France, Switzerland
6.1	Winterstorm Kyrill	54	2007	Germany, United Kingdom, Netherlands, France
5.7	Storms and floods	22	1987	France, United Kingdom.
5.6	Hurricane Frances	38	2004	United States, Bahamas
5.0	Winterstorm Vivian	64	1990	Western/Central Europe
5.0	Typhoon Bart	26	1999	Japan
5.0	Hurricane Gustav	135	2008	United States, Caribbean
4.5	Hurricane Georges	600	1998	United States, Caribbean

Note: *This table excludes payments for flood by the National Flood Insurance Program in the United States.
*In billions, indexed to 2007, except for 2008 which is in current dollars.

Sources: Wharton Risk Center with data from Swiss Re and Insurance Information Institute.

failures in the northeastern US and Canada was an event that occurred in Ohio. A disease in one region of the globe can readily spread to other areas through transportation networks, as was the case with the rapid spread of SARS (Severe Acute Respiratory Syndrome) from China to its trading partners, and as may be the case with avian flu (Heal and Kunreuther,

2007). The meltdown of a nuclear reactor in one country can lead to massive radioactive contamination hundreds of miles away, as illustrated by the Chernobyl nuclear plant disaster in 1986. The initial evidence that a major plume of radioactive material was affecting other countries came not from Soviet sources, but from Sweden, where on 27 April 1986 workers at the Forsmark Nuclear Power Plant (approximately 1100 km from the Chernobyl site) were found to have radioactive particles on their clothes (Mould, 2000). These few examples illustrate the existence of important interdependencies between people and organizations hundreds if not thousands of miles apart.

All these risks have the common feature that individuals and firms are interconnected so that any one unit can create negative 'security externalities'.[2] People, organizations and/or governments may not realize how their failure to operate can affect a large number of agents, often rippling far beyond their direct influence. If the organization is an industrial firm then there is a trade-off between private efficiency and public vulnerability. This source of market failure is often reinforced if there is no coordination mechanism in place to endogenize these externalities. A challenge for public policy is to find a way for the government to provide incentives for the private sector to invest adequately in security (including both technical designs and management practices). Recent major catastrophes also revealed failure in government preparedness, which negatively impacted on the operation of firms in the private sector.

This chapter focuses on mega-terrorism and large-scale natural disasters to highlight the nature of the interdependencies and global nature of the risks. Our particular interest is in examining alternative risk management strategies as well as effective coordination approaches for reducing future losses, and providing adequate protection to potential (direct and indirect) victims of such large-scale disasters.

With respect to terrorism, the attacks of 11 September 2001 and the anthrax crisis have revealed tragically our lack of collective preparedness to deal with such global threats. In the case of 9/11, the security failures at Boston's Logan airport led to the destruction of the World Trade Center (WTC). The failure was embedded within the security protocols promulgated by the Federal Aviation Administration and not with the application of those protocols, that is, checking for bombs in passengers' luggage but not profiling. There was nothing that the Port Authority of New York and New Jersey and firms located in the WTC could have done on their own to prevent these aircrafts from crashing into the Twin Towers. Any protective efforts they might have undertaken would have been rendered useless by the absence of action at a distant site. The anthrax crisis likely challenged all the postal services of most developed countries.

The possible use of so-called weapons of mass destruction (WMD) is even more threatening. A 10-kiloton nuclear bomb planted in a shipping container that explodes in the Port of Long Beach, California could result in total direct costs exceeding $1 trillion, with ripple effects on trade and global supply chains that could lead to a global recession (Meade and Molander, 2006).[3]

Turning to natural disasters, hurricanes Katrina, Wilma and Rita had lasting impacts on energy prices not only throughout the US but also on the energy markets. The growing interdependence of social and economic activities makes it very likely that the next major catastrophe in Florida and/or the Gulf of Mexico would have long-term impacts on both the US economy and other nations. Similarly, a major earthquake in one of the world's financial centers like Tokyo, Japan, is very likely to destabilize financial markets worldwide.

In the next section we will discuss some of the behavioral challenges in managing catastrophes. We then discuss risk management strategies for promoting cost-effective mitigation measures in the context of these challenges that are likely to be exacerbated when we deal with global risks. The fourth section discusses additional and challenging features of global risks by developing a simple model that provides an understanding of the nature of interdependencies and how they affect decisions by agents to invest or not invest in security or protection. Specifically, we highlight the coordination challenge: even though each agent's welfare is improved if everyone invests in security measures, there is no economic incentive for anyone to adopt these measures on their own. The launching of an international global reaction capacity in the aftermath of the anthrax crisis in 2001 illustrates the importance of coordination when developing solutions to tackle global risks. We conclude the chapter by discussing the World Economic Forum's Global Risk Network in which the Wharton Risk Center and several leading companies are currently involved.

HOW INDIVIDUALS BEHAVE WITH RESPECT TO LOW-PROBABILITY EVENTS

In designing risk management strategies, one needs to understand how individuals collect and process information with respect to events that occur with relatively low probabilities. Here, we focus on features of behavior that have been well documented empirically. While not specific to global risks, these features pose challenges for catastrophe risk management in general, which are even more pronounced in the case of global risks as discussed below.

Underestimating or Ignoring Probabilities

Before a disaster, individuals are unlikely to think about the consequences of the event and hence do not consider the trade-offs between the expected benefits and costs of protective measures. Empirical studies indicate that decision-makers often use 'threshold models', whereby if the probability of a disaster is below some pre-specified level, they believe it will not happen to them. In laboratory experiments on the purchase of insurance, many individuals bid zero for coverage, apparently viewing the probability of a loss as sufficiently small that they are not interested in protecting themselves against it (McClelland et al. 1993). People considering protective measures rarely, if ever, have explicit loss probabilities available to them. Often, loss probability does not seem to play a role in their decisions (Camerer and Kunreuther, 1989; Hogarth and Kunreuther, 1995; Huber et al., 1997). When loss probability is considered, it is derived from experience, not from actuarial tables. For example, most people only purchase earthquake insurance after suffering a loss, even though they indicate that it is less likely than before for such an event to occur again in their neighborhood now that the stress on the fault has been relieved.

In the US, even after the 2004 and 2005 hurricane seasons that considerably raised the level of awareness, a large number of residents did not invest in loss-reduction measures with respect to their property, or undertake emergency preparedness measures. In a survey of 1100 adults living along the Atlantic and Gulf coasts undertaken in May 2006, 83 percent had taken no steps to fortify their home that year, 68 percent had no hurricane survival kit and 60 percent had no family disaster plan (Goodnough, 2006).

Turning to terrorism, it took the events of 9/11 for insurers to consider this risk explicitly in their pricing decisions. To our knowledge, there was not an insurer or reinsurer in the world who had conceived of the possibility that a plane crashing into the World Trade Center could cause the structure to collapse. In this sense, such a risk would be considered unknowable. By writing contracts that promised coverage for perils not excluded, insurers were agreeing to provide coverage against losses from presumably unknowable events. Only after such events occur are they priced or explicitly included or excluded from coverage. This is the process followed by insurers with respect to the terrorism risk associated with 9/11 (Kunreuther and Pauly, in press).

Short Time Horizons (Myopia)

In making decisions that involve cost outlays, individuals are often myopic and hence only take into account the potential benefits from such investments over the next year or two. In one study, subjects indicated the maximum they were willing to pay for protective measures such as investing in a deadlock for their apartment door, purchasing a steering wheel lock and strengthening their homes against earthquakes. By varying the number of years that each of the measures provided protection, we could determine how much more the person was willing to invest in the item as a function of time. If a person was willing to pay $50 for a deadlock if he planned to live in his apartment for one year, then he should be willing to pay up to $95.45 if he had a two-year lease and an annual discount rate of 10 percent. Many of the arguments used by respondents suggest that they focused on the cost of the product in determining how much they are willing to pay to invest in a protective measure and do not take into account the expected benefits over more than one year (Kunreuther et al., 1998). These justifications are consistent with experiments by Schkade and Payne (1994) which revealed that the willingness to pay for public goods was affected by cost information.

This tendency toward myopia is one of the most widely documented failings of human decision-making. As a rule, we have difficulty considering the future consequences of current actions over long time horizons. Behavioral research by psychologists has led to the conclusion that most people utilize hyperbolic discount rates (Loewenstein and Prelec, 1992), implying that pay-offs several years in the future are not given very much weight in comparison to exponential discounting. As a general rule, we have difficulty considering the future consequences of current actions over long time horizons (Meyer and Hutchinson, 2001).

Budget Constraints

Short-run budget constraints also discourage individuals from investing in protective measures. More specifically, if individuals have limited disposable income after purchasing necessities, then they will not even consider purchasing insurance or allocating funds for mitigation measures. In focus group interviews to determine factors influencing decisions on whether to buy flood or earthquake coverage, one uninsured worker responded to the question, 'How much does one decide on how much to pay for insurance?' as follows:

> A blue-collar worker doesn't just run up there with $200 [the insurance premium] and buy a policy. The world knows that 90 percent of us live from payday to payday . . . He can't come up with that much cash all of a sudden and turn around and meet all his other obligations. (Kunreuther et al. 1978)

The budget constraint for investing in protective measures may extend to higher-income individuals if they set up separate 'mental accounts' that limit how much they will spend on certain items. Dividing spending into budget categories facilitates rational trade-offs between competing uses of funds and acts as a self-control device. Poorer families tend to have budgets defined over periods of a week or a month, while wealthier families are likely to use annual budgets (Thaler, 1999). Heath and Soll (1996) provide further evidence on the role of budget categories by showing how actual expenses are tracked against these budgets.

Impact of Local Interdependencies

Suppose a family was considering elevating their house on piles so as to reduce flood losses from a future hurricane. If none of their neighbors have taken this step, their house would look like an oddity in a large group of homes at ground level. If the family choose to move, they would be concerned that the resale value of their home would be lower because the house was different from all the others. Given that there is a tendency not to think about a disaster until after it happens, the family may reason that it would be difficult to convince potential buyers that elevating the house should increase its property value.

The question of how the actions of others impact upon one's own decisions relates to the broader question of interdependencies which is a theme of this chapter. If all homes in the neighborhood were elevated, then this family would very likely want to follow suit; if none of them had taken this step, then they would not have an interest in doing so. It is conceivable that if a few leaders in the community elevated their houses then others would do the same. This type of tipping behavior is common in many situations and has been studied extensively by Schelling (1978) and popularized by Gladwell (2000).

Disaster Assistance

One of the arguments that has been advanced as to why individuals do not adopt protective measures is that they assume generous relief will be forthcoming from the government should they suffer losses from a disaster. Under the current system of disaster assistance, the governor of the state(s) can request that the President declare a 'major disaster' and offer special assistance if the damage is severe enough. However, neither the governor nor the President decide the level of federal aid, Congress does.

Federal disaster assistance may create a type of Samaritan's dilemma: providing assistance *ex post* (after hardship) reduces parties' incentives to manage risk *ex ante* (before hardship occurs). If a family residing in a hazard-prone area expects to receive government assistance after a loss, it will have less of an economic incentive to invest in mitigation measures and purchase insurance prior to a disaster. Should a large number of individuals behave in this way, the increased losses from a disaster due to the widespread lack of protection makes it more likely that the public sector will come to the rescue after a disaster.

In fact, the empirical evidence suggests that individuals or communities have not based their decisions on whether or not to invest in mitigation measures by focusing on the expectation of future disaster relief. This behavior seems counter-intuitive and the reasons for it are not fully understood. It will be interesting to see whether Hurricane Katrina changes this view, given the highly publicized commitment by the Bush administration to provide billions of dollars in disaster relief to victims.

Whether or not individuals incorporate an expectation of disaster assistance in their pre-disaster planning process, a driving force with respect to the actual provision of government relief is the occurrence of disasters where the losses are large. If the disaster occurs at a critical time in the political process, it is almost certain that liberal relief will be forthcoming. One has only to look back at earlier disasters, such as the Alaskan earthquake of March 1964 and Tropical Storm Agnes of June 1972, both of which occurred during a presidential election year, to remind oneself of the type of aid the federal government is capable of giving. Following the Alaskan earthquake where relatively few homes and businesses had earthquake-resistant measures and insurance protection, the US Small Business Administration (SBA) provided 1 percent loans for rebuilding structures and refinancing mortgages to those who required funds through its disaster loan program. Hence, the uninsured victims in Alaska were financially better off after the earthquake than their insured counterparts. After the Rapid City, South Dakota floods and Tropical Storm Agnes in June 1972, the SBA offered homeowners forgiveness grants for the first $5000 of their losses (in 1972 prices) and then provided interest rates for the remaining portion of the loan.

Overall, the number of presidential declarations has dramatically increased over the past 50 years, as indicated in Figure 4.2 (Michel-Kerjan, in press). In the case of Hurricane Katrina, which triggered the largest amount of federal aid in the aftermath of a disaster ever, the President declared a 'major disaster' on 29 August, allotting more federal funds to aid in rescue and recovery. By 8 September, Congress had approved $52 billion in aid to victims of Hurricane Katrina. As of August 2006, over $120 billion of federal aid had been approved for victims and rebuilding infrastructure destroyed by the 2005 hurricanes.

The SBA received more than 422,000 applications for disaster loans following Hurricane Katrina and the other Gulf Coast hurricanes in 2005, of which 364,000 were for homes and more than 58,000 were for businesses. The volume of applications, however, overwhelmed the SBA, and many

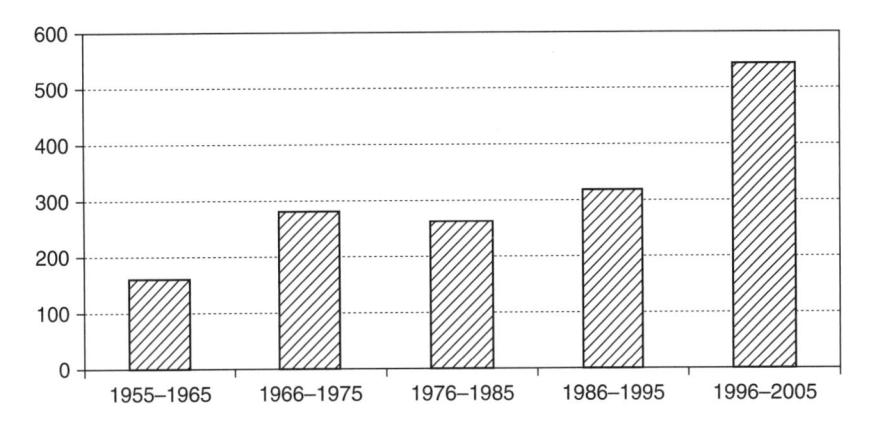

Sources: Data from the US Department of Homeland Security (FEMA) (2006).

Figure 4.2 Total US Declared Disasters (1955–2005)

Gulf Coast homeowners and businesses had to wait months to receive money from the agency. As of May 2006, it took the SBA an average of 74 days to process disaster loan applications, compared with the agency's goal of 21 days. This demand surge needs to be taken into consideration when dealing with large-scale disasters. Through the Accelerated Disaster Response Initiative (ADRI), the SBA reduced the backlog of approved loans in the system from 120,000 in the summer of 2006 to under 28,000 by the year end. As of July 2007, nearly 85 percent of the $6.9 billion in approved SBA disaster loans had been allocated to victims of the 2005 hurricanes (PR Newswire, 2007).

PROMOTING COST-EFFECTIVE MITIGATION MEASURES

If individuals or firms are reluctant to adopt protective measures to reduce the chances of catastrophic losses due to the interdependent links, the private and public sectors may have a role to play in addressing this problem. In this section we illustrate ways in which these issues could be addressed in the context of natural disasters and terrorism.

Reducing Losses from Natural Disasters

One of the principal reasons that individuals in hazard-prone areas do not adopt mitigation measures is that they only consider the short-run returns of the investment, even though it promises to yield benefits over a much longer time horizon. Take the case of a homeowner or firm residing in a hazard-prone area, considering whether to invest in some type of mitigation measure to protect their property. For example, a homeowner could be considering strengthening its roof to reduce the chances of it being blown off in a future hurricane. Suppose the expected annual benefit from this investment (B) occurs at the beginning of each year. If the firm only considers the expected benefits from such an investment over the next two years, then if it undertakes this truncated benefit–cost analysis, it will only undertake this investment as attractive if the upfront cost of mitigation (C) is less than $[B + B/(1 + d)]$ where d is the firm or individual's annual discount rate. An investment viewed as unattractive based on this short-term horizon may actually pass the benefit–cost test if one extended the time horizon.

Long-Term Loans

The insurance industry could partner with banks and financial institutions to encourage investments which are cost-effective when viewed over the long run but are not deemed attractive when evaluated using a short time horizon. Suppose the homeowner at risk had purchased an insurance policy to protect itself against the loss. In fact, banks often normally require some insurance against damage from hurricanes, tornados and floods as a condition for mortgage. The insurer could provide an annual premium reduction to those who undertake the mitigation measure and the bank could provide a 20-year loan for undertaking this measure that could be tied to the mortgage. The annual premium reduction would not be viewed as financially attractive to justify the upfront investment cost if one was only considering the next two years; however, the bank loan now converts this investment cost into an annual payment which is now likely to be lower than the annual premium reduction, assuming that insurers are basing their rates on risk.

To illustrate with an example, suppose the roof mitigation measure considered by a homeowner residing in a hurricane-prone area cost $1500. A 20-year loan of $1500 at an annual interest rate of 10 percent would result in payments of $145 per year. If the annual probability of a hurricane damaging the homeowner's house was 1:100 and the mitigation measure would reduce insured losses by $30,000, then the reduction in the annual insurance premium to reflect these lower claims costs would be $300, which is greater than the annual loan cost. Without the bank loan, the homeowner would never have adopted the mitigation measure had he focused on a two-year time horizon.

A bank should have a financial incentive to provide this type of loan. By linking the expenditure in mitigation to the structure, rather than to the property owner, the annual payments are lower and this would be a selling point to mortgagees. The bank will also feel that it is now better protected against a catastrophic loss to the property, and the insurer knows that its potential loss from a major disaster is reduced. These mitigation loans would constitute a new financial product. Moreover, the general public will now be less likely to have large amounts of their tax dollars used for disaster relief. A win–win–win–win situation for all.

Long-Term Insurance

Today, banks and financial institutions do not routinely provide long-term loans to property owners for undertaking mitigation measures. One way to encourage them to do so would be for insurers to market long-term insurance contracts on properties where the purchase of insurance is a condition for a mortgage. For such a long-term policy to be feasible, insurers would need to charge a rate based on their best estimate of the risk over a 10- to 25-year period. The uncertainty surrounding these estimates could be reflected in the premium as a function of the length of the insurance contract, in much the same way that the interest rate on fixed-rate mortgages varies between 15-, 25- and 30-year loans.

The obvious advantage of a long-term insurance contract from the point of view of policyholders is that it provides them with stability and an assurance that their property is protected for as long as they own it. This has been a major concern in hazard-prone areas where insurers have cancelled policies following severe disasters such as those that occurred during the 2005 hurricane season. One reason that insurers do not renew policies after these events is that state regulators force them to charge premiums in hazard-prone areas that are below the actuarially based estimates.

If insurers were free to charge risk-based rates they might be favorably disposed toward a long-term insurance contract. A key principle guiding a study by the Wharton Risk Center (Kunreuther and Michel-Kerjan, 2009) is that premiums must reflect the risk. The rationale for this principle is that risk-based premiums provide signals to individuals as to the hazards they face, and this encourages them to engage in cost-effective measures to reduce their vulnerability to catastrophes.

Under current insurance contracts, property owners do not have an economic incentive for spending money to guard their homes more effectively from hazards. For example, homeowners might be reluctant to incur the $1500 investment cost because they would only get $300 in return the next year, with no guarantees of future reductions. In addition, they might not know how long they will reside in the area and/or whether their insurer would reward them again when their policy is renewed. With a 20-year insurance contract required as a condition for a mortgage, the premium reduction would be viewed as a certainty.

Of course, there are many issues that have to be addressed if one is to develop long-term property insurance contracts:

- Could one offer adjustable-rate insurance policies similar to these types of mortgage contracts?
- Could a property owner change his or her insurance policy over time in a manner similar to refinancing a mortgage?
- What role would the modeling companies and the scientific community studying climate science play in providing estimates for developing risk-based premiums, and for suggesting a rationale for changes over time as new information becomes available from the scientific community?
- What types of risk transfer instruments would emerge from the reinsurance market as well as from the capital markets to protect insurers against catastrophic losses?
- What role would the federal government play in providing such protection?
- Should property owners be required to purchase insurance or would this be at the discretion of the banks issuing a mortgage?

Although these issues will have to be resolved before such policies are marketed, we feel that the idea should be introduced as a way of dealing with the issue of myopia that often discourages individuals and firms from investing in cost-effective mitigation measures.

CHALLENGES RELATED TO GLOBAL INTERDEPENDENT RISKS

The complexity of world and its evolutionary, adaptive character mean that no definitive list of global risks can be constructed. Every list will be the product of its time and of those who constructed it. Here, we highlight some criteria that a risk must meet to be considered a global risk, with the understanding that it might be challenging to define very clearly the frontier between a global risk and a non-global risk. Moreover, there is often a lot of uncertainty surrounding these global risks.

Defining Global Risks

We use the following criteria proposed by the World Economic Forum's Global Risk Initiative for defining global risks (World Economic Forum, 2006):

- *Global scope:* a global risk has global scope if it has the potential of having primary and/or secondary economic impacts in at least three world regions on at least two continents.
- *Cross-industry impact:* a global risk has cross-industry impact, potentially affecting three or more industries, and which typically results from interdependent actions and/or generates interdependent consequences globally.
- *Economic and social impact*: a global risk has a major economic impact (for example, exceeding $10 billion) and/or a major social impact in terms of human suffering and loss of life, triggering public pressure to respond. There is uncertainty as to how the risk will manifest itself over ten years, and the severity of its impact.
- *Multistakeholder approach:* the risk demands the involvement of a number of interested parties because cooperation is required between the public and private sectors to understand the drivers of the risk, to assess its interdependencies with other risks and its impacts on different industries or countries. In addition, concerted endeavors by governments, multilateral organizations, businesses and civil society institutions are likely to be needed to address the causes or mitigate the effects.

Nature of Global Interdependencies

The nature of the interdependencies needs to be well understood in order to develop risk management strategies. In the case of natural disasters, the interdependencies are primarily a function of the interactions between the individuals who are at risk in hazard-prone areas. As pointed out above, a person may be reluctant to invest in a protective measure, such as elevating their house, if others do not take similar measures. Even if one has taken steps to protect one's house against a future disaster, the structure could be damaged because a neighboring house was unprotected. An unstrapped water heater could be toppled by an earthquake, causing a fire that spreads to other homes in the neighborhood.

Terrorism differs from natural disaster since the threat can come from far away. The existence of growing interdependent systems also translates into levels of security of those systems that strongly depend on the weakest link within a constellation of complex interactions. For example, the crash of Pan America's flight 103 over Lockerbie, Scotland in December 1988 which killed 259 people on board and 11 others on the ground illustrates this point. The explosion was caused by a bomb loaded at Gozo, Malta on Malta Airlines where there were poor security systems, transferred at Frankfurt Airport to a Pan Am feeder and then loaded onto Pan Am flight 103 at London's Heathrow Airport. The bomb was designed to explode only when the aircraft flew higher than 28,000 feet, which would normally not occur until the plane started crossing the Atlantic to its final destination, New York. There was not a thing that Pan Am could have done to prevent this tragedy unless they inspected all transferred bags, which is both a costly and a time-consuming process. The terrorists who placed the bomb knew exactly where to check the bag in. They put it on Malta Airlines, which had minimum security measures, and Pan Am was helpless. Hence, the terrorists took advantage of the weakest link in a chain of interdependencies (Lockerbie, 2001).

While most airlines now check all incoming bags (including those coming from another airline), a similar weak link exists for cargo marine containers. For instance the port of Hong Kong does not screen any container coming from other ports. Terrorists could load a bomb in a container in Karachi, Pakistan where security is very poor; the bomb would then be transferred from Hong Kong to the port of Los Angeles with a very low probability of being inspected, much lower than if the shipment had come directly from Karachi.[4]

Interdependencies are even more pronounced and critical for terrorism since terrorists are likely to take into account the actions of their adversaries when planning an attack strategy. For example, they may respond to security measures undertaken by some of those at risk by shifting their attention to more vulnerable targets. This game-theoretic view of behavior has been studied by Sandler (2003), Keohane and Zeckhauser (2003) and Bier (2007) in determining what costs should be incurred by individuals and firms who are potential victims of a terrorist attack. Rather than investing in additional security measures, firms may prefer to move their operations from large cities to less-populated areas to reduce the likelihood of an attack. Of course, terrorists may choose these less-protected regions as targets if there is heightened security in the urban areas. Terrorists may also change the nature of their attacks if there are protective measures in places which would make the likelihood of success of the original option much lower than another course of action (for example, switching from hijacking to bombing a plane). This substitution effect has to be considered when evaluating the effectiveness of specific policies aimed at curbing terrorism (Sandler et al., 1983). The likelihood and consequences of a terrorist attack are thus determined by a mix of strategies and counterstrategies developed by a range of stakeholders that change over time. This 'dynamic uncertainty' makes the likelihood of future terrorist events extremely difficult to predict (Michel-Kerjan, 2003).

There is an additional challenge related to global risks: the interdependencies exist not only across regions but also across time. People tend to look for local causes to explain events. There is generally little discussion of the numerous actions taken before, far away from, or with little apparent connection to a disaster that can increase risk levels or damage from a given disaster. Kousky and Zeckhauser (2006) introduce the concept of 'JARring actions': those actions that 'Jeopardize Assets that are Remote'. JARring actions impose a particular type of negative externality – one in which the cost is imposed on people who are spatially or temporally distant. Unless there is a system in place that allows victims to hold the responsible parties accountable, internalizing such externalities will be a challenge. This is particularly true if the actions occurred thousands of miles away, or 30 years ago. Greenhouse gas (GHG) emissions illustrate this point, as they typically remain in the atmosphere for decades, and it does not matter whether the emission comes from the US, Europe or China: regardless of their origin, they will have the same marginal impacts on global warming. Unless there is coordination over time and between nations, the incentive for those who reduce their emissions will be reduced, as their actions will have limited effect on the whole system. This raises the question as to how one can provide economic incentives to individuals, organizations and countries so that they will want to invest in protection when they are connected to and dependent on others whose failures may compromise others in the network.

The Coordination Challenge

The vulnerability of one organization, critical economic sector and/or country often depends not only on its own choice of protection or security investments, but also on the actions of other agents. This concept of 'interdependent security' implies that failures of a weak link in a connected system could have devastating impacts on all parts of it, and that as a result there may be suboptimal investment in the individual components (Kunreuther and Heal, 2003; Heal and Kunreuther, 2006).

Consider the problem facing an industrial plant which is part of a global supply chain. Interdependencies exist across supply chains in every industry, and the complexity of these has been growing by leaps and bounds as industry has become more globalized through outsourcing and offshore activities. The result is that global supply chains that utilize sources from one country for manufacturing, or retailing operations in another country, now dominate many of the major economic sectors, from the automotive industry to semiconductors to the huge retail industry represented by giants like Wal-Mart and the Home Depot. The effects of supply chain disruptions (whether from natural disasters, terrorism or other unexpected events) on the profitability of supply chain participants are now recognized as being potentially very large.[5] Coping with the management challenges of such disruptions is, however, a very difficult matter, as the interdependencies involved require cooperative activity and monitoring across the supply chain in ways that are not captured in the traditional intra-supply-chain metrics of price, cycle time and product quality.[6]

To highlight the need for coordination in the context of a supply chain, consider a two-firm example where Firm 1 (F_1) with assets A_1 has outsourced part of its production process to Firm 2 (F_2) with assets A_2. Each firm could invest in measures to protect their operations against damage from some event (for example, a terrorist attack or a natural disaster) that will occur at either one firm or the other but not at both. The cost of a protective measures for each firm i is $c_i, i = 1, 2$. To keep the analysis simple, assume that if both firms undertake this action, the chance of experiencing a loss from this event is zero. If F_1 does not protect itself and F_2 does, then there is a probability p_1 that F_1 will experience a loss L_{11} and will create a loss to F_2 of L_{12}. For example, L_{12} represents the lost profits to F_2 if F_1 experiences damage from an event so that it has reduced its outsourcing activity with F_2. Similarly, if F_2 does not invest in protection but F_1 does, then it has a probability p_2 of experiencing a loss of L_{22}, which will create problems for F_1 which has lost profits from not being able to outsource to F_2 of L_{21}. If both firms do not invest in protection, then there is the possibility that either of the firms will experience a loss with probabilities $p_i, i = 1, 2$ and have a negative impact on the other firm. We assume throughout that the damage that results from multiple security failures is no more severe than that resulting from a single failure. In other words, damage is non-additive.[7] The key issue is actually whether or not there is a failure, not how many failures there are. The loss matrix for the different outcomes is shown by Table 4.2.

In this two-agent game there can be two Nash equilibria (S, S) or (N, N) with it being more profitable for both firms to invest in protection. This may require the two firms to decide together that it would be in their best interests for each to incur these upfront costs to avoid the potential consequences of a disaster to one of the firms. Without such coordination there may be economic incentives for each of the firms not to incur this investment cost. Why? Because even after protecting itself, each firm

Table 4.2 *Expected costs associated with investing and not investing in protection*

		Firm 2 (F_2)	
		S	N
Firm 1 (F_1)	S	$A_1 - c_1$, $A_2 - c_2$	$A_1 - c_1 - p_2 L_{21}$, $A_2 - -p_2 L_{22}$
	N	$A_1 - p_1 L_{11}$, $A_2 - c_2 - p_1 L_{12}$	$A_1 - [p_1 L_{11} + (1 - p_1) p_2 L_{21}]$, $A_2 - [p_2 L_{22} + (1 - p_2) p_1 L_{12}]$

knows that it can suffer an additional loss should the other firm not follow suit. The possibility of experiencing this negative externality may make it more profitable for each firm not to invest in security, and to expend these resources in other ways. As one expands the number of firms in the supply chain, the likelihood of incurring losses from others due to interdependencies in the system increases, and the importance of coordination becomes even greater. We now extend this simple model to the case where n agents make decisions in a global interdependent environment.[8]

Consider A interdependent risk-neutral agents indexed by i. Each is characterized by parameters p_i, L_i, c_i and Y_i. Here p_i is the probability that agent i's actions lead to a direct loss L_i. A direct loss can be avoided with certainty by investing in loss prevention at a cost of c_i. Initial income before any losses are incurred or before expenditure on loss prevention is Y_i. Each agent i has a discrete strategy, X_i, that takes as values either S or N representing investing and not investing respectively. If i incurs a direct loss, then this may also affect other agents' outcomes. We call the loss to them in this case 'an indirect impact'. More specifically, $q_i(K, X_i)$ is the expected indirect loss to agent i when it follows strategy X_i and the agents in the set $\{K\}$ are the only ones investing in loss prevention.

When we use a letter to refer to a set, we will designate it $\{K\}$, except when it is an argument of a function, in which case we omit the brackets. A feature of the IDS problem described above is that an agent who has invested in prevention cannot cause an indirect impact on others, so if everyone other than i invests in prevention, then i cannot suffer indirect impacts. That is, if $\{K\} = \{1, 2, \ldots, i - 1, i + 1, \ldots, A\}$ then $q_i(K, X_i) = 0$ whether $X_i = S$ or N.

If agent i invests in prevention and agents in the set $\{K\}$ are also investing then the expected cost from this is $c_i + q_i(K, S)$ where the first term is the direct cost of investing in prevention and the second is the expected cost (or benefit if negative) of indirect impacts imposed by others who do not invest.

The expected cost of not investing is given by $p_i L + (1 - \alpha p_i) q_i(K, N)$.

Here, the first term is just the expected direct loss and the second is the expected indirect impact. In this second term, the parameter $\alpha \in [0,1]$ indicates the extent to which damages are non-additive. If $\alpha = 0$ then this second term is $p_i L_i + q_i(K, N)$, so that the total expected damage sustained by agent i in the case of non-investment is the sum of the direct and indirect effects.

If however $\alpha = 1$ then we have $p_i L + (1 - p_i) q_i(K, N)$, which means that the indirect effects are conditional on the direct loss not occurring. In this case, the damage from harmful events is non-additive (that is, you only die once). A second plane crashing into one of the towers of the World Trade Center would not have increased the damage from 9/11 significantly, since the two towers entirely collapsed anyway, and a second bomb placed on Pan Am 103 would likewise have inflicted no extra damage.

The agent is indifferent between investing and not investing when:

$$c_i + q_i(K, S) = p_i L_i + (1 - \alpha p_i) q_i(K, N) \tag{4.1}$$

or

$$c_i(K) = p_i L_i + (1 - \alpha p_i) q_i(K, N) - q_i(K, S) \tag{4.2}$$

where $c_i(K)$ in equation (4.2) is the cost of investment at which i is just indifferent between investing and not investing: if $c_i < c_i(K)$ then she will invest and vice versa.

The coordination problem associated with global supply chain security that we discussed above is a case where $q_i(K, N) = q_i(K, S)$ and $\alpha = 1$ so that:

$$c_i(K) = p_i(L_i - q_i(K, N)) \tag{4.3}$$

It follows in this case that $c_i(K)$ increases in K: as more agents invest, the expected indirect loss falls and the cost threshold for investment rises, with $c_i(\emptyset) < c_i(A - i)$ where $c_i(A - i)$ is defined as the critical cost when all agents other than i are investing. In this case the game is supermodular (see Milgrom and Roberts, 1994).

In that context, a Nash equilibrium is a set of strategies $X_1, \ldots X_A$ such that: (1) $X_i = S$ for all $i \in \{K\}$ (which may be empty); (2) if $X_i = S$ then $c_i(K) > c_i$; and (3) if $X_i = N$ then $c_i(K) < c_i$; and (4) if $c_i(k) = c_i$ then i is indifferent between S and N. It is possible to show that should the above four conditions hold, a Nash equilibrium in pure strategies exists. There may be equilibria where all agents invest in loss prevention, those where none do, and asymmetric pure strategy equilibria where some invest and others do not. It is also possible that for some parameter values there is more than one equilibrium.

It is also possible to show that there are Nash equilibria at which all agents invest and also Nash equilibria at which none invest if and only if $c_i(\emptyset) < c_i < c_i(A - i) \forall i$. Also, if both $(N, N, \ldots, N)$ and $(S, S, \ldots, S)$ are Nash equilibria, then $(S, S, \ldots, S)$ Pareto dominates $(N, N, \ldots, N)$ (Heal and Kunreuther, 2007). If there are two equilibria, one with all not investing and the other with everyone investing in protection, then it is obviously interesting to know how we might tip the inefficient $(N, N, \ldots, N)$ equilibrium to an efficient $(S, S, \ldots, S)$ equilibrium. Let's now look into the possibility of tipping the non-investment equilibrium.

Tipping

Let $X_i = N \forall i$ be a Nash equilibrium. A critical coalition CC for this equilibrium is a set $\{M\}$ of agents such that if $X_i = S \forall i \in \{M\}$ then $c_j(M) \geq c_j \forall j \notin \{M\}$.

Let minimum critical coalition MCC be a critical coalition of which no subset is also a critical coalition and let a smallest critical coalition SCC be a minimum critical coalition with the property that no other critical coalition contains fewer members.

Define:

$$q_i^j(K, N) = q_i(K - j, N) - q_i(K, N) \geq 0 \qquad (4.4)$$

This is the change in the expected indirect loss to agent i, who does not invest in loss prevention, when agent j joins the set $\{K\}$ of agents who are already investing in loss prevention. For the remainder of this section we make the following assumption:

Assumption A1: $q_i^j(K, N)$ is independent of i: $q_i^j(K, N) = q^j(K, N) \forall i$

This implies that indirect effects are symmetrically distributed across agents. Also define $q_i^j(\emptyset, S) = q_i(\emptyset, S) - q_i(j, S)$ and $q_i^j(\emptyset, N) = q_i(\emptyset, N) - q_i(j, N)$ and make the additional assumption that:

Assumption A2: $q_i^j(\emptyset, S) = q_i^j(\emptyset, N) = q_i^j(\emptyset) = q^j(\emptyset) \qquad (4.5)$

This indicates that the indirect impact of a change of strategy by agent j on another agent does not depend on the other agent's strategy.

Finally, we shall need the following assumption:

Assumption A3: The ranking of agents by $q^j(K)$ is independent of $\{K\}$

(4.6)

This says in intuitive terms that if agent k creates the largest negative externalities when agents in the set $\{K\}$ are investing in loss prevention, then agent k creates more externalities than any other agent whatever the set investing in loss prevention.

Theorem. Let $X_i = N \forall i$ be a Nash equilibrium. If a smallest critical coalition exists for this equilibrium then for some integer K it consist of the first K agents when agents are ranked in decreasing order of $q^j(\emptyset)$.[9]

What are the policy and strategy implications of these results on critical coalitions in the context of global risks? Clearly one is that an equilibrium with no investment in security may be converted to one with full investment by persuading a subset of the agents to change their policies. Leadership, either through trade associations and/or through influential firms that take the lead, may convince others of the need to adopt adequate mitigation measures. A trade association can play a coordinating role by stipulating that any member must follow certain rules and regulations and has the right of refusal if they are asked to do business with an agent that is not a member of the association and/or has not subscribed to the ruling. Even without such a formal mechanism, if a few organizations voluntarily take action, they could convince others to follow suit and induce 'tipping' in the spirit of Schelling (1978).

There may also be a role for well-enforced government standards and regulations coupled with third-party inspections and insurance.[10] For example, third-party inspections coupled with insurance protection could encourage individuals or organizations to reduce their risks from accidents and disasters that could spill over to others. Such a management-based regulatory strategy would shift the locus of decision-making from the regulator to individual firms. The firms would then be required to do their own planning as to how they would meet a set of standards or regulations. If these individuals or organizations take preventive action, they can encourage the remaining ones to comply with the regulations to avoid being caught and fined. This is another form of tipping behavior. Without some type of inspection, low-risk divisions that have adopted risk-reducing measures cannot credibly distinguish themselves from the high-risk ones that have not.

Application: The Anthrax and Beyond Initiative[11]

The anthrax crisis in the fall of 2001 provides an opportunity to discuss a concrete initiative for addressing the global risk problem in the context of the interdependent environment we described above. Although only four anthrax-contaminated letters were ultimately found in the US postal network, the uncertainty regarding the nature and degree of contamination lasted for weeks. During the crisis, hundreds of false alerts occurred daily in the United States and in many postal services worldwide. The decision to shut down the whole US Postal Service had been seriously considered, but the service handles about 700 million pieces of mail every day and shutting it down for just a week, to measure the scale of the contamination better, would have meant that 1 billion pieces of mail would have to be inspected the following week.

Launching an International Debriefing
The anthrax crisis raised a set of fundamental questions about postal security worldwide and how interdependencies affect global postal operations. The 'Anthrax and Beyond' initiative that Lagadec[12] and Michel-Kerjan designed and implemented began in the winter of 2002. They suggested an international debriefing process to gather ideas and then launch concrete initiatives that would let postal operators better handle future contingencies. This initiative had three objectives: (1) learn about others' experiences and lessons from the anthrax crisis; (2) share ideas and proposals to improve the collective reaction to emerging threats (an *(S, S, . . ., S)* strategy); and (3) establish a platform for crisis management that would link Europe and the United States, so that postal operators could connect immediately with their counterparts and with other international organizations.

In order to achieve this goal, it was important to adopt a different posture than simply organizing another conference. The initiative involved people at the highest level in their organizations, and academic experts who clearly understood not only the emerging risks and crises but also possible conflicts of interest in launching the partnership. These neutral experts play a key role in linking the stakeholders and fostering collective thinking and innovation.

Initially, the initiative was to bring together only a few postal operators from France (LaPoste took a leading role in this initiative), Germany (Deutsch Post), the Netherlands and the United Kingdom (Royal Mail). But as the word spread that a core team had undertaken the initiative, postal operators and external stakeholders from a few additional countries joined in, and after a few months nearly 30 countries across Europe and the United States participated in this initiative; a concrete demonstration of the aforementioned tipping effect.

Since emerging crises in interdependent networks would require high-level involvement, international organizations such as the Universal Postal Union and the Comité Européen de Régulation Postale (European

Committee for Postal Regulation) also sent representatives to the two-day conference that took place in Paris in November 2002, one year after the height of the international postal crisis. Postal sector executives shared their experiences, suggested new avenues for management, and launched a debate on new operational capabilities.[13]

Immediate Measurable Output: Capacity for a Global Reaction

The 'Anthrax and Beyond' initiative produced more than just an opportunity for participants to share experiences. It constituted the first step in improving the overall reaction among postal networks in the event of a new transnational threat. A new international partnership among postal operators was developed to create a global crisis-management network to help allow executives of all the European and US operators to connect instantly. The global information-sharing platform was launched at the start of 2003 so that executives could exchange information about the solutions each country is implementing and work out a concerted strategy.

That new capacity for global reaction had its first test on 15 January 2003, the day it became operational. PostEurop had received an advisory from the US Postal Service about a possible anthrax contamination in the Washington, DC area. The network provided postal services across Europe with accurate and timely information on this potential incident, enabling them to assess the scope of the risk. This was a significant improvement over the situation following the anthrax scare of November 2001 when the chairman of a large postal operator could not talk on the phone with two of his counterparts. The 2003 threat eventually proved to be a false alarm, but it was a dramatic kick-off for the network. This capacity for global reaction is still present today.

The beginning of a crisis is not the time to exchange business cards. The improvised responses during a crisis will be incomplete, if not destructive. Efforts are required in advance of any event to make the institutions flexible enough to allow the interdependent concerned parties to coordinate their actions quickly. The above initiative illustrates successful collective actions because they enable information to be shared, strategy to be coordinated and, most important, the establishment of relationships that can function smoothly after a disturbing event begins. In the process, they produce measurable benefits for all stakeholders in the form of better preparation or cost-sharing. It would have been extremely costly for any operator to launch such a solution alone. The lessons of this initiative are relevant to managing global risks in other interdependent networks such as pandemics which could be spread through transportation networks, global supply chains disrupted by a series of major natural disasters, or terrorist attacks.

Mitigating Global Risks: A Methodology Framework

We conclude this subsection by proposing a framework for decision-makers to start thinking about global risks, and suggest how to mitigate them, while at the same time benefiting from these measures. First, it is important to develop criteria for determining risks and to act upon them throughout a well-specified initiative. The stakeholders affected by these risks must also be well specified. One must then specify the available scientific data by characterizing the nature of the uncertainties and the existing interdependencies. In most cases, it may be easier to specify a limited number of scenarios and case studies so that the nature of potential public–private collaboration emerges more clearly. Finally, one must determine the feasible strategies for forming winning coalitions that have a fair or good chance of being implemented.

Here are some of the open questions to consider in this regard:

1. What are the relevant principles to approach our list of global risks?
   - General principles.
   - Principles specific to a given risk.
2. What are the elements of uncertainty for a given risk?
   - Characterizing probability distribution, ambiguities surrounding these estimates or even ignorance in some cases.
   - Specifying losses and their distribution, and uncertainty associated with them.
3. What is the ultimate goal of our efforts at a local, national or international level?
   - Who are the key stakeholders? What are their agendas and the set of options which they are considering? What are measures of success?
4. What types of programs should be evaluated?
   - Role of private and public sectors.
   - Maintaining the status quo.
5. What types of scenarios should be developed?
   - Nature of interdependencies.
   - Single-period scenarios.
   - Multi-period scenarios.
6. What types of cost- and loss-sharing analyses should be undertaken?
   - Impact on different stakeholders.
   - Reconciling differences between key stakeholders.

To implement this strategy we recommend selecting one pilot study (for example, one industry and several major players from different countries, as was done for the 'Anthrax and Beyond' initiative) to illustrate in a concrete way what can be done, by whom, how, at what costs, what are the potential benefits, and over what period of time.

CONCLUSIONS

More and more decision-makers confront situations that are global in scale, of uncertain importance or consequence, influenced by several different players, and temporally unstable. This increasing globalization of economic and social activities worldwide is reshaping the risk landscape, from the more traditional local and relatively well-defined risks to global and often highly uncertain situations where the impacts can be devastating. The leitmotiv becomes interdependency on a large scale. That will require a paradigm shift from the way that most of the risk management literature has been focused. We believe the research community, working in collaboration with leaders in the private and public sectors, has a lot to offer to help understand this new environment better.

In this spirit, we briefly discuss a new initiative recently launched by the World Economic Forum – the Global Risk Network Initiative. This network was founded by the World Economic Forum in 2004 in response to a concern that the international community and global businesses were not able to respond adequately to a changing global risk landscape. The initiative became the Global Risk Network at the Annual Meeting 2006 in Davos, Switzerland in partnership with Citigroup, Marsh & McLennan, Merrill Lynch, Swiss Re and the Wharton Risk Management and Decision Processes Center at the University of Pennsylvania. One of its main goals is to aggregate information about global risks better and to act as a clearinghouse for future risk mitigation and risk financing solutions. In this sense, this initiative is a work in progress (World Economic Forum, 2006, 2007).

The Global Risk Network methodology selected 23 risks ranging from international terrorism, climate change, natural disasters and pandemics to asset price collapse, liability regimes and critical infrastructure disruption. A survey of experts estimated a range of likelihood and potential losses associated with these risks as depicted in Figure 4.3. The correlation between each of these risks was then estimated through consultations with a number of risk experts. This correlation matrix, which reflects how one risk can affect another risk which in turn affects another, is displayed as Figure 4.4.

Figure 4.4 provides decision-makers with some perspective on other issues that could affect their core business which they may not have

Source: World Economic Forum (2007).

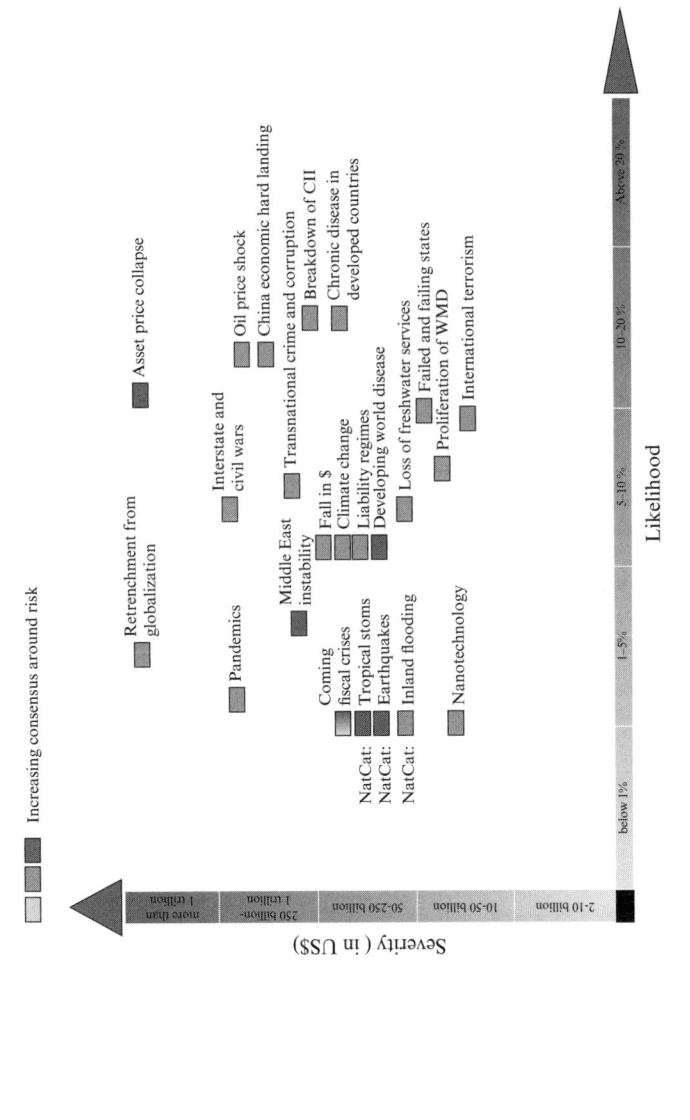

Note: We adopt here the usual approach: likelihood/severity for each risk – no interdependencies.

Figure 4.3 The 23 core global risks

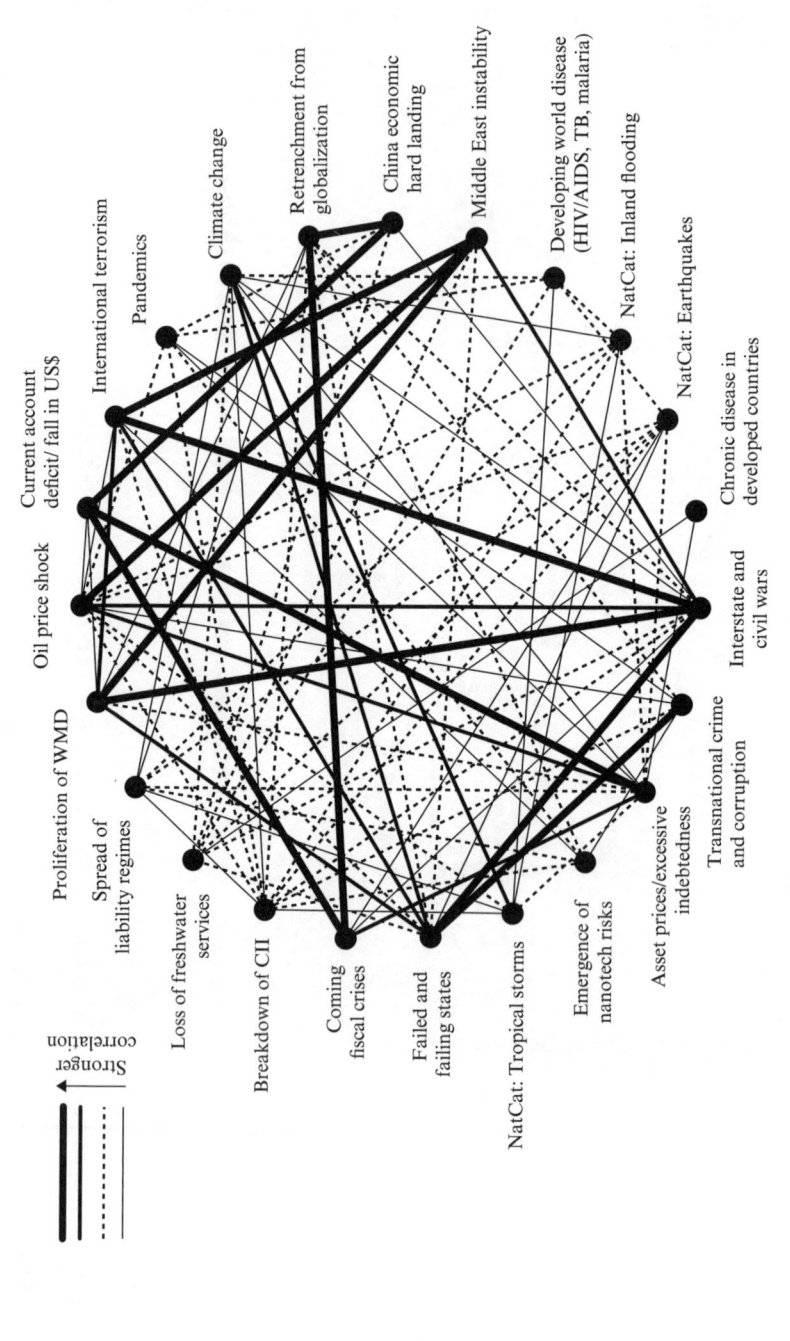

Figure 4.4 New approach to deal with global risks: correlation matrix

considered in their strategic planning process. The large-scale destabilization from events such as the anthrax scare and the SARS epidemic came as a surprise to many managers, signaling that the interdependencies associated with global risks need to be more fully understood and internalized in risk management strategies by firms and governmental organizations.

In fact, it is not yet clear how many key decision-makers in organizations share the view that the above risks are critical ones to consider. For the past ten years the consulting firm PricewaterhouseCoopers (PwC) has undertaken a survey of thousands of chief executive officers (CEOs) worldwide to analyze and understand their concerns regarding the risks that are shaping global business. The PricewaterhouseCoopers Global CEO Surveys are launched annually at the World Economic Forum's Annual Meeting in Davos and the results are widely disseminated. For the tenth edition of the CEO survey in 2007, the Wharton Risk Center collaborated with the firm by including a series of questions related to global risks.

Out of the nearly 1000 CEOs who responded to the survey, more than half indicated that they were not very concerned or not concerned at all by many of the global risks we have discussed above. For instance, 62 percent of them were not very concerned or not concerned at all by the risk of a large pandemics; that proportion was 59 percent in the case of global warming and 51 percent for terrorism risk (PwC, 2007). Whether these responders are focused on their core business and/or whether the experts are overestimating these risks are open questions for future research. If one finds that the first explanation has merit, then what can be done to convince CEOs throughout the world that the risks are real, and induce them to act upon them collectively?

For many companies, these global risks also constitute opportunities to create value by reaching out to new markets and developing new products. Those firms that are capable of developing innovative risk management and risk financing strategies are likely to be the ones to benefit the most from the change in the global risk landscape that is the basis of this chapter. As we point out, proactive cooperation may be a necessary ingredient for understanding the interdependencies associated with global risks and for developing necessary partnerships within a specific industry, across industries, and between the private and public sectors. As national boundaries assume less importance, firms need to take into account interactions at an international level when developing their strategic plans. As is normally the case, proactive leaders will be the ones to glean the benefits from initiatives that reduce the potential impact of future catastrophic events on their activity and those of other affected stakeholders.

NOTES

1. For a discussion on terrorism insurance markets by the authors, see Kunreuther and Michel-Kerjan (2004, 2007a, 2007b) and Michel-Kerjan and Pedell (2006).
2. The notion of 'security externalities' was introduced in Auerswald et al. (2006); see also Kunreuther and Heal (2003), introducing the concept of 'interdependent security'.
3. Gordon et al. (2005) and Rosoff and von Winterfeldt (2006) also analyze the human and economic impacts on the local economy of a dirty bomb exploding in the twin ports of Los Angeles and Long Beach for different attack scenarios. See also Park et al. (2007) for a comparison of the cost of similar terrorist attacks of several US ports (including New York–New Jersey and Houston).
4. There currently is a debate in the US as to whether the federal government should require a 100 percent inspection of incoming cargo containers (the current screening rate is nearly 5 percent). See Martonosi et al. (2005) for a discussion of the feasibility and cost-effectiveness of a 100 percent container inspection policy.
5. See Sheffi (2005) for an analysis of how enterprises can develop protection and coordination mechanisms so that their supply chains are likely to be more resilient to major disruptions such as those discussed in this chapter.
6. For more details on the nature of the risk and interdependencies in global supply chain see Heal et al. (2006).
7. We recognize that there are many scenarios of attack that could inflict additive damage or where the presence of several protection barriers makes a system more unlikely to suffer terrorist attack.
8. This model is based on Heal and Kunreuther (2007).
9. Note that these results on tipping apply only to the type of problems that we introduce here, as these are the ones that have equilibria where all invest and where none invest, so that tipping from the latter to the former is of interest.
10. For a more detailed discussion as to who can use third party inspections and insurance to enforce a regulation, see Kunreuther et al. (2002). They propose this type of public–private partnership as a way of enforcing Sect. 112r of the Clean Air Act Amendments that requires chemical companies and other firms to adopt risk management strategies.
11. This section relies heavily on Lagadec et al. (2006).
12. Patrick Lagadec is with the Ecole Polytechnique in Paris and a founding member of the European Academy of Crisis Management.
13. See *Journal of Contingencies and Crisis Management* Special Issue, 4 (2003), for a detailed description.

REFERENCES

Auerswald, P., L. Branscomb, T. LaPorte and E. Michel-Kerjan (eds) (2006), *Seeds of Disaster, Roots of Response: How Private Action Can Reduce Public Vulnerability*, New York: Cambridge University Press.

Bier, V. (2007), 'Choosing what to protect', *Risk Analysis*, **27** (3), 607–20.

Branscomb, L. and E. Michel-Kerjan (2006), 'Building trust: public–private collaboration on a national and international scale', in P. Auerswald, L. Branscomb, T. LaPorte and E. Michel-Kerjan (eds), *Seeds of Disaster, Roots of Response*, New York: Cambridge University Press.

Camerer, C. and H. Kunreuther (1989), 'Decision processes for low probability events: policy implications', *Journal of Policy Analysis and Management*, **8**, 565–92.

Gladwell, M. (2000), *The Tipping Point*, New York: Little, Brown.
Goodnough, A. (2006), 'As hurricane season looms, states aim to scare', *New York Times*, 31 May.
Gordon, P., J. Moore II, H. Richardson and Q. Pan (2005), 'The economic impact of a terrorist attack on the Twin Ports of Los Angeles–Long Beach', in Harry W. Richardson, Peter Gordon and James E. Moore II (eds), *The Economic Impacts of Terrorist Attacks*, Cheltenham, UK and Northampton, MA, USA: Edward Elgar, pp. 262–86.
Heal, G., M. Kearns, P. Kleidorfer and H. Kunreuther (2006), 'Interdependent security in interconnected networks', in P. Auerswald, L. Branscomb, T. LaPorte and E. Michel-Kerjan (eds), *Seeds of Disaster, Roots of Response: How Private Action Can Reduce Public Vulnerability*, New York: Cambridge University Press.
Heal, G. and H. Kunreuther (2006), 'You can only die once: interdependent security in an uncertain world', in H.W. Richardson, P. Gordon and J.E. Moore II (eds), *The Economic Impacts of Terrorist Attacks*, Cheltenham, UK and Northampton, MA, USA: Edward Elgar, pp. 35–56.
Heal, G. and H. Kunreuther (2007), 'Modeling interdependent risks', *Risk Analysis*, **27** (3), 621–34.
Heath, C. and J.B. Soll (1996), 'Mental budgeting and consumer decisions', *Journal of Consumer Research: An Interdisciplinary Quarterly*, **23**, 40–52.
Hogarth, R. and H. Kunreuther (1995), 'Decision making under ignorance: arguing with yourself', *Journal of Risk and Uncertainty*, **10** (1), 15–36.
Huber, O., R. Wider and O.W. Huber (1997), 'Active information search and complete information presentation in naturalistic risky decision tasks', *Acta Psychologica*, **95** (1), 15–29.
Ibragimov, R., D. Jaffee and J. Walden (2006), 'Non-diversification traps in markets for catastrophic risk', Presented at the National Bureau of Economic Research Insurance group meeting, Cambridge, MA, February.
Keohane, N. and R. Zeckhauser (2003), 'The ecology of terror defense', *Journal of Risk and Uncertainty*, **26** (2/3), 201–29.
Kousky, C. and R. Zeckhauser (2006), 'JARring actions that fuel the floods', in R.J. Daniels, D.F. Kettl and H. Kunreuther (eds), *On Risk and Disaster: Lessons from Hurricane Katrina*, Philadelphia, PA: University of Pennsylvania Press, pp. 59–73.
Kunreuther, H. and G. Heal (2003), 'Interdependent security', *Journal of Risk and Uncertainty*, **26** (2/3), 231–49.
Kunreuther, H., P. McNulty and Y. Kang (2002), 'Improving environmental safety through third party inspection', *Risk Analysis*, **22**, 309–18.
Kunreuther, H. and E. Michel-Kerjan (2004), 'Policy-watch: challenges for terrorism insurance in the United States', *Journal of Economic Perspectives*, **18** (4), 201–14.
Kunreuther, H. and E. Michel-Kerjan (2007a), 'An empirical analysis of the Terrorism Risk Insurance Act (TRIA)', in Harry W. Richardson, Peter Gordon and James E. Moore II (eds), *The Economic Costs And Consequences of Terrorism*, Cheltenham, UK and Northampton, MA, USA: Edward Elgar, pp. 38–64.
Kunreuther, H. and E. Michel-Kerjan (2007b), 'Evaluating the effectiveness of terrorism risk financing solutions', Working Paper, Wharton Risk Management and Decision Processes Center, The Wharton School, August.
Kunreuther, H. and E. Michel-Kerjan (2009), *At War with the Weather*, Cambridge, MA: MIT Press.

Kunreuther, H., A. Onculer and P. Slovic (1998), 'Time insensitivity for protective measures', *Journal of Risk and Uncertainty*, **16**, 279–99.
Kunreuther, H. and M. Pauly (in press), 'Insuring against catastrophes', in F. Diebold, N. Doherty and R. Herring, *Financial Risk Management in Practice: The Known, The Unknown and The Unknowable.*
Lagadec, P., E. Michel-Kerjan and R. Ellis (2006), 'Disaster via airmail: the launching of a global reaction capacity after the 2001 anthrax attacks', *Innovations*, **1** (2), 99–117.
Loewenstein, G. and D. Prelec (1992), 'Anomalies in intertemporal choice: evidence and an interpretation', *Quarterly Journal of Economics*, **107** (2), 573–97.
Lugar, R (2005), 'The Lugar survey on proliferation threats and responses', US Senate, Washington, DC.
Martonosi, S., D. Ortiz and H. Willis (2005), 'Evaluating the viability of 100 percent container inspection at America's ports', in Harry W. Richardson, Peter Gordon and James E. Moore II (eds), *The Economic Impacts of Terrorist Attacks*, Cheltenham, UK and Northampton, MA, USA: Edward Elgar, pp. 218–41.
McClelland, G., W. Schulze and D. Coursey (1993), 'Insurance for low-probability hazards: a bimodal response to unlikely events', *Journal of Risk and Uncertainty*, **7**, 95–116.
Meade, C. and R. Molander (2006), 'Considering the effects of a catastrophic terrorist attack', RAND Corporation, Santa Monica, CA, August.
Meyer, R. and W. Hutchinson (2001), 'Bumbling geniuses: the power of everyday reasoning in multistage decision making', in S. Hoch and H. Kunreuther with R. Gunther (eds), *Wharton on Making Decisions*, New York: John Wiley.
Michel-Kerjan, E. (2003), 'New vulnerabilities in critical infrastructures: a US perspective', *Journal of Contingencies and Crisis Management*, **11** (3), 132–41.
Michel-Kerjan, E. (in press), 'Disasters and public policy: can market lessons help address government failures?' *National Tax Journal*, proceedings of the 99th NTA Conference.
Michel-Kerjan, E. and B. Pedell (2006), 'How does the corporate world cope with mega-terrorism? Puzzling evidence from terrorism insurance markets', *Journal of Applied Corporate Finance*, **18** (4), 61–75.
Milgrom, P. and J. Roberts (1994), 'Comparing equilibria' (with John Roberts), *American Economic Review*, **84** (3), 441–59.
Mould, R. (2000), *Chernobyl Record: The Definitive History of the Chernobyl Catastrophe*, CRC Press.
Park, J., P. Gordon, J. Moore II, H. Richardson and L. Wang (2007), 'Simulating the state-by-state effects of terrorist attacks on three major US ports: applying NIEMO', in Harry W. Richardson, Peter Gordon and James E. Moore II (eds), *The Economic Costs And Consequences of Terrorism*, Cheltenham, UK and Northampton, MA, USA: Edward Elgar, pp. 208–34.
PricewaterhouseCoopers (PwC) (2007), 'Was: within borders. Is: across borders. Will be: without borders?', 10th Annual Global CEO Survey.
PR Newswire (2007), 'Background on SBA's efforts to reduce loan backlog post-Hurricane Katrina', http://sev.prnewswire.com/banking-financial-services/20070725/DC0135525072007-1.html
Rosoff, H. and D. von Winterfeldt (2006), 'A risk and economic analysis of dirty bomb attacks on the ports of Los Angeles and Long Beach', CREATE, University of Southern California, Los Angeles, CA.

Sandler, T (2003), 'Collective Action and Transnational Terrorism', *World Economy*, **26** (6), 779–802.
Sandler, T., J. Tschirhart and J. Cauley (1983), 'A theoretical analysis of transnational terrorism,' *American Political Science Review*, **77** (1), 36–54.
Schelling, T (1978), *Micromotives and Macrobehavior*, New York: Norton.
Schkade, D. and J. Payne (1994), 'How people respond to contingent valuation questions: a verbal protocol analysis of willingness to pay for an environmental regulation', *Journal of Environmental Economics and Management*, **26**, 88–109.
Sheffi, Y. (2005), *The Resilient Enterprise: Overcoming Vulnerability for Competitive Advantage*, Cambridge, MA: MIT Press.
Thaler, R. (1999), 'Mental accounting matters', *Journal of Behavioral Decision Making*, **12**, 183–206.
Wharton Risk Center (2005), *TRIA and Beyond: Terrorism Risk Financing in the US*, Philadelphia, PA: The Wharton School, University of Pennsylvania.
World Economic Forum (2006), *Global Risks Report 2006*, Geneva, Switzerland.
World Economic Forum (2007), *Global Risks Report 2007*, Geneva, Switzerland.

5. NBCR terrorism: who should bear the risk?

Dwight Jaffee and Thomas Russell

INTRODUCTION

The costs to the US economy of the terrorist attacks of 11 September 2001 went considerably beyond the horrendous loss of life and property destruction of that day. The event also triggered disruptions in financial markets which threatened adverse effects on the normal operations of a broad set of newly vulnerable industries.

Immediately following the attacks, the insurance industry, recognizing the new magnitude of this risk, began to place terrorism exclusions in standard commercial property loss contracts. At the same time, mortgage providers and other lenders, aware that collateral was now exposed to terrorist action, refused to make loans unless the borrower obtained terrorism insurance coverage.

In the face of this 'catch-22', the pace of mortgage and other lending slowed, leading to a loss of jobs in construction and other industries dependent on loan markets. Reacting to this, and aware of the obligation to maintain full employment, the US Congress passed the Terrorism Risk Insurance Act of 2002 (TRIA), a temporary measure which made Treasury funds available for three years as a backstop to the private insurance market. The purpose of the Act was to buy time to allow the private market to regain its capacity to handle terrorism events. This did not happen, and the Act was extended by a further temporary (two years) measure, the Terrorism Risk Insurance Extension Act (TRIEA), passed in December 2005.[1] This act expired in December 2007 and was in turn replaced by the Terrorism Risk Insurance Program Reauthorization Act of 2007 (TRIPRA). This act maintains a government presence in the terrorism insurance industry through December 2014.

In passing TRIPRA, Congress recognized that current government arrangements do not fully solve the problem of adequate terrorism coverage. In particular, TRIPRA allows private insurers to continue to exclude terrorism losses that arise from attacks using 'unconventional weapons'.

Consequently, losses caused by nuclear, biological, chemical and radiation (NBCR)[2] attacks remain very difficult to insure.[3] Indeed, the need to close this 'NBCR gap' is a major argument used by supporters of an expanded and permanent government presence in the terrorism insurance line. This chapter discusses the policy issues raised by the absence of NBCR coverage, particularly as they relate to the appropriate sharing of this type of risk between the public and private sectors.

TRIPRA AND NBCR RISKS

Nothing in the language of TRIPRA directly prevents insurers from writing coverage against NBCR attacks. Indeed, if they do offer NBCR coverage, any resulting losses would be backstopped by the Treasury in exactly the same way as losses from conventional terrorist acts. It is also important to note that TRIA and now TRIPRA require insurers in the US to offer coverage against conventional (non-NBCR) terrorism losses to their general commercial insurance customers. So, although TRIPRA provides identical benefits to insurers for all forms of terrorist coverage including NBCR risks, it only requires insurers to provide non-NBCR coverage. As a result, few insurers now offer NBCR coverage. What, then, causes the NBCR gap?

That NBCR coverage can be excluded from terrorist insurance under TRIPRA appears to be accidental, and arises as a consequence of a running together of the specific language of the Act, and historical insurance practice in the US. With respect to terrorism risks in general, the 'must offer' clause in the Act states that insurers:[4]

> Section 103 (B) shall make available property and casualty insurance coverage for insured losses that does not differ materially from the terms, amounts, and other coverage limitations applicable to losses arising from events other than acts of terrorism.

Since insurers in the US have de facto always excluded NBCR losses from their standard policies, their continued exclusion under TRIA was not a 'material difference' and was therefore permitted.

Still, the question arises as to why insurers would refuse to insure this type of loss, particularly given the access to free Treasury reinsurance of losses at the high end made available by TRIPRA. This question is of central importance to current debates on the appropriate role of government. Since the private market refuses to cover NBCR risks under TRIPRA as it now stands, insuring these risks will require either a different type of public–private partnership or, possibly, a new wholly public arrangement. In either case, an understanding of the reluctance of the private sector to write NBCR coverage cannot help but improve the design of any alternative arrangement

WHY IS NBCR COVERAGE LIMITED?

The insurance industry has given a number of reasons why NBCR risk is 'uninsurable' – see GAO (2006, pp. 10–11) – but two concerns dominate the discussion:

1. The potential size of a single NBCR loss is too large to be handled by insurance firms which are constrained to remain profitable on a year-by-year basis.
2. The likelihood of an NBCR loss is difficult to quantify and therefore difficult to price.

We examine each of these in turn.

The Potential Losses from an NBCR Attack are too Large to Handle

Two independent studies confirm the view that an NBCR attack has the potential to cause extremely large aggregate insured losses. Table 5.1 provides RMS Inc. estimates of potential insured losses from specific NBCR attacks. These range from a $28 billion sarin gas attack to a $450 billion tactical nuclear bomb. Property damage represents the larger part of all

Table 5.1 Potential losses from NBCR attacks, $ billion

	Property losses	Workers' compensation	Total
Sarin gas attack (1000 kg ground dispersal)	21	7	28
Dirty bomb (15,000 curies of Cesium-137)	62	0.2	62
Anthrax attack (1 kg anthrax slurry)	35	26	61
Anthrax attack (10 kg anthrax slurry)	112	59	171
Anthrax attack (75 kg anthrax slurry)	266	74	340
Sabotage attack on nuclear power plant	202	15	217
Nuclear bomb (battlefield, 1 kt)	140	100	240
Nuclear bomb (tactical, 5 kt)	250	200	450

Source: Risk Management Systems (2005), Table 2.

Table 5.2 Insured loss estimates, large NBCR terrorist attack ($ billion)

Type of coverage	New York	Washington	San Francisco	Des Moines
Group life	82.0	22.5	21.5	3.4
General liability	14.4	2.9	3.2	0.4
Workers' compensation	483.7	126.7	87.5	31.4
Residential property	38.7	12.7	22.6	2.6
Commercial property	158.3	31.5	35.5	4.1
Auto	1.0	0.6	0.8	0.4
Total	778.1	196.8	171.2	42.3

Source: American Academy of Actuaries (2006), Appendix II.

total losses, although workers' compensation losses are also significant in almost all cases.

Furthermore, these estimates represent only a fraction of total expected losses. First, there would be other forms of insured losses, such as business interruption losses. Second, these are only the direct costs, and do not include any 'multiplier' costs that would arise from economic disruptions across the full economy. For example, estimates put the total losses of the 9/11 attack at more than $190 billion, versus $30 billion in insured losses, and put the economic losses of the London bombing at $4 billion to $6 billion, even though insured losses were minimal; see RMS (2005).

Table 5.2 provides an alternative set of estimates provided in a study by the American Academy of Actuaries of the insured losses from certain NBCR incidents in four US cities. In New York, a large NBCR event could cost as much as $778 billion, with insured losses for commercial property at $158 billion and for workers' compensation at $483 billion. In addition to New York, three other cities were included in the analysis: Washington, DC, San Francisco, CA and Des Moines, IA (see Table 5.2). To give some sense of the scale of these losses, the industry noted that only some $163 billion of the estimated $427 billion policyholder surplus for 2005 was available to cover terrorism risk. Since the surplus in 2006 was in excess of $600 billion, a more current reference scale would seem to be $200 billion. Clearly an NBCR attack could cause insured losses on an unprecedented scale.

The Likelihood of an NBCR Attack

The insurance industry refers to the lack of precision in estimates of the likelihood of an NBCR attack as a second reason why these risks are considered uninsurable. On the one hand, there are commentators who believe that a biological attack in the next ten years is all but certain. In 2005, then US Senate Majority Leader William Frist stated that: 'The greatest existential threat we have in the world today is biological.' He added the prediction that 'an inevitable bio-terror attack' would come 'at some time in the next 10 years'.[5] Views such as these caused the US to spend over $33 billion on bioterrorism countermeasures between 2002 and 2006.

On the other hand, there are experts who point out that such extreme estimates have little scientific underpinning. For example, Mueller (2007, p. 1) points out:

> Even with the September 11 attacks included in the count, however, the number of Americans killed by international terrorism over the period [1975–2003] is not a great deal more than the number killed by lightning – or by accident-causing deer or by severe allergic reactions to peanuts over the same period. In almost all years the total number of people worldwide who die at the hands of international terrorists is not much more than the number who drown in bathtubs in the United States – some 300–400.

The absence of objective analysis is of particular concern, given the well-known tendency to overestimate the probability of easily imagined events. As Tversky and Kahneman (1973) have noted, although there is no necessary correlation between vividness and likelihood, decision-makers are frequently subject to a judgment bias, the availability heuristic, which causes them to make an association between ease of imagining and judged probability even when vividness and frequency are not correlated; see also Sunstein (2003).

Of their nature, events such as terrorist nuclear bomb attacks are very frightening. As Langewiesche (2007) notes of the Hiroshima Nagasaki bombs: 'But the idea was to terrorize a nation to the maximum extent, and there is nothing like nuking civilians to achieve that effect.' This fear is only increased by the frequent use of such events in works of fiction,[6] so it is to be expected that judgments of likelihood are biased upwards; see Slovic (1986). To overcome the availability bias, therefore, it is necessary to pay particular attention to 'base rate' data on the objective likelihood of such attacks. It is clear that even committed nation states such as Iran and North Korea find significant challenges in developing nuclear weapons. So no matter how much they may wish to have them,[7] terrorists on the run from the law face significant – though, as Langewiesche (2007) notes, not insurmountable – obstacles both in developing the weapons and in devising a method of delivery.

With respect to bioterrorism, as Leitenberg (2005, 2006) has noted, a careful analysis of prior bioterrorist attacks raises many questions about the capacity of terrorists to mass deliver the toxic agents. In the Aum Shinrikyo

Tokyo subway gas attack ten terrorists launched five attacks each involving 1 kg of hard-to-get sarin nerve gas. The attack was four years in the planning with an open budget and virtually no monitoring by the Japanese police. Yet the body count was 12 dead total. To be sure this was 12 too many, but in the 2005 London 7/7 backpack-bomb attack, four terrorists with four simple home-made conventional bombs caused 52 deaths.

Again in London, significant international press attention was given to the arrest of a terrorist group in Wood Green accused of a plot to manufacture and distribute ricin gas:

> The group was in possession of 22 castor bean seeds. Their equipment was a coffee grinder, 'with a brown residue' (probably of coffee), a mortar and pestle, and a hand-written recipe taken off the Internet at an Internet café and transcribed into Arabic. The recipe was a derivative of the Maxwell Hutchkinson recipe in the notorious *The Poisoner's Handbook* sold in thousands of copies at US gun shows, a recipe that would very likely not produce ricin, or extremely little of it.
>
> The first tests for ricin in the London apartment were done by a field test kit and apparently registered positive. Within two days, 20 more specific tests were carried out at the British Defence Science and Technology Laboratory, Porton Down, resulting in 17 negatives and three false positives. However, the task of informing the London Metropolitan Police fell to another Porton Down staffer with public liaison responsibilities, who apparently either did not understand or confused the information that he was to relay, with the result that he phoned the press and police saying that 'traces of ricin' had been found. His actions were later attributed to 'incompetence'. (Leitenberg, 2005, p. 27)

Clearly, as economists, we do not possess the expertise to sort through these various viewpoints. But, then, neither do private insurance companies. Thus this risk is not amenable to precise probability calculation and becomes 'ambiguous' in the sense of Ellsberg (1961). It is well known that insurers are 'ambiguity averse' – see Hogarth and Kunreuther (1989), Kunreuther et al. (1995) – preferring to insure risks with known probabilities which are subject to actuarial calculation, rather than risks where it is difficult to attach likelihoods.

When we add to this the fact that insurance executives may also suffer from availability bias and overestimate the likelihood of attack, and that unlike acts of nature, terrorism risks are man made and so subject to manipulation against the insurer, it is not difficult to understand why insurers maintain that NBCR risks are uninsurable.

UNINSURABILITY REVISITED

These facts make the insurer's case for excluding NBCR risk surface plausible, but at a deeper level it is far from clear what principle of profit-driven insurance makes this particularly ambiguous and large risk uninsurable. After all, private insurers currently underwrite conventional terrorism risk, and although the federal government does backstop large losses, a for-profit insurance company such as AIG still has current exposure to terrorist loss in excess of $3 billion.

What is particularly puzzling is why any individual insurance company would ever cite aggregate maximum loss as an argument for not taking at least some part of the risk. Profit-driven insurance companies are free to limit their total exposure on any one class of risk to any amount they wish. In addition (up to state regulatory constraints) they are free to raise the quoted premium to any level which they feel compensates them for the ambiguity in underlying probability.

This would suggest that private insurers should be willing to underwrite at least some amount of NBCR risk. To be sure, the total available from the private sector may then fall short of total demand, but the reaction of the typical private insurer has not been to write limited amounts of insurance, but instead to refuse to write any. In the history of insurance, a pattern of complete withdrawal from a line of insurance following a large loss is well established, and is certainly not unique to NBCR coverage. Private flood insurance, for example, became unavailable after the Mississippi floods of 1927, and private earthquake insurance essentially disappeared in California after the Northridge earthquake of 1994. In both cases it was necessary to develop government programs to support the private insurance market.

THE INSURABILITY OF NUCLEAR REACTORS

The history of private insurance of (non-terrorist) nuclear accidents sheds light on the problem of insuring NBCR risk. At the beginning of nuclear power generation in the US, private insurers refused to insure nuclear plants. Again, doomsday meltdown scenarios were easy to put forward, and since it was a new technology, it was easy to argue that frequency-based probabilities were non-existent. In addition, there can be little doubt that any time the word 'nuclear'[8] is used, special alarm bells sound. Note that private insurers had no problem providing Union Carbide with insurance to cover fertilizer manufacturing plants in India, though the 1984 Bhopal gas tragedy caused approximately 3800 deaths and several thousand other permanent and partial disabilities and cost private insurers $200 million of the final $470 million settlement.

Since the fledgling private nuclear power industry could not expand without insurance, Congress in 1957 passed the Price–Anderson Act to support the private insurance market. Like TRIA, this Act was viewed as a temporary measure providing enough time (ten years), it was thought, to enable the private insurance markets to assess and price this risk. In actuality, the Act was renewed repeatedly, most recently in 2005, extending the Act to 2025.

When passed in 1957, the original Price–Anderson Act provided a $560 million limit on liability for nuclear power plant operators. It was decided that the private insurance industry could provide $60 million of this liability, with the federal government agreeing to cover the next $500 million. The direct role of the federal government was phased out in 1977, and under the current 2005 extension, private insurers are now required to provide $300 million in insurance and the nuclear power industry itself provides further coverage up to a total of $10 billion. Beyond this cover and irrespective of fault, Congress, as insurer of last resort, must decide how compensation is provided in the event of a major accident.

It is interesting that despite the initial cries of uninsurability, private capital now provides $10 billion of insurance to the nuclear industry. The first $300 million of this is provided by an insurance pool, American Nuclear Insurers (ANI), with half of this being reinsured with Lloyd's. The remainder is provided through a contractual agreement administered by ANI, in which payments of $100.6 million per reactor per accident are guaranteed by the operators of nuclear plants, the payments to be collected by an annual assessment of $15 million (inflation adjusted) per operator per year for ten years. In effect this contractual arrangement is just an old form of insurance known as an 'assessable reciprocal mutual'.

By arranging for *ex post* premium assessments, this scheme overcomes the need to set aside large amounts of capital *ex ante*, one of the major impediments to writing catastrophe insurance; see for example Jaffee and Russell (1997). To be sure, as Heal and Kunreuther (2007, p. 13) point out, $10 billion in private insurance is well short of the $100 billion plus in losses which have been estimated to be the cost of a reactor meltdown in a populous state, but an examination of the Price–Anderson Act still establishes a point sufficiently important that we might consider it a general principle of catastrophe insurance. No matter how large the size of aggregate loss, private capital can be induced to flow into any line of insurance so long as the price is right and individual company losses can be limited.

SHOULD TRIPRA BE REWRITTEN TO REQUIRE NBCR COVERAGE?

How can this principle be applied to the problem of the NBCR gap? Clearly the simplest solution would be to rewrite TRIPRA so that the 'must offer' clause no longer permits the exclusion of NBCR losses.[9] This solution, however, is strongly resisted by the insurance industry. The following response by the Aon Corporation to the US Treasury and President's Working Group on Terrorism Insurance is typical:

> As previously stated, despite the fact that TRIA limits an insurer's maximum loss exposure by providing USD100 billion reinsurance facility excess of carrier retentions, NBCR events implicate loss events, that from an economic loss perspective, exceed USD100 billion and the industry's overall policyholder surplus. Given the substantial aggregate retentions associated with TRIEA 2005 for many large commercial lines carriers and their mandatory workers compensation NBCR aggregate exposures, insurers simply do not want to take on catastrophic NBCR event exposure that threatens both the full loss attributable to their TRIA deductible and coinsurance exposures as well as presenting the potential for insured loss exposure in excess of the TRIA annual aggregate reinsurance capacity of USD100 billion. The inclusion of NBCR coverage would also vastly increase the net aggregate Probable Maximum Loss for insurance carriers and require them to cut aggregate capacity for other natural catastrophe exposures as well as standard commercial lines all other peril exposures. Basically, the (re)insurance industry views NBCR event exposure as a 'company killer' where the potential gross aggregate PML is well in excess of the industry's entire capital base. As such, the insurance industry would likely only offer NBCR coverage if it could cap its exposure at a level far below the current USD100 billion plus exposure that these events present. (Aon Group, 2006)

Because this response is so typical, it is worth examining in more detail. In the first place it is difficult to see why the addition of NBCR losses presents 'a potential for insured loss exposure in excess of the TRIA annual aggregate reinsurance capacity of USD100 billion'. Under current TRIPRA provisions, private insured losses are capped at the company's excess of deductible plus 15 percent of its share of aggregate losses up to $100 billion. This is true whether the loss is due to conventional or NBCR terrorist attack, so adding NBCR coverage cannot cause insured loss above this limit.

On the other hand, the industry is correct to note that the addition of NBCR liability would affect the probability of loss within the TRIPRA $100 billion threshold and that this is turn would affect the company's expected loss. In the absence of the $100 billion cap, by standard probability theory, for any joint distribution the expectation, E, of a sum of two random variables X and Y is given by $E(X + Y) = EX + EY$. So, thinking of X as the random variable 'losses by conventional terrorist attack' and Y as 'losses by NBCR', the addition of NBCR coverage would simply add the expectation of that loss to the current level of expected loss with NBCR losses excluded. Assuming firms were free to price this extra risk, additional premiums should exceed the additional expected losses, so net expected profits should be higher when NBCR coverage is provided.

Again, however, it is necessary to consider the role of the $100 billion cap. There are scenarios, albeit unlikely, in which the addition of NBCR risks in fact has no effect on an insurance company's expected loss. If the terrorists view conventional and non-conventional attacks as complements, and conduct a large NBCR attack at the same time as a conventional attack with more than $100 billion in insured loss, the additional NBCR coverage would have no effect on expected loss. In the general case, the additional expected loss from adding NBCR risk will depend on how the joint probability density function of conventional and NBCR loss interacts with the TRIPRA cap.

There are no reliable data with which to make this calculation. Suppose, however, that we accept the industry's view that the addition of NBCR loss would lead to an unacceptable increase in the probability that the deductible will be exceeded together with unacceptable losses in the deductible to $100 billion range. Clearly it is not difficult to rewrite the law to address this concern.

For example, TRIPRA could recognize two forms of terrorist attack, conventional and NBCR. If the attack is certified to be NBCR, then it could be assigned a zero deductible. In that case there is no marginal impact on the current deductible. At the same time, the level of co-pay for NBCR attacks could be set at a lower level, say 10 percent. Note that with these parameters, the maximum loss to the insurance industry is $10 billion on a $100 billion event (less after tax) so that the apportionment of risk as between the public and private sectors is coincidentally of the same order of magnitude as the private–public split for nuclear accidents under the Price–Anderson Act.

Of course, these parameters are just examples. If it is believed that NBCR attacks impose burdens on insurers which require some other special treatment, any combination of deductible and co-pay can be used to reduce the cost of adding this line. This fact was recognized in the failed House Bill, HR 2761. Under this bill, once a loss is certified as being due to an NBCR attack, the industry deductible becomes 7.5 percent (for conventional terrorism it is currently 20 percent) with a step down co-pay to a low of 5 percent for losses above $60 billion (for conventional terrorism the co-pay is 15 percent). The 'make-available' provision for conventional terrorism is extended to NBCR losses. The reduced deductible and co-pay would have gone some way to soften industry objections to adding NBCR to TRIPRA. In addition, these new terms would render moot the conclusion of the recent RAND study (RAND, 2007), that if NBCR risk were to be added to TRIPRA on the same terms as conventional terrorism risk, premiums would need to be raised to such a level that it would have been the equivalent of letting TRIEA expire.

It remains possible, of course, that even with these special NBCR terms, premiums will be increased and demand for terrorism insurance reduced. There is no obvious reason why this needs to happen. We would recommend that if NBCR risk is added to TRIPRA with a 'make available' proviso, it be made clear that insurance companies are allowed to price these risks separately, so that insured individuals could buy this coverage or not as their circumstances dictated. If NBCR risk is unbundled in this way, its inclusion in the extension of TRIPRA would have no effect on the demand for conventional terrorism insurance.[10]

It is also worth noting that since 2001 the financial situation of insurers has improved markedly, and, their protests to the contrary, requiring them to cover NBCR risk with a $100 billion cap ($65 billion after tax) is today a far less burdensome task than it was when TRIA was drafted in 2002. As the Consumer Federation of America (2007) has noted:

> It is clearly within the financial grasp of property casualty insurers to cover an initial $100 billion in losses, or $65 billion after taxes. Insurer retentions under TRIA right now are about $30 billion, plus an additional 15 percent of losses. The President's Working Group on Financial Markets estimates in their report (PWG 2006, p. 26) that there is presently about $6–$8 billion in terrorism reinsurance capacity and $3–$4 billion in private capital from sources like hedge funds.
>
> As this demand for reinsurance and private capital will undoubtedly increase if TRIA coverage is reduced, it is quite conservative to assume that at least $10 billion in reinsurance and $5 billion in private or securitized capital would be available. Thus, property casualty insurers would only have to fill a 'gap' of about $20 billion under this program, which is just over 3 percent of the industry's current $600 billion surplus.

Indeed, with respect to NBCR insurance under workers' compensation, private insurers already provide coverage under the TRIPRA backstop. We turn now to an examination of this problem.

THE SPECIAL PROBLEMS OF WORKERS' COMPENSATION

The workers' compensation line of insurance raises special issues with regard to NBCR attacks. The problems are unrelated to insurance principles, but instead reflect the special history of workers' compensation insurance in the US; see for example Moss (2002, Chapter 6). In order to form the coalition necessary for states to pass workers' compensation insurance legislation, workers and employers made the following deal. Workers would give up the right to sue employers for job-related injury, but workers' compensation insurance would be mandatory for employers and the contract would not be allowed to contain any exclusions. (The Commonwealth of Pennsylvania allows 'acts of war' to be excluded, but the application of that exclusion to 'certified' acts of terrorism has not been tested.)

This means that for the workers' compensation line, private insurers are already providing NBCR coverage, claims of non-insurability notwithstanding. And, as Table 5.2 shows, the exposure to this line is not insignificant. For the scenarios modeled there, workers' compensation losses in New York City (NYC) amount to $483 of the total $778 billion loss, and in all four cities workers' compensation amounts to more than 50 percent of the total loss.

Obviously the breakdown between workers' compensation and other losses depends on the nature of the attack, but unlike conventional terrorism bomb attacks which focus on property, NBCR attacks are particularly hard on any personal insurance line.[11]

THE RAND STUDY OF ANTHRAX ATTACKS

The RAND Corporation, in conjunction with the risk modeling firm Risk Management Systems, has carried out an extensive analysis of the possible losses that would be created from anthrax attacks; see RAND (2005). The RAND study evaluates two different anthrax attacks: one within a single large building; the other released and widely disbursed outdoors. Table 5.3 summarizes the study's major quantitative results. For the indoor anthrax attack, the estimated total insured losses are just under $8 billion, including over $6 billion of workers' compensation claims and

Table 5.3   Allocation of losses by insurance lines from anthrax attacks, ($ billion)

	Indoor attack	Outdoor attack
Property	1.1	100.4
Workers' compensation	6.1	43.5
Group life	0.3	2.5
Individual life	0.2	2.1
Accidental death/dismemberment	0.2	1.5
Health	0.0	22.4
Total	8.0	172.3

Source: RAND (2005), Table S.2.

over $1 billion of property damage claims (primarily the estimated costs of decontaminating the building, including the possibility that the building and its contents would need to be replaced). The total insured losses from an outdoor anthrax attack are estimated to be over $172 billion, more than 25 times as large as the indoor attack. Here the largest component, over $100 billion, is property damage, reflecting the large number of buildings that would become affected and the large costs of decontaminating them. The next-largest component, $43 billion, is workers' compensation claims.

The values in Table 5.3 reflect only insured losses, but these cover all expected workers' compensation claims since, as noted, workers' compensation covers NBCR risk in almost all states. Similarly, the estimates include full coverage of the property damage, since it is assumed that the buildings are all fully insured against such an attack. In reality, a relatively small number of buildings are currently actually insured against the property damage that would be created by an anthrax attack.

The RAND study also evaluates who would be responsible for paying these claims under the 2002 TRIA. For the indoor anthrax attack, the firm(s) insuring the building would initially pay all the claims as a result of their deductibles and co-insurance requirements under TRIA. There would be no taxpayer payments, owing to the relatively small total insured losses of $8 billion. The insured losses would have to reach at least $20 billion before there would be any US taxpayer liability under TRIA.[12]

For the outdoor anthrax attack, the firms insuring the full set of affected buildings would pay virtually the total amount of the claims. Assuming that most of the affected buildings were relatively small, the individual insurers are not expected to exceed their company-specific deductibles. Thus there would no be ability to recoup from future commercial insurance premiums, and US taxpayers would also have no liability. Thus, even though the losses created by the outdoor anthrax attack are 25 times as great as the indoor attack, because they are assumed to be disbursed across a large number of insurers, individual firms cannot recoup their payments from future premium surcharges and US taxpayers continue to have no liability.

Obviously the size of workers' compensation NBCR exposure is not small. If a company in the District of Columbia (where the death benefit is worth approximately $1.8 million) were to lose 300 employees as a result of a terrorist attack, the total claim would equal $500 million (NCCI 2006). However, not all of such claims fall on the private sector. In four states and two territories[13] workers' compensation insurance is provided by a state-run monopoly, and in 13 other states[14] a not-for-profit state enterprise competes with the private sector. Still, the exposure of the private sector is significant. In California, for example, the share of the risk taken by the state enterprise, the State Compensation Insurance Fund, fell sharply between 2005 and 2006 (from over 42 percent to 31 percent) and the state is actively campaigning to attract further private capital.

To the extent that private capital willingly exposes itself to NBCR risk in the workers' compensation line, it would appear that the backstop provided by TRIPRA is already adequate.

GLOBAL RESPONSES TO THE NBCR PROBLEM

Terrorism is a global problem. Some form of government support for terrorism insurance therefore exists in many countries. Prior to 9/11, countries such as the UK, Israel, South Africa and Spain had already experienced terrorist attacks, and in these countries, government programs were already in place to support private markets. The attack on 9/11 caused many other countries – for example France, Germany and Australia – to put in place their own government programs. For an overview of all programs see Guy Carpenter & Co. (2007).

NBCR risk is handled in different ways in different countries. Here is a brief list:

- In the UK, the government-supported terrorism reinsurance pool, Pool Re, makes no distinction between conventional and NBCR risk (a nuclear exclusion was deleted in 2002). The UK also has a sizable non-government supported market and in this market NBCR risk is typically excluded.
- In France the government terrorism insurance scheme GAREAT originally excluded nuclear attacks, but in 2006, nuclear attacks were added so that in France NBCR risk is treated no differently from conventional terrorism risk.
- In Germany NBCR risk is excluded from the government terrorism scheme Extremus.
- In Australia the government-run reinsurance pool ARPC includes chemical and biological loss but excludes nuclear.

As this brief list shows, experience with NBCR risk varies from country to country, but in contrast with the current situation in the US, there are existing public programs (UK and France) which include NBCR risk.

CONCLUSION

The failure of TRIA (and its successor TRIPRA) to sustain a private market in NBCR terrorism insurance is widely recognized as a potentially serious problem for the financing of industries vulnerable to terrorism attacks. Weapons of mass destruction are actively sought by many terrorist groups, and there is little doubt that if such weapons were available, they would be used against targets in the United States.

The easiest way to close the NBCR gap would be to amend TRIPRA to expand the 'make available' clause so that it included NBCR losses, and adjust the deductible and co-payments for these losses as necessary to overcome industry resistance. This was the approach adopted in the failed HR 2761.

A more radical approach would be to take this opportunity to examine the question of whether enough time has now passed for a private market in terrorism insurance (including NBCR insurance) to be viable with less government support. Seven years have passed since 9/11 2001, and in these years insurers' reserves have risen to $600 billion. If the government were simply to cap all terrorism losses at say $100 billion ($65 billion after tax) it does not seem unreasonable to require private insurers to bear this risk.

On the other hand, a completely free market in terrorism risk is probably not viable at this time. If all government support was removed and private providers of workers' compensation insurance were to abandon this line, it is quite probable that the burden of any loss would fall on the public sector anyway. Such a crisis can be avoided by recognizing the special problems of NBCR insurance, requiring that both it and conventional terrorism insurance be 'made available', but capping the losses at some sum (say $100 billion) which is within the capacity of the private market for insurance.

NOTES

1. The pros and cons of permanent government intervention in this industry have been extensively debated; see for example Rand (2007), Wharton (2005) and Jaffee and Russell (2006).
2. A full description of the categories on NBCR loss may be found in GAO (2006), p. 6.
3. Some limited NBCR coverage is available, for example through the Catlin group – see http://production.investis.com/catlin/news/releases/archive2006/2006-06-12/ – but the conditions are very restrictive.
4. AVAILABILITY – Section 103(B) of the Terrorism Risk Insurance Act of 2002 (15 U.S.C. 6701 note; 116 Stat. 2327).
5. Frist (2005).
6. Recently, for example, an episode of the very successful television show *24* featured the detonation of a terrorist nuclear bomb in Los Angeles.
7. Osama bin Laden's desire for such a device has been noted frequently: see, for example,

the testimony of Jamal Ahmad al-Fadl, a native of Sudan and ex-bin Laden associate, in the trial of the earlier World Trade Center bombing: *United States of America* v. *Usama bin Laden, et al.* (S(7) 98 Cr. 1023), prosecuted February–July 2001 in the United States District Court (transcripts at http://cryptome.org/usa-v-ubl-dt.htm).
8. In his economics Nobel Prize acceptance speech, Schelling (2005) explains the non-use of nuclear weapons after World War II in part by the baggage which the word 'nuclear' brings to strategic war analysis.
9. This is the approach that was taken in HR 2761.
10. 'Background risk' could provide an exception in which the demand for conventional terrorism insurance might decline. Under the current system, with NBCR terrorism coverage generally unavailable, organizations might compensate by purchasing additional conventional terrorism coverage – this is the effect of background risk. When NBCR terrorism coverage becomes available, organizations might eliminate this additional conventional coverage, although we would still expect the sum of conventional and NBCR terrorism insurance coverage to rise.
11. According to the Insurance Information Institute, workers' compensation losses made up only 6 percent of total insured losses in the 9/11 conventional attack, http://www.iii.org/media/facts/statsbyissue/terrorism/. This fraction may grow with the growing incidence of respiratory disease associated with the clean-up.
12. The deductible and co-insurance limits have been increased even further under the 2007 extension of TRIA, TRIPRA, and therefore insurers would recoup even less from future premium surcharges, and US taxpayers would become liable only at a threshold even higher than the quoted $20 billion
13. North Dakota, Ohio, Puerto Rico, the US Virgin Islands, Washington and Wyoming.
14. Arizona, California, Colorado, Idaho, Maryland, Michigan, Minnesota, Montana, New York, Oklahoma, Oregon, Pennsylvania and Utah.

REFERENCES

American Academy of Actuaries (2006), Letter to the President's Working Group on Financial Markets; public comment record, US Department of the Treasury, available at http://www.actuary.org/pdf/casualty/tris_042106.pdf.

Aon Group (2006), Response to the US Treasury and President's Working Group: Terrorism Insurance, available at http://www.aon.com/us/busi/risk_management/risk_transfer/terrorism.

Congressional Budget Office (2004), 'Homeland security and the private sector', www.mipt.org/pdf/Homeland-Security-Private-Sector-CBO.pdf.

Consumer Federation of America (2007), 'Testimony before the Senate Committee on Banking, Housing, and Urban Affairs', http://www.consumerfed.org/pdfs/TRIA_Senate_Testimony022807.pdf.

Ellsberg, D. (1961), 'Risk, ambiguity, and the savage axioms', *Quarterly Journal of Economics*, **75**, 643–69.

Frist, W. (2005), 'US senate leader urges "Manhattan project" against bio-terror threat', Agence France Presse, 27 January.

Government Accountability Office (GAO) (2006), 'Terrorism insurance: measuring and predicting losses from unconventional weapons is difficult, but some industry exposure exists', GAO-06-1081, www.gao.gov/new.items/d061081.pdf.

Guy Carpenter & Co. (2007), 'Global terror insurance market', http://gcportal.guycarp.com/portal/extranet/popup/pdf_2007/GCPub/Terror%20Report%202007.pdf?vid=2.

Heal, G. and H. Kunreuther (2007), 'Environmental assets and liabilities', available at http://www.kellogg.northwestern.edu/research/risk/federal/heal-kunreuther.pdf.
Heyes, Anthony and Catherine Liston-Heyes (2000), 'Capping environmental liability: the case of American nuclear power', *Geneva Papers on Risk and Insurance*, **25** (2), 196–202.
Hogarth R. and H. Kunreuther (1989), 'Risk, ambiguity and insurance', *Journal of Risk and Uncertainty*, **2**, 5–35.
Jaffee, Dwight and Thomas Russell (1997), 'Catastrophe insurance, capital markets, and uninsurable risks', *Journal of Risk and Insurance*, **64** (2), 205–30.
Jaffee, Dwight and Thomas Russell (2006), 'Should governments provide catastrophe insurance', *The Economists' Voice*, **3** (5), 1–8.
Kunreuther H., J. Meszaros, R. Hogarth and M. Spranca (1995), 'Ambiguity and underwriter decision processes', *Journal of Economic Behavior and Organization*, **26**, 337–52.
Langewiesche, W. (2007), *The Atomic Bazaar: The Rise of the Nuclear Poor*, New York: Farrar, Straus & Giroux.
Leitenberg, M. (2005), *Assessing the Biological Weapons and Bioterrorism Threat*, http://www.strategicstudiesinstitute.army.mil/pubs/display.cfm?pubID=639.
Leitenberg, M. (2006), 'Bioterrorism, hyped', *Los Angeles Times*, 17 February, http://www.latimes.com/news/printedition/california/la-oeleitenberg17feb17,0,3489887.story?coll=la-headlines-pe-california.
Lyman, Edwin (2004), 'Chernobyl on the Hudson?' a study commission by Riverkeeper, Inc., September.
Moss, D. (2002), *When All Else Fails*, Cambridge, MA: Harvard University Press.
Mueller, J. (2007), 'Reacting to terrorism: probabilities, consequences, and the persistence of fear', http://psweb.sbs.ohio-state.edu/faculty/jmueller/ISA2007T.PDF.
NCCI (2006), 'Workers Compensation Terrorism Impact and Education Study Group issues paper', https://www.ncci.com/NCCI/Media/PDF/TRIA_Study_Group_Jan_06.pdf.
PWG (2006), 'Terrorism risk insurance report of the President's Working Group on Financial Markets', available at http://www.insureagainstterrorism.org/PWGReport.pdf.
RAND Corporation (2005), 'Distribution of losses from large terrorist attacks under the Terrorism Risk Insurance Act', RAND Center for Terrorism Risk Management Policy.
RAND Corporation (2007), 'Trade-offs among alternative government interventions in the market for terrorism insurance', http://www.rand.org/pubs/documented_briefings/2007/RAND_DB525.pdf.
Risk Management Systems (RMS) (2005), 'A risk-based rationale for extending the Terrorism Risk Insurance Act', September.
Schelling, T.C. (2005), 'An astonishing sixty years: the legacy of Hiroshima', Nobel Prize Lecture, http://nobelprize.org/nobel_prizes/economics/laureates/2005/schelling-lecture.html.
Slovic, P. (1986), 'Informing and educating the public about risk', *Risk Analysis*, **6** (4), 403–15.
Sunstein, S. (2003), 'Terrorism and probability neglect', *Journal of Risk and Uncertainty*, **26** (2/3), 121–36.

Tversky, A. and D. Kahneman (1973), 'Availability: an heuristic for judging frequency and probability', *Cognitive Psychology*, 5, 207–32.
Wharton (2005), 'TRIA and beyond: Terrorism risk and financing in the US', available at http://knowledge.wharton.upenn.edu/papers/1299.pdf.

6. The resilient response to economic terrorist targeting in the UK[1]
Jon Coaffee

INTRODUCTION

> The attacks of September 11th indicate a new kind of threat to urban security and imply the need for new urban knowledge's or at least fresh ways to apply older understandings. (Molotch and McClain, 2003, p. 679)

In previous years global cities have been significantly targeted by terrorist groups, in many cases necessitating a counter-response aimed at minimizing the impact of future attacks as well as attempts to reassure international business that the city in question is safe for them to invest and locate in (Rogers, 1996; Chernick, 2005). Today, given the events of September 11th and subsequent acts of terror around the globe, counter-terrorist security and management features are now a regular part of the urban condition in the core cities of the global economy (Coaffee, 2003a; Graham, 2004). However, such 'everyday' counter-terrorist features have a long genesis and have constantly evolved over recent years in response to the changing tactics and targeting philosophies of would-be terrorists.

Although these are international considerations, this chapter uses the response of central London authorities both pre- and post-September 11th as the lens through which to view attempts to reduce the real and perceived threat of terrorist attack against the critical economic infrastructure in the UK – essentially the financial zones of central London. The alterations in the urban landscape and managerial systems of these zones since the early 1990s provide a tangible example of the shifting nature of terrorist threat and response.

1990s ECONOMIC TERRORIST TARGETING AND TACTICS

In the early 1990s important financial centres became prime targets for terrorist attack because of their vast array of new 'designer' office buildings, their increasingly cosmopolitan business communities, the damaging effects of large-scale bombing on commercial activities, and the significant media attention and publicity that could be obtained by the terrorists. Examples of such commercial targeting outside of the UK included attacks in the financial districts of New York in 1993, and Tokyo, Madrid, Paris, Riyadh and Colombo in 1995. In all cases, with the exception of Tokyo,[2] the terrorist tactics employed utilized vehicle-borne improvised explosive devices (VBIEDs) directed against parts of the critical business infrastructure (Coaffee, 2003a).

In a UK context, the main terrorist threat during the early-mid 1990s came from the Provisional Irish Republican Army (PIRA), with its prime target being the City of London (also known as the 'Square Mile' or 'the City') due to its iconic value as the traditional heart of British imperialism and its economic importance at the centre of the British and global financial system (Rogers, 1996).

Large-scale bombs were detonated in the City in the early 1990s, and a number of smaller devices were discovered before detonation. In addition, in the early to mid-1990s, two further bombings targeted the London Docklands – London's secondary financial centre and seen by many as a symbolic extension of the City of London. In all cases, the PIRA attacks were characterized by an attempt to generate maximum disruption to business, gain maximum publicity for its cause and, importantly, to minimize casualties. In all cases the vehicle bombs were 'parked' and warnings were issued.

During the 1990s the threat of such economic terrorism received a good deal of attention from international leaders. For example, the British Prime Minister at the time, John Major, cited the PIRA bombings in London and the Tokyo subway gas attack as examples of how terrorism affects security and freedom, and stated, perhaps prophetically, that 'it is a problem from which no one can hide and on which we must all co-operate. This is the security challenge of the 21st century'.[3]

The threat of terrorist attack in the 1990s served to affect global business centres both materially and symbolically. Urban terrorism created security threats to which municipal and national governments were forced to respond in order to alleviate the fears of their citizens and business community. As a result, security measures similar to those used to 'design out crime' were increasingly introduced, including physical barriers to restrict access, advanced surveillance techniques in the form of security cameras, insurance regulations and blast protection, as well as innumerable indirect measures that operate through activating individual and community responses.

Risk Reduction in 'Fortress London'

In the City of London large PIRA bombs exploded in April 1992 and April 1993 with a number of smaller devices being detonated or discovered. Estimates at the time put the bomb damage for each major blast at between £500 million and £800 million. The City at this time employed around 130,000–140,000 people and generated an estimated output of £10 billion to £15 billion a year for the UK economy (Corporation of London, 1995). In addition the London Docklands was also targeted by the PIRA in November 1992 (unsuccessfully) and successfully in February 1996. These bomb threats in both financial centres, and the subsequent reaction of London authorities and the police, served to highlight the use made of both territorial and technological approaches to counter-terrorist security.

The counter-response employed within the City of London, in particular, drew heavily on lessons learned from attempts to 'beat the bombers' in Belfast in the 1970s and 1980s, with the adoption of 'territorial' approaches to combating terrorism by restricting and monitoring access to vehicular traffic through a series of surveilled checkpoints.[4]

After the first major London bomb in 1992 such a 'fortified' solution to counter terrorism was dismissed as an overreaction by the police and business community. After the second major City bomb in 1993 the adoption of additional security was no longer an option. As such, in July 1993 what was referred to in the media as a Belfast-style 'ring of steel' was activated in the City, securing all entrances to the central financial zone (Burns, 1993; Smith, 1993). Essentially, the entrances into the City were reduced from more than 30 to seven, where road-checks manned by armed police were set up.[5]

The Home Secretary at that time, noting the economic importance of the City, also summed up the situation the City faced, and indicated the delicate balancing act between security and business normality that was required:

> There is a balance to be struck between having roadblocks which will frustrate what the terrorists can do, and creating enormous traffic jams which would disrupt the life out of the City. (cited in Garvey, 1993)

The City's ring of steel represented a far more symbolic and technologically advanced approach to security, which tried to avoid the 'barrier mentality' of Belfast in favour of less overt security measures which would be more acceptable to the international business community. However, the security cordon provided a highly visible demonstration that the City was taking the terrorist threat seriously in order to reassure financial industries that they were doing all they could to stop terrorism and avoid business relocation (Donegan, 1992; Jones, 1993). Indeed, within London, the ring of steel was promoted to the wider London population in terms of traffic management and environmental improvements, which attempted to remove any references to the ongoing terrorist threat (Corporation of London, 1993a, 1993b).[6] Over time the geographical scale of the security cordon increased to a 2001 position where 75 per cent of the Square Mile was covered within the secure zone (this cordon was again expanded in August 2005).

In the City of London the retrofitting of ever-advanced closed circuit television cameras (CCTV) in both private and public spheres backed up territorial approaches to security. Publicly the police, through a partnership scheme called Camera Watch, encouraged private companies to install CCTV in liaison with neighbouring businesses, whilst at the entrances of the ring of steel, as well as strategic points around the Square Mile, the most technologically advanced CCTV cameras available at the time were installed.[7] In the space of less than a decade, where terrorism had been considered a serious threat, the City of London was transformed into the most surveilled space in the UK, and perhaps the world, with over 1500 surveillance cameras operating (Coaffee, 2003b).

The London Docklands, containing the iconic Canary Wharf complex, was also the focus for counter-terrorist planning through the 1990s. Following the thwarted 1992 attack, managers at Canary Wharf initiated their own 'mini-ring of steel', essentially shutting down access to a private estate within the Docklands complex (Coaffee, 2003a). Such an approach combined attempts to 'design out terrorism' with changing approaches adopted by the police and the private security industry. Security barriers were thrown across the road into and out of the complex, no-parking zones were implemented, a plethora of private CCTV cameras were installed and identity card schemes were initiated.

After the 1996 bomb in the southern part of the Docklands, the business community successfully lobbied the Metropolitan Police to set up an anti-terrorist security cordon to cover the whole of the Docklands – the so-called 'iron collar', modelled on the City of London's approach – amidst fears that high-profile businesses might be tempted to relocate away from the area (Finch, 1996; Hyett, 1996; Coaffee, 2003a). Subsequently, a security cordon was initiated for the whole Dockland peninsula comprising four entry points which at times of high-risk assessment would have armed guards stationed at them. High-resolution CCTV cameras were also installed. The most noticeable difference between the scheme initiated in the Docklands and that in the City was the overt advertising of the Docklands security cordon – 'Security cordon – stop if directed' – on large signs at entry points into the cordon, instead of downplaying the zone's anti-terrorism purpose.

Prior to September 11th counter-terrorism measures in the UK, largely deployed to stop VBIEDs, focused almost exclusively on London's financial zones, with these zones becoming synonymous with increasing the 'quality of life' where heightened levels of security were a key selling point in attempting to market the affected economic districts to potential investors and tenants. For example, the London Chamber of Commerce and Industry's *Invest in London* publications highlighted the City of London's cordon as a key contributor to enhanced safety in London, leading to an increase in 'business confidence' (London Chamber of Commerce and Industry, 1994, 1996). Equally, when the 'iron collar' was constructed in the Docklands, it was referred to as a 'ring of confidence' which gave those inside the security zone a feeling of safety, preventing the feared exodus of high-profile tenants to more remote edge-of-city sites (Coaffee, 2004; Coaffee and Murakami Wood, 2006).

Risk and Insurance against Terror

Increased fortification provided material evidence that London's financial zones did all they could to restrict the damage the PIRA could inflict on the UK economy through attacking the reputation and physical infrastructure of London. A less obvious, but equally important, manifestation of the reaction to terrorism in London in the 1990s was the insurance crisis around terrorism cover, whereby the commercial market withdrew coverage, essentially 'redlining' the whole of the UK and, importantly, the financial zones of London.[8]

After the 1992 City bomb, figures released by the insurance industry noted that the cost of damage (initially estimated at around £800 million) was likely to be more than the total cost of damage in Northern Ireland over the previous 22 years (around £600 million).[9] This bomb, according to the insurance industry, demonstrated the potential insurance cost of a major strike against the City or Docklands, bringing home to the PIRA the operational effectiveness of planting a bomb in Britain's financial centres, given the disruption it caused to the UK economy.[10] The net result was that both the British insurance industry and its reinsurers began publicly to express concern about their future liabilities to such risk, and hence their ability to underwrite terrorism insurance in the UK (Gloyn, 1993; Bice, 1994).[11]

Several months after the St Mary Axe bomb, the major European reinsurers wrote to all their ceding companies indicating that they would be excluding terrorism from their standard policies from January 1993. This was a particular worry for the Corporation of London, the local government for the City, which had a large proportion of its buildings portfolio up for renewal on the last day of 1992 (Lapper, 1992). On 12 November 1992, no doubt significantly influenced by the large bomb found and diffused at Canary Wharf in the London Docklands, the Association of British Insurers (ABI) issued a press statement indicating that it had advised its members (the majority of the UK insurers) to exclude terrorism from their commercial policies in line with most other European countries. The statement went on to blame the reinsurers for this scenario in that 'leading world-wide reinsurers have forced this exclusion on the UK market in the light of considerable losses earlier this year in major bombing incidents and the continuation of terrorist bombings in the UK'.[12]

At this time the Lord Mayor of London wrote to the Prime Minister expressing concern over the future economic success of London if the government refused to offer cover against terrorist attack. He argued that the situation could have disastrous effects on London's economic competitiveness through impacts on the UK economy, and by reducing the attractiveness of locating in London (Connan and Durman, 1992). For example, a letter to the Prime Minister from the City Property Association underlined that: 'the City is clearly a prime target, not only because of the value of its buildings, but also because of its importance to "UK LTD"'. The letter continued by indicating that the government should step in to help avoid areas of London becoming 'no-go' areas in terms of occupancy and investment.

This potential crisis was avoided on 21 December 1992 when the government indicated that it was willing to act as the ultimate reinsurer, the so-called 'insurer of last resort', behind a pool of insurers which had agreed to set up a mutual company, Pool Reinsurance (Pool Re), to provide cover in the traditional way (see for example Gunn, 1992). Under this scheme the insurance industry was effectively passing on all the additional premiums in return for the transfer of the terrorist risk to the government, which was reinsuring the scheme. The way that the scheme was set up ensured that the government would not be held responsible for compensation for businesses which were not insured for terrorist risk, and that the premium rate for such terrorism insurance policies would be periodically reviewed in line with political developments in Northern Ireland. The government agreed to meet 90 per cent of further claims not covered by premiums gathered by Pool Re. The insurance companies would collectively cover the remaining 10 per cent. Government involvement effectively aimed to spread the financial risk of further terrorist attack throughout the national economy, and away from the central London markets.

Under Pool Re, areas of the UK were initially designated as either high risk (Zone 1) or low risk (Zone 2). All those in Zone 1 would be charged the highest premium and hence, if there was a large take-up of policies, the pool of premiums could be maximized. This logic relied on all those businesses in Zone 1 regarding themselves as 'at risk' from terrorism.[13] Central London premiums in particular were especially high due to the large number of buildings within the financial zones considered 'target risks'. However, the reality of Pool Re was that insurance risk became concentrated in the financial zones of London due to low take-up from the rest of the country. Potentially, this could have had devastating effects on the economic competitiveness of London in terms of loss of business confidence, and in particular through a terrorist strike against an uninsured building.

Such a concentration of risk in central London continued to increase after the Bishopsgate bomb in April 1993, as the premiums collected at that point by Pool Re were not sufficient to cover the expected bomb damage. The subsequent rate review led to massive increases in terrorism premiums for those in the highest-risk properties – most notably those in London's financial zones. Revisions to the premium structure following the rate review were announced on 3 June 1993 where a number of changes were made in relation to the cost of insurance. These included the creation of four zones (A–D) for the calculation of premiums instead of the two (Zones 1 and 2) that previously existed.[14]

Under the new scheme, Zone A, which comprised most of central London, had a rate of 0.144 per cent per annum of total sum insured. This amounted, in some cases to a 300 per cent increase in premium (see Table 6.1). Zone B (rate of 0.072 per cent; increase of 200 per cent) comprised the rest of London and the central business districts of most other major towns.

In the early to mid-1990s, the concentration of financial risk in the City and Docklands reinforced the view that physical security was necessary, and that the innumerable private security initiatives being undertaken were justified. As will be shown in the next section, such protective measure could also help reduce future insurance costs (Coaffee, 1996).

On 31 August 1994 the Provisional IRA announced a ceasefire that prompted immediate calls to Pool Re regarding possible premium discounts.[15] These began to be offered in 1995 but were suspended as a result of the 1996 PIRA attack on the London Docklands.[16] The Docklands bomb in February 1996 meant that once again uncertainty surrounded the cost and provision of terrorism insurance. In addition it was also reported that some of the worst-affected buildings were not covered by terrorism insurance (Shillum, 1997).[17]

In the latter years of the twentieth century and in the early twenty-first century, as funds for Pool Re grew and the terrorist threat receded,

Table 6.1 Terrorism insurance premium increases as a result of the Pool Re rate review of 1993 (Zone A terrorism premiums, formerly Zone 1)

Value	Premium of previous basis (without target risk loading)	Premium from July 1993	Increase (%)
£0.5M	£450	£720	+60.0
£1.0M	£900	£1 440	+60.0
£5.0M	£4 500	£7 200	+60.0
£10.0M	£8 300	£14 400	+73.5
£25.0M	£17 750	£36 000	+103.5
£50.0M	£31 000	£72 000	+132.5
£100.0M	£51 000	£144 000	+182.5
£250.0M	£102 000	£360 000	+251.5
£500.0M	£175 000	£720 000	+311.5

premium rates fell significantly, and many companies declined to take out cover or took out coverage through alternative market mechanisms. Despite this Pool Re still maintained a sizable membership and by the end of 2000 the company had accumulated a large surplus of £665 million.[18]

The Genesis of 'Resilient Planning' in London

The changing risk agendas of the 1990s brought about a series of changes in the way in which the insurance industry attempted to spread the financial risk of terrorism. At the same time there can be seen to have been a series of relationships developing between the way in which the insurers viewed the risk of terrorism and the way in which it was perceived by those responsible for the physical security enacted around the financial zones in London. The processes involved can be seen to be subtly supportive of one another, as both were concerned with maintaining the reputation of London as a safe and secure business centre. The behaviour of the insurance industry can also be seen to have been important in influencing processes that resulted in the increased fortification of the urban landscape, as well as educating business about the risks faced. In particular, contingency planning was widely utilized as an anti-terrorism measure in order to improve the ability of businesses in the financial zones to 'bounce back' from a terrorist incident: that is, to become more resilient and mitigate potential losses. This was important from an insurance perspective as terrorism insurance covered business interruption as well as material damage.

There were two main elements to such contingency and continuity. First, there was the creation of Crisis Recovery Plans (CRPs) which highlighted how London could bring about a 'business as usual' situation as soon as possible after a large-scale attack (Frost, 1994). This was most noticeably employed in the Square Mile where CRPs were initiated at two levels: first, in relation to individual companies; and second, in respect of a strategic City-wide plan. After the St Mary Axe bomb many companies had been preparing CRPs that made contingency for temporary relocation to peripheral 'disaster recovery space' at short notice. At the time of the Bishopsgate bomb, CRPs instigated by the Corporation of London at a City-wide level were also in evidence. The Corporation's disaster plan had been refined through practice drills and aimed to get people back to work as quickly as possible. For example after the Bishopsgate bomb, Baily (1993, p. 3) highlighted the success of contingency planning, concluding that, 'the juggernaut of the City had shuddered and slowed, but it never stopped moving'. Importantly, the international finance community commended the quick response of the Corporation, indicating that the bomb would not drive them out of the City.

CRPs employed after Bishopsgate were, as noted in the Corporation's *City Research Project* (1995, p. 27), themselves a result of corporate change at a global level to mitigate a variety of risks and develop some form of integrated emergency management. In particular this research project report noted that 'the large institutions which have taken the most extensive measures have not done so solely because of a specific threat [terrorism] but rather as part of a global scheme, not least to counter infrastructural failure such as power cuts and flooding (another danger in London)'. The Corporation continued by indicating that in its opinion its efforts were superior and more proactive to those in other global financial centres:

> The level of contingency planning both by the Corporation and by individual firms is in contrast to centres such as New York, where the response to the World Trade Center blast [in 1993] was impressive but *ad hoc*. (Corporation of London 1995, p. 27)[19]

The second form of contingency planning was the increased importance placed upon developing security plans, which included the risk management response (such as CCTV, access control and stand-off areas, and blast protection) that formed the basis of protective security. Security planning, like CRP, at this time can be expressed on two levels: first, the private response of individual companies in terms of risk management measures; and second, the coordinated response of the police and the local government in constructing strategic security cordons and associated security infrastructure.

A key reason business undertakes risk management measures (CRPs and security plans) is because insurers look upon them favourably. A common complaint made about Pool Re's rating system is that initially it did not provide any premium reduction incentive for companies or local authorities to take risk management measures (Gloyn, 1993). However, the insurance industry can be seen to have contributed to the reinforcement of security in the Square Mile and Docklands through policy changes in the Pool Re underwriting manual that increasingly gave opportunities for premium discounts for occupiers who fortified their buildings through the use of security measures, adequate sprinkler systems or who had up-to-date and tested crisis response plans. The review of Pool Re in July 1993 introduced improved discounts for risk management measures for up to 12.5 per cent of the total policy premium.[20] As well as individual organizations improving risk management with the hope of improving their security and of getting a discount from Pool Re, the Corporation of London also tried unsuccessfully to get a premium discount for its coordinated security response – the ring of steel and associated measures.[21]

The responses in London during the 1990s to terrorist risk elicited a growing awareness of the need to be proactive and prepared for a catastrophic incident. This requirement was further ratcheted up after the events of September 11 which led to a new rhetoric of 'resilience' being used to characterize emergency planning procedures for dealing with terrorist attacks (Coaffee, 2006).

CHANGING RULES OF THE GAME: THE RESILIENT RESPONSE TO SEPTEMBER 11

The unprecedented events of September 11th led to an instant counter-response from London authorities and police forces which initially focused upon the overt fortressing of 'at risk' sites. In central London, the ring of steel and the iron collar swung back into full-scale operation as part of a coordinated London-wide operation, including attempts to 'police-out' terrorism by deploying over 1500 extra police to the streets. In addition certain prominent or iconic buildings were crudely fortified against vehicle-borne bombs, such as the US Embassy and the Houses of Parliament, by so-called 'rings of concrete' (Coaffee, 2004).

The initial strategy adopted in central London was that the police were uniquely prepared to cope with the threat of global terrorism, given over 30 years of active experience of dealing with terrorist threats, and as such, the approach adopted was 'business as usual' with the balancing of security needs with realistic threat assessments. There was also a very real need to reassure global businesses that they should not relocate from London through fear of attack (Coaffee, 2004).

What is clear is that September 11th refocused the minds of London's public authorities and police forces on counter-terrorism, along with the realization that high levels of technical surveillance, which have proved relatively successful against domestic and 'conventional' terrorism, might be ineffective against new terrorist methods such as the use of chemical, biological, radiological or nuclear (CBRN) sources, suicide attack or penetrative vehicle entry into guarded areas. As highlighted in the last section, counter-responses to pre-September 11th threats of terrorism, predominantly seen as emanating from VBIEDs targeting major financial or political centres, often utilized planning regulations and advanced technology to create 'security zones' where access was restricted and surveillance significantly enhanced. September 11th made such counter-terrorist tactics appear inadequate, and security policy began to shift to proactive and pre-emptive solutions, and 'active anticipation and reflexive risk management strategies' (Heng, 2006, p. 70). Post-September 11th, metaphors of 'resilience' have been increasingly used to describe how cities and nations attempt to 'bounce back' from disaster, and to the embedding of security and contingency features into planning systems and critical infrastructure protection in adaptable and flexible ways (Coaffee, 2005).[22]

In London, there was concern not only for 'new' forms of attack but also an extrapolation of conventional methods – most notably car-bombing, which was expected still to make up the majority of planned terror attacks. Most notably, improved fortressing and hostile vehicle mitigation has been developed around and within 'at risk' sites including the addition of crash-proofing measures to stop penetrative vehicle attacks.[23] Such defences, as previously noted, were initially rolled out simply as concrete blocks placed strategically around key buildings, but have over time been replaced by specialist and highly robust steel barriers, often with attempts made to blend them into the streetscape through the use of ornamental design.

Most noticeably, though, September 11th has forced a rethinking of traditional emergency planning and counter-terrorist tactics given the increased magnitude of the threats faced, especially those from CBRN sources which many terrorist groups have expressed significant interest in utilizing in attacks. This realization of a greater and potentially more catastrophic threat profile was also acknowledged by the UK's terrorism insurance scheme, Pool Re, which redefined what it considered to be acts of terrorism to an 'all risks' basis to cover damage caused by CBRN incidents, flooding or aircraft impact. As of January 2003, there was also a doubling of pre-September 11 Pool Re premiums (Kunreuther and Michel-Kerjan, 2004) reflecting the greater risk profile being faced.

A Resilient London

Counter-terrorist experts now talk about the 'new normality' we have entered after September 11th where 'risks can only be managed, not completely eradicated' (Heng, 2006, p. 70). Whereas during the Cold War the 'threat' was perceived as monolithic, with the emergency planning response controlled by central government with response from a small number of public agencies, the new world of 'resilience planning' is focused upon a series of complex threats and hazards (some of which are terrorist related), where local government is expected to take a lead in response, enabled by a far higher level of inclusiveness from multiple stakeholders and business interests.[24]

Prior to September 11th the UK government was already assessing the merits of developing a multiscale emergency planning infrastructure as a result of the failure of institutional cooperation during severe incidents of flooding, fuel protests and the spread of foot-and-mouth disease in cattle (Smith, 2003). The increased threat of terrorism post-September 11th sped up this process, leading to the development of a coordinated multilevel resilience infrastructure replacing previous emergency planning processes (Coaffee, 2006). In particular, the influential Civil Contingencies Act (CCA, 2004) sought to establish a consistent degree of civil protection and emergency preparedness across the UK (Walker and Broderick, 2004). As O'Brien and Read (2005, p. 356) noted, the Act 'clears outdated legislation, re-defines emergencies, clearly identifies the roles and responsibilities of all participatory organisations, introduces a mandatory regime for responders and replaces the previous outdated system for emergency powers'.[25]

In the UK, since the 1970s, London has understandably remained the focus of attention for terrorists, and this did not change after September 11th. As a result, in 2002 and pre-dating the CCA, a specialist emergency planning partnership – the London Resilience forum (or partnership) – was established to address the strategic emergency planning needs of London, which were seen as well developed for dealing with conventional emergencies but required re-evaluating in the light of the September 11th attacks:

> 11 September 2001 brought sharply into focus the need for London to be able to respond quickly and effectively if a similar incident occurred in the capital. A coalition of key agencies – known as the London Resilience Partnership – joined forces in May 2002 to plan and prepare for potential emergencies. This was the first time a strategic, pan-London regime was established that could co-ordinate planning across London. (London Prepared, 2003)

The London Resilience forum operates as a strategic partnership and includes representatives from London's emergency services, transport sectors, the health sector, central and local government (including the Greater London Authority), private utility companies, the military, the business community and the voluntary sector.[26]

The London response post-September 11th was based on restricting the opportunities for terrorists to strike and in preparing the capital for the inevitable attack (which came in July 2005). In broad terms the role of the London Resilience forum in countering the threat and impact of terrorist attack is fourfold and based predominantly on attempts to retain a competitive business edge for London.

First, disseminating information to Londoners and local governments (and tourists) so that they might be better prepared to protect themselves. In the context of the terrorist threat, the development of 'community resilience' or the 'responsible citizen' is seen as increasingly important where advice offered by public authorities is likely in the future increasingly to pass on the responsibility of emergency response to communities and individuals as a supplement to more detailed strategic and institutional strategies (Mythen and Walklate, 2006; Coaffee and Rogers, 2008).

Second, to encourage business continuity planning, which involves liaison with individual business and business associations to promote the updating and regular testing of contingency and security plans which help facilitate a return to 'business as usual' as soon as possible after an incident. This is a particular concern, as in 2004 a survey by the National Counter Terrorism Security Office, the London Chamber of Commerce and Industry and London First[27] indicated that only 58 per cent of London businesses had adequate security and contingency plans in place (Think London,[28] 2004).

Third, the development of a series of strategic emergency plans – for example for mass fatality planning or the development of evacuation plans for London. These plans are regularly validated in tabletop or live simulated tests, which also give an opportunity to test standard procedures and assess staff competencies.

Examples of such London-wide tests have included Exercise Capital Response in 2002 and Exercise Capital Focus in 2003.[29] The most high-profile test conducted since September 11th was Exercise Osiris II in 2003 which aimed to test specific elements of the operational response to a chemical attack on the London Underground. This exercise focused on Bank junction in the heart of the City of London, and followed a desktop exercise, Osiris I.[30] More recently, the biggest post-September 11th transatlantic counter-terrorism exercise, Atlantic Blue, was conducted in April 2005 involving the UK, US and Canada (known as TopOff 3 in the US and Triple Play in Canada). This exercise simulated internationally linked terrorist incidents. The UK used London's transport system as its simulation test bed in order to assess the vulnerability of passengers when bombs were left on buses and the Underground (note: the events of July 2005 followed this pattern).[31] The evaluation of this test also raised serious concerns over 'soft targets' in London (Townsend and Hinsliff, 2005; see also the next section).

Fourth, the London Resilience forum is involved in the emerging security agenda surrounding the 2012 Summer Olympic Games.[32] The London Resilience Partnership has been commissioned to scope the extent of Olympic resilience preparedness activity across agencies in London. The London Resilience Team has undertaken to coordinate pan-London resilience activity for the Olympics including liaison with key agencies such as the Olympic Delivery Authority, the London Organising Committee, various government departments involved in security-related issues, and the Association of Chief Police Officers (London Prepared, 2007).

THE EMERGING THREAT: CONTEST AND THE TARGETING OF CROWDED PUBLIC PLACES

In the UK, and especially London, resilience against terrorism has undoubtedly become a relevant concept for politicians and policy-makers alike (Coaffee and Rogers, 2008). Since early 2003, the UK has had a long-term strategy for developing resilience for counter-terrorism (known within government as CONTEST). Its aim is to reduce the risk of terrorism, so that people can go about their daily lives freely and with confidence. This resilience strategy is divided into four strands: Prevent, Pursue, Protect and Prepare (Home Office, 2006) which aims to both reduce the likelihood of a place being attacked, and assist in the response stages if an attack occurs. This is shown diagrammatically in Figure 6.1.

CONTEST has forced a rethinking of traditional emergency planning and counter-terrorism tactics, given the increased magnitude of the threats faced, especially those from CBRN sources. Equally, CONTEST has focused upon the threat posed by person-borne explosive devices in a multitude of crowded public places. Such a changing mode of terrorist attack is now setting new challenges for the security agencies (Rees, 2006) especially in the 'Protect' and 'Prepare' strands of CONTEST. Although debates continue about the relationship between new and traditional threats, the methods and tactics adopted by terror groups are novel, innovative and increasingly focused on mass casualty strikes or multiple coordinated attacks (such as in Madrid in 2004). Such attacks, often conducted by suicide attackers and tactically aimed at soft targets and more generally crowded places – such as hospitals, schools, shopping

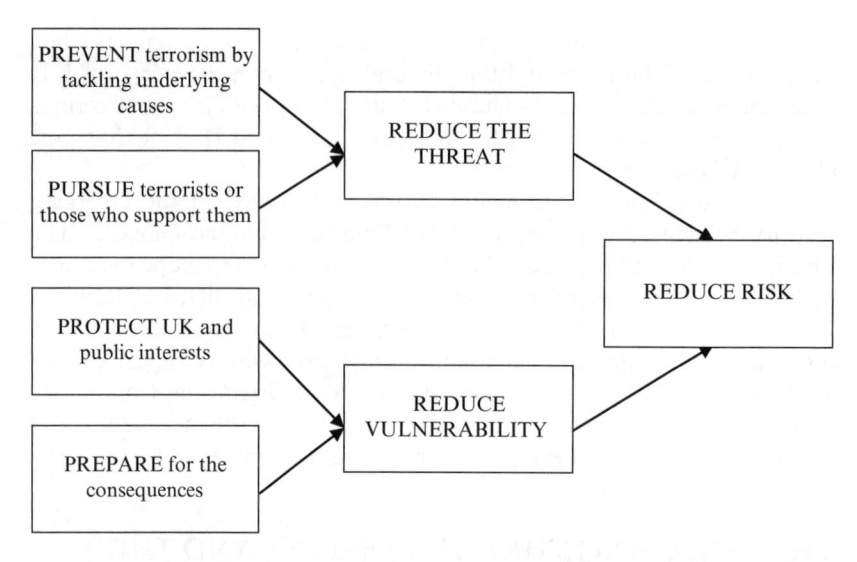

```
┌─────────────────┐
│ PREVENT terrorism by │
│ tackling underlying  │
│ causes          │
└─────────────────┘
                    ┌─────────────────┐
┌─────────────────┐ │  REDUCE THE     │
│ PURSUE terrorists or│→│    THREAT      │
│ those who support them│ └─────────────────┘
└─────────────────┘                        ↘
                                            ┌─────────────────┐
                                            │  REDUCE RISK    │
┌─────────────────┐                         └─────────────────┘
│ PROTECT UK and  │                        ↗
│ public interests│   ┌─────────────────┐
└─────────────────┘ → │    REDUCE       │
                     │ VULNERABILITY   │
┌─────────────────┐   └─────────────────┘
│ PREPARE for the │
│ consequences    │
└─────────────────┘
```

Figure 6.1   The UK Government's CONTEST strategy

promenades, entertainment and leisure complexes, iconic and tourist sites, the rail network and religious sites – have led to considerable ongoing and multidisciplinary research (Silke, 2004; Pedhazur, 2005).

In the UK this concern for the vulnerability of crowded public places has been longstanding but has received greater policy attention at certain times, most notably after the multiple coordinated attacks on the London Underground on 7 July 2005.[33] Importantly, the emergency plans developed by the London Resilience forum that were utilized for this incident appeared to work well, although it was acknowledged that lessons could be learnt (London Resilience, 2006).[34]

The success of the response and recovery planning after the 7/7 explosions was illustrated by the limited economic impact as a result of the bombings. After an initial fall, the FTSE 100 index was only 1 per cent down on the previous day. This deficit was fully recovered on 8 July. The major financial institutions including the Bank of England and the Treasury also revealed in the aftermath of the bomb that the major financial zones in London had been able to keep trading as a result of long-standing contingency planning that has set up a 'secret chatroom' to allow communication between financial institutions and traders (*BBC News*, 2005). The insurance impact of the July 2005 attacks was also minimal, although there was a slight increase in demand for cover. Although the damage caused was substantial, the reserves (over £2 billion built up by Pool Re over the early years of the twenty-first century) meant Pool Re could easily cover the claims made.

Once again, after the unsuccessful coordinated improvised car bomb attacks in central London in June 2007 against a nightclub, the talk was of the need to defend crowded public places.[35] This failed attack and the improvised attack against Glasgow airport the next day[36] has led to an urgent reassessment by Counter Terrorism Security Advisors[37] of other venues where large numbers of people congregate, with a view to providing additional protection. This has been backed up by large and ongoing streams of work being conducted by the National Counter Terrorism Security Office (NaCTSO) on disseminating protective security advice to the managers of crowded public places deemed vulnerable to terrorist targeting.[38]

Balancing Prevention and Recovery

In today's so-called 'age of terrorism' the security challenges facing global business centres are ever changing, necessitating increased attention being given to both preventative and recovery strategies. From a physical and preventative security perspective, on 10 August 2005 the City of London's ring of steel was widened to include more businesses in the City as far as practicable. This was a direct result of a police report post-7/7 that talked of an 'inevitable' attack against 'the obvious target' – the financial zones of London (BBC, 2005). For example the Commissioner of the City of London Police highlighted that there had been 'hostile reconnaissance' of the City on several occasions since the September 11th attacks:

> Potential targets that had been staked out included iconic sites, businesses and prominent buildings. Every successful terrorist group pre-surveys its target. There's no doubt we've been subject to that surveillance. If you want to hurt the Government, hurt people and you want to cause maximum disruption . . . where better to hit than at the financial centre? (Cited in *Edinburgh Evening News*, 2005)

Terrorist targeting against the UK, predominantly by al-Qaeda-linked groups, is still focused upon London, and in particular the financial zones where maximum damage can be done to 'UK plc'. Police sources still see the City of London as the central target. This is an area today that is genuinely an international crowded place – an area that generates 10 per cent of the UK gross domestic product (GDP), has a $500 billion foreign exchange turnover, controls 56 per cent of the global equity market, and has 400,000 workers and more than 5550 foreign banks (Lovegrove, 2007).

However, as most recently seen by the attack against Glasgow Airport, it would be wrong to assume that London is the sole target of would-be terrorist. Since the late 1990s the experience of London in coping with the terrorist threat – through the creation of the London Resilience forum

– has been disseminated across the major provincial cities in the UK and adapted according to the risk profile of individual places (Coaffee, 2006). Equally, the technologies adopted in the financial zones of London in their fight against terrorism – most notably CCTV recording technology and a variety of alert systems – have been utilized by the other main cities in the UK. Likewise, since 2001 counter-terrorist initiatives to assist business and to deal with both traditional and new forms of terrorist attack, which have emerged out of London's experience of dealing with terrorism, have been increasingly rolled out across the UK in order to heighten the speed of response as well as to aid business continuity. Such initiatives include Project Griffin (training private security guards to assist the police in incident control and hostile reconnaissance monitoring)[39] and Project Argus (how business can plan for terrorist attacks in crowded places).[40]

In summary, the UK counter-terrorism strategy (CONTEST) now provides a framework 'to develop and implement plans and programmes to strengthen counter-terrorism capabilities at all levels of Government, the emergency services, business and the wider community' (Home Office, 2006, p. 3). Whereas the greatest threat undoubtedly still focuses upon the central financial zones of London, the threat profile is now shifting towards different types of 'softer' targets and non-London locations.

CONCLUSION: LONDON PREPARED?

Since the early 1990s the UK, and in particular London, has sought to develop a robust and proportionate approach to counter-terrorism. Post-September 11th national UK guidelines and policy rhetoric has sought to provide a balance between democratic rights of access and risk management responses in the new age of terrorism. Today, the response to terrorist risk usually poses the question 'Are we prepared?' rather than 'Can we prevent it?' (Coaffee, 2006). Given the vast array of targets, strategies and technologies available to would-be terrorists, traditional and often static counter-terrorism approaches focused on 'planning-out' terrorism are no longer suitable without appropriate managerial resilience.

Since September 11th, the threat of terrorism has evolved rapidly, and new approaches to counter-terrorism are needed in response. For example, crowded public places are at high risk, and cannot be subject to traditional security approaches such as searches and checkpoints without radically changing public experience. The creation of an environment that is inherently more resilient and less likely to suffer attack, through designing or managing-out different forms of terrorism, offers hope of improving security. As Little (2004, p. 57) notes:

Threats are unpredictable and the full range of threats probably unknowable... Security in this situation needs to be flexible and agile and capable of addressing new threats as they emerge. Protective technologies have a key role to play in making our cities safer but only if supported by organizations and people who can develop pre-attack security strategies, manage the response to an attack, and hasten recovery from it.

In this context there has been a paradigm shift from counter-terrorism towards resilience, which is quickly becoming a key factor in shaping how global cities and their business environments are structured. Likewise, developing resilient urban responses to terrorism is a fluid process and one which must be able to adapt to changing types of terrorist threat. In particular, greater attention and government resources are now being given to the changing nature of threat to 'crowded places', which has forced a rethinking of traditional emergency planning and counter-terrorism tactics given the increased magnitude of the threats faced, especially those from CBRN sources and suicide attacks aimed at 'soft' targets.

At present the UK, and in particular London, is at the forefront of developing resilience policy against terrorism and provides a template that might in the future be adapted by other countries. The London approach attempts to emphasize proportionality of response – that is, trying to maintain business continuity and the functional integrity of urban spaces without creating a sense of undue fear or producing negative social impacts.[41] In short, for resilience (in both the urban design and managerial senses) to be successful and, importantly, sustainable in the long term, it must not only be effective (and cost-effective) but must also be acceptable to the owners, inhabitants and users of particular places. Here, acceptability encompasses complex financial, legal, ethical, social and aesthetic considerations. For example, what is the level of security that the public or business community will tolerate? What is the cost of security for the public and private sectors? What types of security environment are sustainable and create public confidence? What powers should be afforded to police to hunt terrorists? And what are the civil liberty implications of this?

Increasingly, lessons learnt in London are being transferred to other global business centres as well and experiences shared on a mutual basis with other police forces in global cities. Most notably, connections are commonly made between the London Resilience partnership and New York City's Office of Emergency Management. Equally, the respective police forces – the New York City Police Department (NYPD) and the City and Metropolitan police forces in London – share intelligence, have officer exchange programmes, and transfer technology. For example the City of London's 'pager-alert' scheme has been rolled out to New York and great interest is being shown in the City of London Police's Project Griffin initiative.

Likewise, at a national level the terrorism insurance scheme Pool Re has helped pave the way for similar public–private partnerships in the US so that terrorism insurance can be seen as 'an important tile within the mosaic of . . . national security' (Kunreuther and Michel-Kerjan, 2004, p. 212).

Most recently, London-style physical and technological security has also come to New York. This was a process that began almost immediately after September 11th but in more recent years has begun to be strategically developed (Mollenkamp and Haughney, 2006). Although the central business district in New York is now dotted with private security cameras (NYCLU, 2006), in early 2006 wireless CCTV cameras began to be installed on poles 30 feet in the air – the first of nearly 500 cameras to be installed as part of a major drive against crime and terrorism.[42] A key justification for the scheme was the use made of London's 'panoptical' scheme to track the July 2005 bombers' movements across the city on the day of attack (Hays, 2006). In New York such a strategic counter-terrorism programme is constantly evolving. It is claimed that by the end of 2007 over 100 automatic number plate recording cameras were monitoring vehicles moving through Lower Manhattan roadblocks.[43] This will be supplemented, as in the City of London and the London Docklands, by public CCTV and more than 3000 private security cameras. This security system – now called the Lower Manhattan Security Initiative – ultimately aims to 'detect, track and deter terrorists' (Buckley, 2007). The entire New York operation is forecast to be fully in place and running by 2010, in time for the projected completion of several new corporate buildings in the financial district. Civil liberties advocates, however, feel misled about this controversial scheme.[44]

The events of September 11th have served not necessarily to create new urban responses but to reinforce pre-existing trends as a reaction to new forms of terrorist risk (Chernick, 2005). In this sense the financial zones of London have undoubtedly developed a reputation for themselves in terms of their 'bounce-backability' – or resilience – to terrorism. For example, a recent report by the London Chamber of Commerce and Industry (2005) highlighted the remarkably quick return (hours not days) to 'business as usual' after the attacks of 7 July.

London's long history and reputation of effective counter-terrorism is now being branded and used to promote the city and its business centres further on the global stage. Such promotion now plays on the importance of the 'safety' of the city as part of the 'sell' to external investors. A recent statement by London First summed up the commitment of the London business community to work in partnership with the police to enhance preparedness:

> London First aims to make the UK capital the best city in the world to do business. That includes improving our security and our resilience. We aim to help our

members and London businesses generally to improve London's preparations for and protection against terrorist attack. (cited in Think London, 2007)

As opposed to an image of security in 1990s central London of 'checkpoints and cameras', what has emerged in London since September 11th is a well-integrated, properly resourced and proactive style of emergency 'resilience' planning, which is being increasingly utilized by marketing agencies to promote and enhance the 'London Prepared' brand and build confidence in London as an integral part of the global economy.

NOTES

1. The research for this chapter has been supported in part by a UK research council grant (EP/F008635/1) Resilient Design (RE-DESIGN) for Counter-Terrorism: Decision Support for Designing Effective and Acceptable Resilient Places.
2. In Tokyo in 1995 12 people were killed and many injured by the release of the nerve agent sarin into the central Tokyo subway (see for example Juergensmeyer, 1997).
3. Cited in Jones (1996).
4. In the 1970s central Belfast was seen as a laboratory for radical experiments on the fortification and territorializing of urban space as attempts were made to stop persistent car-bombing by encircling the centre with tall steel gates – the original 'ring of steel' (Brown, 1985).
5. Locally, the ring of steel was referred to as the 'ring of plastic' as the temporary access restrictions were initially based primarily on the funnelling of traffic through rows of plastic traffic cones (Coaffee, 2004).
6. The extension to the ring of steel in 1997 was promoted as the 'Traffic and Environment Zone' with no reference made to counter-terrorism (Coaffee, 2003a).
7. In February 1997, 24-hour automatic number plate recording cameras (ANPR), linked to police databases were fitted at entrances to the ring of steel. These digital cameras were capable of processing the information and giving feedback to the operator within four seconds (Norris and Armstrong, 1999).
8. Insurance redlining can be simply defined as the refusal to offer coverage in a geographical area due to adverse risk. Redlining has also been studied in relation to the lending practices of banks, mortgage firms and loan institutions.
9. In Northern Ireland, the government had long accepted responsibility for damage caused by terrorism given the withdrawal of traditional insurance mechanisms in the late 1960s (Greer and Mitchell, 1982).
10. Subsequently it emerged that the initial figures released by the insurance industry were a large overestimation.
11. The insurers' concerns were for two main reasons. First, the large number of catastrophic incidents that had occurred in the years preceding the bombing, which had pushed many insurers and reinsurers near to the limits of insolvency. Second, the nature of terrorist attack defied most of the normal 'laws of insurance', as the insurance industry could not quantify the potential financial exposure of a terrorist bombing when they could not predict where it was going to be located, its explosive force, or how business disruption would affect financial markets. It was also reported that the reinsurers realized that the direct insurers did not have accurate financial risk profiles in place for areas such as the City, and hence adequate information about potential liability could not be accurately calculated. As such given these restrictions the insurance industry felt economically vulnerable.

12. Association of British Insurers (ABI) press release, 12 November 1992.
13. There were nine designated high-risk centres: Birmingham, Glasgow, Leeds, Manchester, London (not just the City and West End, but all London postcodes), Bristol, Liverpool, Edinburgh and Cardiff. In addition, if a property was located next to a high-risk property, such as a government building or a high-profile construction project, an additional 'target risk' premium of 50 per cent was charged. In short, Zone 1 rates were approximately 3–5 times those of Zone 2 without the target risk classification.
14. The ABI commented that already some 20–30 per cent of businesses in London did not have terrorism cover, rising to 70 per cent or more in the provinces. However, to keep the terrorism pool viable, premiums needed to be increased, as the firms taking out cover were predominantly in high-risk locations (see for example Lapper, 1993). The realignment of zones was done to produce a sufficient cash flow into the pool to achieve its stated objectives of nil cost to the government, and to be able to withdraw from the scheme as soon as possible.
15. As a result of the ceasefire a number of changes were made to Pool Re that became effective, in most cases, from 1 January 1995. A deposit premium of 60 per cent of the annual terrorism premium was paid and the 40 per cent balance would only be payable should estimated claims for acts of terrorism exceed £50 million during 1995.
16. From January 2005 a 40 per cent discount was given although this would have to be repaid if claims made against Pool Re reached £50 million. This limit was increased to £75 million in 2006.
17. After this incident, Pool Re announced a considerable increase in the number of clients taking out cover with it. Considerable interest was also being shown in the alternative schemes that had entered the market which in 1995 provided cheaper and more tailored alternatives to Pool Re.
18. However gross premiums fell significantly from a high of £369 million in 1994 to only £39 million at the end of 2000. This reflected a lack of coverage take-up as well as an 85 per cent discount rate given by Pool Re on premiums as a result of no terrorist attacks. At the end of 1999, Pool Re had 213 members spread between UK companies (104), Lloyd's syndicates (32) and insurance companies in the European Union and other parts of the world such as Australia and the US (77).
19. Furthermore, this report highlighted that the City viewed the threat of terrorism as something to be proactive against as opposed to just reactive, and that 'the degree of fatalism with regard to deterring terrorist incidents observed in officials interviewed in the United States was in contrast to the proactive approach of the City after its first bomb' (Corporation of London, 1995, p. 27).
20. For example, the Corporation had to insure around £5 billion–£6 billion of property so any risk management discount was welcomed.
21. Whilst the ring of steel enhanced security in the opinion of most, these risk management measures provided the most concrete example of a proactive security strategy that was unable to elicit a financial discount from Pool Re. However, there was also a strong suspicion that if the ring of steel were removed there would have been significant problems of insuring against terrorism within the Square Mile. In short this meant that whilst the City could not obtain a discount for the ring of steel, its removal would have caused a potential crisis in the market with regard to the provision of insurance cover (Coaffee, 2003a).
22. As Godschalk (2003, p. 137) has noted: 'resilient cities are constructed to be strong and flexible rather than brittle and fragile ... their lifeline systems of roads, utilities and other support facilities are designed to continue functioning in the face of rising water, high winds, shaking ground and terrorist attacks'.
23. Such tactics were used, for example, in the attack against the British Consulate in Istanbul in 2003.
24. 'Resilience' is a term used in many academic disciplines today, but first came forth in ecology literature to describe the way natural ecosystems recover to a steady state or carrying capacity after a perturbation caused by external factors. In the post-September

11th world UK policy-makers adopted it as a positive and proactive term with which to develop new ideas of counter-terrorism (Coaffee and Rogers, 2008).
25. Such a resilience governance infrastructure applies to both terrorist attack (such as July 2005 in central London) but also other risk events such as fears over avian influenza (February 2007) or foot-and-mouth disease (August 2007).
26. The London Resilience Team acts as a secretariat for the forum.
27. London First is a business membership group supported by 300 of the capital's leading businesses with the shared objective of improving and promoting London.
28. Think London is the official inward investment agency for London.
29. This was a table-top exercise which exercised the 'command, control communication and consequence management issues following a catastrophic incident' to ascertain whether current structures and provision could cope with an event on the scale of September 11th (London Prepared, 2006). Exercise Capital Focus in 2003 tested the revised structures in an exercise designed to trail communication arrangements and information flows between the lead Resilience Co-ordinating Group and the Cabinet Office Briefing Room (COBR).
30. For this day-long test the City of London was locked down and London's emergency services were tested for their state of preparedness and their ability to work in a coordinated fashion, giving 'blue-light' services the opportunity to test the effectiveness of new specialist equipment, including chemical suits.
31. The UK Command scenario involved 2000 people from the Metropolitan Police, City of London and British Transport Police services, Ministry of Defence and numerous government departments and agencies, two London borough councils, the fire and ambulance and health services. This provided the opportunity to test the existing procedures for domestic and international incident management and public information dissemination.
32. On 6 July 2005 London was awarded the 2012 Olympic Games by the International Olympic Committee, having persuaded the voting panel that the city could organize the event efficiently and, importantly, safely (Coaffee and Johnston, 2007). This was, however, a security project that had been factored into the bid from the earliest stages and is a central feature of its preparatory planning. The day after this announcement of the Olympic bid result a number of suicide bombers detonated home-made bombs on the London transport system. Almost immediately the estimated cost of security for the 2012 Games increased dramatically from a naively low estimate of $450 million to over $1.5 billion (Coaffee and Johnston, 2007).
33. In this incident four separate but connected bombs exploded – three on the London Underground and one on a bus – killing 56 people (52 commuters and four suicide bombers).
34. Being properly prepared involves planning for a wide range of emergencies, not just terrorist attack. The partnership is currently preparing for how London would respond to pandemic flu, large-scale evacuation and severe weather conditions – incidents that could threaten the capital.
35. On Friday 29 June a car bomb was planted in central London outside a popular nightclub, Tiger Tiger. The car, packed with 60 litres of petrol, gas cylinders and nails, was parked near Piccadilly Circus. Earlier a device only 170 metres away had been removed and impounded by traffic wardens from a nearby street. Both bombs were poorly constructed and luckily failed to explode.
36. On Saturday 30 June a blazing car was driven into Glasgow Airport's terminal building. It is believed this was an improvised attack and that the planned attack was likely to have been similar to failed attacks in London one day before.
37. Counter Terrorism Security Advisors (CTSAs) are specially trained police officers whose primary role is to provide help and guidance on all aspects of counter-terrorism protective security.
38. In support of the crowded places stream of work, NaCTSO has recently developed guidance for sporting stadia, arenas, shopping centres, and bars, pubs and clubs (NaCTSO,

2007). There is also further concern being expressed about the management of the security threat, and in particular the danger from long security checking queues at airports (Milmo, 2007) and other events of arrangements where rigorous security checks are in force.

39. In 2004, the City of London Police and the Metropolitan Police launched Project Griffin. Project Griffin is a joint partnership with the private sector security industry and was developed in London in the post-September 11 era when counter-terrorism was becoming more formalized as the UK shifted from a focus on the PIRA to unconventional terrorism (which has brought with it different challenges and in many cases required a greater number of personnel). The underlying principle of Project Griffin was to train security officers from the major financial organizations in central London, so that they are better equipped to be of assistance to the police in the event of a major incident. The importance of the lessons learnt from the partnership between the City of London Police and the financial industries sector, during the PIRA years, has (at the time of writing in 2007) been rolled out to a further 18 cities in the UK to raise awareness in relation to counter-terrorism and law enforcement issues in order to equip security personnel better to deal with their organizations' security challenges on a day-to-day basis and in the event of a major incident. In particular, Project Griffin is most concerned with trying to disrupt hostile reconnaissance – as well as aiming to provide cordon support and /or high visibility patrols, and supporting the police service during critical incidents. For example on 7 July 2005 in the central financial zones of London an additional 6000 private security guards assisted the police (City of London Police, 2006).

40. This scheme has been influential across the UK in aiding business continuity since 2006–07. Project Argus is a National Counter Terrorism Security Office (NaCTSO) initiative which explores ways to aid businesses in preventing, handling and recovering from a terrorist attack, particularly against crowded public places. This is done through workshop events across the UK which provide an opportunity for local businesses to reflect upon their existing security and contingency plans, and take part in exercises that simulate a terrorist attack similar to that of 7/7. This attempts to build participants' capacity to react in the event of an attack. The event explores the options; what is likely to happen in the event of a terrorist attack; and what the priorities should be. Project Argus highlights the importance of being prepared and having the necessary plans in place to help safeguard staff, customers and company assets (NaCTSO, 2007).

41. Recent scholarship has highlighted the risks that counter-terrorism measures pose for the functional integrity of urban space in terms of their potential to contribute to an atmosphere of fear, a culture of surveillance, consequences for social control and freedom of movement, and a reduction in democratic involvement in urban planning and construction often leading to the increasing militarization of urban design (see for example Graham, 2004).

42. Similar schemes are being installed in other US cities such as Washington, Chicago and Philadelphia.

43. The NYPD has obtained $25 million toward the estimated $90 million cost of the plan ($15 million from the city and $10 million from federal homeland security grants). The rest of the money will, it is hoped, come from additional federal grants. Buckley (2007) also notes that the schemes will cost around $8 million a year to run and that 'the police department is still considering whether to use face-recognition technology, an inexact science that matches images against those in an electronic database, or biohazard detectors in its Lower Manhattan network'.

44. A New York Civil Liberties Union spokesperson noted that: 'this program marks a whole new level of police monitoring of New Yorkers and is being done without any public input, outside oversight, or privacy protections for the hundreds of thousands of people who will end up in NYPD computers' (cited in Buckley, 2007).

REFERENCES

Baily, E. (1993), 'No desks or buildings – but business as usual', *Daily Telegraph*, 26 April, p. 3.
BBC News (2005), 'Banks talked via secret chatroom', 8 July, http://news.bbc.co.uk/1/hi/business/4666225.stm.
BBC (2005), 'City terror attack inevitable', 10 August, http://www.bbc.co.uk/1/hi/busieness/4137068.stm.
Bice, W.B. (1994), 'British government reinsurance and acts of terrorism: the problems with Pool Re', *University of Pennsylvania Journal of International Business Law*, **15** (3), 441–68.
Brown, S. (1985), 'Central Belfast's security segment – an urban phenomenon', *Area*, **17** (1), 1–8.
Buckley, C. (2007), 'New York Plans Surveillance Veil for Downtown', *New York Times*, 9 July, http://www.nytimes.com/2007/07/09/nyregion/09ring.html?ex=1341633600&en=2644be97bd9577f9&ei=5088&partner=rssnyt&.
Burns, J. (1993), 'IRA exploited reduction in spot security checks', *Financial Times*, 26 April, p. 7.
Chernick, H. (ed.) (2005), *Resilient City: The Economic impact of 9/11*, New York: Russell Sage Foundation.
City of London Police (2006), 'Project Griffin', http://www.cityoflondon.police.uk/CityPolice/CT/ProjectGriffin/, accessed 23 July 2006.
Coaffee, J. (1996), 'Terrorism, insurance rhetoric and the City of London', *Association of American Geographers 92 Annual Meeting*, Charlotte, NC, 9–13 April.
Coaffee, J. (2003a), *Terrorism, Risk and the City*, Aldershot: Ashgate.
Coaffee, J. (2003b), 'Morphing the counter-terrorist response: beating the bombers in London's financial heart', *Knowledge, Technology and Power*, **16** (2), 63–83.
Coaffee, J. (2004), 'Rings of steel, rings of concrete and rings of confidence: designing out terrorism in central London pre and post 9/11', *International Journal of Urban and Regional Research*, **28** (1), 201–11.
Coaffee, J. (2005), 'Urban renaissance in the age of terrorism: revanchism, social control or the end of reflection?' *International Journal of Urban and Regional Research*, **29** (2), 447–54.
Coaffee, J. (2006), 'From counter-terrorism to resilience: new security challenges and the multidisciplinary counter-challenge in the "age of terror"', *European Legacy: Journal of the International Society for the Study of European Ideas*, **11** (4), 389–403.
Coaffee, J. and D. Murakami Wood (2006), 'Security is coming home – rethinking scale and constructing resilience in the global urban response to terrorist risk', *International Relations*, **20** (4), 503–17.
Coaffee, J. and L. Johnston (2007), 'Securing spectacle at the Olympics', in J.R. Gold and M. Gold (eds), *Olympic Cities: Urban Planning, City Agendas and the World's Games, 1896 to the Present*, London: Routledge (in press).
Coaffee, J. and P. Rogers (2008), 'Rebordering the city for new security challenges: from counter-terrorism to community resilience', *Social Polity*, **12** (2), 101–18.
Connon, H. and P. Durman (1992), 'Bomb decision threatens property deal', *Independent*, 7 December, p. 20.

Corporation of London (1993a), *The Way Ahead: Traffic and the Environment*, Draft Consultation Paper, London: Corporation of London.

Corporation of London (1993b), *Security Initiatives*, Draft Consultation Paper, London: Corporation of London.

Corporation of London (1995), *City Research Project: Final Report – the Competitive Position of London's Financial Services*, London: Corporation of London.

Donegan, L. (1993), 'City traffic ban to help fight bombers', *Guardian*, 22 May, p. 9.

Edinburgh Evening News (2005), 'Terror attack on finance hub "is inevitable"', http://edinburghnews.scotsman.com/uk.cfm?id=1759222005, 10 August.

Finch, P. (1996), 'The fortress city is not an option', *Architects' Journal*, 15 February, p. 25.

Frost, C. (1994), 'Effective responses for proactive enterprises: business continuity planning, *Disaster Prevention and Management*, **3** (1), 7–15.

Garvey, G. (1993), 'City security boosted in war on terrorism', *Evening Standard*, 29 April, p. 5.

Gloyn, W.J. (1993), *Insurance against Terrorism*, London: Witherby.

Godschalk, D. (2003), 'Urban hazard mitigation: creating resilient cities', *Natural Hazards Review*, **4** (3), 136–43.

Graham, Stephen (ed.) (2004), *Cities, War and Terrorism*, Oxford: Blackwell.

Greer, D.S. and V.A. Mitchell (1982), *Compensation for Criminal Damage to Property*, Belfast: SLS Legal Publications.

Gunn, C. (1992), 'Heseltine backs down on terror bomb cover', *Today*, 21 December, p. 24.

Hays, T. (2006), 'NYPD deploys first of 500 security cameras', http://www.officer.com/article/article.jsp?id=29927&siteSection=8.

Heng, Y. (2006), 'The transformation of war debate: through the looking glass of Ulrich Beck's *World Risk Society*', *International Relations*, **20** (1), 69–91.'

Home Office (2006), *Countering International Terrorism: the UK's Strategy*, London: HMSO.

Hyett, P. (1996), 'Damage limitation in the age of terrorism', *Architects' Journal*, 15 February, p. 29.

Jones, G. (1996), 'Clinton call for alliance to combat terrorism', *Electronic Telegraph*, http://www.telegraph.co.uk/htmlContent.jhtml?html=/archive/1996/06/28/wgsev28.html, 28 June.

Jones, T. (1993), 'Company chiefs want steel gates over roads', *The Times*, 27 April, p. 3.

Juergensmeyer, M. (1997), 'Terror mandated by God', *Terrorism and Political Violence*, **9** (2), 16–23.

Kunreuther, H. and E. Michel-Kerjan (2004), '*Insurability of (Mega)-Terrorism Risk: Challenges and perspectives*', Report for the OECD taskforce on Terrorism Insurance, Paris: OECD.

Lapper, R. (1992), 'Many City buildings may lose bomb insurance cover', *Financial Times*, 11 December, 1.

Lapper, R. (1993), 'City faces rise in terror premiums', *Financial Times*, 29 May, p. 6.

Little, R. (2004), 'Holistic strategy for urban security', *Journal of Infrastructure Systems*, **10** (2), 52–9.

London Chamber of Commerce and Industry (1994), *Invest in London: An International City*, London: EMP plc.

London Chamber of Commerce and Industry (1996), *Invest in London: An International City*, London: EMP plc.
London Chamber of Commerce and Industry (2005), *The Economic Effects of Terrorism on London*, London: LCCI.
London Prepared (2003), 'Emergency advice for London', http://www.londonprepared.gov.uk/londonexercises/, accessed 20 December 2003.
London Prepared (2006), 'London exercises', http://www.londonprepared.gov.uk/londonplans/londonexercises/, accessed 2 December 2006.
London Prepared (2007), 'Emergency plans: Olympics', http://www.londonprepared.gov.uk/londonsplans/index.jsp, accessed 6 February 2007.
London Resilience (2006), 'Looking back moving forward: the multi agency debrief', http://www.londonprepared.gov.uk/downloads/lookingbackmovingforward.pdf, accessed 13 October 2006.
Lovegrove, B. (2007), 'Critical partnership protection in London's financial centre', presentation by the Head of Counter-Terrorism, City of London Police at the Homeland and Border Security event, London, 3 July.
Milmo, D. (2007), 'MPs fear danger in queues at airports', *Guardian*, 26 July, p. 10.
Mollenkamp, C. and C. Haughney (2006), '"Ring of Steel" for New York? To Protect Lower Manhattan, Police Study London's Effort: Cameras, Controlling Access' *Wall Street Journal*, 25 January, available at http://www.mindfully.org/Reform/2006/NYC-Ring-Of-Steel25jan06.htm.
Molotch, H. and N. McClain (2003), 'Dealing with urban terror: heritages of control, varieties of intervention, strategies of research', *International Journal of Urban and Regional Research*, **27** (3), 679–98.
Mythen, G. and S. Walklate (2006), 'Communicating the terrorist risk: harnessing a culture of fear', *Crime, Media and Culture*, **2**, 123–44.
National Counter Terrorism Security Office (NaCTSO) (2007), 'Crowded Places', http://www.nactso.gov.uk/crowdedplaces.php, accessed 13 March 2007.
New York Civil Liberties Union (NYCLU) (2006), 'Who's watching? Video camera surveillance in New York City and the need for public oversight', http://www.nyclu.org/pdfs/surveillance_cams_report_121306.pdf, accessed 3 January 2007.
Norris, C. and G. Armstrong (1999), *The Maximum Surveillance Society: The Rise of CCTV*, Oxford: Berg.
O'Brien, G. and P. Read (2005), 'Future UK emergency management: new wine, old skin?' *Disaster Prevention and Management*, **14** (3), 353–61.
Pedhazur, A. (2005), *The Root Causes of Suicide Terrorism*, London: Routledge.
Rees, W. (2006), *Transatlantic Counter-Terrorism Cooperation: The New Imperative*, London: Routledge.
Rogers, P. (1996), 'Economic Targeting and Provisional IRA Strategy', University of Bradford, Department of Peace Studies, Paper 96.1.
Shillum, R. (1997), 'Terrorism insurance', *Property Management*, **15** (1), 32–37.
Silke, A. (ed.) (2004), *Research on Terrorism: Trends, Achievements, Failures*, London: Frank Cass.
Smith, H. (1993), 'Checkpoints mark Fortress London', *Evening Standard*, 7 June, p. 6.
Smith, J. (2003), 'Civil contingencies planning in government', *Parliamentary Affairs*, **56**, 410–422.
Think London (2004), 'London's business continuity in face of terrorist threat: one

year on', Press Release, 16 March, http://www.thinklondon.com/press_centre/newsreleasedetail.asp?L2=40&NewsReleaseId=2356.

Think London (2007), 'Protect against but be prepared for terrorism', press release, 26 January, http://www.thinklondon.com/press_centre/newsreleasedetail.asp?l2=40&newsreleaseid=3638.

Townsend, M. and G. Hinsliff (2005), 'Anti-terror drill revealed soft targets in London', *Observer*, http://observer.guardian.co.uk/uk_news/story/0,6903,1525247,00.html, accessed 10 July 2005.

Walker, C. and J. Broderick (2004), *The Civil Contingencies Act: Risk Resilience and Law in the United Kingdom*, Oxford: Oxford University Press.

7. Terrorism, news flows and stock markets
Thomas Baumert

INTRODUCTION

That day was not going to be just like any other. When at nine in the morning on 11 March 2004 the European stock markets began their sessions, they did it under the impact of the greatest terrorist attack ever perpetrated in the history of Spain. Scarcely one hour and 20 minutes previously, at 7.39, three rucksack bombs had exploded in a train entering Atocha station, Madrid. In quick succession, they were followed by four more bombs in a train in the Calle Téllez, another on a train that was stopping in Santa Eugenia Station, and two more exploded in a train which had stopped near the Pozo del Tío Raimundo.

As the morning wore on, the news and pictures broadcast by the media recalled to investors' minds the terrible memory of the 9/11 attacks and – to the extent that the turmoil would allow – they recalled the disastrous economic consequences of the latter for the financial sector.

This perception was transformed immediately, both in the Spanish Stock Exchange and in other European bourses, into a clear predominance of sell orders, a trend which was to intensify as the real magnitude of the catastrophe became apparent, and this was maintained, albeit it in a more qualified manner, throughout the following day. During these two days, the stock market indexes reflected – perhaps better than any other indicator – the direct short-term costs estimated by financial agents and how the latter converted the news into economic information which could be incorporated into share prices. The market indicators thus acted as true seismographs of how investors saw the risk and uncertainty.

When, after the weekend, Spanish stock markets got back into action, the Islamist attacks had ceased to be the main impact factor on markets. The previous day's election had produced an electoral upset which gave rise to a scarcely expected change of government.[1] Islamic terror had ceased to be the only factor to be taken into account.[2]

The present work studies the impact of the 11 March attacks upon the main stock markets, with particular emphasis on Spanish share quotations, the evolution of which during 11 and 12 March enables a direct analysis to be made of the way financial agents perceived the economic repercussion of these attacks. Given the mass of news – often incorrect or contradictory – broadcast during those days by the media, it is especially revealing to contrast which of these news items led to the greatest reaction of the above-mentioned markets. The case of 3/11 is singular in this sense, since neither in the case of 9/11 nor in that of 7/7 was it possible to apply an analogous methodology: in the former case because the stock market in New York did not open until ten days after the attacks, and in the latter because the British government applied an 'information embargo'.

To carry out this type of analysis we took as a base the principle of stock market effectiveness,[3] through which as long as liquidity is ensured, the incorporation of information to share prices – that is, the transformation of a news item into quantifiable economic information – takes place immediately. From this is derived, also, that share prices reflect at all times the existing information, so that a reaction only occurs in the face of fresh news (Abadie and Gardeazabal, 2003).[4]

However, it is this very principle which makes it difficult to follow the impact of a particular event beyond the very short term, since the continual flow of news makes it virtually impossible to determine the specific impact of one news item compared to another. Thus, our study centres on the specific days of 11 and 12 March, when the Spanish media devoted practically the whole of their coverage to the Madrid attacks, to an extent that a true '*ceteris paribus*' condition was achieved in the sense that Spanish (and most European) media and news tickers nearly exclusively broadcasted information related to the bombings.

TERRORISM AND STOCK MARKETS: A BRIEF OVERVIEW

Among the rapidly increasing number of articles (Enders and Sandler, 2006; Drakos, 2004) studying the economics of terrorism, those related to the impact of terrorist attacks on capital markets have drawn the attention of many authors. A first step in this direction was made by Abadie and Gardeazabal (2003) who studied the impact of ETA (Euskadi Ta Askatasuna, Basque Homeland and Freedom) terrorism on the evolution of 'Basque' share prices during and after the (false) truce declared by this terrorist group in 1998–99. Another interesting study was published by Chen and Siems (2004), in which the authors analysed stock markets' reaction to 14 armed attacks – a flaw of this work might be the mixing of terrorist attacks and strictly military interventions – detecting an almost immediate and statistically significant impact of these events on world stock markets. The same number of the *European Journal of Political Economy* that published the paper by Chen and Siems also included a study by Eldor and Melnick (2004), which analysed the impact of terrorism on the Israeli stock markets, taking into account the different characteristics of the attacks.[5]

A second group of works we can consider are related to the analysis of the evolution of the beta coefficients – a share's volatility related to the general or sectoral index – of specific shares. A first study of this sort is by Drakos (2004), which centred its attention on the beta alteration experienced by 13 US and non-US airline stocks, showing that the former suffered a bigger rise in the (mainly specific) risk associated to them (53 per cent versus 30 per cent for the non-US airline shares). On the other hand, Choudhry (2005) has analysed changes in the betas of 20 US stocks of different size, location and belonging to different sectors, showing a widely differing impact, depending upon the characteristics of each firm. Finally, Carter and Simkins (2004) have studied to what extent the investor's reaction as a result of 9/11 could be considered 'rational'. The fact that those airlines with the highest capital reserves were less affected than the rest enables them to conclude that the reaction of the investors was rationally differentiated.

For their part, Hon et al. (2004), after analysing the reaction of the world's financial markets in the wake of 9/11, show that a contagion effect took place – an increase in the correlation between them – a result both of their strong interconnection, and the practically simultaneous news flow. This fact has an important consequence, since it demonstrates that it is almost impossible to protect oneself from the consequences of large-scale terrorist attacks by means of the international diversification of portfolios.

For their part, Buesa et al. (2007b) have done a comparative study of impact of the 9/11, 3/11 and 7/7 attacks on stock markets, detecting that, albeit that markets have not desensitized, they present increasingly shorter recovery periods, though these periods vary considerably depending on the sector in question, with the firms belonging to the tourist sector taking the longest to reassert themselves. Shorter reactions, though equally important, are detected in the banking sector – closely linked to the underwriters – and that of the media, since their income from advertising is reduced. This fact, though maybe due in part to the scale of the attacks having been reduced, also appears to indicate a certain 'learning' on the part of the markets. This suggests in turn that the latter react in an increasingly rational manner, overcoming exaggerated reactions and overestimates – in short, the transitory shock – which had characterized the first of these attacks.

Finally, the work by Melnick and Eldor (2006) is especially relevant for the purposes of our research. These authors have studied the role of the media in the impact of terrorism through the response of stock markets to different media coverage of terrorist attacks.[6] After matching 3045 articles related to terrorist attacks in Israeli newspapers and taking into account their characteristics, the authors conclude that media coverage is the main channel by which terrorism produces economic damage.[7]

EMPIRICAL ANALYSIS

The Evolution of the Markets during 11 March

Throughout the following pages we give a detailed analysis of the evolution of the main Spanish share index, the Ibex 35, and the shares which are listed on it, over 11 and 12 March, with special emphasis on the former (see Box 7.1). For that purpose, we compared the share quotations throughout the day with two types of news items which have been shown to have had a direct impact upon the quotations,[8] the magnitude of the attacks – quantified by means of the number of victims that were being counted – and the attribution of who had perpetrated the attack. The case of 3/11 is singular in this sense, since neither in the case of 9/11 nor that of 7/7 was it possible to apply an analogous comparison; in the former case because the stock market in New York did not open until ten days after the attacks, and in the latter because the British government applied an information embargo.

BOX 7.1   DATA SOURCES

The time series with the values for the opening and closing of each session have been obtained from the Madrid Stock Exchange (www.bolsamadrid.es), from Infobolsa (www.infobolsa.es) and Yahoo! Finance (www.yahoo.com). Also, the intraday data have been obtained, for the case of Spanish share quotations, from the Sociedad de Bolsas. Similarly, we have consulted the main national dailies, and libraries of the main radio stations. As our main source for information broadcast throughout the day we have worked with the library of the Europa Press (ep) news agency which, on specific points, we have compared with that of the German Deutsche Presse Agentur (DPA).

Comparing the flow of news on 11 March with market movements (Figure 7.1), we can state that there were two factors which had a significant influence on them: the number of victims – the only objective measurement available to investors when quantifying the magnitude of the attacks; and who was being accused of the attacks. The interpretation made of events by European markets was clear: if it had been an ETA attack, it was a very large-scale one, but this was basically a Spanish problem and, thus, geographically localized, whereas an Islamic attack was an attack on the whole of the European Union (EU), with the possibility of these attacks extending throughout all the Union territory. In other words, and from an investor's point of view, an ETA attack – although certainly not of such magnitude – was a risk already included in stock prices, while the likelihood of a jihadist attack on European soil was considered very remote, thus inducing a major reaction on stock quotations.

In the early morning no one in Spain doubted that it was ETA who were behind the massacre, a fact that was made clear in the rapid succession of institutional and political party statements condemning the attacks and attributing responsibility to ETA. Only a few experts detected details which made ETA participation unlikely, but for the moment these were mere intuitions, which were rejected when the police told the government that the explosive used was Titadine, which was that normally used by ETA. It was true that the spokesman for the illegalized Batasuna – the political arm of ETA – attributed the attack in an early morning radio interview to 'agents of sectors of the Arab resistance' (sic), a hypothesis rejected by the government when CNI (the Spanish Intelligence Service) intercepted a call from him stating that: 'We must play for time. Meanwhile, we must blame the Islamists, later on we'll see.' These statements were not sent out by the press agencies till 12.05, and this intensified the stock market price falls which had commenced some 20 minutes before, when the fact that there were more than 100 victims was publicly announced.

Consequently, the losses were rising most markedly throughout the first half of the day, in the sense that European markets were echoing the likelihood that the attacks could have been carried out by Islamic terrorists, bringing to mind the awful memory of 9/11. This suspicion led to a rush of sales orders on the desks of stock exchange dealers, with heavy falls on all European markets as a result. Nevertheless, the statement by the Interior Minister, confirming 'without any doubt' – and on the basis of information received by state organizations and security bodies – that ETA had been responsible, was backed up almost immediately by the leader of the Popular Party who indicated that 'everything points to it having been ETA', and freshly confirmed by President José María Aznar at 14.30. However, in this case no specific mention was made of ETA. These statements were

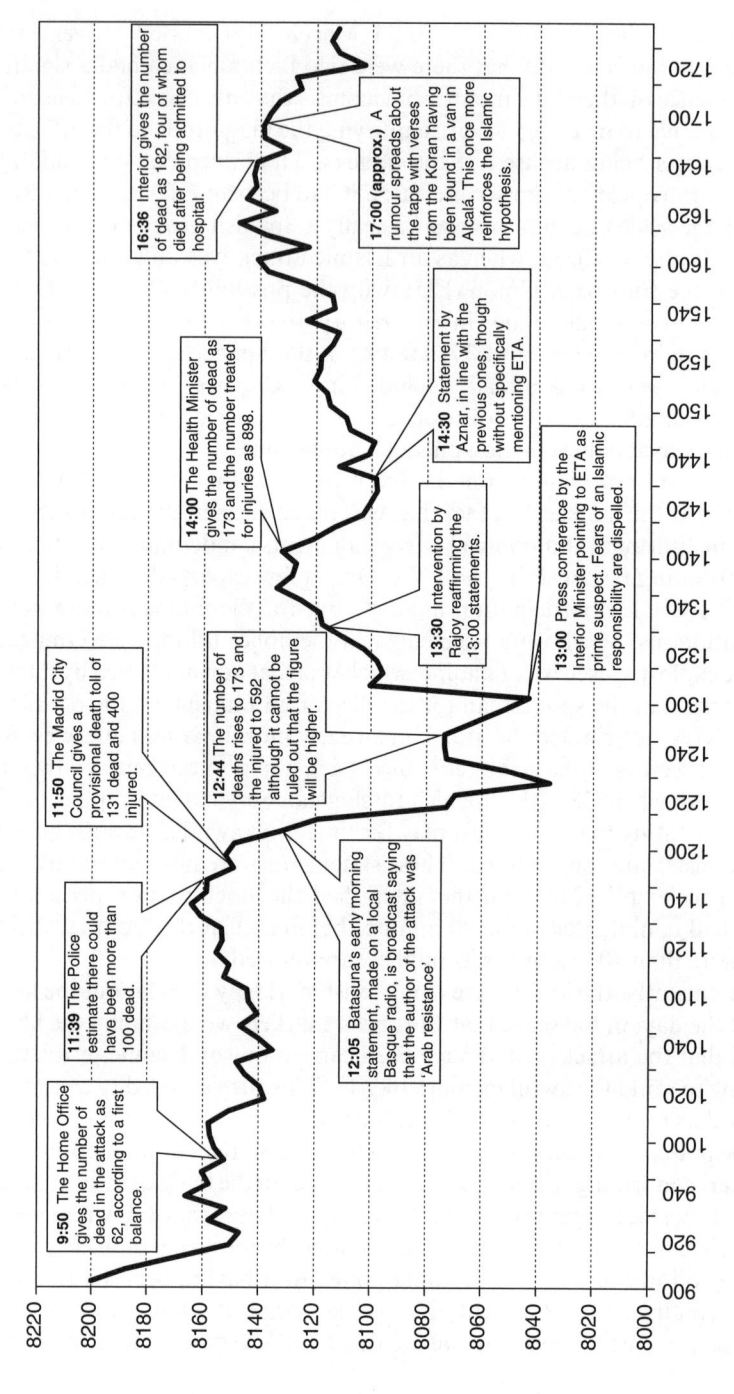

Figure 7.1 IBEX intraday performance 3/11

greeted with relief by the European exchanges, which began to make significant reductions in their losses, albeit that they were still in the red. Indeed, the government had a series of strong arguments – which were conveniently passed to the press and finally reached the ears of financial agents – that gave support to ETA being the perpetrators. According to the State Security Forces and Corps, the explosive found on the trains was Titadine dynamite, the type normally used by ETA, and the police were well aware of ETA's intention to launch an attack precisely in that week. Since the end of the truce in 1999, ETA had attempted on four previous occasions to perpetrate a massacre similar to the one in Madrid, the last of them barely three months before, by placing two suitcase bombs on the Irún–Madrid Intercity; and the CNI had intercepted calls from members of ETA claiming responsibility for 'the firm'. Consequently, at 3 p.m. the CNI continued to state that 'almost certainly the terrorist organisation ETA is the author of these attacks'. This hypothesis was given support, moreover, by the fact that neither the Central Intelligence Agency (CIA), nor the Secret Intelligence Service (MI6), nor Mossad were able to confirm that their agents had detected any noise from al-Qaeda in relationship to an attack in Spain. Only the German government, basing their opinion almost undoubtedly on Bundesnachrichtendienst (BND) data, appeared reluctant to consider the attacks as the handiwork of ETA. This fact probably explains the greater uncertainty reigning in this respect on the German stock exchanges.

Nevertheless, the discovery of a van abandoned by the terrorists, in which a tape was found with verses from the Koran and a box of detonators, gave fresh strength to the arguments pointing against ETA responsibility: the detonators were not of the type used by the terrorist band but, rather, Antigrisú, and the remains of explosives found in the van were not Titadine but Goma 2. These facts once more reinforced the thesis sponsored by some sceptics during the early morning: it was not the habitual modus operandi of ETA, who before an indiscriminate attack usually give warning (in fact, the suitcase bombs on New Year's Eve, 2003 contained a radio-cassette with a tape which was supposed to warn of the attacks minutes before the scheduled explosion – even though it would not have worked, as the terrorists had (intentionally?) forgotten to put batteries in it).

With regard to the effects focusing our attention, we must point out that although the van was found at 10.50 a.m., it was not exhaustively examined, and thus the above-mentioned clues were not discovered till 15.30. The first rumours regarding the van and the fresh evidence confirming Islamic responsibility reached the media around 16.45–17.00, a time when we must also assume it began to spread throughout the stock markets, in which once again and immediately sales orders dominated.

In the end, the day marked by the greatest terrorist attack in the history of Spain finished with the Ibex35 losing 2.2 per cent, to stand at 8112.4 points (all shares stocked in the index closed with losses). After the recovery period and reduction of losses which had begun at 1300 hours – when the provisional number of victims mentioned was nearly at its final total, and at the same time as the government was still indicating ETA as the main suspect of the massacre – the markets once more showed increased losses at the end of the afternoon, when a new count of the number of dead, which raised the total from 173 to 182, coincided with the spread of rumours (about the tape with verses from the Koran found in an abandoned van), thus reinforcing the Islamic hypothesis.

We can conclude, in fact, that the terrorist attacks perpetrated in Madrid increased uncertainty as seen by investors, and this was reflected in significant losses in all the European markets, which all showed even worse results than the Spanish stock exchange. This was due to speculation going around in them during the first half of the session regarding who had been responsible for the attacks: the Frankfurt Stock Exchange – which took the heaviest knock – closed with the Xetra Dax easing 3.46 per cent (3904.95 points); the Footsie 100 of the London Stock Exchange stood at 4445.2 points, with the equivalent of a 2.2 per cent loss, whereas the CAC40 in Paris fell 2.97 per cent (3646.46 points) and the MIB in Milan closed 2.22 per cent down (27,738.00 points). However Wall Street, after a bearish opening, ended the session with more moderate falls, based on the publication of a couple of positive economic data items (increase in retail sales and drop in weekly unemployment benefit claims). Specifically, the Dow Jones – the main indicator of the New York exchange, which encompasses the highest number of stocks – closed at 10,128.38 points, down 1.66 per cent; the Nasdaq, the index of new technology and growth stocks, showed a fall of 1.09 per cent, closing at 1402.2 points; while the Nikkei, the main indicator of the Japanese stock market, fell 1.19 per cent (11,162.75 points).

As for the specific European stocks which showed the highest losses, we can highlight the following. Royal & SunAlliance and British Airways, which are quoted on the London stock market, with −15.5 per cent and −7.93 per cent, respectively; and TUI, which is quoted in Frankfurt, −7.2 per cent. In the case of Royal & SunAlliance and British Airways, the result was seen as significantly influenced by the publication of the year's trading profits which were well below what was expected, whereas in the case of TUI, the market reflected the bad news published by the company in a meeting held that same morning with a group of analysts.[9] On the other hand, the drop suffered by the tour operator TUI must be put down to the heavy fall suffered by all stocks belonging to the tourist sector as a direct consequence of the attacks which, in the Spanish case,[10] was seen in the falls of more than 3 per cent in all the shares.[11] Specifically, Iberia had a drop in share value of 3.7 per cent, closing the session at a share price of 2.62 euros, while the two main Spanish hotel chains, Meliá and NH Hoteles, fell 3.3 and 3.2 per cent, respectively. Furthermore, the booking service centre Amadeus ended the day 3.1 per cent down.

This particular effect on the tourist sector has several possible explanations, which are complementary. Firstly, it is logical for financial agents to recall the strong negative impact on the sector caused by the attacks on the Twin Towers and the Pentagon, and that in some cases it represented a 40 per cent loss in share values (Exceltur, 2004). Secondly, and this aspect could have had a more direct effect, the Madrid attacks coincided with the eve of the inauguration of the International Tourism Exchange (ITB) in Berlin. An early reaction of the Spanish firms and institutions there was to suspend all events and receptions scheduled during the five days the event lasted. This produced a statement from the president of the German Association of Travel Agents and Tour Operators, Klaus Läpple, stating that the Madrid attacks would 'certainly have negative repercussions for the world tourist sector' (Europa Press, 11 March 2004, 17.42). This was in a context of the press informing us over several days of how optimistically the 10,000 exhibitors had got ready to inaugurate the ITB, confident that the effects produced by the 9/11 attacks, the wars in Afghanistan and Iraq, and the SARS epidemic had been overcome. This approach was rapidly changed after the attacks. Nonetheless, and as we shall see in a more detailed manner in the next section, the impact of 3/11 on the tourist sector was in any case less and was more quickly turned round than that after 9/11 (Exceltur, 2004).

Finally, it is worth mentioning the special case of the media, which also suffered a very significant impact as a consequence of the Spanish attacks. It is likely that in this case investors allowed themselves to be carried away by the antecedents of 9/11, insofar as both television and radio stations as well as the press suffered heavy losses through the non-appearance of about $1000 million worth of advertising when the usual programming was replaced by 'blanket coverage' of the events (Navarro and Spencer, 2005).[12]

The Evolution of the Markets during 12 March

As we have already mentioned, the 3/11 stock exchange session concluded for European markets with the suspicion, increasingly more certain, that contrary to what had been hitherto stated by the Spanish government, the Madrid massacre could have been Islamic in origin. This was the conclusion to be drawn from the tape with the verses from the Koran found in a van in Alcalá de Henares.

Throughout the night of 11 March, as the Islamic hypothesis first gathered strength and finally became definitive, markets, especially in the US, and then the Latin American ones, were caught up and carried along by this additional information. Around 20.15 (Central European time), the Dow Jones began to fall sharply in reaction to the Spanish government statement confirming the likelihood that the Madrid attack had been the work of Islamic terrorists. This trend was reinforced even more when rumours that al-Qaeda had claimed responsibility for the attack began to spread. As a result, New York closed the day 1.64 per cent down.

When the European markets opened, they continued the downward trend, thus carrying on the movement which had gathered strength in the final part of the previous day. At the beginning of the morning, the Ibex35 lost 1.8 per cent, the German Dax slipped 0.65 per cent – a much smaller loss than the Spanish one, because the German market, as we mentioned above, had anticipated the likelihood of Islamic responsibility – the London Footsie 100 fell 0.44 per cent, the CAC 40 in Paris slipped 1.33 per cent, and the Italian MIB dropped 1.50 per cent, whilst the euro showed a slight downward trend against the dollar.

In the case of the Madrid exchange, the session began with a steep fall (the slight rise of the early minutes being due to transactions from the previous day being carried out: see Figure 7.2). The growing certainty that Islamists had been responsible was added to the final balance of the scale of the massacre, almost 200 dead and 1400 injured. Nonetheless, at 09.30 hours the beginning of a bullish trend was seen – which was strengthened by the statement from President Aznar, who doubted the credibility of Batasuna's statement putting responsibility for the attacks on 'Islamic resistance' – and was maintained till 16.15 p.m.

Furthermore, Wall Street began the new session (15.30 Central European time) with a clear rise, since the information about the Islamic responsibility for the Madrid attacks had been anticipated in share prices the day before. The bullish opening of the New York stock market helped to reduce losses on the Madrid exchange, but the latter, however, was seen more strongly in the late afternoon, as uncertainty about the result of the elections to be held on Sunday, 14 March spread through the markets. The question of who was responsible took second place. As an agent of a Spanish share bank stated: 'fear that it was Al Qaeda that was responsible is already reflected in the share quotations' (Europa Press, 12 March 2004; 16.51).

Finally, the Madrid Stock Exchange closed the day with a 0.98 per cent fall, leaving it at 8032.60 points, and with nine of the stocks making up the Ibex35 showing a positive balance. Thus the higher than 2 per cent losses at the opening were mitigated, driven in part by the recovery of the other European markets and the bullish start of the New York Stock Exchange.

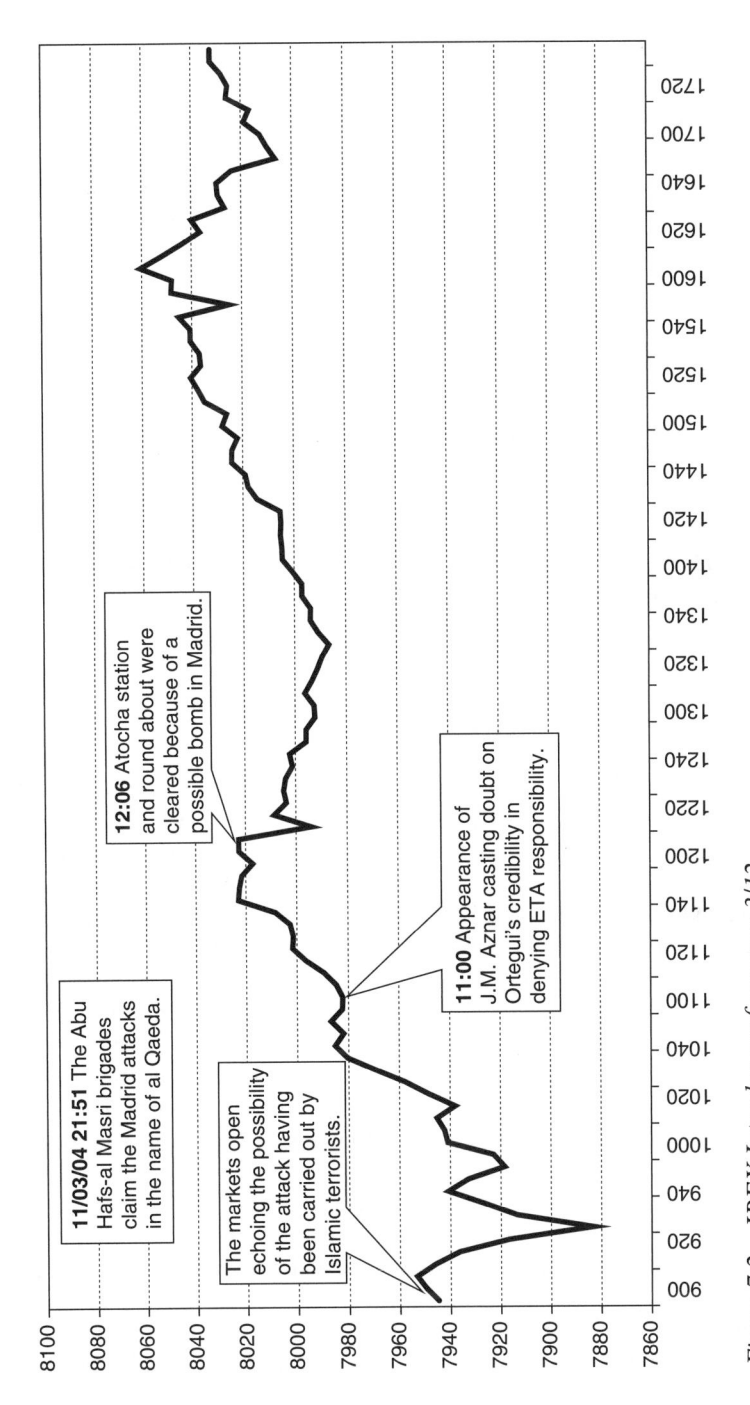

Figure 7.2 IBEX Intraday performance 3/12

The greatest falls apart from Metrovacesa (−4.36 per cent) and Unión Fenosa (−2.28 per cent) were shown by the three stocks belonging to the tourism sector: NH Hoteles fell 2.92 per cent (throughout the day it had lost as much as 5.51 per cent); Iberia slipped 2.67 per cent (8.75 per cent at the worst moment of the session); and Amadeus fell 2.31 per cent (throughout the day it had been quoted at up to 5.66 below the previous closing). This recovery of tourism stocks throughout the day has a possible explanation, beyond the general trend followed by the market, in the repeated statements by important presidents of tour operator associations and the like, going back on their comments of the day before and now talking of the slight or non-existent impact that the attacks were going to have for the sector.[13]

Moreover, it is probable that European investors, as well as seconding the bullish trend set by New York, took advantage of the high volume of trading on the stock markets to improve their investment portfolio, profiting from low stock prices (Europa Press, 12 March 2004, 18.05). Consequently, the Dax gained 0.27 per cent (3661.78 points), London's main index rose 0.5 per cent (4467.4 points) and the Paris exchange CAC40 showed an improvement of 0.42 per cent (3661.78 points). Only the Milan MIB fell 0.6 per cent (27,575 points).

The Aftermath

The week after the attacks began with a 4.15 per cent fall on the Ibex35, leaving it standing at 7.699.1 points – an annual minimum;[14] the loss was much higher than that experienced by the rest of the European markets. Meanwhile Wall Street lost 1.34 per cent on the Dow Jones – its lowest level since 17 December – and 2.29 per cent on the Nasdaq, even though the figures for industrial production published that day were highly positive. Given that we start from the assumption of market efficiency, we must put these falls down to the result of the incorporation of new information to the share prices. Specifically, it seems reasonable to consider that this reaction of the Spanish market was simply the markets' reaction to the electoral upset which took place on 14 March, still under the shadow of the terrible events of 11 March (see for this Michavilla, 2005).

The change of government increased investors' uncertainty for three main reasons. Firstly, it was by any standards unexpected, so the markets could not have anticipated it. Secondly, the election results obliged the PSOE (the Spanish socialist party) to form a coalition government, a fact that normally produces a negative stock market reaction. And, finally, there was great uncertainty over what the economic policy to be adopted by the new government was going to be. Though the idea cannot be dismissed that part of the losses could still be due to information regarding Islamic responsibility for the attacks, a comparison between the fall of the Ibex35 and the rest of the markets leads one to think that this was at best residual. In fact, among the Ibex35 shares, the most affected were those belonging to the most regulated economic sectors, none of which, in principle, should have been directly affected by the 3/11 massacre. Similarly, stocks from the tourist sector took a severe knock as did the financial one – the latter closely tied to the insurers – although in this case, it seems reasonable to consider the losses as a belated consequence of the attacks.

To sum up, we can conclude that the Spanish stock market reacted with higher losses in the face of the PSOE election victory than it had done on 11 and 12 March following the attacks. Nonetheless, the uncertainty brought about by the new government did not last long. The calming messages and announcements given out throughout 16 March by socialist leaders, giving assurance that the new government would not intervene in the management of privatized firms and would encourage mergers in the energy sector, led to a rapid recovery of the Ibex35, which was also backed by a positive evolution in international markets, and closed the session with a 1.45 per cent rise (7810.7 points).

One final point deserves to be taken into account, that which refers to the number of derivatives traded during these days. As we pointed out in the introduction, once the markets get used to terrorist actions and recover from their effects, uncertainty is transferred to the derivatives markets, which by means of the risk premium, evaluate long-term instability. Indeed, Table 7.1 shows how the volume of traded derivatives increased noticeably, doubling in the case of the mini options and futures on the Ibex35 and multiplying tenfold in the case of futures on shares.[15] However, they recovered to the volumes of January 2004 throughout the second half.[16]

Table 7.1   Volume of derivatives traded, first semester 2004

	Futures Mini on Ibex35	Options Mini on Ibex35	Futures on Ibex35	Futures on stocks	Options on stocks
Jan-04	79918	269347	342397	170072	690727
Feb-04	85875	223735	361766	194254	612291
Mar-04	169147	424117	453673	2260566	1021104
Apr-04	119464	180792	362313	208827	384316
May-04	106612	197673	375730	202580	600876
Jun-04	100584	233675	348389	2609543	702510

Source: Bolsa de Madrid (2004).

CONCLUSIONS

As for the determining elements of the Stock Exchange reaction in the specific case of the 11 March attacks, it can be seen that there were two factors which impinged mainly on the market trend: the number of victims – the only objective measurement which was available to investors when quantifying the magnitude of the attacks; and who was responsible for them – certainty over which allowed the risk of the attacks being repeated or spreading to the rest of Europe to be measured.

Both elements were subject to important variations in respect of the information pouring out to market operators during the days of 11 and 12 March. This was a source of instability in share quotations. In consequence, it can be argued that the communication policy followed by governments after an attack can be considered – along with the need for guaranteeing the liquidity of the markets (OECD, 2002; Saxton, 2002) – a fundamental element when minimizing uncertainty amongst investors. If excess instability in markets is considered to be harmful for the real sector of the economy, it is fair to point out that it would be desirable to develop joint action and communication protocols,[17] which would permit the risk as perceived by markets to be reduced (Frey, 2004), in line with the procedure applied by the British authorities after 7/7. This, it may be remembered, was to suspend electronic trading and impose strict control over information protocols, which could equally be extended to the political area (for example, after 3/11, the American government considered reforming the electoral law so that it was allowed to postpone elections if they might be affected by an attack taking place near that time). And it is especially recommendable that such measures be coordinated internationally, as international portfolio diversification is no longer an alternative that allows investors protection from the impact of terrorism. This sort of international coordination effort would allow a reduction of the uncertainty perceived by investors after an important terrorist attack. As a London financial analyst stated after 7 July (BBC News, 8 July 2005, 16.01): 'Investors know how to deal with good and bad news. What they can't get over is uncertainty.'

NOTES

1. The left-wing daily paper *El País* described it in its edition on 16 March as an 'unexpected political turn', adding that 'no analysis mentioned in its forecasts the possibility of a change of government after eight years'. For the effect of the attacks on the election result, see Moreno (2004), Michavilla (2005) and Olmeda (2005).
2. From among the growing literature referring to the 11 March attacks and the political

consequences stemming from them, we can highlight the works of Álvarez de Toledo (2004) and García Abadillo (2004).
3. See the seminal work of Fama et al. (1969), as well as Fama (1970, 1991). We distinguish between weak, semi-weak and strong efficiency. The latter includes insider trading.
4. It might be argued that the stock market's response to a terrorist attack is a result of volatility, that is, a mere psychological and not an economic reaction. Nevertheless, the real question is whether it is a rational reaction or not. As long as this can be agreed – and the work by Carter and Simkins (2004) heavily supports this hypothesis – we have to assume that investors' behaviour is driven by rational economic expectations, the psychological component of his response mainly accounting for a sort of 'overreaction'.
5. Eldor and Melnick estimated a 30 per cent decline of the Israeli TA100 Index between 2000 and 2003. Abadie and Gardeazabal (2003) detected a 10 per cent reduction of the gross domestic product (GPD) per capita of the Basque Country relative to a control area, while Eckstein and Tsiddon (2004) found a 5 per cent reduction of the GDP in Israel as a result of terrorism.
6. An interesting question is – and we are not going to delve further into it because of lack of space – to what extent is it precisely the media coverage which is one of the aims pursued by terrorists. As pointed out by Münkler (2002), terrorist activity, beyond material and human damage caused, is focused as a communications strategy which attempts to spread a particular message in a particularly spectacular way. This message often consists of showing up the vulnerability of the alleged 'enemy'. Simultaneously, the media tend to give broad coverage to terrorist events, not only because of their intrinsic relevance, but also because 'terrorism sells' (although publicity incomes are usually reduced), thus somehow accomplishing the terrorist objectives. This complex interaction between terrorism and the media is studied, among others, by Ganor (2005), Frey (2004) and Frey and Rohner (2006).
7. According to the authors, the media coverage achieved by Islamic terrorism in Israeli newspapers during 2002 is the equivalent of $11 billion, a sum twice larger than the Procter & Gamble advertisement budget, and ten times larger than that of McDonald's or Coca-Cola.
8. After comparing the different news items published in those days by Europa Press, we have been able to state clearly that there were two types of news items which provoked an almost immediate reaction on the stock markets.
9. The airline stocks, despite being amongst the most affected, showed in all lesser falls than those of British Airways: thus, the Dutch KLM lost 4.84 per cent, the German Lufthansa fell 4.73 per cent, the French airline Air France dropped 3.9 per cent, Iberia fell 3.7 per cent and Swissair saw its quotation fall by 1.85 per cent.
10. Nonetheless, and just as the TUI spokesman Mario Koepers said the day after, the Madrid attacks would not have repercussions for his firm in either the short or long term, given that despite having had calls from customers after they heard news of the attacks, no trip booked for Spain had been cancelled. Therefore, there would not have been an underlying economic reality which might justify the change in perception of investors' results (Europa Press, 12 March 2004, 14.03).
11. Contrary to the case with other sectors, the repercussion of terrorism on tourism has attracted a relatively large number of studies.
12. Let it be noted, however, that this fact is circumscribed basically to the Spanish media, and only to a lesser extent to that of the rest of Europe. This is because the latter, instead of replacing their previously scheduled programme by 24-hour coverage of the events, simply inserted special news items and news tickers in the existing programmes.
13. Thus, the president of the German Tourist Association, Klaus Laepple, stated that the attacks 'would not have consequences for tourism'. Moreover, the president of the biggest German tour operator, Volker Bröttcher, said that after the attacks, 'bookings [continued] at a completely normal rate'. He was seconded in this sense by the spokesman of Lufthansa Airlines who stated that 'there have been no cancellations or changes

of bookings'. This statement was backed by spokespersons of British Airways and Air France. See Comas (2004).
14. At the same time, the highest amount of trading of the year was achieved, with 4428 million euros' worth.
15. Given the rapid recovery of the markets, it seems debatable to what extent this speculation on futures was profitable for the sellers.
16. The volume of derivatives traded might be worth deeper analysis, as it could point to an abuse of 'insider information' about the attacks in order to speculate with falling stock prices, a hypothesis that was first raised in the aftermath of 9/11 (see Napoleoni, 2004), and that we have analysed elsewhere (Buesa et al., 2007a). This sort of market observation might become increasingly relevant as an instrument for terrorist prevention (Navarrete, 2004).
17. Contrary to what is often believed, information protocols are not aimed at controlling the media or censoring information, but to assure that under certain circumstances – like a major terrorist attack – the media agree to broadcast and publish only information that has been officially confirmed, thus deterring them from spreading rumours or 'insider information'. Of course the effectiveness of this sort of protocol relies heavily on restricting it to very specific circumstances and limiting it in time (usually up to a maximum of 48 hours). Although it might seem that this might not work, due to the natural inclination of the media to release any 'new information', it has to be remembered that the British information protocol ran extraordinarily well on 7/7.

REFERENCES

Abadie, A. and J. Gardeazabal (2003), 'The economic costs of conflict: a case study of the Basque Country', *American Economic Review*, **93** (1), 113–32.
Álvarez de Toledo, C. (2004), *4 días de marzo. De las mochilas de la muerte al vuelco electoral*, Barcelona: Planeta.
Bolsa de Madrid (2004), *Cifras del mes, abril de 2004*, www.bolsamadrid.es.
Buesa, M., T. Baumert, A. Valiño, J. Heijs and J. González (2007a), '¿Pueden servir los atentados como fuente de financiación del terrorismo?', *La Ilustracion Liberal*, **31**, 61–6.
Buesa, M., T. Baumert, A. Valiño, J. Heijs and J. González (2007b), 'El impacto de los atentados terroristas sobre los mercados de valores. Un estudio comparativo de la repercusión financiera de los ataques islamistas contra Nueva York, Madrid y Londres', *Información Comercial Española*, **835**, 253–71.
Buesa, M., A. Valiño, J. Heijs, T. Baumert and J. González (2006), 'The economic cost of March 11: measuring the direct cost of the terrorist attack on March 11, 2004 in Madrid', Working Paper no. 54, Instituto de Análisis Industrial y Financiero, Universidad Complutense Madrid, www.ucm.es/bucm/cee/iaif.
Carter, D. and B. Simkins (2004), 'The market's reaction to unexpected, catastrophic events: the case of airline stocks returns and the September 11th attacks', *Quarterly Review of Economics and Finance*, **44**, 539–58.
Chen, A.H. and T. Siems (2004), 'The effects of terrorism on global capital markets', *European Journal of Political Economy*, **20**, 349–66.
Choudhry, T. (2005), 'September 11 and time-varying beta of United States Companies', *Applied Financial Economics*, **15** (17), 1227–42.
Comas, J. (2004), 'Las cadenas hoteleras e Iberia sufren los mayores recortes', *El País*, 13 March.
Drakos, K. (2004), 'Terrorism-induced structural shifts in financial risk: airline

stocks in the aftermath of the September 11th terror attacks', *European Journal of Political Economy*, **20**, 435–46.

Eckstein, Z. and D. Tsiddon (2004), 'Macroeconomic consequences of terror: theory and the case of Israel', *Journal of Monetary Economics*, **51** (1), 971–1002.

Eldor, R. and R. Melnick (2004), 'Financial markets and terrorism', *European Journal of Political Economy*, **20**, 367–86.

Enders, W. and T. Sandler (2006), *The Political Economy of Terrorism*, Cambridge, New York: Cambridge University Press.

Exceltur (2004), 'Valoración empresarial de los atentados del 11-M en le sector turístico espanõl', in *Perspectivas turísticas Exceltur*, No. 8, Abril de 2004, www.exceltur.org.

Fama, E., L. Fisher, M.C. Jensen and R. Roll (1969), 'The adjustment of stock prices to new information', *International Economic Review*, **10**, 1–21.

Fama, E. (1970), 'Efficient capital markets: a review of theory and empirical work', *Journal of Finance*, **25** (2), 383–417.

Fama, E. (1991), 'Efficient capital markets II', *The Journal of Finance*, **45** (5), 1575–1617.

Frey, B. (2004), *Dealing with Terrorism: Stick or Carrot?*, Cheltenham, Northampton: Edward Elgar.

Frey, B. and D. Rohner (2006), 'Blood and ink! The common-interest-game between terrorists and the media', Working Paper No. 285, Institute for Empirical Research in Economics, University of Zurich.

Ganor, B. (2005), 'Dilemmas concerning media coverage of terrorists attacks', in R. Howard and R. Sawyer (eds) (2006), *Terrorism and Counterterrorism. Understanding the New Security Environment*, Dubuque, IA: McGraw-Hill.

García Abadillo, C. (2004): *11-M. La vengaza*, Madrid.

Hon, M., J. Strauss and S.-K. Young (2004), 'Contagion in financial markets after September 11: myth or reality', *Journal of Financial Research*, **27** (1), 95–114.

Melnick, R. and R. Eldor (2006), 'Small investment and large returns: terrorism, media and the economy', Intelligence and Terrorism Information Center at the Israel Intelligence Heritage & Commemoration Center (IICC), 22 January.

Michavilla, N. (2005), 'Guerra, terrorismo y elecciones: incidencia electoral de los atentados islamistas en Madrid', Real Instituto Elcano, Documento de Trabajo 13/2005, www.realinstitutoelcano.org.

Moreno, L. (2004), 'The Madrid bombings in the domestic and regional politics of Spain', CSIC – Unidad de políticas comparadas; Working Paper 04-13, www.iesam.csic.es.

Münkler, H. (2002), *Die neuen Kriege*, Reinbek bei Hamburg: BPB.

Napoleoni, L. (2004), *Terror Inc.: Global Terrorism*, London: Penguin.

Navarrete Rojas, F.F. (2004), 'La obtención de inteligencia antiterrorista en los mercados de valores', *Boletín de Información Centro Superior de Estudios de la Defensa Nacional*, **286**, 57–84.

Navarro, P. and A. Spencer (2005), 'September 11, 2001: assessing the costs of terrorism', *The Milken Institute Review*, fourth quarter 2001.

OECD (2002), *OECD Economic Outlook*, **71**, Paris: OECD.

Olmeda, J.A. (2005), 'Miedo o engaño: el encuadramiento de los atentados terroristas del 11-M en Madrid y la rendición de cuentas electorales', Real Instituto Elcano, Documento de Trabajo 13/2005, www.realinstitutoelcano.org.

Saxton, J. (2002), 'The economic costs of terrorism', Joint Economic Committee, United States Congress.

8. Dancing with wolves: avoiding transnational corporation interactions with terrorist groups
Dean C. Alexander

INTRODUCTION

US-headquartered Chiquita Brands International (CBI) admitted in 2007 engaging in transactions with Colombian terrorist groups. The case provides an example of how unintended interactions may arise between transnational companies and terror groups based in host countries.

This chapter provides an analysis of the CBI case and sheds light on the challenges transnational corporations (TNCs) face in doing business in politically unstable environs. It addresses the disparate steps global firms may pursue should they face similar circumstances. The chapter then analyzes the multifaceted implications of such interactions for TNCs, and various alternatives firms may undertake. The chapter concludes that terrorist activity injects another layer of complexity that TNCs must contend with while doing business abroad.

CHIQUITA BRANDS INTERNATIONAL CASE

Background and US Government Investigation of CBI

By all accounts, CBI is an important transnational corporation: a New York Stock Exchange-listed 'international marketer and distributor of high-quality fresh and value-added food products – from energy-rich bananas and other fruits to nutritious blends of convenient green salads', with $4.5 billion in annual revenues. 'The company markets its products under the Chiquita and Fresh Express premium brands and other related trademarks. Chiquita employs approximately 25,000 people operating in more than 70 countries worldwide', including Colombia. (Chiquita, 2007a).

For over six years – from 1997 to 4 February 2004 – CBI paid Autodefensas Unidas de Colombia (AUC) extortion funds in two banana-producing regions of Colombia, Uraba and Santa Maria. The hundred-plus payments, made by CBI's Colombian subsidiary, Banadex, totaled over US$1.7 million (DOJ, 2007a). Banadex's payments to the AUC were done in response to AUC threats of 'physical harm to Banadex personnel and property' (DOJ, 2007, p. 2). Banadex's payments to the AUC were reviewed and approved by senior executives of CBI (DOJ, 2007a).

On 10 September 2001, the US government designated the AUC a Foreign Terrorist Organization (FTO) and a 'specially designated global terrorist' (SDGT) on 31 October 2001. As evidenced above, prior to and subsequent to these dates CBI made payments to AUC. Payments made subsequent to these designations became federal crimes (DOJ, 2007, p. 1).

From the date of the AUC's designation as an FTO to 4 February 2004, CBI 'made 50 payments to the AUC totaling over $825,000' (DOJ, 2007a, p. 3). In February 2003, CBI's outside counsel advised the firm to stop making the payments as they were improper under US law. On 24 April 2003, CBI disclosed to the US Department of Justice (DOJ) that it had made extortion payments to AUC. The DOJ informed CBI that such payments were illegal and should not continue (DOJ, 2007). Nevertheless, from that date to 4 February 2004, CBI 'made 20 payments to the AUC totaling over $300,000. Chiquita sold Banadex to the Colombian buyer in June 2004' (DOJ, 2007, p. 3).

On 24 June 2004, CBI completed the sale of its banana-producing and port operations in Colombia to Invesmar Ltd, a holding company of a Colombia-based producer and exporter of bananas and other fruit products called C.I. Banacol S.A. CBI's operations in Colombia accounted for some 9 percent of its worldwide banana production (Chiquita, 2004).

Under the terms of the deal, Chiquita received US$28.5 million in cash, about US$15 million in notes and deferred payments, with the buyer assuming some US$8 million in pension liabilities. In order to ensure that CBI continued to have ample access to Colombian bananas, the transaction allowed for Chiquita to purchase 11 million boxes of Colombian bananas per year and 2.5 million boxes of Costa Rican golden pineapples per year, over an eight-year period, from the buyer's affiliates (Chiquita, 2004).

The net book value of the assets and liabilities transferred in the deal was about US$37 million. Chiquita expected to have an after-tax loss of some US$5 million (Chiquita, 2004). According to Chiquita spokesman Michael Mitchell the sale was made 'in order to extricate ourselves from the legal dilemma that we faced in Colombia' (Otis, 2007).

On 14 March 2007, the US Department of Justice indicted CBI for engaging in transactions with a specially designated global terrorist, the AUC (Indictment, 2007). In March 2007, Fernando Aguirre, CBI chairman and chief executive officer, admitted that:

> In 2003, Chiquita voluntarily disclosed to the Department of Justice [DOJ] that its former banana-producing subsidiary had been forced to make payments to right- and left-wing paramilitary groups in Colombia to protect the lives of its employees. The company made this disclosure shortly after senior management became aware that these groups had been designated as foreign terrorist organizations under a US statute that makes it a crime to make payments to such organizations. (Chiquita, 2007a)

CBI contends that the payments 'were always motivated by our good faith concern for the safety of our employees' (Chiquita, 2007a).

On 19 March 2007, CBI pleaded guilty to 'one count of engaging in transactions with a specially-designated global terrorist' organization, in the US District Court for the District of Colombia (DOJ, 2007a). Under the terms of the plea agreement, CBI sentence includes 'a $25 million criminal fine, the requirement to implement and maintain an effective compliance and ethics program, and five years' probation' (DOJ, 2007a). Also, CBI pledged to cooperate in the ongoing investigation (DOJ, 2007).

On 11 September 2007, Fernando Aguirre, CBI chairman and chief executive officer (CEO), announced that the DOJ 'formally recommended that the US District Court for the District of Colombia approve' the March 2007 plea agreement (Chiquita, 2007b). Also, according to Aguirre, the DOJ 'decided not to prosecute any current or former company executives in connection with its investigation' (Chiquita, 2007b). The $25 million fine 'will be paid in five annual installments' (Chiquita, 2007b).

With reference to the future, Aguirre noted: 'Chiquita looks forward to putting this difficult chapter behind it, and remains committed to the highest standards of corporate responsibility, ethical conduct and legal compliance, in the United States and around the world' (Chiquita, 2007b).

Other Potential Claims Against CBI

In addition to the US government investigation of CBI, other potential claims might be in store for CBI by the Colombian government and private citizens. More specifically, on 21 March 2007, Mario Iguaran, Colombia's Attorney General, stated that he would seek to extradite to Colombia Chiquita-connected individuals as the company had paid extortion payments and had allowed (via a Banadex ship) for the transfer of 3000 AK47s and ammunition to the AUC (Baena, 2007). Attorney General Iguaran requested the US government to provide 'the names of the Chiquita executives who approved or participated in the payments, which lasted from 1997 to 2004' (Marx, 2007).

Iguaran expressed that Chiquita's activities were:

> not one of the extortionist [AUC] and the extorted [Chiquita] but a criminal relationship. It's a much bigger, more macabre plan. Who wouldn't know what an illegal armed group like the AUC does ... by exterminating and annihilating its enemies. When you pay a group like this you are conscious of what they are doing. (Marx, 2007)

On 16 March 2007, Colombia's Interior and Justice Minister, Carlos Holguin, said: '[t]he possibility exists that Colombia will request the United States to extradite the US citizens' connected with CBI–AUC extortion payments (EFE, 2007).

Additionally, on 7 June 2007, 144 heirs of individuals allegedly killed by Colombian terrorist groups the AUC and the Revolutionary Armed Forces of Colombia (FARC) sued CBI and ten CBI employees in the US District Court for the District of Colombia under the Alien Tort Claims Act (ATCA), Torture Victim Protection Act (TVPA) and state tort law. In summary, the causes of actions alleged in the suit are as follows: the statutes ATCA and TVPA for extrajudicial killings, wrongful death, negligence, negligent hiring, negligent supervision, intentional infliction of emotional distress, battery and assault (Doe, 2007).

More specifically, the suit claims that CBI provided material support, 'hired, armed, contracted with, or otherwise directed terrorist paramilitary security forces', including the AUC (Doe, 2007, p. 2). The AUC allegedly 'used extreme violence and murdered, tortured, unlawfully detained or otherwise silenced individuals believed to be interfering with' CBI's business in Colombia or who resided 'in the path of Defendants' paramilitary agents' (Doe, 2007, p. 2). The plaintiffs also claim that CBI made payments to the AUC and FARC (Doe, 2007, p. 2). According to the suit, the defendants 'were aiding and abetting all acts of violence committed with the material support provided by Defendants to the terrorist groups they supported' (Doe, 2007, p. 44).

The suit claims that CBI's subsidiary and 'alter ego' in Colombia was Banadex, its subsidiary sold in June 2004 (Doe, 2007, p. 36). 'Although it no longer has a Colombian subsidiary, Chiquita remains one of the largest buyers of bananas in Colombia, purchasing bananas from Colombian companies' (Doe, 2007, p. 36). In addition to CBI, ten current (or former) employees, officers and directors of CBI and Banadex were listed as defendants (Doe, 2007).

The plaintiffs also cited a 7 November 2001 Organization of American States report stating that in Colombia, a 'shipment of arms [AK47s] and ammunition was unloaded by a shipping company called Banadex S.A., at the request of a [sic] the shipping agent Turbana Ltd, and the AUC took possession of the weaponry' (OAS, 2007, p. 18).

DIFFICULTIES TRANSNATIONAL CORPORATIONS FACE IN POLITICALLY UNSTABLE ENVIRONMENTS

As the CBI case illustrates, complying with terror group extortion (in the form of 'revolutionary payments' or protection money) may initially afford a TNC the opportunity to continue doing business. Ultimately, though, such 'defensive' measures – somewhat akin to bribery payments as a 'cost of doing business' – may result in far-reaching operational, financial and legal consequences. Other diverse challenges, including substantial economic and foreign policy implications, may also be a consequence of such acts.

Indeed, extortion tactics used to fund terror groups – whether undertaken by ETA (Euskadi Ta Askatasuna, Basque Homeland and Freedom) in Europe, Abu Sayef in Asia, or narco-terror groups in Colombia – merit closer attention as they inject another layer of complexity that TNCs must contend with while doing business abroad (extortion may also occur in a TNC's home country, including by domestic terror groups) (Alexander, 2004). In the face of extortion, a TNC must weigh up several poor options: pay terrorists the extortion; refuse to pay them and possibly suffer physical damage to in-country assets; stop operations temporarily; or sell operations, most likely at a loss. A TNC's decision to make protection payments will undermine its status in home and host countries, while encouraging such conduct by terrorists against business worldwide.

Terror group extortion payment pressures may have diverse negative operational effects on TNCs: declining levels of production, often with poorer-quality deliverables; higher costs of production due to heightened labor, security and transportation costs; lower efficiencies; underutilization of assets; production stoppages and threats to business continuity; adjustments to and pressures on supply chains; and corporate governance complexities including which entities (parent or subsidiaries) and executives (CEO or host-country manager) approved the illicit payments.

At the extreme, companies may forego doing business in a country or reduce exposure to that region by utilizing any of the following steps: licensing technology rather than greater investment commitments; establishing joint ventures instead of wholly owned approaches; or purchasing products from the host country or suppliers based in third countries.

Concurrently, disparate unhelpful financial implications may arise when terror extortion attaches, such as: higher costs for labor, security, capital, inputs and insurance; reduced profitability; loss of goodwill and declining stock price; financial penalties and/or liabilities arising from host and home country litigation initiated by government, private sector, employees and/or other citizens.

Likewise, civil and criminal litigation against TNCs and their management may occur along the following lines:

- Host or home country government suits for collaborating with or funding terrorists and accounting or tax fraud charges, as often such 'security payments' are not reported or are mischaracterized.
- Global business suits for breach of contract, as production cannot be fulfilled due to business interruption, and even claims of unfair trade practices.
- Host and home country suits by employees and citizens injured or killed through terror acts funded by extortion money.
- Investor suits against management for breach of fiduciary care.

Among other difficulties firms may face in politically unstable environments are having disparate parties perceive that they are favoring one group in a fractured political environment (for example, government versus 'rebels'), potentially resulting in victimization for the TNC. Given a highly fractious and fluid political environment, it is possible for a TNC to be viewed as too aligned with particular power brokers, the military, labor or opposition parties. Unwise TNC interactions in the host country may also result in undermining home country interests vis-à-vis the host country.

STEPS TRANSNATIONAL CORPORATIONS MAY UNDERTAKE TO REDUCE RISKS UNDER SUCH CONDITIONS

Although substantial negative ramifications may arise when a TNC encounters terror extortion, the risks can be lessened by following distinct steps. Initially, the entity must analyze whether it should do business in the host country.

What is the benefit for the TNC to do business in Country X? Does the country offer the TNC the following:

- Unique and/or competitive natural resources, land, or inputs?
- Attractive manufacturing or production variables due to lower labor, energy or taxes?

- A strategic geographical location for supply chain or distribution?
- A large domestic market?

Next, what level of physical presence (and assets) – from a representative office, joint venture or portfolio investment to a wholly owned subsidiary – does the TNC need in the host country? The TNC's industry sector, and whether it will offer products, services or both there, relate to the degree of assets that should be put at risk. Other variables ranging from the country's political and economic stability, legal and business environment, infrastructure and labor relations should be included in the TNC's calculations as to whether (or how) to do business in a host country.

Once a determination to pursue business in the host country is made, it is useful to reduce the TNC's own risks by exploring whether land grants or subsidized loans are available from the host country or development agency (for example, the World Bank or regional development bank), respectively. Political risk insurance covering war, civil disturbance, terrorism, expropriation, breach of contract and inconvertibility of currency offered by commercial, government (for example, the US government's Overseas Private Investment Corporation) and non-governmental organizations (for example, the World Bank's Multilateral Investment Guarantee Agency) is worth considering.

OPIC

OPIC is a US government agency that 'helps US businesses invest overseas, fosters economic development in new and emerging markets, complements the private sector in managing risks associated with foreign direct investment, and supports US foreign policy' (OPIC, 2007a).

OPIC's 'political violence coverage compensates for property and income losses caused by violence undertaken for political purposes. Declared or undeclared war, hostile actions by national or international forces, civil war, revolution, insurrection, and civil strife, including politically motivated terrorism and sabotage' (OPIC, 2007b).

> An investor may choose to insure for all these risks, or to exclude civil strife. Actions undertaken primarily to achieve labor or student objectives are not covered. OPIC pays compensation for two types of losses: damage to tangible assets, and business income loss caused by damage to tangible assets. An investor may purchase one or both coverages. (OPIC, 2007c)

With an 'off-site' rider, OPIC also may compensate for 'income losses resulting from damage to specific sites outside the insured facility, such as critical railway spur, power station, or supplier' (OPIC, 2007c).

OPIC had several political risk claims for activities taking place in Colombia. In fiscal year 2004, OPIC paid Sector Capital Corp. three separate cash settlements of $114,426, $114,408 and $36,923 for compensation for 'civil strife' coverage for its activities in Colombia. In fiscal year 2003, OPIC paid the same firm four separate cash settlements of $170,979, $114,565, $114,419 and $114,447 for compensation for 'civil strife' coverage for its activities in Colombia (OPIC, 2007d). In fiscal year 2001, OPIC paid Sector Resources $2,430,759.59 for compensation for 'civil strife' coverage for its activities in Colombia (OPIC, 2002). Clearly, firms that obtain political risk insurance may receive compensation should they experience in the host-country.

MIGA

'MIGA provides non-commercial guarantees (insurance) for investments made in developing countries. MIGA's guarantees protect investors against the risks of transfer restriction (including inconvertibility), expropriation, war and civil disturbance, and breach of contract' (MIGA, 2007a).

In addition, MIGA's participation in a foreign investment transaction can aid as follows:

- Assisting in resolving disputes in the host country.
- Aiding in obtaining project finance for otherwise difficult-to-fund projects.
- Lowering borrowing costs as risk-capital ratings of projects often decline due to MIGA's involvement.
- Increasing length of loans due to extended insurance contracts.
- Extensive knowledge of the host country (MIGA, 2007b).

'Since its inception in 1988, MIGA has issued 774 guarantees for projects in 91 developing countries, totaling $14.7 billion in coverage. 43 percent of MIGA's gross outstanding portfolio is in IDA-eligible (world's poorest) countries. MIGA's gross exposure stands at $5.1 billion' (MIGA, 2007c).

During fiscal years 1997 and 2001, MIGA provided political risk insurance relating to expropriation and transfer risk for Spanish (Banco Santander Hispano S.A.) and American (Citibank) entities, respectively, providing loans in Colombia (MIGA, 2007d). In fiscal year 1999 the Dutch company Dunriding Compant N.V. obtained $62.4 million in MIGA insurance, covering the risks of transfer restriction as well as war and civil disturbance (including terrorism). The deal insured the firm's 'acquisition, expansion, and modernization of a 150-megawatt coal-fired thermal plant near Cucuta city, Colombia' (MIGA, 2007e).

Two years beforehand, the American firm Motorola and Dutch bank ABN Amro obtained MIGA insurance covering '$5 million and $30 million, respectively, of equity and loan investments in a wireless digital trunk communications system in Colombia' (MIGA, 2007f). The insurance covered the risks of 'expropriation, transfer restriction, and war and civil disturbance' (including terrorism) (MIGA, 2007f).

Speaking of politically unstable countries, MIGA also established the Afghanistan Investment Guarantee Facility, which provides political risk insurance for '[n]ew investments associated with the expansion, modernization, or financial restructuring of existing projects' and 'privatizations of state enterprises' (MIGA, 2007g).

Other Steps

As terror extortion may lead to the kidnapping of TNC personnel, the need for kidnapping and ransom insurance, along with other insurance products (for example, property and casualty, business interruption, life, disability and health insurance), should be contemplated. Integral, too, is the applicability of disparate security products, services and methodologies – from risk and vulnerability assessments to business and risk intelligence data reports – that can aid in lessening the likelihood, frequency and severity of terrorism in general, and terror extortion in particular.

Staffing potentially high-risk countries with seasoned expatriate employees, coupled with expert host country talent, will prove fruitful. Undertaking background checks and using contract workers are other steps that should aid in protecting TNC interests.

Developing alliances and gathering support from host country government, business, civic and labor entities, along with home country representatives (for example, the US Embassy) and non-governmental institutions (for example, the World Bank, MIGA and the International Centre for the Settlement of Investment Disputes), are further steps to aid TNCs against terror extortion. Engendering support for bilateral economic and political relations between host and home countries (for example, trade and investment agreements) will assist TNC efforts abroad as well.

IMPLICATIONS FOR TNC ACTIVITIES AND ALTERNATE STEPS

As noted above there are many negative issues that may arise due to extortion-related entanglements between TNCs and terror groups. Among the implications for TNCs are whether (or how) to invest and do business in an unstable host country. Given the risks, should the TNC avoid it completely or choose less risky operational, financial and legal structures? Also, this case allows for TNCs to have a great appreciation of risks and possible victimization to their assets, including their employees.

Consequences for TNCs

If one TNC sets the precedent that paying terrorists is a permissible cost of doing business, then terror groups will approach other businesses in the future. This trend would result in adding costs to all TNCs as well as risking their assets. If a TNC avoids doing business in Country X due to extortion threats, or reduces its level of activities in that country, then the TNC firm will generate less revenue overall. Concurrently, though, this lessened commitment to doing business in Country X will allow for new opportunities for other TNCs and local businesses in the home country. So too, the TNC that otherwise would invest in Country X may pursue opportunities in third countries or expand its efforts in its home country rather than risk terror extortion in Country X.

Ramifications for the Host Country

Should terror extortion and concomitant violence rise to a noticeable level, it is highly likely that there will be less TNC investment there. As such, less economic development will take place there, including fewer jobs created. Worsening economic conditions may exacerbate an already risky political atmosphere, while aiding terror groups in their quest for chaos.

In contrast, should TNCs prove able to refrain from paying extortion payments, coupled with weakening terror group power, then increases in foreign investment in the home country should occur. This, in turn, would aid the business climate, contribute to economic development and growth, increase stability and further undermine terror groups. Also, lower levels of foreign investment would result in less transfer of technology and slow the development of labor skills in the home country.

Foreign Policy Implications

TNC violations of host country law relative to contacting or aiding terror groups could undermine host–home country relations. For instance, the two countries may have complex counter-terrorism activities that might be weakened by a TNC funding – through extortion payments – a terror group.

Analogously, it will look odd for the home country to berate weak counter-terrorism efforts in the host country, when a TNC from the former is aggravating instability in the latter. Another thorny issue that might arise would be calls for the host country to extradite senior management of the TNC based in the home country. Denial of such requests would appear to be hypocritical should the home country seek the extradition of terrorists based in the host country who undertook terror-related (including financing) activities in the home country.

Impact on Global Business

If terror activities, including extortion, cause TNCs to reduce their activities in high-risk areas then that would undermine global business. So too, higher costs for inputs and final products would be expected as business activities would be less efficient. Bilateral, regional and global trade and investment would be reduced. Lower levels of foreign investment would result in less transfer of technology and undermining the development of human skill sets in the home country.

CONCLUSION

As business prefers predictable, stable settings, complex, difficult environments are abhorred. Terrorist activity injects another layer of complexity that companies must contend with while doing business abroad. And yet, the foregoing illustrates that while terror group extortion can have substantial pernicious operational, financial and legal effects on TNCs, a variety of alternatives and instruments are available to lessen such occurrences. In doing so, TNCs can aid in enhancing global trade, investment and business while contributing to the reduction of terrorism internationally, by eliminating a source of terror funding.

REFERENCES

Alexander, Dean C. (2004), *Business Confronts Terrorism: Risks and Responses*, Madison, WI: University of Wisconsin Press.
Baena, Javier (2007), 'Colombia seeks 8 in Chiquita payments', AP, http://abcnews.go.com/International/wireStory?id=2967203, 20 March.
Chiquita (2004), 'Chiquita agrees to sell operations in Colombia', Chiquita Brands International Press Release, 11 June.
Chiquita (2007a), 'Chiquita statement on agreement with US Department of Justice', Chiquita Brands International Press Release, 14 March.
Chiquita (2007b), 'Chiquita Brands Int'l statement on US Department of Justice sentencing memorandum', Chiquita Brands International Press Release, 11 September.

Does (2007), Jane/John Does 1–144, Colombia, South America v. Chiquita Brands International, Filed in the US District Court for the District of Colombia, http://www.iradvocates.org/chiquita.html, 7 June.

DOJ (2007), 'Chiquita Brands International pleads guilty to making payments to a designated terrorist organization and agrees to pay $25 million fine', US Department of Justice Press Release.

EFE (2007), 'Colombia might ask US to extradite Chiquita execs', EFE.

Indictment (2007), United States of America v. Chiquita Brands International, Inc., US District Court for the District of Columbia, 14 March, http://www.secinfo.com/d14D5a.u1XUq.d.htm.

Marx, Gary (2007), 'Colombian official seeks US papers on Chiquita', *Chicago Tribune*, 22 March.

Multilateral Investment Guarantee Agency (MIGA) (2007a), 'Frequently asked questions', http://www.miga.org/quickref/index_sv.cfm?stid=1587, retrieved 30 September 2007.

Multilateral Investment Guarantee Agency (MIGA) (2007b), Guarantees Overview, http://www.miga.org/guarantees/, retrieved 30 September 2007.

Multilateral Investment Guarantee Agency (MIGA) (2007c), 'Guarantees projects', http://www.miga.org/guarantees/index_sv.cfm?stid=1546, retrieved 30 September 2007.

Multilateral Investment Guarantee Agency (MIGA) (2007d), 'Project name: Grupo del Istmo de Papagayo', S.A., http://www.miga.org/sitelevel2/level2.cfm?id=1073, retrieved 24 June 2007.

Multilateral Investment Guarantee Agency (MIGA) (2007e), Guarantee Holder: Drummond Company, http://www.miga.org/sitelevel2/level2.cfm?id=1075, retrieved 24 June 2007.

Multilateral Investment Guarantee Agency (MIGA) (2007f), Guarantee Holder: ABN AMRO, Motorola, http://www.miga.org/sitelevel2/level2.cfm?id=10754, retrieved 24 June 2007.

Multilateral Investment Guarantee Agency (MIGA) (2007g), 'Afghanistan investment guarantee facility', www.miga.org/documents/ACFHTAM3a47l.pdf, retrieved 24 June 2007.

OAS (2003), 'Report of the General Secretariat of the Organization of American States on the diversion of Nicaraguan arms to the United Defense Forces of Colombia', Organization of the American States, 6 January.

Otis, John (2007), 'Critics question Chiquita's claim that it was forced to pay Colombia's paramilitaries', *Houston Chronicle*, 2 April.

Overseas Private Investment Corporation (OPIC) (2002), 'Memo of Determinations, Political Violence Claims of Sector Resources, Ltd', Contract Insurance No. F030 and No. F074.

Overseas Private Investment Corporation (OPIC) (2007a), 'About us: overview', http://www.opic.gov/about/index.asp, retrieved 24 June 2007.

Overseas Private Investment Corporation (OPIC) (2007b), 'Insurance overview', http://www.opic.gov/insurance/index.asp, retrieved 24 June 2007.

Overseas Private Investment Corporation (OPIC) (2007c), 'Insurance: political violence', http://www.opic.gov/insurance/coverage/violence/index.asp, retrieved 24 June 2007.

Overseas Private Investment Corporation (OPIC) (2007d), 'Insurance: claims and arbitral awards', http://www.opic.gov/insurance/claims/index.asp, retrieved 24 June 2007.

9. The impact of 9/11 on airport passenger density and regional travel

Garrett R. Beeler Asay[1] and Jeffrey Clemens[2,3]

INTRODUCTION

9/11's impact on the observed quantity of air travel can be characterized as an immediate, sharp downturn in the two months following the event, followed by a gradual but incomplete recovery towards the original trend. The relative sizes of both the temporary and permanent aspects of the decline in air travel were estimated by Ito and Lee (2005b) using monthly data (through much of 2003) at the national level. In this chapter we use data that are disaggregated at the airport level to look not only at the impact of September 11th on the quantity of air travel, but also at its composition.

We explore several hypotheses related to the impact of September 11th on the composition of air travel in the United States. First, we ask whether large airports were more affected by 9/11 than small airports. Second, we ask whether New England and Mid-Atlantic destinations were impacted more strongly than destinations in other regions. In future work, we also intend to explore the extent to which (if at all): (1) US origin passengers have shifted away from international and toward domestic travel; and (2) foreign-origin passengers have shifted away from US destinations.

The answers to these questions have implications which extend beyond the relatively narrow scope of air travel, as they touch on the ability of terrorism to bring about short-, medium- and long-run changes in patterns of economic activity. The large airport hypothesis, for example, addresses the broader question of terrorism's impact on the density of economic activity. Glaeser and Shapiro (2002) point out two potentially important effects of terrorism on density that would work in opposite directions. On the one hand, the fact that terrorists tend to target high-density areas suggests that an increase in terrorism risk will discourage density. On the other hand, increases in transportation costs brought about by terrorism will tend to encourage density. Recent research provides mixed results on the net impact. Abadie and Dermisi (2006) find evidence that demand for office space in several of Chicago's landmark buildings has fallen since the September 11th attacks. Redfearn (2005), on the other hand, finds no evidence of reductions in home prices in areas surrounding likely terrorist targets in Los Angeles following the attacks. Together, this work may suggest that while the threat is sufficient to discourage activity in very high-density central business districts, it is not sufficient to impact the form of the remainder of the urban area.

Additionally, the impact of the terrorist threat on the air travel industry itself is important in its own right. To the extent that terrorism is responsible for increasing the perceived risks of air travel, it results in several unique costs which all contribute to its total economic impact. Resulting increases in security are costly both in terms of the direct costs of funding the security effort and in terms of the longer security delays imposed on travelers. Trips not taken on account of the increased hassle or increased fear of flying also add to the welfare losses. Substitution away from air travel towards alternative modes of transportation (or towards telecommunications) also involves a loss of benefits conferred by air travel.

There are many studies that have documented the effects of 9/11 on air travel. Most recently, Gordon et al. (2007) studied the impact of 9/11 on the aggregate economy by predicting air travel as if 9/11 did not happen, and then comparing the current economic activity with the predicted economic activity. Further, Becker and Rubinstein (2007) use a similar method in their comparison of air travel before and after the attacks. Specifically, they find that air travel fell by about 15 percent and had still not recovered by 2003. The estimates made by Ito and Lee (2005b) suggest a permanent decrease of around 7 percent.

Still other effects changed the behavior of individual travel modes; for instance, Gigerenzer (2006) shows that individuals substituted driving for flying after 9/11. From a personal safety standpoint this was not a good decision. Much of the risk associated with flying is concentrated in take-offs and landings, while the risk associated with driving increases with the number of miles driven. In fact, in order for flying and driving to have the same risk, a 9/11-like attack would have to happen 12 times a year (Sivak and Flannagan, 2003). Nevertheless, Gigerenzer (2006) shows that an estimated additional 1500 deaths occurred because individuals chose to drive instead of fly.

We suggest that large airports could also be subject to a 'fear factor'. This could cause a shift of passengers from large airports to small airports. Further, business trends in the airline industry could also promote smaller airports. The rise of low-cost carriers with a different business model could decrease the percentage of passengers passing through large airports. Low-cost carriers (LCCs) fly from smaller, less congested airports with fewer travelers and generally cheaper take-off and landing fees. Further, LCCs depart early in the morning or late at night to take advantage of cheaper airport fees. This method also minimizes delays. One other LCC characteristic is the utilization of more point-to-point routes instead of the hub-and-spoke business model. The hub-and-spoke business model tends to utilize large airports. (Travelers are flown to one large airport and then boarded on other flights to their final destinations. In the point-to-point method, travelers are flown directly from their origin to their destination.) Because LCCs use more point-to-point routes, this could have lessened the volume of traffic to large airports. Though we do not test this hypothesis directly, we do include a measure of LCC market share.

Other factors that could increase the appeal of smaller airports come from large airports being nearer to their full capacity. That is, large airports may (both prior to 9/11 and currently) be relatively constrained in their ability to expand, making additional flights and passengers more costly. In addition, the costs imposed on flying by 9/11 (security measures and so on) could be more costly at large airports because of their high volumes of travel both in absolute terms and relative to capacity.

ANALYTICAL FRAMEWORK AND DATA

This study is meant to estimate the impact of the September 11th terrorist attacks on patterns of air travel within the United States. We view 9/11 as an exogenous shock to the airline system. We proceed by estimating a variety of models which are designed to parameterize the periods before and after the event. For controls, our focus is on controlling: (1) general economic factors which are relevant to the size of the market for air travel; and (2) pre-existing trends which, if not accounted for, could result in inappropriate characterizations of the pre- and post-event periods. We use state-level economic data to measure 'demand-side' impacts on airport passenger levels. These data are supplemented by time-related factors (primarily time trends and controls for seasonality), special events and, in some specifications, two 'supply-side' factors for which we have national data.

Following Ito and Lee, our quantitative analysis is of the following form:

$$Q_{Air\_Travel} = \beta_0 + \alpha(economic\_factors) + \gamma(time\_factors)$$
$$+ \phi(other\_special\_events) + \delta(September\_11th\_factors)$$

The following paragraphs describe the variables included in each of the above categories and the data used to account for each of these variables.

Our quantity variable is a measure of the number of passenger enplanements in a given month. The data were collected at the airport level using the US Department of Transportation (2008), T-100 databank, henceforth referred to as US DOT, which accounts for all certified US air carriers. Because the data are not readily available from the databank website, we created a computer program using the Python programming language to query the BTS site and retrieve the data.

Our research differs from Ito and Lee (2005b) (henceforth referred to as I&L) in several respects. First, because we are concerned with geographic and airport-level hypotheses, we use disaggregated data. I&L measure quantity using revenue passenger miles at the national level from the Air Transport Association (ATA), which only collects data from some of the largest US airlines. As a robustness check, we ran our regressions using pooled data from the US DOT 100 databank and found similar significance and effect size of 9/11 in the data. See Table 9.1 for summary statistics of our disaggregated data.

The economic factors include two variables that can be viewed as demand-side variables and, in some specifications, two variables that can be viewed as supply-side variables. The demand-side variables are the unemployment rate (which accounts for the effects of the business cycle) and the level of employment (which is a proxy for the level of economic activity). Both variables are measured using data from the Bureau of Labor Statistics. We collect these data at the state level and, where appropriate,

Table 9.1 Summary statistics

	Mean	Std. Dev.	Min	Max	N
Passengers per month per airport	368 322	763 343	0	7 229 013	49 510
Real jet fuel price ($)	89.81	47.87	37.38	225.40	48 098
Passenger share of non-major carriers (%)	21.48	7.31	11.01	35.30	49 510
Unemployment rate (%)	5.35	1.39	2.00	11.50	48 422
Total employment	4723	3764	195	15 248	48 415
Passengers per month (15 largest airports)	2 548 049	1 263 193	711 374	7 229 013	3 120
Passengers per month (non-large airports)	221 723	416 596	0	3 768 055	46 390

apply state-level unemployment rates and employment levels to each airport within the state. This contrasts with I&L who, again, use nationally aggregated data throughout. As I&L observe, it would be preferable to use gross domestic product (GDP) data to measure the level of economic activity, but GDP is reported on a quarterly, rather than monthly, basis. Most notably, employment-level data will fail to pick up increases in economic activity and incomes due to productivity gains, which were a particular key component of economic growth during the early 2000s. When using the state-level employment data for our disaggregated regressions we typically include a linear time trend to help account for trend productivity growth and other upward-trending factors that may not be accounted for by our other controls.

The primary supply-side economic variables used by I&L are: (1) a measure of the share of air travel that is provided by low-cost carriers; and (2) a measure of the price of jet fuel. As I&L note, past studies have identified the emergence of LCCs as possibly the most significant development in the airline industry in recent decades. This variable is, in a sense, a measure of the extent of competition within the industry. Jet fuel prices are naturally important as they constitute a significant input cost in the provision of air travel. We have developed a measure of the LCC share which appears to behave similarly to I&L's in terms of both its summary statistics and its impact on our regression analysis. This measure also uses the US Department of Transportation (2008)'s T-100 databank. It is based on the fraction of passengers in each month who are not attributed to a major carrier.[4] To account for the price of jet fuel, we have also collected monthly data on the spot price of jet fuel in Los Angeles from the Department of Energy's website (in cents per gallon). We have also experimented with the use of other input cost variables such as the Producer Price Index for the production of civilian aircraft and the wages of pilots, airline mechanics and transportation attendants as reported annually in the National Compensation Survey.

The time variables used in our regressions fall into two categories: the traditional seasonality and trends variables, and the additional accounting for calendar irregularities. The intensity of air travel is very clearly affected by seasonality, with holiday and vacation seasons driving the amount of air travel above its yearly mean level. Consequently we include month-dummy variables in all of our regressions. As noted above, there is also reason for concern that our typical proxy for the level of economic activity (the employment level) will fail to account for trend productivity growth, which is a key determinant of incomes and hence demand for air travel. Consequently we include a linear time trend in most of our specifications.[5] We also include dummy variables to account for two specific calendar irregularities. The first is for Februaries during leap years which, since they have an extra day, will be expected to involve a larger volume of passenger travel within that month. The second, perhaps less obvious, source of irregularities is for Novembers and Decembers in years during which the Sunday after Thanksgiving occurs in December. This Sunday typically involves a large volume of air travel, and its irregular inclusion in December would hinder efforts to account fully for seasonality if it were not independently accounted for. Both of these irregularities are accounted for in I&L's previous work.

We also include dummy variables for the first Gulf War, the Iraq War, and the SARS epidemic.[6] Finally, we account for September 11th in several ways that differ across specifications. In most of the specifications presented, September 11th is accounted for by two variables. The first is a dummy variable that takes a value of 0 in each month prior to September 2001 and a value of 1 in September 2001 and each subsequent month. This variable seeks to identify the size of any permanent shift in the amount of air travel following the terrorist attacks. The second is an effort to account for the post-September 11th shock that proved to be transitory. This variable, which takes the form of a post-September 2001 time decay, is similar to the time decay variable used by Ito and Lee. If, as in Ito and Lee, we define T as the number of months since August 2001 (so that $T = 1$ in September 2001, 2 in October, and so on), then we can define our post-September 2001 time decay variable as being equal to 0 in all months prior to September 2001, and equal to $1/T$ in all subsequent months.

Before moving on to present our regression analysis and results, a word should be said regarding plausible interpretations of our regression equations.[7] Though we control for various supply and demand factors, we interpret our results as reflecting the impact of various factors on market equilibrium rather than on demand or supply specifically. We think that identifying the impacts of September 11th on market equilibrium is sufficiently interesting to make the claim of identifying shifts in demand unnecessary. Having the luxury of leaving it at this is, perhaps, a benefit of studying the impact of a clearly exogenous event on observed quantities rather than, say, trying to identify the impact of an increase in prices on the quantity demanded.

To model September 11th's impact on demand explicitly, it would be necessary to distinguish between the factors that impact upon supply and demand, perhaps as sketched below:

$$Q_D = D(income, economic\_activity, P_{air\_travel}, P_{substitutes}, Risk\_factors)$$

$$Q_S = S(input\_prices, other\_S\_side\_factors, P_{air\_travel}).$$

If input prices truly only belong in the supply equation, then they could feasibly be used as instruments for identifying exogenous price shocks from the perspective of the demand equation. We may pursue this approach in future work, but have not yet had the opportunity to compile price data that are disaggregated at the airport level.

REGRESSION ANALYSIS AND RESULTS

In this section we discuss and present our regression results. First we summarize the main differences between our data and the data used by I&L. Then we present specifications similar to those used by I&L, but making use of our disaggregated dataset. In subsection C we move on to test the hypothesis that the September 11th terrorist attacks had a more severe impact on passenger traffic at particularly large airports than at smaller airports.

Differences from Ito and Lee's Analysis

Since our basic regression specifications closely follow those of I&L, we begin by highlighting the primary differences between our data and theirs. First, we measure quantity using passenger enplanements while I&L use revenue passenger miles. Second, we use US DOT (2008) data that only go back to 1990 (but that have the benefit of coming in a highly disaggregated format) while I&L use ATA data going back to 1986. Third, the two supply-side variables may not be constructed in the same manner as I&L's, as the descriptions of their data collection was not particularly detailed in these two cases. (Because of uncertainty about the quality of the data used for these two variables more generally, we present most of the specifications in this chapter both with and without these supply-side variables.) Fourth, we define our Iraq War dummy differently, setting it equal to one from March 2003 to the present rather than only setting it equal to one during the 'major combat operations' phase. Finally, we did not collect a measure of airline fatalities, as this variable appears with a coefficient of 0.000 in all of I&L's regressions.

In summary, our attempted replication results are qualitatively similar to I&L's, although there are certainly some notable quantitative differences.

Initial Results using the Disaggregated Data

In this section we briefly present results for regressions that use specifications similar to those of I&L, but which make use of data disaggregated at the airport level. A word should be said about the airports included in the sample. Many airports in the data as initially collected have months in which they either do not report a number of passengers or report zero passengers. Many other airports report very small numbers of passengers, and these smaller airports tend to experience wilder fluctuations (in percentage terms) from month to month than larger, more established airports. Consequently, it was desirable to set a minimum cut-off for inclusion in our final sample. The cut-off used in the regressions that appear below is the requirement that an airport account for at least 0.1 percent of the total passenger count. This leaves 126 airports in the sample, accounting for approximately 95 percent of the total passenger count in January 1990 (the first month in our sample).

To quickly summarize the specifications shown in Table 9.2, columns 1–3 exclude the supply-side variables (the share of passengers accounted for by non-major airlines and the consumer price index (CPI) adjusted real price of jet fuel), while columns 4–6 include them. Columns 1 and 4 include no time trend variables. Columns 2 and 5 add a general time trend (ending with April 2007). Columns 3 and 6 also allow for the possibility of a break in the time trend after September 11th. The employment level and unemployment rate variables are collected at the state level, with the state-level values applied to each airport within the state. All regressions include airport- and month-specific dummy variables. The standard error estimates allow for prediction errors to be serially correlated at the airport level.

The coefficients on the demand-side economic variables are all of the expected sign. Increases in the log of the employment level are positively linked to air travel, and the coefficients are statistically significantly different from zero in all cases. Increases in the unemployment rate are always negatively linked to the level of air travel, although the coefficients are only statistically significantly different from zero in specifications that do not include a general time trend. When included, the general time trend is significant and always has a coefficient close to 0.002, suggesting an upward trend in air travel of about 0.2 percent per month. When included, the LCC share is positive and statistically significantly different from zero. This is also the case for the price of jet fuel, suggesting that for this variable reverse causality is at work since high fuel prices would normally be expected to negatively impact upon both the supply of and demands for air travel.

It is noteworthy that in these specifications there is a clear difference between the coefficients estimated for the post-September 2001 dummy variable when we do and do not allow for a general time trend. We think that allowance for a general time trend is appropriate, as the log of the employment level is otherwise the only variable used to explain the upward

Table 9.2 Estimates of the impact of 9/11 on air travel using data disaggregated at the airport level

ln(passengers)	(1)	(2)	(3)	(4)	(5)	(6)
% of non-major passengers				1.116***	0.658***	0.741***
				(0.15)	(0.11)	(0.15)
Ln(Real jet fuel)				0.0697***	0.0368***	0.0339***
				(0.010)	(0.0081)	(0.0093)
Unemployment (%)	−0.0247**	−0.0110	−0.0121	−0.0261**	−0.0106	−0.0104
	(0.0099)	(0.0077)	(0.0079)	(0.010)	(0.0086)	(0.0087)
Ln(Employment)	1.052***	0.506**	0.494**	0.822***	0.454**	0.457**
	(0.16)	(0.22)	(0.22)	(0.18)	(0.23)	(0.23)
9/11	0.0533**	−0.0639***	−0.0518**	−0.00719	−0.0915***	−0.0990***
	(0.026)	(0.021)	(0.022)	(0.023)	(0.023)	(0.028)
Time decay (9/11)	−0.414***	−0.353***	−0.377***	−0.331***	−0.312***	−0.298***
	(0.020)	(0.021)	(0.021)	(0.022)	(0.022)	(0.026)
Time		0.00207***	0.00211***		0.00190***	0.00184***
		(0.00039)	(0.00040)		(0.00042)	(0.00044)
Post-9/11 time trend			−0.00115**			0.000536
			(0.00047)			(0.00068)
February leap year	0.0270***	0.0263***	0.0200***	0.00992**	0.0219***	0.0236***
	(0.0048)	(0.0047)	(0.0041)	(0.0048)	(0.0041)	(0.0040)

Gulf War	−0.0759***	−0.00398	−0.00193	−0.0869***	−0.0120	−0.0102
	(0.018)	(0.011)	(0.011)	(0.017)	(0.015)	(0.014)
Iraq War	0.0650***	0.0267	0.0633***	−0.00248	−0.00723	−0.0233
	(0.014)	(0.016)	(0.012)	(0.014)	(0.014)	(0.018)
SARS	−0.0267**	−0.0117	−0.0386***	−0.0329***	−0.0191**	−0.0119
	(0.012)	(0.013)	(0.0070)	(0.0090)	(0.0089)	(0.0074)
Thanksgiving Dec.	0.0489***	0.0573***	0.0601***	0.0337***	0.0487***	0.0477***
	(0.0081)	(0.0071)	(0.0071)	(0.0086)	(0.0068)	(0.0069)
Thanksgiving Nov.	−0.0454***	−0.0351***	−0.0324***	−0.0548***	−0.0408***	−0.0422***
	(0.0066)	(0.0056)	(0.0056)	(0.0069)	(0.0055)	(0.0056)
Constant	4.578***	8.011***	8.094***	6.063***	8.291***	8.291***
	(1.34)	(1.65)	(1.66)	(1.46)	(1.72)	(1.72)
N	20197	20197	20197	19472	19472	19472
R-squared	0.97	0.98	0.98	0.98	0.98	0.98

Notes:
Standard errors are in parentheses. They are robust to heteroskedasticity and allow for autocorrelation at the airport level.
*** p <0.01, ** p <0.05, * p <0.1.
Coefficients for airport and month dummy variables suppressed.

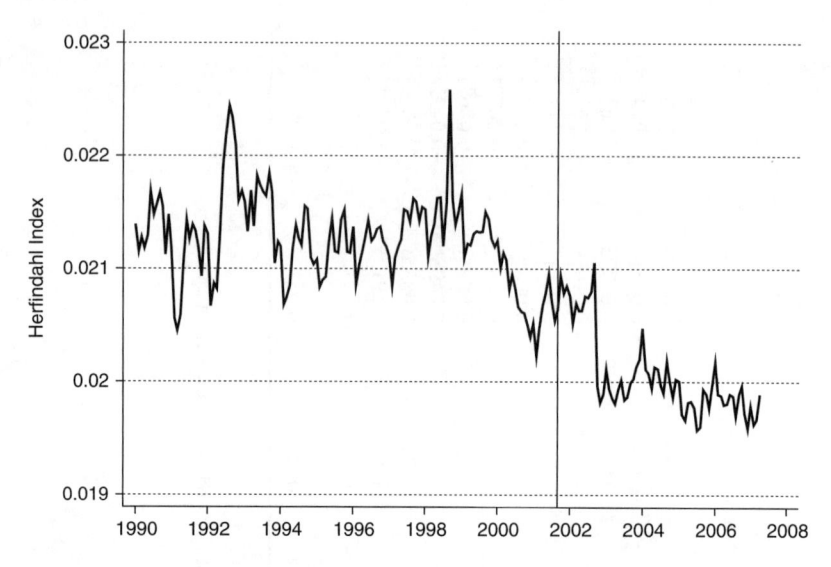

Figure 9.1 Monthly Herfindahl index approach to measuring airport concentration

trend in air travel over time. Increases in the usage of air travel over time could also reflect increases in incomes resulting from, say, productivity growth, or simply an increase in preference for air travel. When the general time trend is included the coefficient on the post-September 2001 dummy variable ranges from −0.052 to −0.099, implying a permanent downward shift of around 5–10 percent. The coefficients on the time decay variable range from −0.312 to −0.377, implying an additional transitory shock of around 31–38 percent. In model 3, the coefficient on the post-September 2001 time trend variable is negative and statistically significant, but in model 6 it is neither of these things. Model 3's coefficients suggest that the trend growth rate was about 0.1 percent less per month after September 2001.

To illustrate the effect of 9/11, we created a simple prediction plot. This plot ignores some shift factors, only taking into account the time effects on the natural logarithm of passengers. From Figure 9.1 you can see the initial drop and then the slow recovery. However, one can see that the post-9/11 trend line never reaches the pre-9/11 trend line.

Large Airport Hypothesis

In this section we present estimates from specifications which explore the hypothesis that passenger traffic through large, hub airports may have been more adversely affected by the events of September 11th than passenger traffic through smaller airports. The basis for this hypothesis lies in the fact that areas of high economic and population density make attractive targets for terrorist attacks. Increased perceptions of terrorism risk, the hypothesis goes, will then discourage the use of high-density transportation nodes more than low-density transportation nodes. It may also reduce travel to high-density cities more generally, as these cities are homes to relatively large numbers of high-value potential terrorist targets.

In assessing this hypothesis, it is important to account for pre-existing trends and other idiosyncratic characteristics that apply to large airports. It is apparent from looking at the data that large airports have at least been declining in relative importance since prior to September 2001. This can be seen in Figure 9.1, which plots a monthly Herfindahl Index-style measure of passenger concentration at airports over time. The higher the Herfindahl Index, the more passengers are concentrated at a few airports. As the index drops, passengers are more disaggregated across airports. (The Herfindahl measure is not being used here as an index of 'monopoly' in the usual sense of concentration of firm market power. The shares being used are the shares of passengers using each airport.) Although the index fluctuates fairly significantly over time, there is clearly a decline that takes place around 1999 and 2000. It does, however, appear to have stabilized and even increased somewhat during the months surrounding September 2001. It then drops off substantially and, it would seem, permanently in October 2002. As we move on to the regression results, it should be kept in mind that this concentration index provides a measure of the relative importance of large airports, while the regressions focus on absolute shifts in passenger volumes.

The results shown in Table 9.3 explore these changes in the relative importance of large airports in a regression context. Fifteen of the 126 airports in the sample are designated as large airports. These airports are not necessarily the traditional hubs of the 'hub-and-spoke' system used by the major airlines over the years. They were selected solely on the basis of the volume of travel flowing through them. This cut-off is based loosely on the airport accounting for at least 2 percent of all passenger traffic in January 1990 (the first month in the sample). The fifteenth airport (Honolulu National Airport) accounted for 1.99 percent of passenger traffic in that month, and is included in part because there is a substantial drop to 1.87 percent to the sixteenth-ranked airport.

To summarize difference across specifications, models 1–3 do not include the two supply-side variables while models 4–7 do. All specifications include a general time trend specific to the large airports (without which September 11th consistently appears to have had an unrealistically large impact on

Table 9.3 Estimates of the impact of 9/11 on large airports relative to other airports

Ln(passengers)	(1)	(2)	(3)	(4)	(5)	(6)	(7)
% of non-major passengers				1.126***	0.659***	0.735***	0.732***
				(0.15)	(0.11)	(0.15)	(0.15)
Ln(Real jet fuel)				0.0702***	0.0368***	0.0342***	0.0341***
				(0.0097)	(0.0081)	(0.0092)	(0.0092)
Unemployment (%)	−0.0122	−0.0133*	−0.0133*	−0.0272**	−0.0118	−0.0116	−0.0116
	(0.0076)	(0.0078)	(0.0078)	(0.010)	(0.0085)	(0.0086)	(0.0086)
Ln(Employment)	0.488**	0.476**	0.476**	0.815***	0.437*	0.440*	0.440*
	(0.22)	(0.22)	(0.22)	(0.18)	(0.23)	(0.23)	(0.23)
9/11	−0.0459*	−0.0333	−0.0356	0.0186	−0.0740***	−0.0809***	−0.0826***
	(0.023)	(0.024)	(0.023)	(0.024)	(0.024)	(0.029)	(0.029)
Time decay (9/11)	−0.371***	−0.394***	−0.390***	−0.357***	−0.330***	−0.317***	−0.314***
	(0.026)	(0.025)	(0.023)	(0.026)	(0.027)	(0.030)	(0.027)
Time	0.00217***	0.00222***	0.00221***		0.00201***	0.00195***	0.00195***
	(0.00041)	(0.00041)	(0.00042)		(0.00043)	(0.00045)	(0.00045)
Post 9/11 time trend		−0.00119**	−0.00111**			0.000484	0.000544
		(0.00047)	(0.00052)			(0.00068)	(0.00071)
Large airport * 9/11	−0.0973*	−0.0965*	−0.0782**	−0.142***	−0.0952*	−0.0955*	−0.0817***
	(0.053)	(0.053)	(0.030)	(0.051)	(0.051)	(0.051)	(0.028)
Large airport * time decay (9/11)	0.0583	0.0492	0.0117	0.112	0.0801	0.0848	0.0558*
	(0.090)	(0.091)	(0.027)	(0.090)	(0.089)	(0.090)	(0.029)
Large airport time trend	−0.000621	−0.000626	−0.000584	−0.000201	−0.000655	−0.000653	−0.000615
	(0.00041)	(0.00042)	(0.00046)	(0.00041)	(0.00043)	(0.00043)	(0.00048)

Large airport post 9/11 time						-0.000457
						(0.0012)
February leap year	0.0269***	0.0204***	-0.000587	0.0100**	0.0223***	0.0239***	0.0239***
	(0.0047)	(0.0041)	(0.0012)	(0.0047)	(0.0041)	(0.0040)	(0.0040)
Gulf War	-0.00456	-0.00246	0.0204***	-0.0886***	-0.0127	-0.0110	-0.0110
	(0.011)	(0.011)	(0.0041)	(0.018)	(0.014)	(0.014)	(0.014)
Iraq War	0.0252	0.0629***	-0.00246	-0.00327	-0.00809	-0.0225	-0.0224
	(0.016)	(0.012)	(0.011)	(0.014)	(0.015)	(0.018)	(0.018)
SARS	-0.0107	-0.0385***	0.0628***	-0.0327***	-0.0185**	-0.0120	-0.0121
	(0.013)	(0.0071)	(0.012)	(0.0089)	(0.0089)	(0.0077)	(0.0075)
Thanksgiving Dec.	0.0573***	0.0601***	-0.0386***	0.0334***	0.0488***	0.0479***	0.0479***
	(0.0071)	(0.0071)	(0.0070)	(0.0086)	(0.0069)	(0.0069)	(0.0069)
Thanksgiving Nov.	-0.0351***	-0.0324***	0.0600***	-0.0550***	-0.0407***	-0.0419***	-0.0420***
	(0.0056)	(0.0056)	(0.0071)	(0.0070)	(0.0055)	(0.0057)	(0.0056)
Constant	8.158***	8.244***	-0.0325***	6.132***	8.431***	8.430***	8.433***
	(1.64)	(1.65)	(0.0056)	(1.46)	(1.72)	(1.72)	(1.72)
			8.246***				
			(1.65)				
N	20197	20197	20197	19472	19472	19472	19472
R-squared	0.98	0.98	0.98	0.98	0.98	0.98	0.98

Notes:
Standard errors are in parentheses. They are robust to heteroskedasticity and allow for autocorrelation at the airport level.
*** p <0.01, ** p <0.05, * p <0.1
Coefficients for airport and month dummy variables suppressed.

passenger traffic at these airports). Model 5 does not include a general time trend. Models 1 and 6 add in a general time trend to complement the already-included hub-specific time trend. Columns 2 and 6 allow for a break in the general time trend following September 2001, and columns 3 and 7 allow for a distinct break in the time trend for large airports only (in addition to the break already allowed for the general time trend).

Results for the September 2001 variables are generally similar to those from the previous tables. Estimates for the post-September 2001 time decay variable range from -0.314 to -0.442 across the seven specifications, suggesting a transitory drop in the number of passengers of about 31–44 percent. In the six specifications which include a general time trend, the coefficients on the post-September 2001 dummy variable range from -0.033 to -0.083, suggesting a permanent decrease in the number of passengers of 3–8 percent. Interestingly, when no general time trend is included, the coefficient on the post-September 2001 dummy variable is positive with the coefficient in column 4 being positive to a statistically significant degree. This specification also includes abnormally large, negative estimates of the coefficients on the post-September 2001 large airport dummy interaction, suggesting the possibility of a small increase in small airport traffic and a decrease in large airport traffic post-September 11th. In the remaining five specifications, all of which include time trends, the post-September 2001 large airport dummy interaction estimates range from -0.078 and -0.097. This suggests a permanent post-September 2001 decrease in large airport passenger traffic of 8–10 percent beyond the decreases experienced by other airports. Neither the interaction between the post-September 2001 time decay variable and the hub dummy variable, nor the variable allowing for a hub-specific break in trend following September 2001, are statistically significantly different from zero in any of the specifications. These results suggest that, to the extent that September 11th exerted a differential impact on large airports, it is best captured as a permanent shock to the level of passenger traffic when other factors are held constant.

To illustrate the difference between the large and smaller airports we created Figure 9.2. In this figure, we can see that large airports have higher levels of passengers on average; this is represented by the higher trend line for large airports. However, the 9/11 shock also causes a larger drop in percentage terms at large airports than at smaller airports. Again, this implies that the initial effect is stronger for large airports. In the longer term, we suggest that large airports could be more affected than smaller airports. This could be the result of higher perceived risk associated with large airports as well as other factors including capacity constraints as large airports become more limited in their expansion.

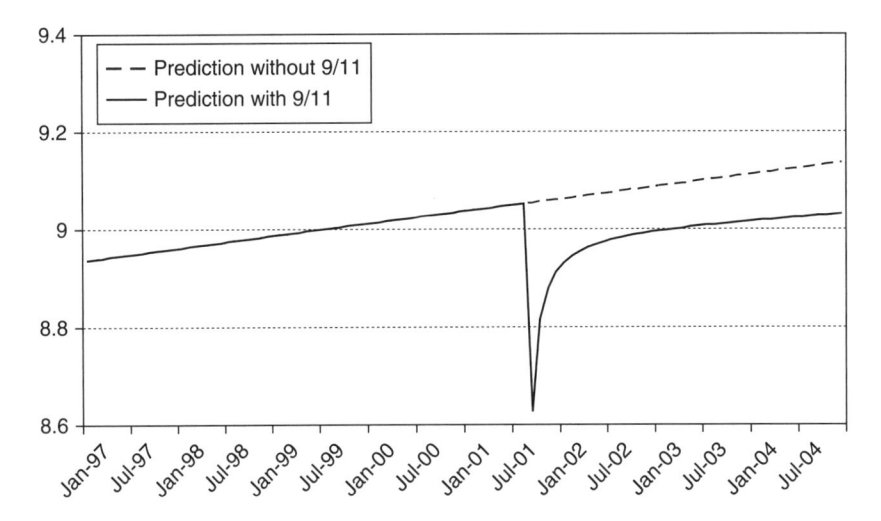

The impact of 9/11 on airport passenger density 163

Figure 9.2   Illustration of 9/11 effect using regression model 6 from Table 9.2

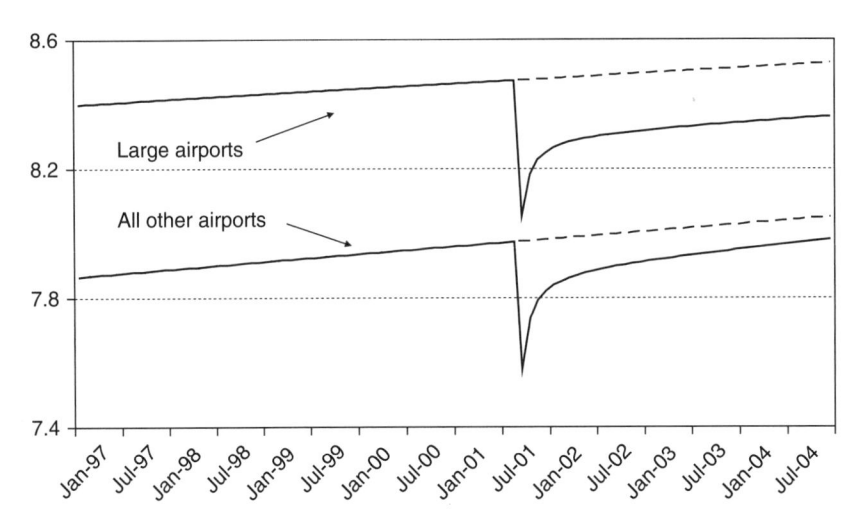

Figure 9.3   Comparison of large versus all other airports using regression model 7 from Table 9.3

Tourism Destination and East–West Coast Hypotheses

In this section we explore the possibility that East Coast cities might have been more affected by the 9/11 attacks than other cities, given their

Table 9.4 Region effects

Ln(passengers)	(1)	(2)	(3)	(4)	(5)*
East Coast	0.491**	0.452*	0.452*	0.507**	
	(0.24)	(0.24)	(0.24)	(0.25)	
West Coast	0.328	0.266	0.265	0.350	
	(0.40)	(0.41)	(0.41)	(0.41)	
East Coast * 9/11		0.107	0.152*		
		(0.11)	(0.087)		
West Coast * 9/11		0.158	0.0581		
		(0.16)	(0.12)		
Large Airport Dummy				0.464**	−0.190**
				(0.21)	(0.089)
East Coast * Large Airport * 9/11				−0.789**	0.00789
				(0.37)	(0.10)
West Coast * Large Airport *9/11				−0.704	−0.144
				(0.47)	(0.10)
East Coast * Post 9/11 Time Trend			−0.00130		
			(0.0021)		
West Coast * Post 9/11 Time Trend			0.00292		
			(0.0035)		

Table 9.4 (continued)

Ln(passengers)	(1)	(2)	(3)	(4)	(5)*
Constant	8.661***	8.612***	8.601***	8.713***	4.019
	(1.25)	(1.26)	(1.26)	(1.25)	(2.72)
Observations	46652	46652	46652	46652	46652
R-squared	0.22	0.22	0.22	0.22	0.95

Note:
Robust standard errors in parentheses, clustered by airport.
*** $p<0.01$, ** $p<0.05$, * $p<0.1$
Coefficients for airport dummy variables suppressed.
*Model 5 includes airport fixed effects.
Coefficients for airport dummy variables, month dummy variables, and other explainatory variables supressed.

proximity to New York and Washington, DC. In general, East and West Coast airports can also be viewed as serving different markets. This is particularly true with respect to incoming international travelers, as West Coast airports tend to serve travelers from Asia while East Coast airports are more likely to serve passengers from Europe. Although we do not estimate international travel directly, it is possible that international passengers board domestic connection flights after they land at a US destination.

To try and capture this idea in our regression model, we created dummy variables to represent the East Coast and West Coast airports. We then interacted these with our post-9/11 dummy variable. Table 9.4 depicts the regression results. There does not appear to be any relationship between the regions and the impact of 9/11 as is shown by the insignificance of the interaction terms. However, this could also be due to our data, which focus on domestic travel. International data could see more significant differences between these two regions.

DISCUSSION AND CONCLUSION

We have used airport-level data to study the impact of the September 11th terrorist attacks on domestic air travel in the United States. Our initial estimates of 9/11's effects are similar to those made by Ito and Lee, who used nationally aggregated data in previous work. We have also found evidence suggesting that 9/11 may have had a more adverse impact on large airports than on small airports. This could be the result of 9/11's various impacts (including its impact on risk perceptions and security procedures) being relatively severe in the case of large airports. It is also possible, however, that this result is due to pre-existing trends in the market for air travel. We hope, in future work, to further tease out the extent to which these results can be attributed to 9/11 itself. We found no evidence that East Coast airports were more adversely affected than West Coast airports. We think it is more likely that such an effect would be discernible in data on international passenger traffic.

NOTES

1. Center for Risk and Economic Analysis of Terrorism Events, University of Southern California, garrett.asay@usc.edu.
2. Summer Scholar, Center for Risk and Economic Analysis of Terrorism Events, University of Southern California.
3. We would like to thank Tatiana Kichkaylo, Peter Gordon, Jim Moore, Harry Richardson,

Adam Rose, Detlof van Winterfeidt and the members of the planning and economics discussion group at USC for their helpful comments and support.
4. We have some misgivings about the economic content of this particular measure, but report it because of its apparent consistency with I&L's measure. Fortunately, the inclusion or exclusion of this measure does not significantly affect the estimates associated with the variables that are of primary interest in this study. Our misgivings are based on the fact that the US DOT's definition of a major carrier is based on annual operating revenues, with major carriers defined as those with annual operating revenues exceeding $1 billion. Consequently, as low-cost carriers expand, they cease to be defined as low-cost carriers (as would be the case for carriers like Southwest and JetBlue). We have also experimented with an alternative measure of the low-cost carrier share which is based on the fraction of total enplanements accounted for by airlines that are considered to be the traditional low-cost carriers. At present, however, we have only been able to compile these data on an annual basis, and the coefficients on the low-cost carrier share are both volatile across specifications and generally of the incorrect sign. Importantly, however, as with the other measure of the low-cost carrier share, the inclusion of this alternative measure does not significantly affect the coefficients on the primary variables of interest.
5. Ito and Lee do not include a time trend in their specification and, in fact, we are able to replicate their results fairly closely when we also use data aggregated at the national level. When using our disaggregated data, however, it typically seems necessary to include a linear time trend to obtain reasonable coefficients on the September 11th-related variables. In some specifications without the time trend, for example, a dummy variable that is equal to 1 during all months following September 11th will have a highly positive coefficient. This suggests that our controls for the level of economic activity fail to account sufficiently for upward-trending factors that drive increases in airline demand over time.
6. We differ from Ito and Lee only in that while they account for the current Iraq War solely in terms of the 'major combat operations' phase (that is, February to April 2003), we account for the Iraq War as an ongoing event from March 2003 (which marks the actual commencement of major combat operations) to the present.
7. I&L refer to their quantity equation as a demand equation. They express awareness that the quantities used in their (and our) regressions are, in fact, market equilibria influenced by both supply- and demand-side factors, but they are comfortable with interpreting these quantities as the quantities demanded. We are not willing to make this jump and instead focus on the equilibrium interpretation.

REFERENCES

Abadie, Alberto and Sofia Dermisi (2006), 'Is terrorism eroding agglomeration economies in central business districts? Lessons from the office real estate market in downtown Chicago', National Bureau of Economic Research, Inc., NBER Working Papers: 12678.

Becker, Gary S. and Yona Rubinstein (2007), 'Fear and the response to terrorism: an economic analysis,' Working Paper, University of Chicago.

Gigerenzer, Gerd (2006), 'Dread risk, September 11, and fatal traffic accidents', *American Psychological Society*, **15** (4), 286–7.

Glaeser, Edward L. and Jesse M. Shapiro (2002), 'Cities and warfare: the impact of terrorism on urban form', *Journal of Urban Economics*, **51** (2), 205–24.

Gordon, Peter, S. Kim, J. Moore, J. Park and H.W. Richardson (2007), 'The economic impacts of a terrorist attack on the US commercial aviation system', *Risk Analysis*, **27** (3), 505–12.

Ito, Harumi and Darin Lee (2003), 'Low cost carrier growth in the US airline

industry: past, present, and future', Unpublished Working Paper, Brown University, RI.
Ito, Harumi and Darin Lee (2005a), 'Comparing the impact of the September 11th terrorist attacks on international airline demand', *International Journal of the Economics of Business*, **12** (2), 225–49.
Ito, Harumi and Darin Lee (2005b), 'Assessing the impact of the September 11 terrorist attacks on US airline demand', *Journal of Economics and Business*, **57** (1), 75–95.
Redfearn, Christian (2005), 'Land markets and terrorism: uncovering perceptions of risk by examining land price changes following 9/11', in Harry W. Richardson, Peter Gordon and James E. Moore II (eds), *The Economic Impacts of Terrorist Attacks*, Cheltenham, UK and Northampton, MA, USA: Edward Elgar, pp. 152–69.
Sivak, Michael and Michael J. Flannagan (2003), 'Flying and driving after the September 11th attacks', *American Scientist Online*, January–February.
US Department of Transportation (2008), *Bureau of Transportation Studies, Air Carrier Statistics (From 41 Traffic), Table T-100 (All Carriers)*.

10. The effect of transnational terrorism on bilateral trade
Quan Li

Since the 9/11 terrorist attacks, the economic consequences of terrorism have attracted wide public and scholarly attention. The global 'war on terror' has led to tightened security almost around the world, increasing the costs of conducting international business. Many are concerned that international trade, an important component of the global economy, will suffer due to terrorism and counter-terrorism. A 2003 report, prepared by the Australian Department of Foreign Affairs and Trade and delivered at an Asia-Pacific Economic Cooperation (APEC) trade and security forum in Bangkok in 2003, estimated that the United States economy is losing up to US$75 billion a year because of terrorism. The popular view is that terrorism leads to lost business.

Several econometric studies (Nitsch and Schumacher, 2004; Fratianni and Kang, 2006; Blomberg and Hess, 2006) demonstrate that terrorism reduces the volume of trade. According to these studies, a doubling in the number of terrorist incidents in two countries of a dyad is associated with a decrease in bilateral trade by about 4 percent. The presence of terrorism together with internal and external conflict is equivalent to as much as a 30 percent tariff on trade in a given country year. And the negative effect of terrorism for trade is stronger for contiguous countries.

In this chapter, I re-examine the effect of terrorism on trade. Previous studies have ignored the direction of terrorist attacks, failed to control for dyad-specific unobserved characteristics, and treated pairs of countries at different development stages equally. This research corrects for these issues. I investigate both the impact of the total number of terrorist events within countries and the effect of terrorist attacks between citizens of two countries in a dyad. I also test the implications of controlling for dyad-specific unobservables, political ties between governments of country pairs and subsamples based on development stage. Using the same data of annual bilateral trade flows from 1968 to 2000, I find no consistent evidence that the total number of terrorist incidents within countries reduces bilateral trade flows, once controlling for dyad-specific unobservables or across subsamples of different development stages. But bilateral terrorist attacks reduce trade in country pairs that involve at least one advanced economy. Overall the econometric evidence is too weak to support the view that transnational terrorism on average reduces bilateral trade flows. The findings suggest caution in understanding and estimating the impact on transnational terrorism on international commerce.

The rest of the chapter proceeds as follows. The next section discusses the logic of why terrorism reduces trade, as identified in the literature, and further develops the implication that conventional logic ought to lead one to expect that bilateral terrorist attacks reduce bilateral trade flows. The third section presents the empirical methodology and data, and fourth section discusses the findings. The final section conjectures why terrorism may not consistently reduce bilateral trade, and concludes the chapter.

HOW DO TERRORIST INCIDENTS AFFECT BILATERAL TRADE?

Terrorism is argued to reduce the volume of trade through several mechanisms (Nitsch and Schumacher, 2004; Fratianni and Kang, 2006; Blomberg and Hess, 2006). First, because terrorism threatens human life, it increases the sense of insecurity among the public. Consequently, it leads to changes in consumption and production patterns in the economy and disrupts existing business plans. Tourism, shopping and business investment may all be affected. The costs of doing business and risks for firms will rise, and the appeal of the market to international traders and producers will decline. Second, to deal with terrorism, governments have to strengthen security measures, which often involve extensive inspections and sometimes border shutdowns. This obviously will cause delays in the delivery of traded goods and increase the expenses of conducting trade. Home transactions may be substituted for international commerce. And trade may also be diverted toward countries with less demanding border inspections.[1] Third, terrorism may directly damage traded goods, either as collateral damage or as the target of terrorist attacks. Consequently, trading costs and the volume of trade will decline.

If one accepts the above logic in the literature, further implications can be inferred. A widely used definition of terrorism is the premeditated or threatened use of extra-normal violence or force to obtain a political, religious or ideological objective through the intimidation of a large audience (for example, Enders and Sandler, 1999, 2002). The focus of previous research and this analysis has been on transnational terrorism. Terrorist attacks in one country become transnational when they involve victims, perpetrators, targets or institutions of another country. Based on the incident venue, transnational terrorist incidents can involve: (1) terrorist attacks initiated by foreign terrorists against some domestic target in a country; (2) attacks by domestic terrorists against some foreign target in a country; or (3) attacks by foreign terrorists against some other foreign target in a country. Therefore, many terrorist incidents involve perpetrators from one country against victims of another or several others.

Following the theoretical logic in the literature, direct attacks between citizens of two countries should have an even clearer negative effect on bilateral trade flows. In addition to working through the above theoretical mechanisms, direct attacks between citizens of two countries may be the result of strained relations and ought to generate further animosity between their citizens. As citizens are consumers, producers and traders, they may be reluctant to trade with citizens of another country who may turn out to be terrorist perpetrators against themselves. Furthermore, governments are more likely to target security measures and counter-terrorist efforts at the citizens of countries of terrorist perpetrators. Finally, where state-sponsored terrorism is involved, governments may strengthen export controls and exchange sanctions against each other.

For example, the fact that 15 of the 19 hijackers of 9/11 were Saudi Arabians has not only strained political and economic relations between the US and Saudi Arabia but also generated wide criticism among the American public against Saudi Arabia. The US bombing of Libya and the US invasion of Iraq are also cases in point. Therefore, if one accepts the logic in the literature, it is plausible to expect that terrorist attacks exchanged between citizens of two countries in a dyad should have a negative effect on their bilateral trade flows. Figure 10.1 illustrates this implication graphically. As some citizens of countries A and B trade with each other, some other citizens in these two

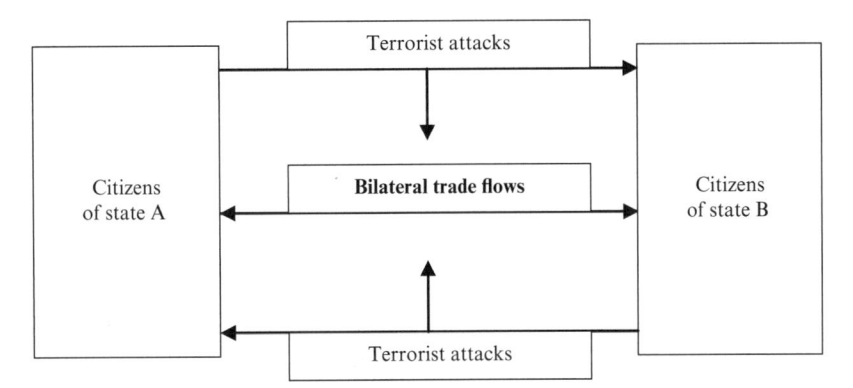

Figure 10.1 Terrorist attacks between countries and bilateral trade

countries may turn into terrorists and attack each other. Following the logic in the literature, such attacks should reduce the bilateral trade flows.

One may even argue that where the focus of analysis is bilateral trade flows, the effect of bilateral terrorist attacks on trade ought to be even stronger and more relevant than that of the total numbers of terrorist incidents within countries in general. Bilateral trade flows are directly affected by relations between citizens of the two countries. In contrast, the total numbers of terrorist incidents within countries in general often reflect the general risk environments in these countries. The direct empirical implication of the logic in the literature is that bilateral terrorist attacks reduce bilateral trade flows.

EMPIRICAL METHODOLOGY AND DATA

To test the effect of terrorism on trade, I employ the gravity model of international trade, as in Nitsch and Schumacher (2004), Fratianni and Kang (2006) and Blomberg and Hess (2006). International trade economists usually employ the gravity model to estimate the normal level of trade between states (Aitken, 1973; Anderson, 1979; Deardorff, 1998; Frankel, 1997). The model posits that bilateral trade is a function of incomes, populations and distance between countries.

Following earlier work on the impact of terrorism on trade, I also employ the gravity model specification of Glick and Rose (2002) and Rose (2004) as well as their data for the sake of comparison, with some slight modifications. The empirical model is specified as follows:

$$Ln(TRADE_{ij,t+1}) = \beta_0 + \beta_1 ln(GDP_{i,t}*GDP_{j,t})$$

$$+ \beta_2 ln(GDP_{i,t}*GDP_{j,t}/POP_{i,t}*POP_{j,t}) + \beta_3 ln(Distance_{ij,t})$$

$$+ \beta_4 Language_{ij} + \beta_5 Border_{ij} + \beta_6 Landlocked + \beta_7 Island$$

$$+ \beta_8 ln(Area_i*Area_j) + \beta_9 Common\text{-}Colonizer_{ij} + \beta_{10} RTA_{ij,t}$$

$$+ \beta_{11} GSP_{ij} + \beta_{12} Current\text{-}Colonial\text{-}Tie_{ij,t}$$

$$+ \beta_{13} Former\text{-}Colonial\text{-}Tie_{ij,t} + \beta_{14} Currency_{ij,t}$$

$$+ \beta_{15} ln(Terror_i*Terror_j)_t + \beta_{16} ln(Terror_{ij,t}) + \beta_p T + e_{ij,t}$$

The gravity model variables are defined as those in Rose (2004). $TRADE_{ij,t+1}$ is the average value of real bilateral trade between countries i and j at time $t + 1$; GDP is real GDP; POP is population; Distance is the distance between i and j; *Language* is a dummy variable indicating that i and j share a common language; *Border* is a dummy variable indicating that i and j share a land border; *Landlocked* is the number of landlocked countries in the country pair; *Island* is the number of island nations in the country pair; *Area* is the area of a country in square kilometers; *Common-Colonizer* indicates that i and j shared the same colonizer after 1945; *Current-Colonial-Tie* indicates that i and j are colonies at time t; *Former-Colonial-Tie* indicates that i and j were ever in a colonial relationship; *RTA* is a dummy variable indicating that i and j belong to the same regional trade agreement; *GSP* (US Generalized System of Preferences) is a dummy variable indicating that i extends the GSP to j or vice versa; *Currency* is a dummy indicating that i and j use the same currency; T denotes the set of year fixed effects dummy variables; $e_{ij,t}$ denotes the error term. The two terrorism variables are defined as follows. $ln(Terror_i * Terror_j)_t$ is the log of product of (1 + the number of terrorist incidents) in countries i and j, respectively, as in previous work (for example, Nitsch and Schumacher, 2004). $ln(Terror_{ijt})$ is the number of attacks perpetrated by citizens of the two countries against each other as victims. Data are from the ITERATE database (Mickolus et al., 2002). Following the logic of the literature, we should expect both terrorism variables to reduce bilateral trade flows.

The model is estimated using ordinary least squares (OLS) with year fixed effects and robust standard errors clustered over dyad. None of the previous econometric studies (Nitsch and Schumacher, 2004; Fratianni and Kang, 2006; Blomberg and Hess, 2006) has modeled the influence of dyad-specific unobservables. Cheng and Wall (2005), however, have demonstrated that in the gravity model of trade, it is important to control for heterogeneity in bilateral country-pair fixed effects. Failing to control for such heterogeneity leads to overestimated effects of the right-hand side variables. To examine whether past models are sensitive to this possible confounding effect, I also estimate models that control for dyad fixed effects.

Another modeling difference in this analysis is that the dependent variable is one year, leading the independent variables to allow terrorist incidents some time to affect traders and to control for possible reverse causality. Previous research has the dependent variable contemporaneous with the independent variables. In robustness tests, I will also use the contemporaneous trade variable.

FINDINGS

Table 10.1 presents the statistical results of four models. Model 1 is the OLS model with year fixed effects, the same estimator and similar model

Table 10.1 Effect of Terrorist Attacks on Log of Real Bilateral Trade$_{t+1}$ (1968–2000)

	OLS year fixed effect	OLS dyad & year fixed effects	OLS year fixed effect	OLS dyad & year fixed effects
Log of product of 1+number of terrorist incidents$_{i,j,t}$	−0.070 (7.44)**	0.002 (0.38)	−0.074 (7.87)**	0.002 (0.41)
Log of (1 + terrorist attacks$_{ij}$)$_t$	0.125 (2.44)*	−0.026 (1.13)	0.161 (2.89)**	−0.021 (0.88)
Log distance$_{ij}$	−1.165 (47.19)**		−1.164 (44.45)**	
Log of product of real GDPs$_{ijt}$	0.938 (84.04)**	0.576 (10.95)**	0.955 (84.38)**	0.572 (10.39)**
Log of product of real GDPs per capita$_{ijt}$	0.407 (24.77)**	0.206 (3.92)**	0.427 (25.38)**	0.235 (4.25)**
GSP dummy	0.820 (24.81)**	−0.037 (1.30)	0.803 (23.67)**	−0.012 (0.39)
Dummy for RTA	0.995 (9.25)**	0.456 (7.00)**	1.034 (9.21)**	0.499 (7.91)**
Currency	1.021 (6.68)**	0.601 (3.77)**	1.008 (6.39)**	0.568 (3.17)**
Common language	0.429 (9.67)**		0.439 (9.55)**	
Land border dummy	0.728 (6.33)**		0.784 (6.74)**	

# Landlocked	−0.465 (13.81)**	−0.477 (14.01)**
# Islands	0.059 (1.50)	0.023 (0.59)
Product of land areas	−0.078 (8.43)**	−0.078 (8.35)**
Dummy for common colonizer post 1945	0.737 (9.43)**	0.704 (8.96)**
Dummy for pairs currently in colonial relationship	1.254 (2.76)**	−2.517 (21.95)**
Dummy for pairs ever in colonial relationship	1.277 (11.56)**	1.347 (11.74)**
Military alliance		0.065 (3.12)**
Interstate military dispute		−0.480 (1.77)
Common political interest (S score)		0.407 (6.27)**
Constant	−18.560 (49.72)**	−20.046 (48.90)**
	−13.260 (12.00)**	−13.342 (11.46)*
Observations	170659 170659	163448 163448
R-squared	0.66 0.87	0.66 0.87

Notes:
Robust t statistics (clustering by country-pairs) in parentheses.
* significant at 5%; ** significant at 1%.

specification applied by previous empirical studies. Results for the gravity model variables are consistent with both model expectations and previous research findings. Geographic distance hinders bilateral trade flows, and both real GDPs and real GDPs per capita increase the volume of bilateral trade. Furthermore, regional trade agreement joint membership, GSP concession within a dyad, currency union membership, common language, land contiguity, the number of island nations in the dyad, and historical and current colonial ties all have statistically significant and positive impact on bilateral trade, consistent with expectations. Also as expected, the number of landlocked countries in the dyad and the log product of land areas in the dyad are negatively associated with trade. The model also demonstrates good fit for data, explaining about 66 percent of the variations in bilateral trade flows. These results indicate that this is a reasonably well-specified model.

We are most interested in the effects of the terrorism variables in model 1. The log product of the numbers of terrorist incidents of two countries in a dyad is the same variable employed in Nitsch and Schumacher (2004). Its effect is identical to that in Nitsch and Schumacher (2004) in terms of sign and significance, but the size of effect is slightly larger. The effect is statistically significant and negative, and the coefficient −0.07 indicates that a doubling in the number of terrorist incidents (that is, a 100 percent increase) will lead to a decline in bilateral trade by 7 percent, all else being equal.

The second terrorism variable, however, the number of terrorist attacks between citizens of two countries in a dyad, produces a somewhat surprising finding that is inconsistent with the commonly held logic. The number of terrorist attacks between countries has a statistically significant but positive impact on bilateral trade. The size of the coefficient (0.125) is very large, indicating that a 100 percent increase in the number of terrorist attacks between two countries is associated with a 12.5 percent rise in bilateral trade flows.[2]

Model 2 in Table 10.1 additionally controls for dyad fixed effects with dyad-specific intercepts. This dyad fixed effect within estimator controls for dyad-specific unobserved attributes following Cheng and Wall (2005), and it also allows the analyst to focus on temporal variations, that is, how changes in terrorist incidents affect changes in bilateral trade flows. Since the estimator does not permit time-invariant dyad-specific variables, variables such as common language, distance, and so on are excluded from model 2.

In model 2, the log product of the numbers of terrorist incidents of two countries in a dyad now no longer has any statistically significant impact on bilateral trade flows. The size of the effect is much smaller than that in model 1. While the finding is puzzling, and we will turn to it in the next section, it is clear that the number of terrorist incidents within countries no longer reduces trade once dyad-specific unobservables attributes are controlled for.

The effect of the bilateral terrorist attacks also is statistically insignificant. On the one hand, the result is not surprising given that the dyad-specific fixed effects absorb the variations to be explained by this dyadic terrorist attack variable. On the other hand, the fact that it turns insignificant once we control for dyad-specific unobserved attributes indicates that the effect of bilateral terrorist attacks on trade flows is probably not very strong.

Models 1 and 2 in Table 10.1 produce surprising findings with respect to the effect of terrorism on trade. One may wonder whether the results are spurious. It is possible that the dyadic terrorist attacks variable captures the influence of other dyadic political variables that have been found to affect trade. For example, states that share common interests tend to trade more with each other (Dixon and Moon, 1993; Morrow et al., 1998, 1999). This is because traders expect less political risk to future trade and the transaction costs are lower (Pollins, 1989; Morrow et al., 1998, 1999). Alliance contributes to the increase in bilateral trade under a bipolar system, but not under a multipolar system (Gowa, 1989; Gowa and Mansfield, 1993; Mansfield and Bronson, 1997). Military conflict reduces bilateral trade (Li and Sacko, 2002).

Models 3 and 4 in Table 10.1 present the results of controlling for military alliance, dyadic military dispute and common political interests, as suggested by the political science literature. Data are from EUGene (Bennett and Stam, 1999). The two models produce results for the terrorism variables that are consistent with those in models 1 and 2. The total number of terrorist incidents in countries reduces trade in model 3 (without controlling for dyad fixed effects), but the effect is statistically insignificant in model 4 (after controlling for dyad fixed effects). As in model 1, dyadic terrorist attacks are positively associated with trade in model 3; but as in model 2, the effect is statistically not different from zero in model 4.

One may plausibly argue that countries at different development stages have different trade patterns. Trade among less-developed countries (LDCs) is relatively smaller than that among advanced economies or between less-developed and advanced economies. Since trade flows among less-developed countries are relatively small to begin with, the risk of terrorism for trade may not result in large behavioral changes by traders. In contrast, the volume of trade is relatively large in country pairs that involve advanced economies. In this context, the risk of terrorism is likely to lead to larger changes in the volume of trade.

To assess the possible confounding impact of development stages, models in Table 10.1 are re-estimated for two subsamples – the non-OECD (Organisation for Economic Co-operation and Development) country pairs and the OECD–OECD or OECD–LDC country pairs. The results are presented in Tables 10.2 and 10.3, where models in Table 10.3 also

Table 10.2 Effect of Terrorist Attacks on Log of Real Bilateral Trade$_{t+1}$ (1968–2000) for subsamples

	Non-OECD pairs		At least one OECD country	
	OLS year fixed effect	OLS dyad & year fixed effects	OLS year fixed effect	OLS dyad & year fixed effects
Log of product of 1 + number of terrorist incidents$_{i,j,t}$	−0.115 (7.64)**	−0.005 (0.62)	−0.042 (3.62)**	−0.006 (1.35)
Log of (1+terrorist attacks)$_{ij,t}$	0.176 (1.45)	0.044 (0.67)	0.033 (0.70)	−0.052 (2.34)*
Log distance$_{ij}$	−1.253 (35.19)**		−0.994 (31.54)**	
Log of product of real GDPs$_{i,j,t}$	0.944 (49.71)**	0.635 (6.75)**	0.948 (70.65)**	0.558 (7.00)**
Log of product of real GDPs per capita$_{i,j,t}$	0.318 (11.84)**	0.070 (0.77)	0.448 (20.00)**	0.333 (4.34)**
GSP dummy	0.008 (0.08)	−0.293 (3.12)**	0.683 (17.33)**	−0.119 (3.64)**
Dummy for RTA	1.191 (7.87)**	0.182 (1.45)	0.847 (6.01)**	0.571 (9.76)**
Currency	0.762 (4.46)**	0.583 (2.68)**	1.726 (4.78)**	0.585 (3.41)**
Common language	0.324 (4.92)**		0.507 (9.34)**	

Land border dummy	0.895	−0.061
	(6.88)**	(0.32)
# Landlocked	−0.551	−0.428
	(9.92)**	(10.72)**
# Islands	0.068	−0.050
	(1.04)	(1.04)
Product of land areas	−0.089	−0.091
	(5.61)**	(8.32)**
Dummy for common colonizer post-1945	0.743	2.963
	(8.92)**	(16.03)**
Dummy for pairs currently in colonial relationship	3.813	0.991
	(7.68)**	(2.09)*
Dummy for pairs ever in colonial relationship	−0.457	1.215
	(0.95)	(11.40)**
Constant	−16.320	−20.588	−14.357
	(26.88)**	(41.03)**	(8.59)**
	−13.427		
	(7.15)**		
Observations	85919	85919	84740	84740
R-squared	0.47	0.80	0.77	0.92

Notes:
Robust t statistics (clustering by country-pairs) in parentheses.
* significant at 5%; ** significant at 1%.

179

Table 10.3 Effect of Terrorist Attacks on Log of Real Bilateral Trade$_{t+1}$ (1968–2000) for Subsample Country Pairs, with Political Controls

	Non-OECD pairs		At least one OECD country	
	OLS year fixed effect	OLS dyad & year fixed effects	OLS year fixed effect	OLS dyad & year fixed effects
Log of product of 1 + number of terrorist incidents$_{i,jt}$	−0.107	−0.007	−0.052	−0.003
	(7.19)**	(0.86)	(4.40)**	(0.72)
Log of (1+terrorist attacks$_{ij}$)$_t$	0.154	0.054	0.063	−0.049
	(1.25)	(0.83)	(1.30)	(2.16)*
Log distance$_{ij}$	−1.160		−1.006	
	(27.74)**		(31.22)**	
Log of product of real GDPs$_{ijt}$	0.965	0.628	0.961	0.595
	(51.07)**	(6.33)**	(70.50)**	(6.93)**
Log of product of real GDPs per capita$_{ijt}$	0.352	0.103	0.465	0.336
	(12.68)**	(1.07)	(20.35)**	(4.07)**
GSP dummy	0.170	−0.292	0.674	−0.105
	(1.76)	(3.10)**	(16.79)**	(3.02)**
Dummy for RTA	1.480	0.259	0.752	0.600
	(9.49)**	(2.11)*	(4.92)**	(10.36)**
Currency	0.898	0.597	1.134	0.324
	(5.15)**	(2.66)**	(3.67)**	(2.17)*
Common language	0.279		0.536	
	(4.05)**		(9.85)**	
Land border dummy	1.009		0.038	
	(7.68)**		(0.19)	

# Landlocked	−0.565		−0.418
	(10.20)**		(10.20)**
# Islands	0.013		−0.074
	(0.21)		(1.53)
Product of land areas	−0.092		−0.090
	(5.85)**		(8.05)**
Dummy for common colonizer post 1945	0.682		2.778
	(8.10)**		(14.32)**
Dummy for pairs currently in colonial relationship	0.000		−2.762
	(.)		(24.96)**
Dummy for pairs ever in colonial relationship	−0.403		1.257
	(1.00)		(11.40)**
Military alliance	0.091	−0.074	0.025
	(3.21)**	(1.90)	(0.90)
Interstate military dispute	−0.637	−0.513	−0.327
	(1.93)	(2.87)**	(0.90)
Common political interest (S score)	1.100	−0.383	0.129
	(8.10)**	(2.55)*	(1.78)
Constant	−19.475	−13.199	−21.473
	(28.31)**	(6.60)**	(39.43)**
Observations	83812	83812	79636
R-squared	0.47	0.80	0.77

−0.061	
(2.53)*	
−0.017	
(0.08)	
−0.155	
(1.86)	
−15.495	
(8.54)**	
79636	
0.92	

Notes:
Robust t statistics (clustering by country-pairs) in parentheses.
* significant at 5%; ** significant at 1%.

control for alliance, conflict and political relations. In both Tables 10.2 and 10.3, the results for the non-OECD country pairs are largely consistent with those in Table 10.1. The total number of incidents in the country pair reduces trade in the absence of controlling for dyad fixed effects in model 1 of both Tables 10.2 and 10.3, but it does not have any significant impact after controlling for dyad fixed effects in model 2 of both tables. The dyadic terrorist attacks are positively associated with bilateral trade in models 1 and 2 in both Tables 10.2 and 10.3, but the effect is statistically insignificant.

The results for the OECD–OECD or OECD–LDC country pairs are somewhat different from those in Table 10.1. Similarly, in both Tables 10.2 and 10.3, terrorist incidents within countries reduce trade in model 3 (without dyad fixed effects), but the effect disappears in model 4 (after controlling for dyad fixed effects). In contrast, bilateral terrorist attacks now have a statistically significant negative impact on bilateral trade flows in model 4 (with dyad fixed effects) of both Tables 10.2 and 10.3. According to the estimates, a doubling in the number of bilateral attacks leads to a decline in bilateral trade flows by about 5 percent. Once we control for country pair heterogeneity, dyadic terrorist attacks reduce bilateral trade flows in country pairs that involve at least one advanced economy.

As noted, we lag the independent variables one year to allow time for terrorist attacks to affect trade contracts and to control for possible reverse causality. One may wonder whether this modeling choice makes a difference to the results. When we re-estimate all the models in Tables 10.1–10.3 using contemporaneous independent variables, all the results remain consistent, except that the significant impact bilateral attacks for one advanced economy country pair now becomes statistically insignificant.[3]

Overall, the econometric evidence in this analysis supports the conclusion that the effect of terrorism on bilateral trade is not always negative, as perceived by the public and presented in the literature. The effect is sensitive to development stages and, particularly, country pair heterogeneity. Most troubling is the fact that the effect of bilateral terrorist attacks, which should be highly significant and negative according to the theoretical logic in the literature, is only significant in some particular model specification.

WHY TERRORISM MAY NOT REDUCE BILATERAL TRADE

Econometric evidence in this analysis does not support the view in the literature that terrorism reduces bilateral trade. So what explains the inconsistency between evidence and logic? One empirical possibility is that all existing analyses fail to distinguish terrorist attacks in terms of severity. Events that are hoaxes and attacks that take lives should have very different implications for traders, but they are lumped together and treated with equal weight in analysis. This data lumping, however, should not have caused our finding that bilateral terrorist attacks increase trade by a significant economic magnitude. It is hard to imagine that even minor terrorist actions should be good for the economy at large, even though certain counter-terrorism-related businesses may boom.

The issue is probably more theoretical than empirical. There are several possible conjectures. First, consumers, producers and traders are rational economic agents. Their consumption and business decisions depend on their ability to anticipate risks. Their decisions and behavior are most likely modified *ex ante* where terrorist attacks are anticipated; but their behavior is most likely modified *ex post* where terrorist attacks are unanticipated. Terrorist events need to be distinguished if we are to estimate their *ex post* effect on trade. To the extent that agents overanticipate the risks *ex ante*, they may expand consumption and business *ex post*.[4]

Second, terrorism tends to concentrate in particular geographic hot spots (Braithwaite and Li, 2007). In these hot spot countries, trade is likely to suffer, but the effect has already been taking place for a long time. Additional new attacks in the long-existing terrorism hot spots are not likely to have any large further impact on economic behavior, as their costs have been anticipated and internalized and trade levels have been suppressed for a long time already. If one were to estimate the immediate impact of terrorist attacks on trade, as is currently done, there is unlikely to be supporting evidence. This does not mean that terrorism does not reduce trade, but that the effect is localized, and over the long run.

Third, existing research has failed to consider the gigantic magnitude of international trade in the global economy and the huge opportunity cost of private agents and governments stopping trade to evade terrorism. Indeed, most analysts appear to agree that the contemporary global economy is probably the most integrated in history (see, for example, Frankel, 2000). As the global economy becomes more integrated, it also becomes more competitive. Businesses that locate elsewhere to avoid terrorism may find their competitors snatch their abandoned market. More and more national governments liberalize their economies to expand international trade and investment in order to increase national economic growth. The pressures to maintain trade and keep commerce functioning smoothly are high. Indeed, more than $1.4 billion worth of goods cross the borders of the North American Free Trade Agreement (NAFTA) countries every day (McDonald, 2002). In 2001 alone, cargo vessels offloaded roughly 18 million 40-foot long cargo containers at American ports, often in single batches as large as 8000. Ports and border crossings around the world have similarly experienced an increasing volume of daily shipping and trucking activities. Even though terrorist events occur, catastrophic ones are rare. For profit-oriented firms that operate in an increasingly competitive global market, the cost of abandoning trade due to terrorism may far exceed its benefit. Governments also face the mounting pressure of balancing between counter-terrorist measures and expanding trade. These pressures are reflected in the fact that the US stock market quickly bounced back to the pre-9/11 level. To the extent that terrorist attacks lead to temporary delays in trade, we probably should expect to see a quick bounce-back and recovery in trade volume right after terrorist attacks. The statistical findings here may have reflected this trade recovery phenomenon.

Overall the econometric evidence is too weak to support the view that transnational terrorism on average reduces bilateral trade flows. This does not mean that terrorism does not reduce trade. Even at the aggregate level, bilateral terrorist attacks still reduce trade among country pairs that involve at least one advanced economy. Most likely the effect of terrorism on trade is localized and depends on context.

NOTES

1. Both Nitsch and Schumacher (2004) and Fratianni and Kang (2006) cite the temporary closing of US borders right after the 9/11 attacks as evidence of disrupted trade.
2. This result is quite robust. When the two terrorism variables are entered one by one into the models, the results do not change. One also may wonder whether the findings are due to collinearity. The bivariate correlation between the two terrorism variables in the estimation sample is only 0.21. Collinearity is not a source of the results.
3. These results are not reported due to space constraint, but are available upon request.
4. Li and Sacko (2002) demonstrate that *ex post*, unexpected interstate military disputes reduce bilateral trade substantially but anticipated ones do not. Li (2006) studies these *ex ante* and *ex post* effects of political violence on foreign direct investment and finds no evidence of significant impact by terrorism.

REFERENCES

Aitken, N.D. (1973), 'The effect of the EEC and EFTA on European trade: a temporal and cross section analysis', *American Economic Review*, **63** (December), 881–92.
Anderson, J.E. (1979), 'A theoretical foundation for the gravity equation', *American Economic Review*, **69** (March), 106–16.
Bennett, D.S. and A.C. Stam (1999), EUGene: expected utility generation and data management program, http://wizard.ucr.edu/cps/eugene/welcome.html.

Blomberg, S. Brock and Gregory D. Hess (2006), 'How much does violence tax trade?' *Review of Economics and Statistics*, **88** (4), 599–612.
Braithwaite, Alex and Quan Li (2007), 'Transnational terrorism hot spots: identification and impact evaluation', *Conflict Management and Peace Science*, **24** (4), 281–96.
Cheng, I-Hui and Howard J. Wall (2005), 'Controlling for heterogeneity in gravity models of trade and integration', *Federal Reserve Bank of St Louis Review*, **87** (1), 49–64.
Deardorff, A.V. (1998), 'Determinants of bilateral trade: does gravity work in a neoclassical world?' Jeffrey A. Frankel (ed.), *The Regionalization of the World Economy*, Chicago, IL, USA and London, UK: University of Chicago Press, pp. 7–28.
Dixon, W.J. and B.E. Moon (1993), 'Political similarity and American foreign trade patterns', *Political Research Quarterly*, **46** (1), 5–25.
Enders, Walter and Todd Sandler (1999), 'Transnational terrorism in the post-Cold War era', *International Studies Quarterly*, **43**, 145–67.
Enders, Walter and Todd Sandler (2002), 'Patterns of transnational terrorism 1970–99: alternative time series estimates', *International Studies Quarterly*, **46**, 145–65.
Frankel, J.A. (1997), *Regional Trading Blocs in the World Economic System*, Washington, DC: Institute of International Economics.
Frankel, Jeffrey (2000), 'Globalization of the economy', in Joseph Nye and John Donahue (eds), *Governance in a Globalizing World*, Washington, DC: Brookings Institution Press.
Fratianni, Michele and Heejoon Kang (2006), 'International terrorism, international trade, and borders', in Michele Fratianni and Alan M. Rugman (eds), *Research in Global Strategic Management*, Vol. 12, *Regional Economic Integration*, Oxford: Elsevier, pp. 203–24.
Glick, Reuven and Andrew Rose (2002), 'Does a currency union affect trade? The time-series evidence', *European Economic Review*, **46** (6), 1125–51.
Gowa, J. (1989), 'Bipolarity, multipolarity, and free trade', *American Political Science Review*, **83** (4), 1245–56.
Gowa, J. and E.D. Mansfield (1993), 'Power politics and international trade', *American Political Science Review*, **87** (2), 408–20.
Li, Quan (2006), 'Political violence and foreign direct investment', in Michele Fratianni and Alan M. Rugman (eds), *Research in Global Strategic Management*, Vol. 12, *Regional Economic Integration*, Oxford: Elsevier, pp. 225–49.
Li, Quan and David Sacko (2002), 'The (ir)relevance of interstate militarized disputes to international trade', *International Studies Quarterly*, **46** (1), 11–44.
Mansfield, Edward and Rachel Bronson (1997), 'Alliances, preferential trading arrangements, and international trade', *American Political Science Review*, **1**, 94–107.
McDonald, Michael (2002), 'Checkpoint terror: border searches snarl the free flow of goods', *US News and World Report*, 11 February.
Mickolus, Edward F., Todd Sandler, Jean M. Murdock and Peter Fleming (2002), *International Terrorism: Attributes of Terrorist Events, 1991–2000 (ITERATE 5)*, Dunn Loring, VA: Vinyard Software.
Morrow, J.D., R.M. Siverson and T.E. Tabares (1998), 'The political determinants of international trade: the major powers, 1907–90', *American Political Science Review*, **92** (3), 649–61.

Morrow, J.D., R.M. Siverson and T.E. Tabares (1999), 'Correction to "The political determinants of international trade"', *American Political Science Review*, **93** (4), 931–4.
Nitsch, Volker and Dieter Schumacher (2004), 'Terrorism and international trade: an empirical investigation', *European Journal of Political Economy*, **20** (2), 423–33.
Pollins, B.M. (1989), 'Does trade still follow the flag?', *American Political Science Review*, **83** (2), 465–80.
Rose, Andrew (2004), 'Do we really know that the WTO increases trade?', *American Economic* Review, **94** (1), 98–114.

11. A global business strategy for North Korea

Harry W. Richardson and
Chang-Hee Christine Bae

INTRODUCTION

The United States government has consistently followed a somewhat narrow path in the war against terror: protect the United States at home (hence the huge role for the Department of Homeland Security), while abroad the approach has been military action and cooperation with foreign governments in seeking out international terrorists. However, there are other options. The possibility explored here is whether global business, backed up by the support of interested national governments and IFIs (international financial institutions), might be able to deter terrorism via a program of foreign investment from countries directly, indirectly or potentially involved in pro-terrorist activities. For example, could a more even-handed allocation of US resources, both public and private, between Israel and Palestine in recent decades have avoided or at least mitigated terrorist threats from the Middle East? This is a complex question that is difficult to answer and, from a political perspective, probably much too late to explore. This chapter takes a future view of a simpler case, that of North Korea (we will use the acronym DPRK, that is, the Democratic People's Republic of Korea, and we will refer to South Korea as ROK, that is, the Republic of Korea).

Although the DPRK has been involved in terrorist activity in the past, we do not consider that it is currently a terrorist state in the strict sense. Apart from occasional military skirmishes with the ROK (usually at sea), its actions in the past two decades have been relatively peaceful. The last direct terrorist attack was the bombing of a ROK airplane in 1987. The major terrorist threat from the DPRK is indirect: the sale of military equipment (most dangerously, nuclear material) either to states supportive of terrorism or to terrorists themselves. Given the widespread assumption that a nuclear terrorist attack would be the worst-case scenario (probably inaccurate, because there are some types of bioterrorist attack that could kill many more people), the analysis has become inextricably involved in the denuclearization of the DPRK issue. However, despite the views of the United States government, denuclearization is much less of a problem than proliferation. If we can prevent the export of nuclear material from the DPRK by maritime embargos, controls on air freight and sealing (with China's help) the very porous Chinese–DPRK border, denuclearization becomes a separate, even a secondary issue (we will explain this later). The DPRK may threaten more missile tests, but it is more of a political ploy than an aggressive act.

On 13 February 2007 the Six Parties (the two Koreas, the United States, China, Japan and Russia) signed an agreement under which the DPRK agreed to dismantle its nuclear operations in return for gifts of oil and other benefits. In July 2007 it shut down the Yongbyon nuclear reprocessing plant. In September 2007, the DPRK government agreed to total denuclearization by the end of 2007. It never happened. Nevertheless, a major step occurred in late June 2008 when the DPRK declared details of its nuclear program and demolished the cooling tower at Yongbyon. In return, the United States removed the DPRK from the terrorist nation list and waived it from the provisions of the Trading with the Enemy Act. These concessions are more or less symbolic, and only the first of many required actions, but are nevertheless significant. However, the DPRK has a long reputation of one step forward followed by two steps back. From our viewpoint, full denuclearization is not a very critical issue. However, unless the modifications of United States policy are extended into the future, the strategy suggested here will never be implemented.

To explore the feasibility of our proposed strategy, we examine two case studies, the Kaesong Industrial Complex begun in 2004 and the Tumen River Project started more than two decades ago. These case studies have different implications: how do we weigh the prospects for successful economic growth against the difficulties of multilateral cooperation?

THE PATH TO DENUCLEARIZATION

Despite promising recent events, many Korean experts remain skeptical about the timeline to full denuclearization (Kihl, 2007). The Yongbyon plant closure is only the first of many steps. There is processed fuel already in existence and probably 6–10 bombs. There are possibly other reprocessing plants, either operating or under construction. Even if everything was dismantled or confiscated, monitoring and verification for years would be necessary to ensure that reprocessing operations could not be restarted at some other location at a later date. The DPRK promised full denuclearization, and in return for some initial steps, the United States has removed the DRPK from the list of terrorist states and relaxed some of the trade restrictions. If the trend continues, the strategy suggested in this chapter will be easier to implement.

There are two answers to the question of whether the DPRK still poses a threat. The first is that we would still need to ensure that the DPRK toes the line. There have been too many examples of retrogression in the past. The second, and perhaps the most important, is that more investment in the DPRK would ensure that a future reunification process would go much more smoothly. Elsewhere (Richardson and Kim, 2007), we have argued that infrastructure (and business) investment in the DPRK is the key to successful reunification. There are two main scenarios: sudden R-Day (Reunification Day) following the German pattern and a TP (Transition Phase) approach. The German experience illustrates that the sudden R-Day approach is fraught with difficulties. The TP strategy is more complex, but in its fundamentals implies substantial ROK, multilateral and IFI investments in the DPRK (especially in infrastructure) combined with a partial closure of the border (on the China–Hong Kong model) after reunification to discourage migration south. If global business activity in the DPRK, on the lines suggested here, can alleviate any future threats it may also fulfill a dual function by stabilizing the Korean peninsula (both North and South) in the event of reunification.

A standard objection in some quarters to the strategy recommended here is that efforts to improve the DPRK economy pander to the regime and reward its bad behavior in the past. Certainly, the DPRK government has been clever, if not masterful, in extorting payments (both in money and in kind) in return for political concessions via bilateral bargaining. However, that is beside the point. Stabilizing the DPRK is in the self-interest of the ROK, the United States, China and everyone else, even if it helps the regime to survive. The United States, for example, has supped with many devils, albeit sometimes, if not always, with a long spoon. In the war against terror, pragmatism deserves a bigger break than ideological rhetoric.

THE STATE OF THE DPRK ECONOMY

Although not in such a desperate state as in the 1990s, the DPRK economy remains in a serious plight. Surprisingly, before 1970 the DPRK was richer and more productive than the ROK, and experienced an economic growth rate of 14 percent per annum in the late 1950s and into the 1960s. Then, the situation was reversed. The DPRK economy began to suffer from the constraints of a top-down central planning system, while in the ROK

190   *Global business and the terrorist threat*

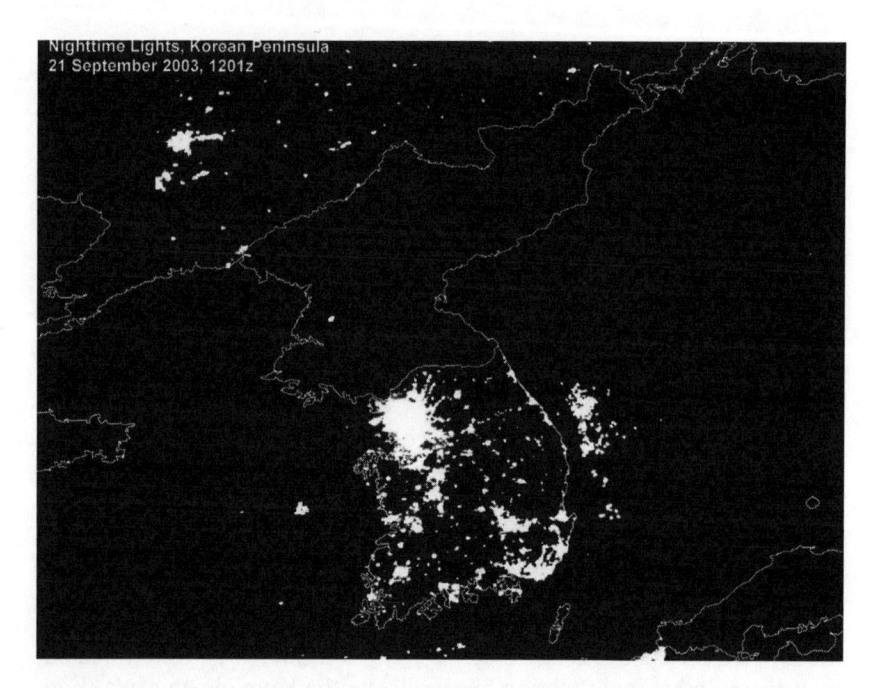

Source: http://www.globalsecurity.org/military/library/news/2006/10/061011-d-6570c-001.jpg.

Figure 11.1   Night over the two Koreas

President Park Chung Hee initiated an export-led industrialization process that became known as the 'Miracle of the Han River'. The DPRK economy continued to deteriorate, especially in the 1990s. Russia withdrew most of its aid after the collapse of the Soviet Union in 1991. China began to demand payments in hard currency in return for its exports. Drought and famine afflicted the DPRK, especially in 1995–96. Most major sectors performed poorly. Infrastructure gaps became more severe, and the existing infrastructure stock became more dilapidated. Minimal electricity service was available (see Figure 11.1 for a visual comparison of nighttime electricity in the two Koreas), and the sector's position was aggravated by a partial cut-off in oil supplies. Industry suffered from underinvestment in the capital stock, a lack of spare parts for machinery and raw material shortages.

The state of agriculture was even worse: food shortages for more than a decade, insufficient arable land, fuel scarcities, too few tractors and the inefficiencies of collective farming. There was severe flooding in 2006, followed by drought. The economy experienced negative growth between 1990 and 1998, with growth rates ranging between −1.1 percent and −6.3

percent. However, after the adoption of the ROK President Kim Dae Jung's 'sunshine policy' in 1999, the economic situation in the DPRK improved somewhat, and the economic growth rate became positive again (growing at 2.7 percent per annum, 1999–2004).

Nevertheless, the gaps in economic indicators between the DPRK and the ROK remain vast. The DPRK's gross domestic product is only about 3 percent of that of the ROK; its per capita ratio is one-fifteenth; and its foreign trade is much less than 1 percent of that of the ROK, $4.06 billion as opposed to $635.3 billion (Park, 2007). Its economic growth rate is also much lower; even with the slowdown in recent years, the ROK economy is growing 2.7 times as fast. However, ROK government aid to the DPRK more than doubled in 2006, and the number of visitors to the North (excluding tourists to Mount Geumgang) have more than quadrupled in recent years. The problems associated with the economic integration of the DPRK, not only with the ROK but with the rest of the world, are a little less severe because of its modest population, 23.3 million compared with the ROK's 49 million.

The DPRK government initiated an economic reform program in 2002, but it had minimal effects on economic efficiency. Rationing was ended, except for grain. Price effects were massive: rice increased 550-fold, other commodities 18 times, and wages 25 times. The major explanation was a deep devaluation of the DPRK won, by 60 times at the official rate and by more than 1000 times on the black market. There had been some hope initially that the reforms might lead to an adoption of the Chinese economic model, but there was little follow-up. A major problem is that relaxing price controls alone without complementary institutional reforms to free up markets and establish property rights will not work. However, there were two significant consequences: the development of some small-scale private markets (for example open-air markets, street food stalls and convenience stores) and an unintended surge in imports from China.

THE PROPOSED STRATEGY

The central argument of this chapter is that the involvement of the global business sector (broadly defined) in the pacification of the DPRK may be a viable and desirable strategy for all parties (especially the Six Parties involved in the DPRK discussions and the IFIs), regardless of the progress of denuclearization and whether or not a full-scale proposed dismantling ever becomes permanent. If the DPRK economy can be substantially improved, it may dramatically reduce any incentive for the government to sell arms or related materials (whether conventional or nuclear) to terrorists or to governments that support terrorism.

There are mutual benefits to both Koreas from this approach. The gains to the DPRK from more foreign direct investment are obvious. If these investments come from the ROK, they represent an opportunity to divert ROK's investment priorities from countries such as China and Vietnam to the DPRK, that offers advantages such as proximity, language and possibly quality of labor. The match between ROK capital, technology and managerial know-how and cheap DPRK labor is a compelling combination.

However, the burden cannot be placed on the ROK alone. China is already investing in the DPRK, especially in mining and other natural resource activities. If we consider the DPRK territory as a whole, there is some sense (at least initially) in China focusing on the northern border of the DPRK and for the ROK to continue giving most of its attention to the southern border. However, even China and the ROK cannot do the job. The two largest economies in the world, the United States and Japan, would need to get involved. The United States has committed itself to the position of no normalization without full denuclearization. Japan is keeping the DPRK at arm's length, primarily because of the continuing, very long controversy about the alleged abduction of Japanese citizens in the 1970s and the 1980s. One very obvious consequence has been the veto of both the United States and Japan on the DPRK's entry into the IFIs, such as the World Bank and the Asian Development Bank (however, the relaxation of trade restrictions by the United States in late June 2008 made the DPRK eligible for World Bank loans). The role of the IFIs is of critical importance via the financing and provision of infrastructure, essential to the success of a global business strategy and unlikely to be supplied by the private sector. Thus, a key element in the strategy is public–private participation; broadly speaking, governments and the IFIs would build the infrastructure while foreign direct investment (FDI) (primarily multinational corporations) would stimulate the DPRK economy (American business investment in North Korea is still restricted). Other countries could participate, but probably only as components of a broad multilateral effort. A multilateral approach is needed (rather than merely bilateral economic cooperation with the ROK), because the scale of the problem is so big. As for other countries, Russia's direct involvement is highly problematic, while the European Union and other parts of the developed world seem wholly disengaged in spite of the argument that permanent pacification of the DPRK is a global issue.

There are several pros and cons associated with the proposed strategy. The pros include:

1. If it permanently stops a nuclear proliferation leak, it would make a significant contribution to global security.
2. There has been much discussion about cementing a North East Asia regional production and trading bloc, and the DPRK remains a 'major gap' in putting that bloc together (Kim, 2006). Filling in that major gap would have major regional and even global economic impacts.
3. It might accelerate Korean reunification. Such a step would have important political stability implications for East Asia as a whole and produce substantial military defense savings for the United States.
4. A multilateral program of economic cooperation would help to relieve what appears to an intolerable burden on the ROK.
5. As pointed out above, economic growth in the DPRK for most of the 1990s was negative, but turned moderately positive after 1999. If the proposed strategy produces a surge in growth in the DPRK, it might have a powerful influence on future decision-making in the DPRK.
6. Although this strategy may support the DPRK goal of regime survival, an offsetting benefit is the improvement in the welfare of the 23.3 million, largely impoverished, DPRK citizens (at least outside Pyongyang). Of course, the implementation of economic cooperation would have to be undertaken very carefully, with frequent and detailed audits to ensure that the benefits are trickling down to the population at large.
7. If the IFIs and several multinational corporations can get together in designing a solid public–private investment program for the DPRK, it might serve as a demonstration test for an effective strategy that might be replicated in other countries, especially in the developing world.
8. If a global business strategy can create a lasting peace on the Korean peninsula, and if lack of peace is a major global threat, it might be considered a bargain, especially when compared with the war in Iraq. The infrastructure component of a strategy for the DPRK might cost less than $100 billion over 15 years (Kim, 2005; Wolf and Akramov, 2005) whereas the cost of the Iraq War up to now is probably more than $600 billion (Joseph Stiglitz, using a very broad calculus, says $3 trillion) (Stiglitz and Bilmes, 2008).

However, the strategy also has a few cons:

1. The DPRK government has been very clever and manipulative in obtaining bilateral concessions. The 'do not reward bad behavior' principle might be a disincentive to participation.
2. Despite the promises, denuclearization may be incomplete or be reversed, and in that case the preconditions for normalization of

relations will not be met. Without US involvement, both public and private, the strategy will fail.
3. The argument that a strategy of economic cooperation and aid will change political behavior may be based on a rose-tinted view of the underlying situation.
4. Continuing political instability (reinforced by the overarching goal of regime survival) may inhibit private investors from entering the DPRK economy, with the partial exception of those from the ROK and China.

CASE STUDIES

There are two applications of some version of this strategy in the DPRK that we would like to discuss: the Kaesong Industrial Complex near the DMZ (De-Militarized Zone) on the DPRK's southern border and the Tumen River Project in the northeast corner of the DPRK (see Figure 11.2). A third possible application might be the Mount Keumgang tourist zone (Park, 2005), but we chose not to examine it because it is very likely to remain solely an inter-Korean venture.

Kaesong

Kaesong is located within the DPRK, closer to Seoul (60 km) and Incheon International Airport (50 km) than to Pyongyang (100 km). It is a very important historic city, being the capital of all Korea during the Koryo Dynasty for eight centuries up to 1392. We (Richardson and Bae, 2004) argued that Kaesong might be considered a candidate for a new capital in a reunified Korea to prevent a squabble over Seoul versus Pyongyang. It could be justified in terms of low construction costs compared with the ROK's original plan for a new capital in Chungcheong. Although this plan was declared unconstitutional by Korea's Supreme Court, the proposal persists in a somewhat modified form as a New Administrative City. It could also be an important appeasement to the DPRK in the event of reunification, and its location in the center is almost perfect.

It was chosen as an industrial complex that would begin an era of inter-Korean cooperation, based on ROK capital and technology and DPRK labor. Surprisingly, it was not the first choice; both Haeju and Shinuiju were considered (and favored by the DPRK) in the late 1990s. However, the DPRK and the ROK signed an agreement to establish the Kaesong Industrial Complex (KIC) in mid-2003 and construction began in April 2004. The initiative was taken by the chief executive officer (CEO) of

A global business strategy for North Korea 195

Source: http://www.lib.utexas.edu/maps/cia97/korea_north_sm97.gif.

Figure 11.2 North Korea

Hyundai (the ROK's largest chaebol), but with the support of both governments. Hyundai was designated the developer and given the land use rights. However, some of the development rights were later shared with the ROK's most important land banking agency, the KLC (Korea Land Corporation), in effect converting the KIC into a public–private sector enterprise. This is consistent with the strategy suggested here.

The original plan was on a massive scale. The area of the project was 66.1 km^2, 43 percent of it as an industrial park and the remainder for tourism and residential development. About 57 percent of the latter area would be in two new towns, the rest in the form of expanding the existing city. The industrial park was planned to be built in three phases over eight years (73 percent of the development is in the third phase); however, the plan is behind schedule. The initial focus is on low-wage, labor-intensive industries such as textiles (although machinery, electronics and chemicals are also prominent). Later, attention will be shifted to information technology sectors and tourism. Currently, although all raw materials come from the ROK, there are some restrictions on bringing in some types of computers and mobile communication devices (so-called 'strategic materials').

The pace of industrial expansion remains slow; as of April 2007, there were 22 firms in operation, employing 13,000 workers with a gross output of about $13 million per month. However, at a recent auction 344 firms bid for about 140 sites, so the speed of development may pick up. Nevertheless, the initial estimate of the ultimate scale, 19,000 mainly small companies with about 725,000 jobs, seems much too high. Even a more modest forecast of 200,000 jobs seems ambitious. Given the ambiguities about the rates of growth, the numbers quoted in early studies (Park, 2004), such as a cost of the first phase of $185 million, total construction costs of $1.9 billion, lease income of $136 million and $2.3 billion of corporate and labor tax revenues for the DPRK, all seem questionable. There will also be both direct and indirect economic impacts in the ROK running into billions of dollars and hundreds of thousands of jobs, again too difficult to quantify pending the ultimate scale of development.

The key question is: how competitive is Kaesong compared with its main competitors, for example, in China and Vietnam? Certainly, there have been some limited infrastructure improvements. The road between the ROK and the DPRK opened in 2004. The Seoul–Shinuiji railway was operated once in May 2007. A doubling of electricity capacity at Kaesong was also announced in mid-2007.

Wages are low ($57.50 per month, including 15 percent fringe benefits), much cheaper than in China ($100–$200) and even lower than in Vietnam ($60). Wages were much higher in the ROK (about $425 per month); not fully offset by much higher labor productivity (perhaps about 25 percent higher). The work week was somewhat longer than in China, 48 hours as opposed to 44 hours. On the other hand, land prices were higher than in China – $150 per pyong (1 pyong = 3.954 sq. yards) vs. $50 – but much lower than in the ROK ($410 per pyong in small low-cost cities).

Firms in Kaesong benefit from substantial corporate tax relief: five years' full exemption followed by three years' 50 percent exemption. Also, taxes are lower than in the ROK (10–14 percent compared to 23–28 percent), and slightly lower than in China (15 percent).

Overall, therefore, Kaesong is very competitive. Its long-term future depends upon many considerations: continued inter-Korean cooperation with perhaps the promise of reunification; the location, relocation and new plant siting decisions of ROK firms; its attraction to firms from other countries; and a change in the terms of the Korea–United States (KORUS) Free Trade Agreement (FTA) if it is confirmed. In the short run, much depends on the behavior of ROK firms. How many existing firms will either relocate to or establish branch plants in Kaesong, how many new firms will choose Kaesong in preference to a ROK location, and how many firms will divert their attention from China, Vietnam or other countries? In April 2007, a relatively modest amount of land (about 30 acres) was opened up as a site for foreign manufacturing firms, but it is difficult to predict the response, especially in the short run, given the prevailing political uncertainties. The exclusion of Kaesong from the benefits of the KORUS FTA, ostensibly because of non-conformity with ILO environmental and labor laws but much more likely because of United States government opposition, could be a major blow to rapid industrial expansion at Kaesong, and it is vital that this should be changed in the near future if the FTA is implemented. Another requirement for the strategy to work is a diversification of industrial locations beyond Kaesong; this reinforces the case for multilateralism.

The Tumen River Project

The Tumen River development area is a vast natural resource region in Northeast Asia which crosses national borders (the DPRK, Russia, China and a small part of Mongolia). It has largely been an intergovernmental project, but the ROK and Japan have a limited amount of foreign direct investment there. The planning has been there for a long time (since the 1980s). A multilateral agreement was signed in 1991 and the project was jump-started by a $30 billion United Nations Development Plan in 1993 (although this was later abandoned). The discussion here is primarily to illustrate the difficulties involved in a multilateral approach to economic development.

The basic idea was that the region has abundant natural resources including energy, minerals, agriculture and fisheries, and could be developed as a 'natural economic zone' with multilateral cooperation that might have a future pay-off in terms of increased political and economic security. However, hitherto, the results have been disappointing, primarily because of political obstacles. Russia and Japan continue to have territorial disputes over the four islands between Hokkaido and the Kamchatka Peninsula (named the Southern Kurils by the Russians and the Northern Territories by the Japanese), and find it difficult to cooperate. China, on the other hand, has given much priority to South China and other project areas such as the Three Gorges Dam. The DPRK is much more interested in the region and had plans to develop a Free Economic Zone at Rajin, hoping to attract foreign domestic investment there (especially from Japan). However, resolution of the dispute over the alleged abduction of Japanese citizens many years ago by DPRK agents remains a major obstacle to close cooperation. The ROK's interest has faded with the development of Kaesong and other opportunities in the DPRK closer to home. Mongolia's role is as a very minor player.

Lu (1993) suggested that the Tumen River region is in the 'shadow belt' of each of the involved countries. In other words, the region is so geographically peripheral that it has difficulty getting the parties' attention. Hughes (2000), on the other hand, argues that the problem is the inherent conflict between regionalization and regionalism. By 'regionalization' he means the prospects for multilateral cooperation in a transborder economic development region that, in the abstract, could be considered substantial. However, the obstacle is regionalism, that is, the inability of the constituent countries to come together and resolve their political disagreements. Even more serious is that provincial and local governments have a strong interest in developing the region (after all, it is not a shadow belt to them), but have been given little freedom by their national governments to engage in promoting economic development and pursuing project opportunities. Although it may be too early to write off the Tumen River even after two decades of minimal activity, it does not augur well for a multilateral approach to the DPRK as a whole. Perhaps the implications are 1) to give more emphasis to the private sector, less constrained by national governments; and 2) to strengthen the eligibility of the DPRK for infrastructure loans/grants from the IFIS.

CONCLUSIONS

The United States has focused on a narrow approach to fighting the war on terror: dealing with homeland protection at home (reinforced by cooperation with intelligence agencies abroad) and military action abroad, as in Iraq and Afghanistan. However, both these approaches have limitations. Complete protection of the homeland is impossible: there are too many targets, too many loopholes and too few resources. The military action method is both very expensive and very unpopular, and contributes to the spread of anti-American sentiment. Hence, this chapter suggests a third way: positive actions internationally to deter terror or potentially terrorist activities. Although we use the DPRK as a case study, the global business strategy may be applicable to other countries in other parts of the world. One objection to its extension to the Middle East is that promoting economic development would make no difference to radical Islam. In the absence of an experiment, it is impossible to evaluate this position. Although it is probably much too late, a much more balanced allocation of

United States aid between Israel and Palestine in the past could have had a substantial impact on the Middle East political situation.

Although there is little hope that the timeline for full denuclearization is now settled, there is no strong reason – other than United States stubbornness – why it should be a precondition for this type of strategy to take place. The risk of proliferation is the threat, rather than nuclearization itself. Expert opinion suggests that the nuclear technology that the DPRK was developing is highly unreliable, so its nuclear presence may have been much more symbolic than substantive.

The two case studies that we have examined are mixed in terms of their implications for the success of the proposed strategy. The Tumen River Project has been very slow to develop, with many stumbles along the way. Regardless of its ultimate results, its history illustrates the dangers and risks of multilateral cooperation when the main parties involved have unrelated issues that divide them. The Kaesong Industrial Complex holds more promise as an exemplar, but hitherto only the ROK is involved, the original planned scale was much too ambitious, and its exclusion from the KORUS Free Trade Agreement discussions is a major disadvantage. On the other hand, it is already an excellent illustration that a business-oriented strategy might work in the DPRK.

Finally, it is worth emphasizing that the DPRK government's past aggression, extortionist tactics and current apparent lack of concern for the welfare of its citizens are insufficient reasons for dismissal of this strategy out of hand. The primary rationale is the self-interest of all the parties involved (particularly, but not limited to, the ROK) and the importance of a viable DPRK economy to the success of a North East Asia regional production and trading bloc. Obviously, the connection and updating of the internationally linked transportation network through the DPRK is an important step in achieving this objective.

REFERENCES

Hughes, Christopher (2000), 'Tumen River Area Development Programme: frustrated micro-regionalism as a microcosm of political rivalries', Coventry: University of Warwick, Centre for the Study of Globalization and Regionalization, WP57/00.

Kim, Won Bae (2005), 'Infrastructure development in North Korea', Seoul: Korea Research Institute of Human Settlements.

Lu, Zhongwei (1993), 'Northeast Asian economic cooperation in the post-Cold War era: economic relations between China, the ROK, the DPRK, Japan and Russia', University of California Multi-Campus Research Unit, Institute on Global Conflict and Cooperation, PP06.

Park, Jiyoung (2005), 'Guidelines for economic integration of the Korean peninsula', Los Angeles, CA: University of Southern California, School of Policy, Planning and Development.

Park, Suhk-Sam (2004), 'Creating a visible bridge: the economic impact of Kaesong Industrial Complex construction', *East Asia Review*, **16** (3), 87–104.

Richardson, Harry W. and Chang-Hee Christine Bae (2004), 'The location and relocation of national and state capitals in North America and the rest of the world', Seoul: International Symposium on Capital Relocation.

Richardson, Harry W. and Won Bae Kim (2007), 'A spatial infrastructure strategy for Korean reunification', Honolulu: East–West Center.

Stiglitz, Joseph and Linda Bilmes (2008), *The Three Trillion Dollar War*, London: Allen Lane.

Wolf, Jr., Charles and Kamil Akramov (2005), *North Korean Paradoxes: Circumstances, Costs and Consequences of Korean Unification*, Washington, DC: RAND Corporation, National Defense Research Institute.

12. The economic impacts of international border closure: a state-by-state analysis

Peter Gordon, James E. Moore II, Jiyoung Park and Harry W. Richardson

INTRODUCTION

Recurrent reminders that an international avian influenza epidemic is a real possibility have prompted a variety of public policy discussions. A recent World Bank study estimated that the global economy would lose $2 trillion from an outbreak, or 3 percent of world gross domestic product (GDP). Another report in the *Lancet* (by the Harvard Initiative for Global Health Group – see Murray et al., 2006), largely based on an analogy drawn from the Spanish flu epidemic of 1918–20, presented various estimates of possible US fatalities. These included a low threshold of 114,483, a median threshold of 297,883, a mean threshold of 383,881 and a high threshold of 744,226. Applying the US Environmental Protection Agency's valuation of a statistical life, $5.8 million, these fatalities amount to large imputed dollar amounts: $664 billion, $1.728 trillion, $2.227 trillion and $4.317 trillion, respectively. These estimates, astronomical though they are, ignore the treatment costs of those who get sick but do not die, quarantine costs, and other disaster management costs.[1] While the *Lancet* study argues that a future pandemic might be even worse than in 1918–20, it also accepts that fatalities might be lower because of improved medical management (although the health care system could be overwhelmed), anti-virals, quarantine and vaccination. Yet, it is probably safe to say that terrorists with an admitted interest in acquiring and using weapons of mass destruction have taken note of these magnitudes as well as the recent reports that the H5N1 strain can be spread by human-to-human contact.

The closure of the US to international trade and travel for as long as one year has been proposed as an extreme policy that might be justified by such an extreme threat. In this research we ask whether such extreme measures can be justified. We attempt to measure the economic impacts of a one-year border closure. The hypothetical disruptions are obviously severe, well beyond anything that the US economy has ever experienced, and raise analytical issues that we take up briefly at the end of this chapter.

Our modeling approach (reported in some of our previous papers; see Gordon et al., 2007 and Park et al., 2007) enables us to report most of the impacts at the level of the individual states (and DC). Political decision-making in a federal system requires spatially disaggregated information. We utilized NIEMO (National Interstate Economic Model), the only operational multi-regional input–output model of the US, that provides estimates for 47 sectors (the 'USC Sectors'), and the 50 states plus DC. We applied demand-side and supply-side versions of NIEMO whenever direct spatial impacts could be located (stopping international air travel, trade and cross-border shopping). We also used USIO, a 47-sector aggregation of the national IMPLAN model[2] where the locations of direct spatial impacts are not known. Our simulations are for 2001, the year for which we had access to the most relevant data. We did not address the costs or the feasibility of implementing border closures.

In round numbers, the bottom line from the summing of our most optimistic scenarios is that a one-year border closing results in a total output loss of $2.359 trillion. Dividing our low-end estimated output loss by an aggregate multiplier of approximately 1.655 (from our results), we get an overall GDP loss of approximately $1.425 trillion, or approximately 14 percent of 2001 GDP.

These are the aggregated impacts from five kinds of disruptions: a one-year shutdown of all international air travel, in and out of the US; a one-year shutdown in international commodity trade (except gas and oil); a one-year shutdown of legal as well as illegal immigration; and a one-year disruption of all cross-border shopping. In each case, we tried to model and include various plausible mitigations. Also in the interests of conservatism, we restricted our reporting to Type I multiplier results. Multiplier results would be approximately 50 percent greater if Type II multipliers were used. Given the limited mitigations that we were able to model, the more conservative results are most plausible. Nevertheless, such a very large event is difficult to model, and the results must be understood in light of many caveats. Also our models are linear, so shorter-duration border closings would simply produce proportionately smaller impacts.

INTERNATIONAL AIR TRAVEL LOSSES

Air travel losses can be estimated for various scenarios. We report on the most optimistic, which includes the assumed diversion of 65 percent of

Table 12.1 Top three impacted sectors across 50 states and DC ($ million)

Sectors		Losses	
Transportation	USC 33	−71 237.45	(62.80%)
Accommodations, food services	USC45	−19 499.01	(17.19%)
Retail trade	USC35	−16 321.99	(14.39%)
Total (all 47 sectors)		−113 428.83	(100.00%)

US-based overseas travel to US travel (for domestic vacations) and a 25 percent increase in telecommunications activities as substitutions for canceled business trips. Direct losses such as hotel, food, shopping and ground transportation were located at major airports (including an average 5 percent local airport revenues from ticket sales taxes; 95 percent of ticket sales revenue losses were allocated nationally).

The various modeling steps involved: (1) calculating annual passenger volumes for four trip types (US-based international inbound, US-based international outbound, abroad-based international inbound, abroad-based international outbound) for each of the US international airports and aggregating each of the four volumes to the 50 states and DC (Tables 12.A1 and 12.A2); (2) calculating per-passenger spending patterns for each of the representative trip types by major USC sector (Table 12.A3). The resulting estimated direct losses for the whole nation are shown in Table 12.A4. The national effects of just the lost air ticket sales (these revenues accrue to airline owners and managers who are scattered over the whole US) are shown in Table 12.A5. This creates an overall loss of nearly $84 billion.

However, the two proposed mitigations (substituting telecommunications and domestic travel) reduce losses substantially, with most of the positive offsetting impacts coming from the increased use of telecommunications. In light of the mitigations, direct losses were estimated to be just over $58 billion. These prompted more than $113 billion of total losses. As expected, almost 95 percent of the losses would be felt in three of the USC sectors and almost two-thirds of that would impact upon the transportation sector (Table 12.1).

These results are in light of both assumed mitigations. Taking these one at a time, the results of the assumed telecommunications offset are shown in Table 12.A6; these are results for the nation as a whole because the location of telecommunications offset impacts is unknown.

We also modeled the state-level mitigations from lost international tickets sales to US travelers made up by the increased sales of domestic air travel. To the extent that there are geographic effects, they are shown in Table 12.A7, where the effects of differences in local purchases are shown.

TRADE LOSSES

The most optimistic international trade loss scenario allows for the continuation of energy imports (USC sector 10) and it also includes the presumption of substantial economic resilience by assuming that canceled exports replace canceled imports to the maximum extent possible. To plausibly model that possibility, we had to disaggregate to the maximum extent possible; this analysis was conducted at the six-digit Harmonic System of industrial classification (HS) code level for each state. These data by port of entry were available from WISERTrade. At this disaggregated level, we assumed that if local exports are greater than imports, then local exports are sold to local importers; and exporting sectors experience only partial losses and the importing sectors are not disrupted. We applied the NIEMO demand-side model. On the other hand, if exports were less than imports, then the local importing industries purchase from local exporting industries, and importing sectors experience partial losses; the exporting sectors are not disrupted. We then applied the NIEMO supply-side model.

The results of international trade losses for the most impacted states and sectors are shown in Tables 12.2a and 12.2b. Table 12.A8 shows the state-by-state effects of trade losses, both with and without the two assumed mitigations.

LEGAL IMMIGRATION LOSSES

Annual legal net immigration per year is approximately 1.5 million. We assume that the labor force participation rate of immigrants is 67 percent, and that there are 1 million workers among them. There are also estimates of the occupations of this group. Our first step was to assign occupations to industries, using the US Department of Labor Statistics (BLS) information. We then applied Borjas's labor supply elasticity (−0.3). This raised wages in selected sectors. We then used a national input–output (I–O) price model to calculate sector-level price effects and used these to reduce final demands. Table 12.3 shows the major impacted sectors and Table 12.A9 provides the state-by-state details for price effects (left side of the table) and reduced final demand effects (right side of the table).

Table 12.2a *Top three impacted states from trade losses across 47 sectors ($ million)*

State	Losses	
California	−220 685.56	(9.93%)
Texas	−148 719.02	(6.69%)
Illinois	−90 465.95	(4.07%)
Total (all states)	−2 223 037.28	(100.00%)

Table 12.2b *Top three impacted sectors from trade losses across 51 states ($ million)*

Sectors		Losses	
Electronic and other electrical equipment, components and office equipment	USC24	−285 665.30	(12.85%)
Misc. manufactured products, scrap and mixed freight	USC29	−248 300.23	(11.17%)
Motorized and other vehicles	USC25	−206 953.18	(9.31%)
Total (47 USC sectors)		−2 223 037.28	(100.00%)

Table 12.3 *Top three impacted sectors, lost legal immigration across 51 states ($M)*

Sectors		Losses	
Health care and social assistance	USC43	−1 090.68	(10.78%)
Construction	USC31	−995.60	(9.84%)
Retail trade	USC35	−678.86	(6.71%)
Total (47 USC Sectors)		−10 121.90	(100.00%)

ILLEGAL IMMIGRATION LOSSES

This part of the analysis was similar to our treatment of legal immigration. Of course, the magnitudes involve less precision; the mid-level estimate of annual illegal immigration is 628,000. We allocated most of these people to some of the 47 USC sectors, based on proportions of illegal employment predominantly working in agriculture, construction, retail, other production, and other services sectors. We then followed the same estimation procedure as in the case of legal immigrants. The results on the most

Table 12.4 Top three impacted sectors, lost illegal immigration across 50 states ($ million)

Sectors		Losses	
Construction	USC31	−479.30	(23.51%)
Retail trade	USC35	−342.87	(16.82%)
Real estate and rental and leasing	USC38	−96.06	(4.71%)
Total (47 USC sectors)		−2038.91	(100.00%)

impacted sectors are shown in Table 12.4. Table 12.A10 shows sector-level detail, with price effects in the left columns and final demand effects in the right columns.

ANNUAL INCOMING BORDER-CROSSING SALES LOSSES

Data for annual inbound border-crossings by state are available from the US Bureau of Transportation Statistics. Based on various reports, we assumed that 60 percent of these are foreign visitors crossing over to shop in the US and spending $100 per shopping visit. We also assumed that 40 percent of the crossings are returning US shoppers who would shop domestically instead. The results for the most impacted states and sectors are shown in Tables 12.5a and 12.5b. State-level details are shown in Table 12.A11.

SUMMARY OF LOSSES

The total projected losses mentioned in the introduction are the sum of the losses documented in the previous five sections (see Table 12.6). As might have been expected, the loss of commodity trade, even with the major mitigations that we were able to model included, accounts for the overwhelming share of the disruption.

CONCLUSIONS

Our approach is based on the simple idea that border closure effects vary from place to place and that local (state-level, in this case) effects are what most political decision-makers consider. This motivated our applying approaches to estimate state-level effects where possible.

Table 12.5a   Top three impacted states, lost cross-border shopping across 47 sectors ($ million)

States	Losses	
Texas	−3553.20	(35.74%)
Arizona	−2533.17	(25.48%)
California	−986.02	(9.92%)
Total (51 states)	−9941.23	(100.00%)

Table 12.5b   Top three impacted sectors, lost cross-border shopping across 50 states ($ million)

Sectors		Losses	
Retail trade	USC35	−6139.92	(61.76%)
Professional, scientific, and technical services	USC39	−615.75	(6.19%)
Real estate and rental and leasing	USC28	−530.84	(5.34%)
Total (47 USC sectors)		−9941.23	(100.00%)

Table 12.6   Summary of losses

Loss types	Losses ($ million)
International air travel	113 429
International trade	2 223 037
Legal immigration	10 122
Illegal immigration	2 039
Cross-border shopping	9 941
Total	2 358 568

Interestingly, the magnitude of estimated costs is close to the cited median dollar value of expected loss of life. Until other information becomes available, our 'first-cut' estimates suggest that the total costs of the proposed border closure policy match the magnitude of the cost of the threat.

But many questions remain. For example, can we really model extreme events? How do we model extreme events? Available models, by definition, highlight perturbations at the margin. Yet, policy-makers are compelled to think about events beyond the margin. Work by RAND researchers on the effects of nuclear attack makes use of 'scenario analysis' and 'strategic gaming' exercises that basically rely on expert judgment (Meade and Molander, 2007; see also Carter et al., 2007).

Complex global repercussions, especially via capital markets, that might further multiply economic impacts are missing from our models and may simply be unknowable, given the magnitudes involved. We are also missing enforcement costs as well as the welfare losses from reduced consumer choice (Broda and Weinstein, 2004). But on the other hand, the natural resiliency of market economies is also left out of our approaches. The value of our exercise, then, rests on the possibility that the many positives as well as the many negatives that are beyond the models used might roughly balance.

NOTES

1. The Harvard group's loss estimates are also much higher than Meltzer et al. (1999) who estimated US losses in the range of $71–$166 billion.
2. IMPLAN refers to the software and data files made available by Minnesota Implan Group (implan.com).

REFERENCES

Borjas, G.J. (2003), 'The labor demand curve is downward sloping: reexamining the impact of immigration on the labor market', *Quarterly Journal of Economics*, November, 1335–74.

Broda, C. and D.E. Weinstein (2004), 'Globalization and the gains from variety', Federal Reserve Bank of New York, Staff Report #180.

Carter, A.B., M.M. May and W.J. Perry (2007), 'The day after: action following a nuclear blast in a US city', *Washington Quarterly*, **30** (4), 19–32.

Gordon, P., J.E. Moore, II, J.Y. Park and H.W. Richardson (2007), 'The economic impacts of a terrorist attack on the US commercial aviation system', *Risk Analysis*, **27** (3), 565–72.

Maplesden, H.C., F.X. Wang, T.X. Tian and S.D. Cook (2002), 'Expenditure patterns of travelers in the US: 2002 edition', Research Department of the Travel Industry Association of America, Washington, DC.

Meade, C. and R.C. Molander (2007), *Considering the Effects of Catastrophic Terrorist Attack*, Santa Monica, CA: RAND, Center for Terrorism Risk Management Policy.

Meltzer, M.I., N.J. Cox and K. Fukuda (1999), 'Modeling the economic impact of pandemic influence in the US: implications for setting priorities for intervention', *Emerging Infectious Diseases*, **5**, 659–71.

Murray, C.L., A.D. Lopez, B. Chin, D. Feehan and K.H. Hill (2006), 'Estimation of potential global pandemic influenza mortality on the basis of vital registry data from the 1918–20 pandemic: a quantitative analysis', *Lancet*, **368**, 2211–18.

Park, J.Y., P. Gordon, J.E. Moore II and H.W. Richardson (2007), 'Simulating the state-by-state effects of terrorist attacks on three major US ports: applying NIEMO (National Interstate Economic Model)', in H.W. Richardson, P. Gordon and J.E. Moore II (eds), *The Economic Costs and Consequences of Terrorism*, Cheltenham, UK and Northampton, MA, USA: Edward Elgar, pp. 208–34.

Zimmerman, R., C.E. Restropo, J.S. Simonoff and L.B. Lave (2007), 'Risk and economic costs of a terrorist attack on the electric system', in H.W. Richardson, P. Gordon and J.E. Moore II (eds), *The Economic Costs and Consequences of Terrorism*, Cheltenham, UK and Northampton, MA, USA: Edward Elgar, pp. 273–90.

APPENDIX

Table 12.A1   Lost passenger volumes

	US-based		Based abroad
Case 1. International inbound Total number: 44 205 247 Source: BTS-OTTI	Case 2. International outbound Total number: 36 957 710 Source: OTTI	Case 3. International inbound Total number: 27 421 952 Source: OTTI	Case 4. International outbound Total number: 34 557 016 Source: BTS-OTTI

Note: T-100 International Market (All Carriers, 2005) from Bureau of Transportation Statistics (BTS), which are downloaded from http://www.transtats.bts.gov/. We also used OTTI (http://tinet.ita.doc.gov) to calculate foreign arrivals and outbound trips of the US residents.

Table 12.A2 Estimated state-by-state number of passengers

State	Dsum (inbound)	Proportions of total or international arrivals[1,3] (%)	Arrivals of international passengers (AIP)	Proportion of AIP to total (%)	International arrivals of US residents (IAUS)	Proportion of IAUS to total	Osum (outbound)	Proportions of total or US residents departure[2,3] (%)	Departure of international passengers (DIP)	Proportion of DIP to total (%)	International departure of US residents (IDUS)	Proportion of IDUS to total (%)
AL	1475	0.021[3]	1227	0.004	248	0.001	2021	0.014[3]	759	0.002	1262	0.003
AK	52435	0.750[3]	43620	0.159	8815	0.020	64232	0.434[3]	24133	0.070	40099	0.109
AZ	890631	1.929[3]	528910	1.929	361721	0.818	909656	6.146[3]	341768	0.989	567888	1.537
AR	509	0.007[3]	423	0.002	86	0.000	666	0.005[3]	250	0.001	416	0.001
CA	12597191	16.4[3]	4495735	16.395	8101456	18.327	12648021	20.000[2]	5256479	15.211	7391542	20.000
CO	849231	1.039[3]	284798	1.039	564433	1.277	820241	5.542[3]	308173	0.892	512068	1.386
CT	48006	0.686[3]	39936	0.146	8070	0.018	46631	0.315[3]	17520	0.051	29111	0.079
DE	–	0.000[3]	0	0.000	0	0.000	4	0.000[3]	2	0.000	2	0.000
DC	2580552	36.9[3]	2146737	7.829	433815	0.981	2555433	4.000[2]	1077125	3.117	1478308	4.000
FL	10224178	14.99[1]	4109224	14.985	6114954	13.833	10262260	6.000[2]	8044797	23.280	2217463	6.000
GA	3676131	2.226[1]	610281	2.226	3065850	6.935	3647994	24.649[3]	1370591	3.966	2277403	6.162
HI	2108498	30.148[3]	1754039	6.396	354459	0.802	2118845	14.317[3]	796073	2.304	1322772	3.579
ID	126	0.002[3]	105	0.000	21	0.000	524	0.004[3]	197	0.001	327	0.001
IL	5616636	3.932[1]	1078163	3.932	4538473	10.267	5551295	5.000[2]	3703409	10.717	1847886	5.000
IN	34550	0.494[3]	28742	0.105	5808	0.013	30898	0.209[3]	11609	0.034	19289	0.052
IA	524	0.007[3]	436	0.002	88	0.000	2278	0.015[3]	856	0.002	1422	0.004
KS	645	0.009[3]	537	0.002	108	0.000	774	0.005[3]	291	0.001	483	0.001
KY	546907	7.820[3]	454967	1.659	91940	0.208	558455	3.773[3]	209818	0.607	348637	0.943
LA	37980	0.543[3]	31595	0.115	6385	0.014	33367	0.225[3]	12536	0.063	20831	0.056
ME	6454	0.092[3]	5369	0.020	1085	0.002	5495	0.037[3]	2065	0.006	3430	0.009

Table 12.A2 (continued)

State	Dsum (inbound)	Proportions of total or international arrivals[1,3] (%)	Arrivals of international passengers (AIP)	Proportion of AIP to total (%)	International arrivals of US residents (IAUS)	Proportion of IAUS to total	Osum (outbound)	Proportions of total or US residents departure[2,3] (%)	Departure of international passengers (DIP)	Proportion of DIP to total (%)	International departure of US residents (IDUS)	Proportion of IDUS to total (%)
MD	286920	0.816[1]	223770	0.816	63150	0.143	291562	1.970[3]	109543	0.317	182019	0.493
MA	1983484	2.967[1]	813708	2.967	1169776	2.646	1983037	3.000[2]	874306	2.530	1108731	3.000
MI	1938839	1.113[1]	305140	1.113	1633699	3.696	1900136	12.839[3]	713902	2.066	1186234	3.210
MN	1306762	0.371[1]	101713	0.371	1205049	2.726	1308609	8.842[3]	491658	1.423	816951	2.211
MS	749	0.011[3]	623	0.002	126	0.000	265	0.002[3]	100	0.000	165	0.000
MO	167179	0.519[1]	142399	0.519	24780	0.056	164058	1.109[3]	61638	0.178	102420	0.277
MT	58	0.001[3]	48	0.000	10	0.000	95	0.001[3]	36	0.000	59	0.000
NE	2567	0.037[3]	2135	0.008	432	0.001	1449	0.010[3]	544	0.002	905	0.002
NV	856052	12.240[3]	712141	2.597	143911	0.326	838183	5.663[3]	314914	0.911	523269	1.416
NH	10056	0.144[3]	8365	0.031	1691	0.004	9862	0.067[3]	3705	0.011	6157	0.017
NJ	4598623	3.412[1]	935764	3.412	3662859	8.286	4569535	5.000[2]	2721649	7.876	1847886	5.000
NM	295	0.004[3]	245	0.001	50	0.000	505	0.003[3]	190	0.001	315	0.001
NY	10131931	20.846[1]	5716297	20.846	4415634	9.989	10082301	21.000[2]	2321182	6.717	7761119	21.000
NC	1071051	0.964[1]	264455	0.964	806596	1.825	1068898	7.222[3]	401596	1.162	667302	1.806
ND	127	0.002[3]	106	0.000	21	0.000	2176	0.015[3]	818	0.002	1358	0.004
OH	176570	2.525[3]	146887	0.536	29683	0.067	172409	1.165[3]	64776	0.187	107633	0.291
OK	1051	0.015[3]	874	0.003	177	0.000	4767	0.032[3]	1791	0.005	2976	0.008
OR	256533	0.593[1]	162742	0.593	93791	0.212	259889	1.756[3]	97643	0.283	162246	0.439
PA	1938357	2.151[1]	589938	2.151	1348419	3.050	1925884	3.000[2]	817153	2.365	1108731	3.000
RI	18027	0.258[3]	14996	0.055	3031	0.007	17763	0.120[3]	6674	0.019	11089	0.030
SC	9925	0.142[3]	8257	0.030	1668	0.004	10130	0.068[3]	3806	0.011	6324	0.017

SD	711	0.010[3]	591	0.002	120	0.000	821	0.006[3]	308	0.001	513	0.001
TN	218 559	3.125[3]	181 817	0.663	36 742	0.083	209 548	1.416[3]	78 729	0.228	130 819	0.354
TX	5 956 051	3.264[3]	895 079	3.264	5 060 972	11.449	6 001 647	6.000[2]	3 784 184	10.951	2 217 463	6.000
UT	178 024	2.545[3]	148 096	0.540	29 928	0.068	193 382	1.307[3]	72 656	0.210	120 726	0.327
VT	2	0.000[3]	2	0.000	0	0.000	11	0.000[3]	4	0.000	7	0.000
VA	5739	0.082[3]	4774	0.017	965	0.002	5431	0.037[3]	2040	0.006	3391	0.009
WA	1 143 749	1.261[1]	345 826	1.261	797 923	1.805	1 135 398	2.000[2]	396 244	1.147	739 154	2.000
WV	28	0.000[3]	23	0.000	5	0.000	132	0.001[3]	50	0.000	82	0.000
WI	96 515	1.380[3]	80 290	0.293	16 225	0.037	97 742	0.660[3]	36 723	0.106	61 019	0.165
WY	6	0.000[3]	5	0.000	1	0.000	11	0.000[3]	4	0.000	7	0.000
Total	71 627 199		27 421 952	100	44 205 247	100	71 514 726		34 557 016	100	36 957 710	100

Notes:

1. Proportions of international (overseas) arrivals to the US are available at http://tinet.ita.doc.gov/cat/F-2005-45-541.html.
2. Proportions of (overseas) departures of the US residents to the other countries are available at http://tinet.ita.doc.gov/view/m-2005-O-001/index.html.
3. The undefined proportions for each state are calculated, based on the difference between 'total inbound or outbound passengers' and 'sum of preliminary fixed inbound or outbound passengers available from OTTI'. Distribution of the unidentified passengers from the OTTI to the recalculated proportions are conducted. For example, the gap of inbound between the selected major states and all states of inbound passengers would be 6,993,722 (71,627,199 − 64,633,477), and the gap is used to recalculate the proportions unspecified by OTTI. The recomputed proportions are used to calculate new international passengers by multiplying the remained passengers (5,818,011) which are not specified with the information provided by OTTI. Similarly, the US-based outbound passengers are calculated.

* Base year: 2005

** Because the approach combines different two data sources and estimate four types of passenger numbers, we found there were some gaps between inbound and outbound numbers of international (or US residents) passengers. Although we can explain part of the reasons as having to do with different durations of periods of passengers and base year of 2005, we keep the numbers as is, because we did not find a better source or better information.

Table 12.A3 Calculation of spending patterns of international passengers

USC sectors	Descriptions[1]	US-based		Based abroad	
		$ per passenger for international inbound (IAUS)[4]	$ per passenger for international outbound (IDUS)[4]	$ per passenger for international inbound (AIP)[4]	$ per passenger for international outbound (DIP)[4]
33	Airline tickets[2]	333.33	333.33	333.33	333.33
33	Transportation	90.67	90.67	143.50	143.50
45	Accommodation	0.00	0.00	686.00	0.00
35	Foods	0.00	0.00	267.31	0.00[3]
45	Grocery stores	0.00	0.00	60.69	0.00[3]
35	Gifts/shopping	0.00	0.00	406.00	0.00
44	Amusement	0.00	0.00	264.00	0.00
	Total	424	424	2160.83	476.83

Notes:
1. Transportation, accommodation, food, gifts/shopping, and amusement expenditure is based on US expenditures per round trip, proprietary data purchased from the Travel Industry Association (www.tia.org). See Table 12.A1 for the calculations and references.
2. These are all international boardings or alightings at US airports in 2005 (www.bts.gov). We assume that the average cost of an international round trip is $1000. We assume two-thirds of this value to account for the share of tickets that may have been purchased in US carriers. See http://www.lawa.org/lax/statistics/tcom-1201.pdf. We separately consider both of these trips and assume that half are made by US residents and half by foreign residents.
3. Based on $328 for food/beverage sector (Maplesden et al., 2002, p. 74), we separate the sector into two USC sectors, because spending on the food/beverage sector is similar to the spending pattern of domestic travelers (Maplesden et al., p. 73). The applied proportions are shown in Table 3, as 81.5 percent for the Foods sector and 18.5 percent for the grocery stores sector.
4. AIP = arrivals of international passengers; IAUS = international arrivals of US residents; DIP = departure of international passengers; IDUS = international departure of US residents

Table 12.A4 Direct losses in light of two mitigations, increased telecommunications and domestic travel diversion

One year	USC sectors	Contents	Amount
Mitigations	36	Telecommunication[1]	43 596.65
Mitigations	33, 35, 44, 45	Diversion	8 381.50
Direct losses	33, 35, 44, 45	Total direct loses	−110 145.09
		Net direct losses	−58 166.94

Note: 1. We assume final demand for telecommunication services (available from 2001 IMPLAN sector 422) increases by 25 per cent during the one-year international travel ban.

Table 12.A5 National air ticket sales loss effects ($ million)

Classification	USC sectors	Direct impact	Indirect impact	Total impact
Commodity sectors	USC01	0.0	−57.1	−57.1
	USC02	0.0	−36.2	−36.2
	USC03	0.0	−12.2	−12.2
	USC04	0.0	−38.2	−38.2
	USC05	0.0	−80.8	−80.8
	USC06	0.0	−53.1	−53.1
	USC07	0.0	−0.1	−0.1
	USC08	0.0	−36.6	−36.6
	USC09	0.0	−12.5	−12.5
	USC10	0.0	−4 021.2	−4 021.2
	USC11	0.0	−93.9	−93.9
	USC12	0.0	−6.4	−6.4
	USC13	0.0	−16.2	−16.2
	USC14	0.0	−163.6	−163.6
	USC15	0.0	−380.4	−380.4
	USC16	0.0	−157.6	−157.6
	USC17	0.0	−248.4	−248.4
	USC18	0.0	−618.1	−618.1
	USC19	0.0	−67.0	−67.0
	USC20	0.0	−97.8	−97.8
	USC21	0.0	−174.9	−174.9
	USC22	0.0	−397.2	−397.2
	USC23	0.0	−488.4	−488.4
	USC24	0.0	−384.3	−384.3
	USC25	0.0	−826.6	−826.6
	USC26	0.0	−454.2	−454.2

Table 12.A5 (continued)

Classification	USC sectors	Direct impact	Indirect impact	Total impact
		National air ticket impacts		
Non-commodity sectors	USC27	0.0	−53.2	−53.2
	USC28	0.0	−29.4	−29.4
	USC29	0.0	−87.8	−87.8
	USC30	0.0	−389.6	−389.6
	USC31	0.0	−264.2	−264.2
	USC32	0.0	−2 281.6	−2 281.6
	USC33	−45 327.8	−6 268.2	−51 596.0
	USC34	0.0	−850.0	−850.0
	USC35	0.0	−596.0	−596.0
	USC36	0.0	−1 710.7	−1 710.7
	USC37	0.0	−2 902.5	−2 902.5
	USC38	0.0	−2 889.2	−2 889.2
	USC39	0.0	−3 559.8	−3 559.8
	USC40	0.0	−647.2	−647.2
	USC41	0.0	−2 783.8	−2 783.8
	USC42	0.0	−48.9	−48.9
	USC43	0.0	−88.3	−88.3
	USC44	0.0	−103.8	−103.8
	USC45	0.0	−731.2	−731.2
	USC46	0.0	−645.7	−645.7
	USC47	0.0	−2 617.9	−2 617.9
Total		−45 327.8	−38 471.7	−83 799.5

Table 12.A6 Mitigation effects from 25 percent increased telecommunications ($ million)

	USC sectors	Direct impact	Indirect impact	Total impact
		Mitigation from increased telecommunication		
Commodity sectors	USC01	0.0	19.6	19.6
	USC02	0.0	12.9	12.9
	USC03	0.0	5.0	5.0
	USC04	0.0	12.1	12.1
	USC05	0.0	28.7	28.7
	USC06	0.0	21.0	21.0
	USC07	0.0	0.0	0.0
	USC08	0.0	12.7	12.7
	USC09	0.0	7.7	7.7
	USC10	0.0	213.2	213.2

Table 12.A6 (continued)

		Mitigation from increased telecommunication		
	USC sectors	Direct impact	Indirect impact	Total impact
	USC11	0.0	40.1	40.1
	USC12	0.0	5.1	5.1
	USC13	0.0	7.6	7.6
	USC14	0.0	132.2	132.2
	USC15	0.0	227.3	227.3
	USC16	0.0	130.7	130.7
	USC17	0.0	282.1	282.1
	USC18	0.0	1 065.7	1 065.7
	USC19	0.0	38.4	38.4
	USC20	0.0	129.6	129.6
	USC21	0.0	150.0	150.0
	USC22	0.0	267.7	267.7
	USC23	0.0	219.8	219.8
	USC24	0.0	2 894.0	2 894.0
	USC25	0.0	111.8	111.8
	USC26	0.0	6.2	6.2
	USC27	0.0	26.6	26.6
	USC28	0.0	36.4	36.4
	USC29	0.0	55.9	55.9
Non-commodity	USC30	0.0	261.2	261.2
sectors	USC31	0.0	256.3	256.3
	USC32	0.0	832.9	832.9
	USC33	0.0	427.3	427.3
	USC34	0.0	400.7	400.7
	USC35	0.0	174.8	174.8
	USC36	43 596.7	8 205.4	51 802.0
	USC37	0.0	1 161.2	1 161.2
	USC38	0.0	2 195.2	2 195.2
	USC39	0.0	3 174.6	3 174.6
	USC40	0.0	257.6	257.6
	USC41	0.0	923.0	923.0
	USC42	0.0	51.1	51.1
	USC43	0.0	58.8	58.8
	USC44	0.0	706.1	706.1
	USC45	0.0	231.1	231.1
	USC46	0.0	177.4	177.4
	USC47	0.0	1 089.3	1 089.3
Total		43 596.7	26 744.0	70 340.7

Table 12.A7 Air travel disturbances ($ million)

State	Without diversion Direct impacts	Without diversion Indirect impacts	Without diversion Total impacts	With diversion Direct impacts	With diversion Indirect impacts	With diversion Total impacts
AL	−2.5	−235.4	−237.9	−2.3	−210.5	212.8
AK	−89.6	−114.7	−204.2	−80.5	−101.9	−182.4
AZ	−1129.9	−683.6	−1813.5	−1001.1	−604.5	−1605.6
AR	−0.9	−182.1	−182.9	−0.8	−161.5	−162.3
CA	−10795.8	−7083.3	−17879.0	−9119.7	−6064.2	−15183.8
CO	−690.1	−551.1	−1241.2	−574.0	−468.5	−1042.5
CT	−80.4	−159.1	−239.5	−73.8	−141.8	−215.7
DE	0.0	−46.0	−46.0	0.0	−40.7	−40.7
DC	−4336.7	−1935.6	−6272.3	−4001.5	−1779.3	−5780.8
FL	−9761	−5759.9	−15520.9	−9258.1	−5456.7	−14714.8
GA	−1918.5	−1501.3	−3419.8	−1402.1	−1187.7	−2589.8
HI	−3542.3	−1969.3	−5511.6	−3242.3	−1794.4	−5036.7
ID	−0.3	−75.1	−75.4	−0.2	−65.9	−66.0
IL	−3267	−2420.6	−5687.5	−2847.9	−2132.6	−4980.5
IN	−57.6	−302.9	−360.5	−53.2	−268.5	−321.6
IA	−1.1	−259.5	−260.6	−0.8	−227.0	−227.8
KS	−1.1	−169.2	−170.3	−1.0	−148.8	−149.8
KY	−919.9	−722.6	−1642.5	−840.9	−654.1	−1495.0
LA	−63.2	−376.2	−439.4	−58.5	−335.1	−393.6
ME	−10.7	−70.9	−81.6	−9.9	−62.2	−72.1
MD	−456.5	−448.4	−904.9	−415.3	−407.1	−822.3
MA	−1885.2		−3043.9	−1633.8	−1008.1	−2641.9
MI	−979.8	−948.9	−1928.7	−710.8	−754.9	−1465.7
MN	−483.4	−630.6	−1114.0	−298.1	−485.3	−783.4
MS	−1.2	−126.4	−127.6	−1.2	−110.9	−112.0
MO	−286.1	−375.8	−662.0	−262.9	−337.4	−600.3
MT	−0.1	−45.8	−45.9	−0.1	−40.2	−40.3
NE	−4.2	−220.1	−224.3	−4.0	−195.6	−199.6
NV	−1435.4	−715.2	−2150.6	−1316.7	−652.7	−196934
NH	−16.9	−44.2	−61.4	−15.5	−39.4	−54.9
NJ	−2753.1	−1856.2	−4609.4	−2334.1	−1603.0	−3937.1
NM	−0.5	−59.2	−59.7	−0.5	−52.2	−52.7
NY	−12220.6	−6447.9	−18668.5	−10460.7	−5523.8	−15984.5
NC	−710.2	−764.2	−1474.4	−558.9	−643.8	−1202.7
ND	−0.5	−62.9	−63.4	−0.2	−55.1	−55.3
OH	−296	−669.6	−965.6	−271.6	−594.3	−865.8
OK	−2.2	−192.3	−194.5	−1.6	−168.0	−169.6
OR	−343.2	−332.9	−676.1	−306.5	−294.7	−601.2
PA	−1482.6	−1431.8	−2914.4	−1231.2	−1223.1	−2454.3

Table 12.A7 (continued)

State	Without diversion			With diversion		
	Direct impacts	Indirect impacts	Total impacts	Direct impacts	Indirect impacts	Total impacts
RI	−30.2	−51.8	−82.0	−27.7	−46.6	−74.4
SC	−16.7	−150.3	−167.0	−15.3	−132.6	−147.9
SD	−1.2	−54.8	−56.0	−1.1	−48.0	−49.1
TN	−365.9	−421.7	−787.6	−336.2	−379.2	−715.4
TX	−3038	−3519.1	−6557.1	−2535.2	−3062.9	−5598.1
UT	−300.9	−255.9	−556.8	−273.5	−230.7	−504.2
VM	0.0	−32.5	−32.5	0.0	−28.6	−28.6
VA	−9.6	−217.5	−227.1	−8.8	−193.6	−202.5
WA	−866.2	−747.0	−1613.3	−698.6	−624.3	−1322.9
WV	−0.1	−72.9	−73.0	0.0	−63.2	−63.3
WI	−162.2	−493.9	−656.1	−148.4	−436.1	−584.5
WY	0.0	−54.6	−54.6	0.0	−49.4	−49.4
US subtotal	−64817.3	−47221.7	−112039.0	−56436.8	−41390.7	−97827.4
Foreign	0.0	−24420.5	−2420.5	0.0	−2142.5	−2142.5
Total	−64817.3	−49642.2	−114459.5	−56436.8	−43533.2	−99970.0

Table 12.A8 International trade losses ($ billion)

State	Imports (A) Direct impacts	Imports (A) Indirect impacts	Imports (A) Total impacts	No substitution effects — Imports, except energy sector (USC 10) (B) Direct impacts	Indirect impacts	Total impacts	Exports (C) Direct impacts	Indirect impacts	Total impacts	Total (B)+(C) Total impacts	Substitution effects Direct impacts	Indirect impacts	Total impacts
AL	−19.4	−7.8	−27.2	−18.2	−6.5	−24.7	−10.8	−13.2	−24.0	−48.7	−22.4	−14.1	−36.5
AK	−3.2	−1.4	−4.7	−2.9	−1.3	−4.2	−0.7	−1.2	−1.9	−6.1	−2.6	−1.8	−4.4
AZ	−18.5	−8.7	−27.1	−17.5	−7.3	−24.7	−13.3	−8.6	−21.9	−46.6	−22.4	−11.4	−33.8
AR	−11.0	−4.7	−15.7	−10.4	−3.9	−14.3	−7.2	−8.9	−16.1	−30.4	−17.2	−11.0	−28.2
CA	−151.2	−57.3	−208.5	−130.6	−43.8	−174.5	−107.9	−83.9	−191.8	−366.2	−144.4	−76.2	−220.7
CO	−20.6	−9.9	−30.5	−19.6	−8.9	−28.5	−9.7	−8.9	−18.7	−47.2	−21.7	−13.0	−34.7
CT	−18.4	−7.7	−26.0	−17.4	−6.2	−23.6	−15.2	−11.4	−26.6	−50.2	−25.2	−13.2	−38.3
DE	−5.0	−2.2	−7.2	−4.2	−1.7	−6.0	−2.0	−2.2	−4.2	−10.2	−4.2	−2.8	−6.9
DC	−4.5	−2.2	−6.7	−4.0	−1.5	−5.5	−0.3	−0.3	−0.7	−6.1	−2.9	−1.3	−4.2
FL	−57.6	−29.0	−86.7	−55.0	−25.7	−80.7	−18.1	−15.9	−34.0	−114.7	−41.2	−25.3	−66.5
GA	−36.7	−16.6	−53.3	−34.3	−13.9	−48.2	−17.5	−18.0	−35.5	−83.7	−36.6	−21.3	−57.9
HI	−4.4	−2.6	−6.9	−3.5	−1.9	−5.4	−0.7	−0.8	−1.5	−7.0	−3.7	−2.2	−6.0
ID	−5.4	−2.4	−7.8	−5.2	−1.9	−7.1	−3.7	−3.0	−6.7	−13.8	−6.9	−3.7	−10.6
IL	−59.6	−28.2	−87.8	−53.4	−21.5	−74.9	−34.7	−36.8	−71.5	1−46.4	−54.7	−35.8	−90.5
IN	−32.4	−13.5	−45.9	−29.9	−10.5	−40.4	−23.9	−28.4	−52.3	−92.6	−41.2	−26.7	−67.9
IA	−14.3	−6.5	−20.8	−13.3	−5.4	−18.7	106	−11.5	−22.1	−40.8	−23.8	−14.9	−38.6
KS	−16.5	−7.7	−24.2	−15.5	−6.7	−22.3	−12.0	−11.9	−23.8	−46.1	−25.8	−16.3	−42.2
KY	−23.5	−8.7	−32.2	−22.3	−7.8	−30.2	−13.1	−15.4	−28.5	−58.7	−28.3	−15.6	−43.9
LA	−22.8	−10.3	−33.0	−15.4	−6.9	−22.3	−9.6	−13.8	−23.4	−45.7	−16.1	−13.1	−29.2
ME	−5.1	−2.3	−7.4	−4.8	−2.0	−6.9	−2.9	−3.0	−5.9	−12.8	−5.7	−3.5	−9.2
MD	−22.7	−10.7	−33.3	−21.5	−9.1	−30.6	−6.9	−6.6	−13.5	−44.1	−22.6	−11.5	−34.1
MA	−34.4	−14.0	−48.4	−32.6	−11.9	−44.5	−23.2	−17.4	−40.6	−85.1	−37.6	−19.5	−57.1

220

MI	-65.2	-25.6	-90.8	-62.9	-22.7	-85.6	-35.8	-37.7	-73.5	1-59.1	-44.6	-29.4	-74.0
MN	-28.3	-12.5	-40.7	-26.0	-9.8	-35.7	-15.2	-15.9	-31.1	-66.8	-31.5	-18.9	-50.4
MS	-11.7	4.9	-16.5	-10.2	-3.7	-13.9	-5.9	-7.4	-13.3	-27.2	-13.4	-8.5	-21.9
MO	-28.8	-12.8	-41.6	-27.1	-10.8	-37.8	-14.0	-14.7	-28.8	-66.6	-34.4	-18.8	-53.3
MT	-4.0	-2.2	-6.3	-3.1	-1.6	-4.7	-1.1	-1.9	-3.0	-7.7	-2.6	-2.2	-4.8
NE	-8.2	4.6	-12.7	-7.3	-3.5	-10.8	5.3	6.1	-11.4	-22.2	-11.8	-8.3	-20.1
NV	-7.5	-4.2	-11.7	-7.1	-3.5	-10.6	-1.7	-1.6	-3.2	-13.8	-7.6	-4.2	-11.8
NH	-6.3	-2.5	-8.7	-6.0	-2.1	-8.1	-4.4	-3.9	-8.3	-16.4	-10.4	-5.2	-15.5
NJ	-38.0	-18.8	-56.7	-33.9	-14.1	-48.0	-19.7	-18.9	-38.5	-86.5	-35.9	-19.6	-55.5
NM	-8.1	-3.1	-11.3	-7.7	-2.8	-10.5	-2.7	-2.4	-5.2	-15.7	-8.4	-4.0	-12.4
NY	-75.5	-34.6	1-10.1	713	-29.0	1-00.2	-34.9	-29.8	-64.7	1-64.9	-51.4	-31.7	-83.0
NC	-35.6	-15.0	-50.5	-33.8	-12.5	-46.3	-26.2	-23.8	-50.0	-96.4	-47.3	-26.9	-74.2
ND	-3.6	-1.7	-5.3	-3.2	-1.3	-4.5	-2.2	-2.3	-4.5	-8.9	-3.6	-2.6	-6.2
OH	-63.4	-24.1	-87.5	-60.5	-20.6	-81.2	-39.3	-44.0	-83.4	1-64.6	-52.3	-36.2	-88.5
OK	-15.7	6.7	-22.4	-13.8	-5.8	-19.6	-7.7	-9.8	-17.6	-37.1	-21.1	-13.3	-34.4
OR	-15.9	6.3	-22.2	-15.0	-5.0	-20.0	-12.4	-9.3	-21.7	-41.6	-19.3	-9.7	-29.0
PA	-53.6	-23.8	-77.4	-48.9	-19.1	-67.9	-32.1	-33.6	-65.7	1-33.6	-50.1	-31.9	-81.9
RI	-4.8	-1.8	-6.7	-4.5	-1.5	-5.9	-3.1	-2.7	-5.9	-11.8	-7.5	-3.6	-11.2
SC	-16.9	-6.7	-23.6	-16.0	-5.5	-21.5	-11.6	-12.2	-23.8	-45.3	-18.4	-11.0	-29.4
SD	-3.5	-1.8	-5.2	-3.3	-1.5	-4.7	-2.1	-2.3	-4.4	-9.1	-4.3	-3.0	-7.3
TN	-29.3	-11.9	-41.2	-27.9	-10.2	-38.1	-16.3	-17.7	-34.0	-72.0	-32.7	-19.2	-52.0
TX	-96.1	-42.8	1-39.0	-82.1	-35.3	1-17.4	-59.8	-63.7	1-23.5	2-41.0	-87.3	-61.4	1-48.7
UT	-8.7	-4.2	-12.9	-7.7	-3.3	-11.0	-5.0	-5.2	-10.2	-21.2	-10.8	-6.8	-17.5
VM	-2.8	-1.1	-3.9	-2.6	-0.9	-3.6	-2.5	-1.6	-4.2	-7.7	-3.0	-1.6	-4.6
VA	-34.2	-14.4	-48.6	-32.8	-12.6	-45.4	-13.1	-12.6	-25.7	-71.1	-32.8	-17.4	-50.3
WA	-33.1	-15.0	-48.1	-30.2	-11.3	-41.4	-23.9	-19.8	-43.7	-85.2	-39.3	-22.2	-61.6
WV	-6.7	-2.8	-9.5	-6.2	-2.4	-8.6	-4.7	-6.6	-11.3	-19.9	-10.9	-7.6	-18.4
WI	-30.6	-12.0	-42.6	-29.0	-10.1	-39.1	-18.9	-21.6	-40.5	-79.6	-38.9	-22.6	-61.6
WY	-2.4	-1.2	-3.6	-1.9	-1.0	-3.0	-0.8	-1.5	-2.2	-5.2	-2.7	-2.2	-4.8
US subtotal	-1325.2	-573.5	-1898.8	-1213.3	-469.8	-1683.2	-766.3	-751.9	-1518.2	-3201.4	-1341.4	-804.0	-2145.3
Foreign	0.0	-41.9	-41.9	0.0	-38.5	-38.5	0.0	-83.8	-83.8	-122.3	0.0	-77.7	-77.7
Total	-1325.2	-615.5	-1940.7	-1213.3	-508.3	-1721.7	-766.3	-835.8	-1602.1	-3323.7	-1341.4	-881.7	-2223.0

Table 12.A9 Legal migration reduction

Classification	USCsec.	Leontief price model			Total industry output	Demand-side USIO		
		Job losses (1000)	Increased wage	Increased price		Direct impact	Indirect impact	Total impact
Commodity sectors	USC01	−17.506	0.0036%	0.0184%	173097	−31.928	−53.292	−85.220
	USC02	−15.599	0.0032%	0.0135%	118853	−16.100	−30.619	−46.720
	USC03	−4.087	0.0008%	0.0161%	44785	−7.193	−15.563	−22.757
	USC04	−8.019	0.0017%	0.0137%	84392	−11.594	−20.559	−32.153
	USC05	−17.407	0.0036%	0.0173%	286070	−49.480	−71.343	−120.823
	USC06	−1.710	0.0004%	0.0109%	61546	−6.715	−15.704	−22.420
	USC07	−0.773	0.0002%	0.0076%	52637	−4.009	−0.186	−4.195
	USC08	−3.251	0.0007%	0.0077%	19049	−1.459	−12.258	−13.718
	USC09	−0.968	0.0002%	0.0079%	9129	−0.718	−3.894	−4.612
	USC10	−12.860	0.0027%	0.0135%	371603	−50.313	−145.066	−195.379
	USC11	−3.033	0.0006%	0.0115%	76034	−8.740	−25.064	−33.804
	USC12	−6.282	0.0013%	0.0098%	134457	−13.218	−16.569	−29.787
	USC13	−0.831	0.0002%	0.0103%	16209	−1.665	−5.881	−7.546
	USC14	−6.736	0.0014%	0.0115%	142133	−16.389	−42.933	−59.322
	USC15	−19.663	0.0041%	0.0149%	203666	−30.293	−90.718	−121.011
	USC16	−12.398	0.0026%	0.0133%	101676	−13.477	−73.066	−86.542
	USC17	−10.040	0.0021%	0.0133%	142353	−18.924	−61.830	−80.754
	USC18	−22.982	0.0048%	0.0132%	203883	−26.905	−87.329	−114.233
	USC19	−23.036	0.0048%	0.0163%	172998	−28.277	−29.044	−57.322
	USC20	−10.892	0.0023%	0.0117%	97801	−11.422	−67.565	−78.987
	USC21	−8.249	0.0017%	0.0129%	121498	−15.660	−50.146	−65.806
	USC22	−24.032	0.0050%	0.0143%	184519	−26.448	−88.621	−115.069
	USC23	−32.231	0.0067%	0.0169%	331350	−55.988	−65.114	−121.102
	USC24	−42.166	0.0087%	0.0169%	601195	−101.766	−96.724	−198.490
	USC25	−24.500	0.0051%	0.0185%	447184	−82.700	−65.058	−147.758

	USC26	−9.550	0.0020%	118010	−14.683	−4.403	−19.087
	USC27	−11.311	0.0023%	114130	−12.995	−13.696	−26.691
	USC28	−13.267	0.0027%	73637	−9.536	−16.183	−25.719
	USC29	−13.410	0.0028%	282474	−31.340	−23.446	−54.786
	USC30	−10.323	0.0021%	296699	−30.432	−75.830	−106.263
Non-commodity	USC31	−386.254	0.0800%	1013114	−951.797	−43.806	−995.603
sectors	USC32	−90.127	0.0187%	875258	−233.021	−260.171	−493.192
	USC33	−50.485	0.0105%	502771	−119.428	−141.814	−261.243
	USC34	−23.662	0.0049%	162269	−19.786	−85.979	−105.765
	USC35	−238.062	0.0493%	942803	−549.591	−129.268	−678.859
	USC36	−28.886	0.0060%	586269	−80.457	−185.599	−266.056
	USC37	−68.963	0.0143%	1287273	−313.909	−338.570	−652.479
	USC38	−35.227	0.0073%	1681503	−246.257	−383.897	−630.153
	USC39	−104.510	0.0216%	1008257	−278.631	−371.406	−650.037
	USC40	−26.512	0.0055%	210209	−23.881	−104.940	−128.821
	USC41	−191.282	0.0396%	443881	−212.121	−228.778	−440.899
	USC42	−162.262	0.0336%	85680	−41.535	−4.248	−45.782
	USC43	−376.519	0.0780%	1188873	−1065.819	−24.860	−1090.679
	USC44	−50.143	0.0104%	154279	−30.940	−20.977	−51.917
	USC45	−354.587	0.0734%	498852	−417.576	−58.896	−476.472
	USC46	−218.761	0.0453%	1288980	−607.182	−40.334	−647.516
	USC47	−93.648	0.0194%	755883	−228.573	−179.859	−408.432
Total		−2887.000	0.5979%	17769757	−6150.873	−3971.107	−10121.98

Notes:
1. Impact unit: $ millions.
2. Legal employment data are obtained from recent year of entry (2000 to 2004) of Table 2.8 in US Census Bureau, Current Population Survey, Annual Social and Economics Supplement, 2004. We distributed the employment numbers to the USC sectors, based on occupation-industry data sets available at the Bureau of Labor Survey web page and conversion bridge of 2-digit NAICS to USC sector developed by authors (Park et al. 2007).
3. Total employment (144850 million) from US Department of Labor (2006).
4. Low-end labor supply elasticity is assumed to be −0.3 (Borjas, 2003).
5. Total industry output is available from 2001 IMPLAN and the authors aggregated 509 IMPLAN sectors to 47 USC sectors according to the process of Park et al. (2007).

Table 12.A10 Median value illegal migration reduction

Classification	USCsec.	Leontief price model			Total industry output	Demand-side USIO		
		Job losses (1000)	Increased Wage	Increased Price		Direct impact	Indirect impact	Total impact
Commodity sectors	USC01	−24.477	0.0051%	0.0101%	173 097	−17.466	−10.141	−27.607
	USC02	−44.443	0.0092%	0.0112%	118 853	−13.284	−6.954	−20.239
	USC03	−9.338	0.0019%	0.0065%	44 785	−2.922	−4.512	−7.434
	USC04	−0.000	0.0000%	0.0028%	84 932	−2.395	−1.547	−3.942
	USC05	−13.198	0.0027%	0.0064%	286 070	−18.267	−11.098	−29.365
	USC06	−0.727	0.0002%	0.0016%	61 546	−0.996	−2.270	−3.266
	USC07	−1.061	0.0002%	0.0011%	52 637	−0.591	−0.050	−0.640
	USC08	−0.029	0.0002%	0.0012%	19 049	−0.222	−4.747	−4.970
	USC09	−0.309	0.0001%	0.0010%	9 129	−0.095	−1.028	−1.124
	USC10	−4.307	0.0009%	0.0025%	371 603	−9.133	−33.883	−43.016
	USC11	−1.264	0.0003%	0.0017%	76 034	−1.278	−4.656	−5.933
	USC12	−2.635	0.0005%	0.0015%	134 457	−1.986	−0.845	−2.831
	USC13	−0.347	0.0001%	0.0012%	16 209	−0.196	−1.536	−1.732
	USC14	−2.809	0.0006%	0.0019%	142 133	−2.742	−11.310	−14.052
	USC15	−8.207	0.0017%	0.0032%	203 666	−6.563	−22.194	−28.757
	USC16	−10.137	0.0021%	0.0041%	101 676	−4.154	−28.239	−32.393
	USC17	−4.185	0.0009%	0.0025%	142 353	−3.516	−13.289	−16.804
	USC18	−11.972	0.0025%	0.0036%	203 883	−7.295	−17.423	−24.718
	USC19	−12.314	0.0026%	0.0044%	172 998	−7.559	−6.791	−14.350
	USC20	−4.546	0.0009%	0.0022%	97 801	−2.133	−26.967	−29.101
	USC21	−3.569	0.0007%	0.0020%	121 498	−2.489	−15.412	−17.901
	USC22	−10.399	0.0022%	0.0034%	184 519	−6.305	−31.243	−37.548
	USC23	−13.924	0.0029%	0.0044%	331 350	−14.579	−21.311	−35.890
	USC24	−20.422	0.0042%	0.0055%	601 195	−33.342	−26.007	−59.349
	USC25	−10.584	0.0022%	0.0045%	447 184	−19.913	−15.644	−35.557

	USC26	−4.132	0.0009%	118010	−2.922	−0.791	−3.712
	USC27	−4.894	0.0010%	114130	−2.528	−2.327	−4.856
	USC28	−5.741	0.0012%	73637	−2.022	−6.303	−8.325
	USC29	−8.413	0.0017%	282474	−8.334	−5.380	−13.714
	USC30	0.000	0.0000%	296699	−4.226	−16.460	−20.686
Non-	USC31	−207.570	0.0430%	1013114	−472.204	−7.098	−479.302
commodity	USC32	0.000	0.0000%	875258	−7.427	−62.525	−69.952
sectors	USC33	0.000	0.0000%	502771	−6.570	−32.776	−39.347
	USC34	0.000	0.0000%	162269	−1.315	−17.880	−19.195
	USC35	−145.299	0.0301%	942803	−295.085	−47.783	−342.868
	USC36	−0.397	0.0001%	586269	−6.207	−38.087	−44.294
	USC37	−1.272	0.0003%	1287273	−10.640	−53.140	−63.780
	USC38	−0.930	0.0002%	1681503	−24.536	−71.522	−96.058
	USC39	−1.786	0.0004%	1008257	−8.747	−85.541	−94.288
	USC40	−0.282	0.0001%	210209	−1.977	−28.798	−30.775
	USC41	−1.547	0.0003%	443881	−5.781	−38.806	−44.586
	USC42	−0.325	0.0001%	85680	−1.673	−0.638	−2.311
	USC43	−2.556	0.0005%	1188873	−20.218	−2.653	−22.871
	USC44	−0.529	0.0001%	154279	−1.814	−3.391	−5.204
	USC45	−1.861	0.0004%	498852	−12.556	−9.015	−21.572
	USC46	−3.695	0.0008%	1288980	−15.420	−7.491	−22.911
	USC47	−20.937	0.0043%	755883	−47.074	−42.712	−89.786
Total		−628.371	0.1301%	17769757	−1138.696	−900.216	−2038.91

Notes:
1. Impact unit: $ million.
2. 2006 total employment (144,850 million) from US Department of Labor.
3. Low-end labor supply elasticity is assumed to be −0.3 (Borjas, 2003).
4. Illegal job proportions are available at http://en.wikipedia.org/wiki/Illegal_immigrant_population_of_the_United_States.
5. Total industry output is available from 2001 IMPLAN and the authors aggregated 509 IMPLAN sectors to 47 USC sectors according to the process of Park et al. (2007).

Table 12.A11 Borders closed to cross-border shopping, based on the instead shopping of US residents

State	Direct impacts	Indirect impacts	Total impacts
AL	0.0	−7.4	−7.4
AK	−9.2	−6.0	−15.2
AZ	−655.1	−330.9	−986.0
AR	0.0	−6.3	−6.3
CA	−1685.7	−847.5	−2533.2
CO	0.0	−5.4	−5.4
CT	0.0	−3.3	−3.3
DE	0.0	−0.8	−0.8
DC	0.0	−0.3	−0.3
FL	0.0	−7.3	−7.3
GA	0.0	−7.2	−7.2
HI	0.0	−0.8	−0.8
ID	−7.7	−5.6	−13.3
IL	0.0	−16.8	−16.8
IN	0.0	−10.8	−10.8
IA	0.0	−4.5	−4.5
KS	0.0	−3.9	−3.9
KY	0.0	−6.6	−6.6
LA	0.0	−16.7	−16.7
ME	−139.6	−80.4	−220.0
MD	0.0	−2.3	−2.3
MA	0.0	−7.2	−7.2
MI	−351.7	−195.8	−547.4
MN	−57.7	−38.4	−96.0
MS	0.0	−4.8	−4.8
MO	0.0	−7.1	−7.1
MT	−30.2	−19.9	−50.1
NE	0.0	−1.7	−1.7
NV	0.0	−1.9	−1.9
NH	0.0	−2.7	−2.7
NJ	0.0	−9.2	−9.2
NM	−42.7	−27.1	−69.8
NY	−456.1	−230.8	−686.9
NC	0.0	−7.5	−7.5
ND	−33.1	−20.7	−53.8
OH	0.0	−19.5	−19.5
OK	0.0	−13.5	−13.5
OR	0.0	−7.9	−7.9
PA	0.0	−14.3	−14.3
RI	0.0	−0.9	−0.9

Table 12.A11 (continued)

State	Direct impacts	Indirect impacts	Total impacts
SC	0.0	−4.9	−4.9
SD	0.0	−0.8	−0.8
TN	0.0	−7.4	−7.4
TX	−2315.7	−1237.5	−3553.2
UT	0.0	−3.5	−3.5
VM	−45.3	−25.7	−71.1
VA	0.0	−4.8	−4.8
WA	−213.4	−119.4	−332.8
WV	0.0	−2.9	−2.9
WI	0.0	−13.1	−13.1
WY	0.0	−1.1	−1.1
US subtotal	−6043.3	−3422.8	−9466.0
Foreign	0.0	−475.2	−475.2
Total	−6043.3	−3898.0	−9941.2

Notes:
1. Impact unit: $ million.
2. Input data of number of incoming cross-border, not by air, are obtained from http://www.transtats.bts.gov/Fields.asp?Table_ID=1358.
3. We assume 40 percent of incoming people crossing the border to be US residents (see http://www.bts.gov/publications/us_international_travel_and_transportation_trends/2006/html/chapter_03/table_03_02.html). Those substitute domestic purchase for shopping abroad if the US borders were closed.
4. We assumed $100 expenditure on the retail industry (USC sector 35) per incoming person crossing an international border.

13. Macroeconomic impacts of shutting down the US borders in response to a security or health threat

Adam Z. Rose, Garrett R. Beeler Asay, Dan Wei and Billy Leung

INTRODUCTION

Several threats to the United States may raise the consideration of a partial or complete shutdown of our borders to people and goods. Such threats would include a coordinated terrorist attack or an influenza outbreak, and could last anywhere from just a few days to several months. Given that the US economy is highly dependent on international mobility of goods and people, the economic impacts of a partial or total border closure are likely to be significant. Major economic impacts would stem from four factors. First, the US imports a significant amount of both intermediate and final goods, many of which either cannot be readily replaced or can be replaced only at a significantly higher cost of domestic substitutes. Second, export demand is an important stimulus to the US economy, and it may face retaliation in the form of import bans on US goods if it imposes restrictions on goods coming in from other countries. Third, international visitors inject a significant amount of spending into the US economy. Fourth, migration provides workers at all skill levels.

We will analyze the impacts of the curtailment of all of these actions using the REMI Economic-Demographic Simulation Model (REMI, 2006). The analysis is performed through a set of comparative static simulations to isolate the impact of each aspect of a curtailment, as well as a comprehensive simulation to identify interaction effects. The extreme nature of the shock to the US economy posed a major challenge to the REMI model, which is typically applied to marginal policy changes. We explain the several major refinements we made to enable the model to be used for a policy simulation of a complete shutdown of the US borders to goods and people. In various stages of the simulations, we analyzed the effects of resilient responses to the potential shock at both individual business and market levels. These include use of inventories, excess capacity, conservation, domestic input substitution in response to price changes, redirecting exports to domestic input needs, and rescheduling lost production to a later date (Rose, 2007).

Our overall results indicate that a complete shutdown of the US borders to people and goods for one year would result in a loss of gross domestic product (GDP) of about $1.4 trillion (2006$) and a loss of employment of more than 22 million. Most analysts, however, surmise that a shutdown is likely only to be implemented for three to six months, so these figures should be pro-rated accordingly. Moreover, for a policy decision, the costs of the shutdown need to be carefully weighed against the expected value of its benefits (avoided terrorist damage or health effects).

BACKGROUND

Only a limited number of studies have expressly analyzed the effects of major shutdowns of the US border to goods and/or people. The most comprehensive is that of Gordon et al. (Chapter 12, this volume), which parallels the analysis in this chapter. That study used a sophisticated input–output approach to the problem, based on a 47-sector US Input–Output Table (MIG, 2006), including refinements to allow for price responses and supply-side multiplier effects, and the key interactions between them are shown in the National Interstate Economic Model (NIEMO), capable of analyzing the impacts on all 50 states (Gordon et al., 2007). The simulations were performed in a comparative static mode for the following border closure components: imports, exports, air travel, in-migration (both legal and illegal) and cross-border shopping. Some forms of resilience to this shock were modeled, such as the diversion of exports to replace imports, and the substitution of telecommunications for air travel. The major findings of the study are a projected reduction in US GDP of $1.4 trillion (in 2001$), with international trade aspects accounting for about 95 percent of the total. This contrasts with our estimates of $1.2 to $1.8 trillion losses in GDP (2000$), 92 percent and 90 percent of which are trade-related, respectively. Though there are differences in some of the lesser types of factors modeled (for example, we did not include cross-border shopping, nor telecommunications substitution for international air travel; and Gordon et al. did not include utilization of excess capacity as we did, and excluded oil and gas imports from the ban), the data inputs were otherwise very similar, and the differences are mainly attributable to the type of model used. For example, an inherently linear model, such as input–output (I–O), is more likely to lead to higher estimates of a shock to the system than a non-linear model, in part because the former stunts several types of adjustments. However, this difference wanes as the shutdown period decreases.

Very few other studies of border shutdown have been undertaken. The major exception is the case of oil embargoes and related supply dislocations, which do provide some insights to the more general considerations modeled in this chapter. The first contemporary oil price shock was instigated by the Arab country members of the Organization of Petroleum Exporting Countries (OPEC) in the form of an embargo that lasted from September to December 1973, during which these members reduced their production by 4.2 million barrels per day. With this reduction in quantity, price nearly tripled. There was also a second, larger decrease in production from 1979 to 1980 during the Iranian Revolution. In general the impacts of the embargo are summarized in two ways (Greene et al., 1998). First, there is a transfer of national wealth to oil-producing states. Second, there is a loss in potential GDP and accompanying unemployment increases. Greene et al. (1998) also use consumer and producer surplus models to estimate the impacts of a hypothetical two-year reduction in oil output similar to the prior oil shocks. They find a range of values from $720 billion to $1.14 trillion.[1] However, if the world were able to increase short-term elasticity of supply and demand substantially, these shocks could be cut by more than half. We should note that this case is not directly comparable to a complete shutdown of imports, because imports to the US were offset somewhat by imports from non-Arab oil-producing countries. Also, most of the impacts manifested themselves through increases in price, a combination of OPEC demonstrating its market power, an increase in tension in the oil markets, and irrational consumer behavior (for example, hoarding of gasoline). A shutdown of all imports to the US is similar, however, in that the market adjustment to the shortages would generally increase the price of domestic substitutes.

Other studies have empirically estimated the elasticity of GDP growth and inflation to the price of oil within the US (Hunt et al., 2001; Dalsgaard et al., 2001; Jimenez-Rodriguez and Sanchez, 2004; Abeysinghe, 2001; Ciscar et al., 2004). These estimates range from 0 to a −0.17 percent change in GDP for a 10 percent permanent increase in oil prices (Schneider, 2004). Further, a 10 percent permanent increase in oil prices was associated with a 0.02 to 0.18 percent increase in inflation.

REMI MODEL ANALYSIS

REMI Policy Insight is a structural economic forecasting and policy analysis model. It integrates input–output, computable general equilibrium, econometric and economic geography methodologies. The model is dynamic, with forecasts and simulations generated on an annual basis and behavioral responses to wage, price and other economic factors.

The REMI model consists of thousands of simultaneous equations with a structure that is relatively straightforward. The exact number of equations used varies depending on the extent of industry, demographic, demand and other detail in the model. The overall structure of the model can be summarized in five major 'blocks': (1) Output and Demand; (2) Labor and Capital Demand; (3) Population and Labor Supply; (4) Wages, Prices and Costs; and (5) Market Shares. The blocks and their key interactions between them are shown in Figures 13.1 and 13.2.

The Output and Demand block includes output, demand, consumption, investment, government spending, import, product access and export concepts. Output for each industry is determined by industry demand in a given region and its trade with the US market, and international imports and exports.

For each industry, demand is determined by the amount of output, consumption, investment and capital demand on that industry. Consumption depends on real disposable income per capita, relative prices, differential income elasticities and population. Input productivity depends on access to inputs because the larger the choice set of inputs, the more likely that the input with the specific characteristics required for the job will be formed. In the capital stock adjustment process, investment occurs to fill the difference between optimal and actual capital stock for residential, non-residential and equipment investment. Government spending changes are determined by changes in the population.

The Labor and Capital Demand block includes the determination of labor productivity, labor intensity and the optimal capital stocks. Industry-specific labor productivity depends on the availability of workers with differentiated skills for the occupations used in each industry. The occupational labor supply and commuting costs determine firms' access to a specialized labor force.

Labor intensity is determined by the cost of labor relative to the other factor inputs, capital and fuel. Demand for capital is driven by the optimal capital stock equation for both non-residential capital and equipment. Optimal capital stock for each industry depends on the relative cost of labor and capital, and the employment weighted by capital use for each industry. Employment in private industries is determined by the value added and employment per unit of value added in each industry.

The Population and Labor Supply block includes detailed demographic information about the region. Population data is given for age and gender, with birth and survival rates for each group. The size and

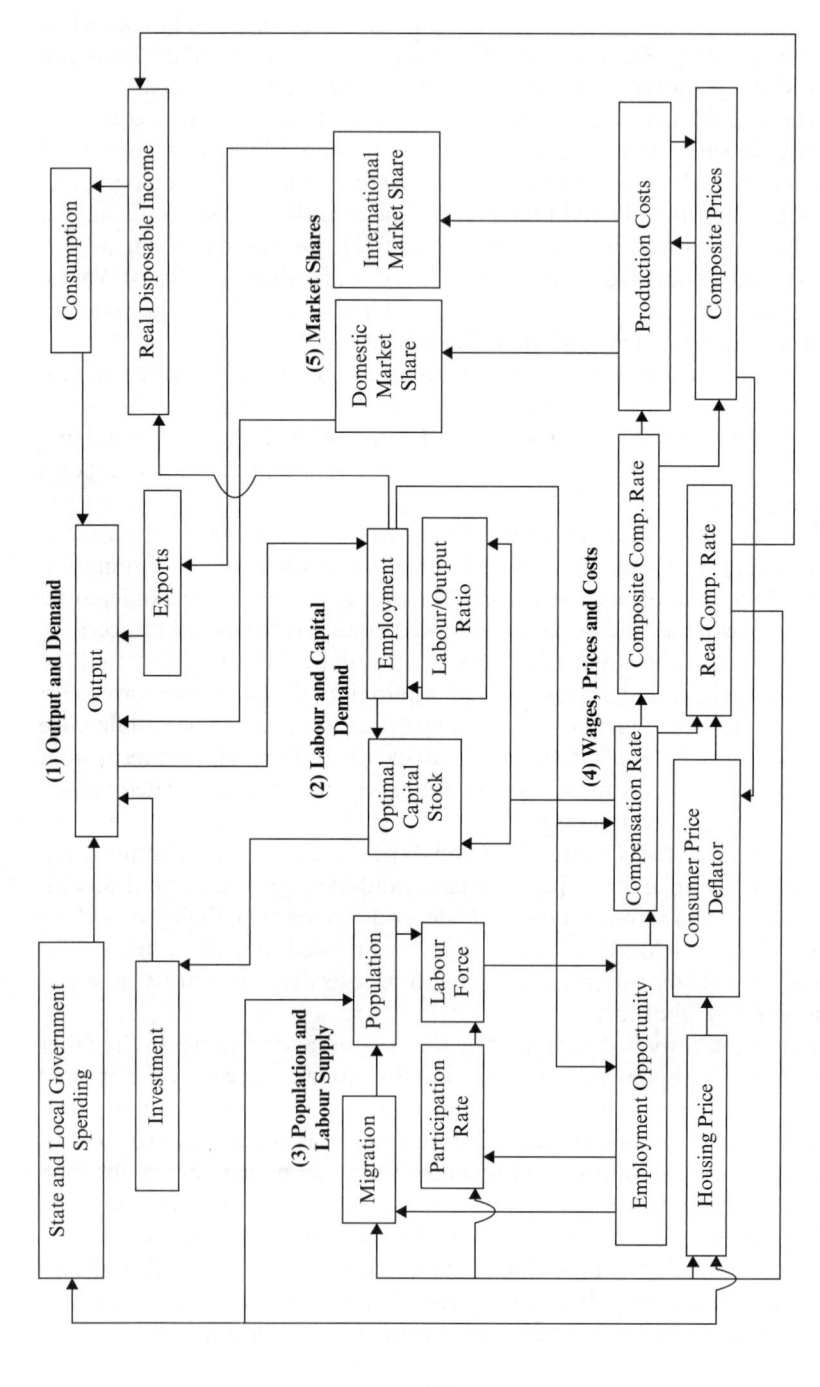

Figure 13.1 REMI model linkages (excluding economic geography linkages)

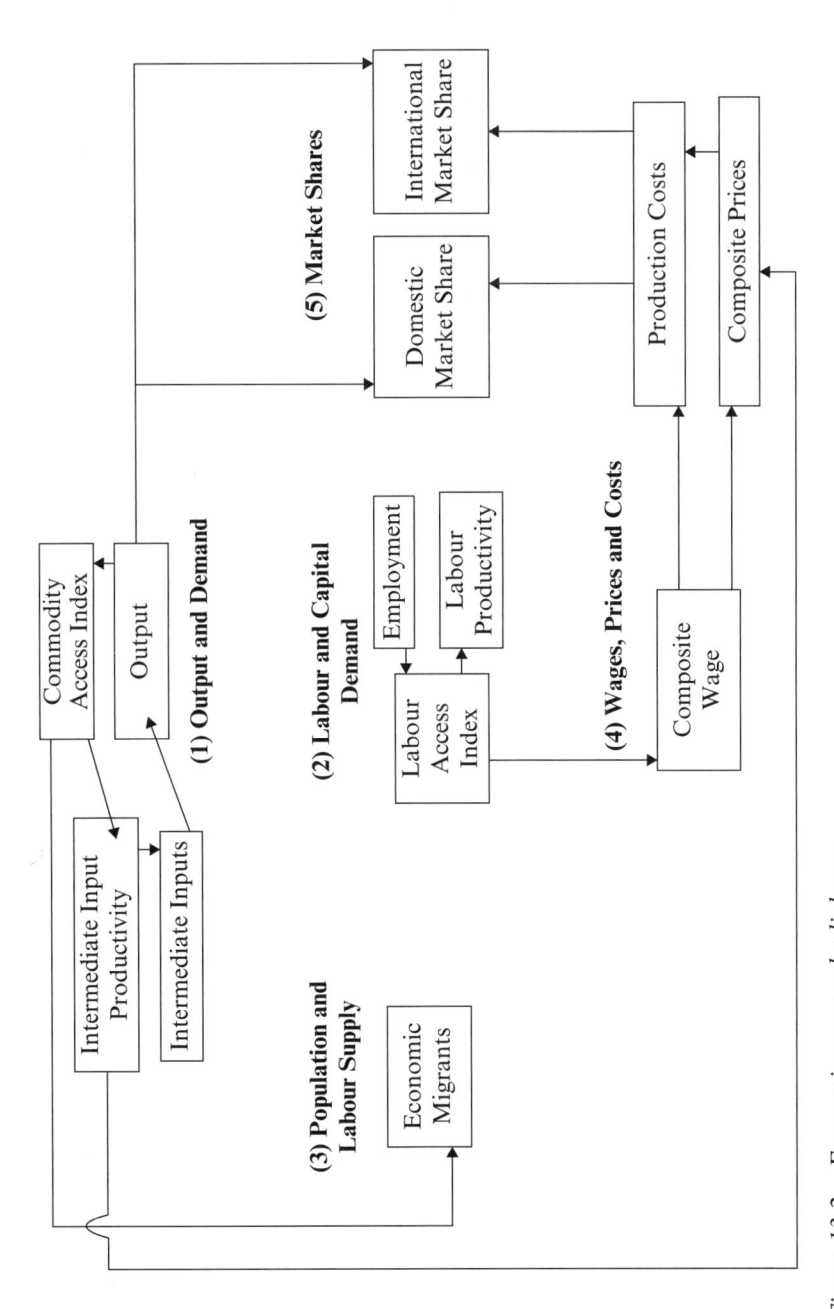

Figure 13.2 Economic geography linkages

labor force participation rate of each group determines the labor supply. These participation rates respond to changes in employment relative to the potential labor force and to changes in the real after-tax compensation rate. Migration includes retirement, military, international and economic migration. Economic migration is determined by the relative real after-tax compensation rate, relative employment opportunity and consumer access to variety.

The Wages, Prices and Costs block includes delivered prices, production costs, equipment cost, the consumption deflator, consumer prices, the price of housing and the wage equation. Economic geography concepts account for the productivity and price effects of access to specialized labor, goods and services.

These prices measure the value of the industry output, taking into account the access to production locations. This access is important due to the specialization of production that takes place within each industry, and because transportation and transaction costs of distance are significant. Composite prices for each industry are then calculated based on the production costs of supplying regions, the effective distance to these regions, and the index of access to the variety of output in the industry relative to the access by other uses of the product.

The cost of production for each industry is determined by cost of labor, capital, fuel and intermediate inputs. Labor costs reflect a productivity adjustment to account for access to specialized labor, as well as underlying compensation rates. Capital costs include costs of non-residential structures and equipment, while fuel costs incorporate electricity, natural gas and residual fuels.

The consumption deflator converts industry prices to prices for consumption commodities. For potential migrants, the consumer price is additionally calculated to include housing prices. Housing price changes from their initial level depend on changes in income and population density. Regional employee compensation changes are due to changes in labor demand and supply conditions, and changes in the national compensation rate. Changes in employment opportunities relative to the labor force and occupational demand change determine compensation rates by industry.

The Market Shares equations measure the proportion of local and export markets that are captured by each industry. These depend on relative production costs, the estimated price elasticity of demand, and effective distance between the home region and each of the other regions. The change in share of a specific area in any region depends on changes in its delivered price and the quantity it produces compared with the same factors for competitors in that market. The share of local and external markets then drives the exports from and imports to the home economy.

As shown in Figure 13.2, the Labor and Capital Demand block includes labor intensity and productivity, as well as demand for labor and capital. Labor force participation rate and migration equations are in the Population and Labor Supply block. The Wages, Prices and Costs block includes composite prices, determinants of production costs, the consumption price deflator, housing prices and the wage equations. The proportion of local, interregional and international markets captured by each region is included in the Market Shares block.

In this chapter we have used a version that bifurcates the US economy into border states and interior states, which provides a better spatial resolution of the analysis. However, because of limitations of space, we present only the national-level aggregation of the results. Unfortunately, the REMI model has several limitations in its application to estimating the economic impacts of a complete border closure. It should be noted, however, that practically all models would have trouble yielding credible estimates of such an extreme policy as this. In addition, REMI is generally oriented toward regional analysis within the US, as opposed to international analysis, and thus it has limited international trade features. Therefore, REMI does not include any explicit balance-of-payments or interest rate variables, nor does it measure international competitiveness. Moreover, it omits any explicit constraints on some major factors of production. The model does not contain some key 'price feedback loops' as well.[2] These limitations are also applicable to input–output models, and some of them are applicable to computable general equilibrium models as well (see Rose, 2005).

SIMULATIONS AND COMPARATIVE STATIC RESULTS

Shutdown of Imports

Major assumptions and simulation results
This simulation estimates the economic impacts on the US economy of a one-year halt in all imports from the rest of the world in response to an external threat to the US. The simulation is run in a 'comparative static' mode, meaning that this shock is analyzed in isolation, with business as usual proceeding in the rest of the economy with respect to exports, travel and migration. In 2005, US imports reached $1.53 trillion (2000$), or 13.3 percent of GDP. Hence, we would expect an import ban to have significant impacts.

An initial application of REMI for a complete shutdown of all imports yielded high positive economic impacts for the US. The major reason for this counter-intuitive outcome is that the REMI model automatically offsets all import losses by domestic production increases. In actuality, given labor and production capacity limitations and imperfect substitution in many sectors, it is impossible to offset all import losses by increasing domestic production. In many sectors, domestic goods substitution can only be achieved at a relatively higher cost (for example in oil and gas extraction and apparel manufacturing, where the majority of US domestic consumption is produced abroad).

Therefore, it is necessary to incorporate constraints such as capacity and production cost differentials into the REMI model to reflect the difficulty in expanding domestic production. We first assume that excess capacity can be utilized to make up part of the import shortfalls. Of course, not all excess capacity can be accessed due to reasons such as maintenance downtime. However, we believe it is reasonable to assume that excess capacity of 20 percent on average can be accessed in our simulated case (USDOC and USCB, 2006). We also assume that the utilization of excess capacity at this level will not result in noticeable production cost increases.

Next we calculate the gap of import replacement for each REMI sector after the use of excess capacity. For those sectors that have a remaining import replacement gap, we incorporate a cost penalty into the model to reflect the higher production cost that domestic producers will face for further expansion of their production. The calculation of this cost penalty involves two steps: (1) the calculation of cost differentials between imported goods and domestic counterparts at current production levels of the latter; and (2) further increases in these differentials with increased domestic output, reflecting upward-sloping supply curves.

Note that there is another likely adjustment to an import shock, and that is the diversion of exports as replacements. This strategy could be implemented whether US exports were embargoed by other countries or not. It will be discussed at greater length below.

Major economic impacts of an import shutdown with loss replacement by the use of excess capacity include: (1) a reduction of $666.3 billion in GDP, or a 5.8 percent decline from the baseline level in the year 2005; (2) a decrease in employment of about 19 million jobs, or a reduction of around 11 percent; (3) a decrease in total personal income of $427.3 billion, or −4.1 percent. These results indicate that a closure of all imports will cause significant negative impacts to the US economy. Though the increased demand for domestic substitutes would stimulate the economy, the production cost increase more than offsets the positive impacts (see Table 13.1 for simulation results for other economic indicators).

Table 13.1 Impacts of a complete import shutdown in the US for one year

Economic indicator	Difference from baseline	
	Level	%
Total employment (thousands)	−19 040	−10.99
Total GDP (billion 2000$)	−666	−5.82
Personal income (billion nominal $)	−427	−4.14
PCE price index	32.3	29.02
Real disposable personal income (billion 2000$)	−2087	−25.54
Demand (billion 2000$)	−2162	−11.89
Output (billion 2000$)	−812	−4.60
Labor productivity index	11.6	9.64
Relative delivered price index	0.426	42.58
Relative cost of production index	0.39	39.72
Imports from rest of world (billion 2000$)	−1525	−100.00
Self-supply (billion 2000$)	−637	−3.82
Exports to rest of world (billion 2000$)	−175	−17.72
Population (thousand)	0.563	0.00
Labor force (thousand)	−2187	−1.47

Note: Assumes import replacement after the use of excess capacity at the level of 20% in each sector.

Simulation method and data inputs

Before running the REMI simulation, policy variables that represent the direct impacts of the simulated events are determined. To simulate a complete shutdown of the US border to imports, the share of 'Imports from rest of world' for each sector is reduced by 100 percent for each of the relevant 66 REMI sectors. To incorporate the domestic production cost increases, we also changed the 'Production cost' variable for each REMI sector producing import substitutes. Appendix 13.A describes the methods and assumptions we followed to obtain the vector of sectoral production cost increases. The overall (weighted average) production cost increase for the case where only excess capacity was used and exports were not diverted is 52.45 percent. This represents an overall economy-wide 4.82 percent price increase.

Shutdown of Exports

Results and major assumptions

This simulation estimates the economic impact on the US of a one-year border cessation of all its exports to the rest of the world. Of course exporting goods from the US does not generate either a health or a security threat.

Table 13.2 Impacts of a complete export shutdown for the US for one year

Economic indicator	Difference from baseline	
	Level	%
Total employment (thousands)	−17240	−9.92
Total GDP (billion 2000$)	−1360	−11.89
Personal income (billion nominal $)	−787	−7.63
PCE price index	−0.817	−0.73
Real disposable personal income (billion 2000$)	−544	−6.66
Demand (billion 2000$)	−1832	−10.07
Output (billion 2000$)	−2603	−14.74
Labor productivity index	−4.1	−3.42
Relative delivered price index	−0.007752	−0.77
Relative cost of production index	−0.007759	−0.78
Imports from rest of world (billion 2000$)	−182	−11.94
Self-supply (billion 2000$)	−1649	−9.90
Exports to rest of world (billion 2000$)	2.6	0.27
Exogenous industry sales (billion 2000$)[a]	−956	n/a[b]
Population (thousand)	−0.06	0.00
Labor force (thousand)	−1966	−1.32

Notes:
[a] 'Exogenous industry sales' is used as the policy variable to zero out exports in the REMI model.
[b] The 2005 control level of 'Exogenous industry sales' is zero. Therefore, the calculation of percentage change is not applicable here.

However, a shutdown of US exports is relevant for three reasons. First, some US exports may be considered likewise contaminated. Second, other countries may retaliate against the shutdown of their imports to the US. Finally, the US may wish to divert some major portion of its exports to replace lost imports (for example, automobiles, clothing).

The simulation was among the most straightforward of all to run with the REMI model, requiring only a constraint that exports of all sectors equal zero. This simply represents a downward shift in a major element of final demand in the model.

Table 13.2 presents major economic impacts on the US economy: (1) GDP is predicted to decline about $1.36 trillion, or a decrease of 11.9 percent from the baseline level in 2005; (2) employment is reduced by about 17.2 million jobs, or −9.9 percent; and (3) total personal income decreases $0.79 trillion, or −7.6 percent.

The simulation results indicate that the negative impacts on the US economy from terminating the exports to the rest of the world are sizeable. The contraction in GDP results from the loss of demand from the international market, which in turn reduces employment opportunities and total personal income. The simulation results also show a decrease in imports of nearly 12 percent when exports are completely shut down. The major reason is that a decrease in production of exports reduces the demand for various production inputs from both domestic and international suppliers.

Simulation method and data inputs

Again, policy variables that affect the direct impacts of the simulated events are first specified. In this case, 'Industry Sales / International Exports (amount)' for each of the 66 REMI sectors are used to simulate the complete shutdown of exports to rest of the world. The 2005 base year export values are obtained from the REMI 'control model' for each sector and are used as the initial input data. 'Exogenous industry sales' is used as the policy variable to zero out exports in the REMI model in order to simulate a major export reduction. The simulation results in Table 13.2 show that the sum of 'Exogenous industry sales' and 'Exports to rest of world' is −$953.6 billion, which is equivalent to a 97 percent reduction in total exports in 2005. Though the simulation did not reach an outcome of 100 percent exports reduction, even after several iterations, we view this as a close representation of a total export shutdown.

Shutdown of International Travel

Results and major assumptions

We apply the international travel ban to both outbound and inbound traffic. In the case of outbound travel this reflects both the concern that disease may be contracted abroad, and possible retaliations by other countries to US border closure. A drop in international travel would reduce demand for US airlines, as well as other services and goods within the country. This would further reverberate throughout the economy in the form of general equilibrium effects. A mitigating effect that we modeled is a change in destinations by US residents, for example, substituting domestic for foreign visitors. In order to capture this effect we assumed that those who would have traveled outside the US, instead traveled within the country. This slight offsetting effect reduces the overall economic impacts associated with the loss of international travel to the US.[3] Assuming that the United States cuts off all international travel (outbound and inbound), we estimate economic impacts to be a loss of about $175 billion in GDP and a reduction in employment of about 3.4 million jobs (see Table 13.3).

Table 13.3 Impacts of complete shutdown of international travel with domestic substitution

Economic indicator	Difference from baseline	
	Level	%
Total employment (thousands)	−3375	−1.95
Total GDP (billion 2000$)	−175	−1.53
Personal income (billion nominal $)	−106	−1.02
PCE price index	−0.17	−0.15
Real disposable personal income (billion 2000$)	−68	−0.83
Demand (billion 2000$)	−329	−1.81
Output (billion 2000$)	−304	−1.72
Labor productivity index	0.72	0.59
Relative delivered price index	−0.002	−0.16
Relative cost of production index	−0.002	−0.16
Imports from rest of world (billion 2000$)	−24	−1.60
Self-supply (billion 2000$)	−305	−1.83
Exports to rest of world (billion 2000$)	0.53	0.05
Population (thousand)	−0.16	0.00
Labor force (thousand)	−384	−0.26

These impacts are considerably lower than those of both the import and export shutdowns.

Inputs and other assumptions

Our input data come from two sources: the Travel Industry Association of America (TIAA) (2002) and the US Department of Transportation (2005). The first source provides data on levels of tourism and total expenditure by international tourists within the US, as well as a regional breakdown of expenditure statistics. Unfortunately, the statistics provided are for 2000, while the REMI base year is 2005. In order to scale the level of international travel from 2000 to 2005, we compared the number of international flights in 2000 to 2005 using the US Department of Transportation (2000 and 2005) data, and found that international travel (inbound and outbound) grew by about 5.1 percent from 2000 to 2005. We then scaled the statistics provided by the TIAA (2002) by this growth rate to yield an estimate of 2005 expenditure and adjusted for inflation (see Appendix 13.B for detailed computations).

The two-region nature of the REMI model required that we disaggregate the airline travel data spatially. The TIAA breaks the US up into nine regions: New England, Middle Atlantic, East North Central, West

North Central, South Atlantic, East South Central, West South Central, Mountain and Pacific. Unfortunately, no state designation was provided for each region, so we assumed that the Pacific, South Atlantic, Middle Atlantic and New England regions would comprise the border states, and the East North Central, West North Central, East South Central, West South Central and Mountain regions would comprise the rest of the US. With this bifurcation, border states accounted for 79.3 percent of total spending of international travelers. For domestic travelers, this number is lower, with 55.9 percent of spending in border states and the rest in the interior states.

Shutdown of Immigration

Results and major assumptions

Documented migrant simulation   Documented migration provides the US with skilled and unskilled labor and this is reflected by REMI through its 'International migrant' policy variable. In 2005, REMI predicted that roughly 1 million international migrants entered the US. To implement this in REMI, we reduced documented international migration by 1 million workers. The results of this scenario were a drop in employment of 277,200, and a $17.7 billion reduction in GDP (see Table 13.4).

Figure 13.3 depicts how our policy simulation is incorporated into the REMI model. Circles, dotted lines and shaded text depict our modifications and inputs into the REMI model. Starting with documented migration, we adjusted the international migration policy variables that feed into the 'Demographic block' of the REMI model.[4] Once this change is made to the demographic block, it is translated to the other REMI blocks through the functional relationships represented by the solid arrows in Figure 13.3. Eventually, linkages in the model (again represented by the solid arrows) translate our changes in migration (represented by the dashed arrows) to changes in output.

Undocumented migrant simulation   While documented international labor was relatively easy to implement in the REMI model, undocumented migration required some different assumptions. From an economic perspective, undocumented labor benefits the economy through lower wages. If the US government is able to reduce or cut off this source of labor, we assume that producers will hire documented labor, thereby paying a higher wage for services with two macroeconomic effects: (1) demand is stimulated because labor has more income; and (2) production costs increase as wages increase.

Table 13.4 Impacts of shutdown of documented and undocumented migrants in 2005

Economic indicator	Documented migration difference from baseline		Undocumented migration difference from baseline	
	Level	%	Level	%
Total employment (thousands)	−277	−0.16	−394	−0.23
Total GDP (billion 2000$)	−18	−0.16	−24	−0.21
Personal income (billion nominal $)	−17	−0.17	−5	−0.05
PCE price index	0.02	0.02	0.27	0.24
Real disposable personal income (billion 2000$)	−15	−0.19	−23	−0.29
Demand (billion 2000$)	−27	−0.15	−46	−0.25
Output (billion 2000$)	−26	−0.15	−44	−0.25
Labor productivity index	0	0.00	0.02	0.02
Relative delivered price index	0	0.02	0	0.25
Relative cost of production index	0	0.02	0	0.25
Imports from rest of world (billion 2000$)	−2	−0.11	−2	−0.16
Self-supply (billion 2000$)	−26	−0.15	−43	−0.26
Exports to rest of world (billion 2000$)	−0.06	−0.01	−0.54	−0.06
Population (thousand)	−1012	−0.34	−0.03	0.00
Labor force (thousand)	−548	−0.37	−44	−0.03

Looking at Figure 13.3, two dashed arrows lead from the circle encompassing undocumented migration towards block number 4. The REMI model interprets an increase in wages as an increase in demand (the first effect we are modeling), but not necessarily an increase in production costs. For this reason we had to apply two sets of policy changes to the model, represented by the two dashed lines. The first policy change represents the increase in demand associated with replacing undocumented labor with documented labor. The second policy change represents the increase in production costs associated with replacing undocumented labor with documented labor.

To implement these changes, we made three major assumptions. First, we assume that 850,000 undocumented migrants must be replaced by documented labor. The number of undocumented migrants is based on the research by Passel (2006).[5] Second and third, we assume that undocumented labor earns about $330 per week (Passel, 2006) and documented

Note: Ovals, dashed lines and shaded text denote inputs and modifications to REMI.

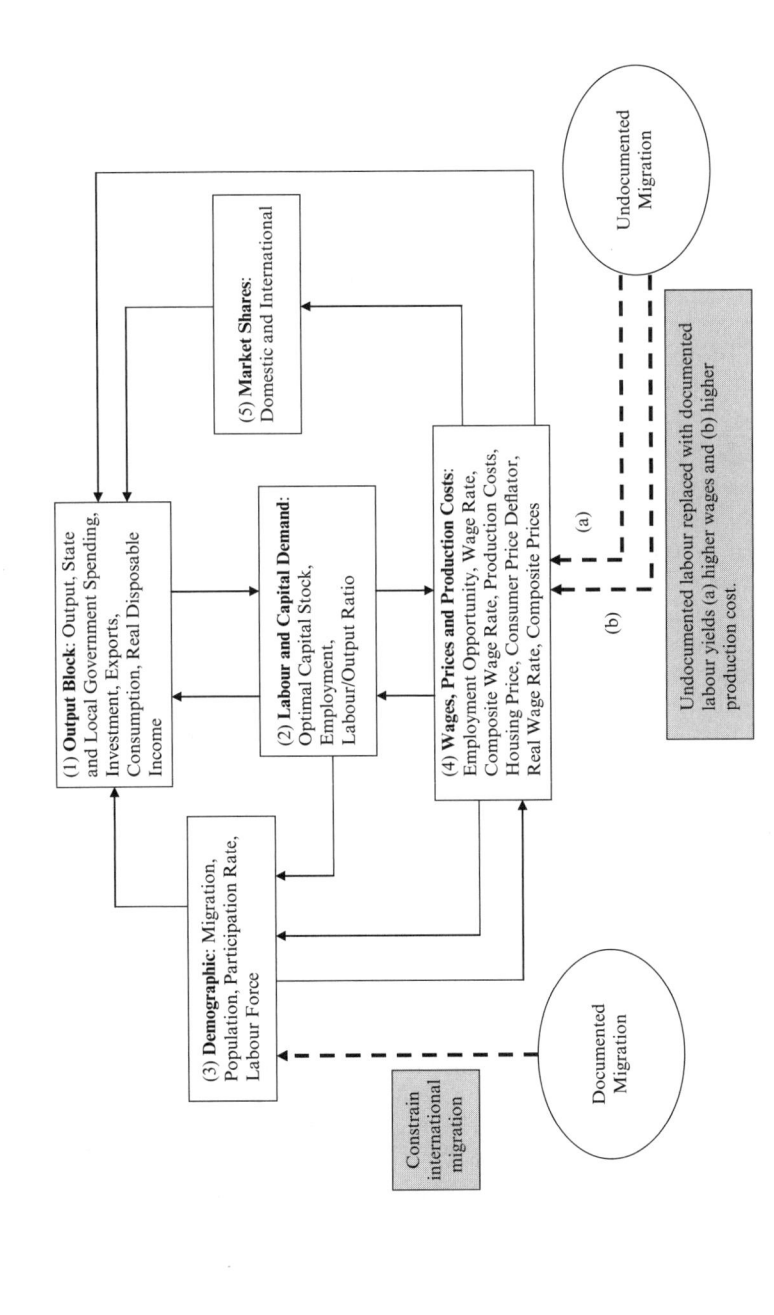

Figure 13.3 Migration linkages

labor earns about $609 per week (US Census 2005; the average wage of a high school graduate). Given these assumptions we find that a complete border closure is expected to reduce employment by 393 thousand jobs and GDP by $23 billion (see Table 13.4, 'Undocumented migration' column for more detailed results).

TOTAL IMPACTS

Shutdown of All Cross-border Activities: Simple Summation

In this and the next section, we examine the total effects of shutting down all cross-border activities. Simple summations of the economic impacts of the four individual closure simulations presented in the above sections are summarized in Table 13.5. The impact summations show that the total effects of a border closure to both goods and people result in a reduction in GDP of about $2.2 trillion, or about −20 percent and a reduction in employment of about 40.3 million jobs, or about −24 percent.

In a simultaneous shutdown of all cross-border activities, it is legitimate to assume export substitution for imports, that is, goods originally intended for export would be diverted to substitute for the lack of corresponding imports. A country the size of the US engages in a great deal of international 'cross-hauling' (that is, import and export of the same kinds of goods in the same period). If the US border is shut down for international trade, it is reasonable to assume that the exporters would instead sell their goods to the importers as middlemen, or directly to domestic customers. As an intermediate step to a simultaneous shutdown simulation that will be presented in the next section, we present a second version of simple summation that incorporates the consideration of export diversion to substitute for imports. Recall that earlier we utilized a vector of sectoral production cost increases to reflect the difficulty in further expansion of domestic production beyond 20 percent excess capacity. Under an import–export substitution case, the vector of sectoral production cost change is adjusted downward from 4.82 percent to 3.92 percent because the import replacement gap for most sectors is reduced with export substitution.[6] This second version of the simple summation of individual closure impacts is presented in Table 13.6. The differences in economic impacts are reflected in the 'Imports' and the 'Sum' columns. From a comparison of the 'Imports' column of Tables 13.5 and 13.6, inclusion of the resilience adjustment of export substitution reduces the loss in GDP associated with the import ban from $666 billion to $278 billion. The total ('Sum') column impact is reduced from $2.2 trillion to $1.8 trillion, or a lowering of the

Table 13.5 Simple summation of elements of complete shutdown of US borders: Version I (No export diversion)

| Economic indicator | Difference from baseline level ||||||
	Imports	Exports	Travel	Documented migrants	Undocumented migrants	Sum
Total employment (thousands)	−19 040	−17 240	−3375	−277	−394	−40 326
Total GDP (billion 2000$)	−666	−1360	−175	−18	−24	−2243
Personal income (billion nominal $)	−427	−787	−106	−17	−5	−1342
PCE price index	32	−0.82	−0.17	0.02	0.27	31
Real disposable personal income (billion 2000$)	−2087	−544	−68	−15	−23	−2737
Demand (billion 2000$)	−2162	−1832	−329	−27	−46	−4396
Output (billion 2000$)	−812	−2603	−304	−26	−44	−3789
Labor productivity index	11.61	−4.12	0.72	0.00	0.02	8.23
Relative delivered price index	0.43	−0.01	0.00	0.00	0.00	0.42
Relative cost of production index	0.40	−0.01	0.00	0.00	0.00	0.39
Imports from rest of world (billion 2000$)	−1525	−182	−24	−2	−2	−1735
Self-supply (billion 2000$)	−637	−1649	−305	−26	−4	−2621
Exports to rest of world (billion 2000$)	−175	3	0.53	−0.06	−0.54	−172
Population (thousand)	0.56	−0.06	−0.16	−1012	−0.03	−1012
Labor force (thousand)	−2187	−1966	−384	−548	−44	−5129

Table 13.6 Simple summation of elements of a complete shutdown of US borders: Version II (Export diversion)

Economic indicator	Difference from baseline level					
	Imports	Exports	Travel	Documented migrants	Undocumented migrants	Sum
Total employment (thousands)	−13110	−17240	−3375	−277	−394	−34396
Total GDP (billion 2000$)	−278	−1360	−175	−18	−24	−1855
Personal income (billion nominal $)	−200	−787	−106	−17	−5	−1115
PCE price index	27	−0.82	−0.17	0.02	0.27	26
Real disposable personal income (billion 2000$)	−1717	−544	−68	−15	−23	−2367
Demand (billion 2000$)	−1464	−1832	−329	−27	−46	−3698
Output (billion 2000$)	−80	−2603	−304	−26	−44	−3057
Labor productivity index	11	−4	0.72	0.00	0.02	7.74
Relative delivered price index	0.35	−0.01	0.00	0.00	0.00	0.34
Relative cost of production index	0.33	−0.01	0.00	0.00	0.00	0.32
Imports from rest of world (billion 2000$)	−1525	−182	−24	−1.70	−2.45	−1735
Self-supply (billion 2000$)	61	−1649	−305	−26	−43	−1962
Exports to rest of world (billion 2000$)	−142	3	0.53	−0.06	−0.54	−139
Population (000)	0.50	−0.06	−0.16	−1012	−0.03	−1012
Labor force (000)	−1503	−1966	−384	−548	−44	−4445

impact of more than 17 percent. The reduction in employment drops from 40.3 to 34.4 million jobs.

Shutdown of All Cross-border Activities: Simultaneous Simulation

Results and major assumptions
In the final scenario, we simulate a simultaneous shutdown of all cross-border activities to the US for one year. We assume that import losses are replaced by the use of excess capacity at a level of 20 percent, and by export substitution. This simulation will be contrasted with the prior comparative static simulations to determine whether the 'whole' is different from the sum of the parts, that is, whether the economic impacts of a simultaneous border closure of goods and people would be different from the sum of the individual shutdowns that we simulated and summarized earlier. Differences can arise from non-linearities and/or synergies. The latter would stem from complex functional relationships and non-linearities in the REMI model. This is in direct contrast to an I–O model, which is linear and relatively simple in terms of structure (for example, an absence of price–quantity interaction).

Simulation results for this 'simultaneous' case are presented in Table 13.7. Major economic impacts include: a reduction in GDP of about $1.19 trillion, or −10.4 percent from the baseline level; and a reduction in employment of about 22.1 million jobs, or a decrease of 12.8 percent. Overall, our results indicate that a closure of US borders to both goods and people will result in considerable impacts to the US economy. However, a comparison between the simultaneous simulation and the second version of simple summation (both of them incorporate the export substitution effects) shows that the simultaneous simulation yields smaller negative impacts to the economy, on the order of a 35 percent lower estimate than our second simple summation estimate. The differences between the comprehensive (simultaneous) simulation and the ordinary sum are due primarily to the non-linearity and/or synergies of the REMI model. With respect to the latter, the sectoral production cost increases affect all four factors (import, export, tourism and immigration) in a simultaneous closure simulation, and their interactive effects result in the different outcomes from the sum of individual simulations. Note that a price increase at the margin, given the law of one price, affects all units sold, and has a much greater effect than if one focuses only on the increment of goods production associated with the shutdown.

Simulation method and data inputs
Policy variables used in this simulation are a combination of all the variables we used in the previous four individual closure simulations:

Table 13.7 Simultaneous simulation of elements of a complete shutdown of the US borders to people and goods

Economic indicator	Difference from baseline Level	%
Total employment (thousands)	−22130	−12.77
Total GDP (billion 2000$)	−1194	−10.44
Personal income (billion nominal $)	−712	−6.90
PCE price index	16.68	14.98
Real disposable personal income (billion 2000$)	−1534	−18.78
Demand (billion 2000$)	−2319	−12.75
Output (billion 2000$)	−1860	−10.53
Labor productivity index	6.411	5.32
Relative delivered price index	0.218	21.73
Relative cost of production index	0.182	18.20
Imports from rest of world (billion 2000$)	−1523	−99.89
Self-supply (billion 2000$)	−796	−4.78
Exports to rest of world (billion 2000$)	−103	−10.45
Exogenous industry sales (billion 2000$)	−960	n/a[a]
Population (thousand)	−1012	−0.34
Labor force (thousand)	−3045	−2.04

Note: [a] The 2005 control level of 'Exogenous industry sales' is zero. Therefore, the calculation of percentage change is not applicable here.

(1) imports are constrained to zero by reducing 100 percent the share of 'Imports from rest of the world' for each sector; (2) exports are constrained to zero by reducing the amount of 'Industry sales / International exports' by the value of total exports to the rest of world in each sector; (3) a net loss in international travel is simulated by reductions in 'Exogenous final demand'; (4) the border closure of legal immigrants is simulated by a decrease in 'International migration of all ages and all groups' by 1 million; and (5) the border closure of illegal immigrants is simulated by considering two effects in the model: (a) the increase in 'Wage compensation'; and (b) the 'Production cost' increase due to the higher labor costs. Also, in this comprehensive border closure case, we used the vector of sectoral production cost change that is derived under the assumption of both 20 percent excess capacity utilization and the diversion of exports to substitute for import shortfalls.

INTERPRETATION OF THE RESULTS

Border Closure Duration

Thus far all of our simulations have been performed on an annual basis. This is due more to the standard features of the REMI model than to policy considerations. That is, REMI – as is the case with other models – is normally geared to simulating annual impacts. In fact, REMI projects impacts on an annual basis beyond the initial impact year, because some effects are dynamic or include lags. However, because these effects were less than a few percentage points different from those reported in Tables 13.1–13.7, they have not been presented here.

In all likelihood, a shutdown of the US borders to a terrorist or health threat would not last as long as one year. More realistic are durations of three to six months. Accordingly, we have adjusted our major results of a simultaneous shutdown to these time periods in Table 13.8. The figures represent an arithmetic interpolation of the annual results. They also include an updating to 2006 current dollars from the base of 2000 constant dollars reported earlier.

For a six-month shutdown, GDP impacts are estimated to be just under $700 billion, or a little over 5 percent downturn in annual terms. Employment losses are estimated at just over 11 million, or just over 6 percent. For the three-month shutdown, GDP losses are estimated at about $350 billion, or about 2.6 percent. Employment losses are estimated

Table 13.8   Economic impacts of a complete shutdown of the US borders for various time periods

Economic indicator	One year Level	One year %	Six months Level	Six months %[a]	Three months Level	Three months %[a]
Gross domestic product (billion 2006 constant dollars)	−$1392	−10.44	−$696	−5.22	−$348	−2.61
Total employment (thousands)	−22,130	−12.77	−11,065	−6.39	−5533	−3.19
Personal income (billion 2006 constant dollars)	−$830	−6.90	−$415	−3.45	−$207	−1.73

Note: [a] Percent calculated on an annual basis.

to be about 5.5 million, or slightly above 3 percent. To put these results in context, most post-World War II recessions resulted in unemployment increases of between 2 and 4 percent of base levels, so the three-month shutdown would fall into the ordinary recession range if viewed in terms of an annual averaging. At the same time, the losses still represent a 12.77 percent reduction in employment during the three-month period, and from that perspective come close to what would be referred to as a brief 'depression'.

How realistic is our simple arithmetic adjustment of the annual REMI results for shorter timescales? It is likely to underestimate the impacts as the duration gets shorter, because there is less time to adjust to the dislocation. At the same time, various resilience adjustments to be noted below are likely to be more effective in the short run. Still, we do not have sufficient information to know the extent to which these factors offset each other.

Investment Uncertainty

One source of realism that is not modeled by REMI is the financial market. REMI has an investment equation that is a function of the last period's capital stock, the current demand for capital, the depreciation rate and a measure of how quickly investment is turned into capital. This measure of investment ignores several major predictors of borrowing, namely the interest rate and uncertainty. Here we discuss the impacts of these two factors on our results.

First, large shocks can increase uncertainty. With greater uncertainty, firms' calculations of future profits become more difficult, making borrowing less attractive. For instance, currently China is the United States' fastest-growing importer (*The Economist*, 2007). A sudden cut in trade between these two countries would seriously harm the trade-related industries and their investment. Further, with higher uncertainty in the economy, asymmetric information increases, thereby reducing credit and lending, further reducing investment.

Second, the interest rate can be affected in a less obvious manner. If the government constrains all imports and exports, it sets the current account deficit to zero. This account is related to the capital and investment account through the balance of payments. Prior to the government shutdown, countries which sold goods in the US recycled the dollars they earned by purchasing US government bonds, which in turn kept yields relatively lower. Cutting imports reduces this cycle, driving bond prices lower and yields higher.

Looking at Figure 13.4, we see that the import and export shutdown affects REMI's 'Market Shares' block. This activates the linkages within

Figure 13.4 Investment linkages

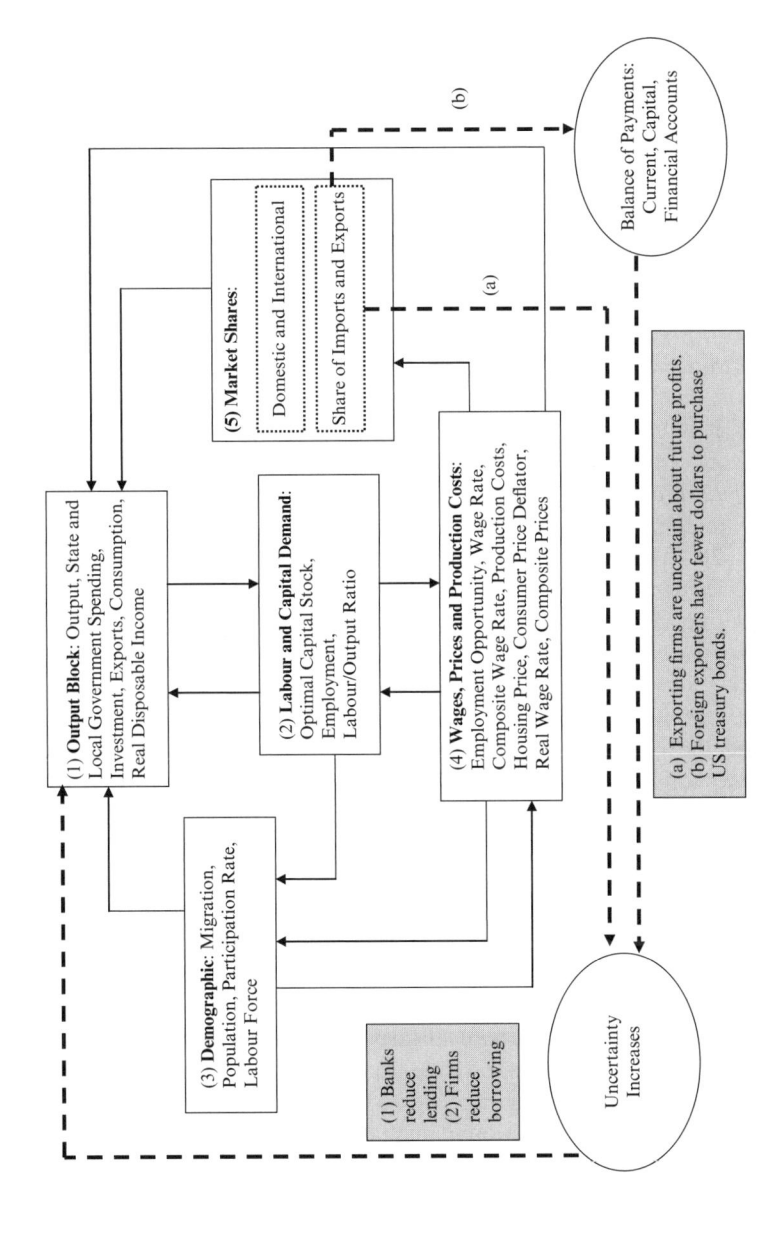

Note: Ovals, dashed lines and shaded text denote inputs and modifications to REMI model.

the model represented by the solid arrows (note, however, that these exclude geographic linkages). As imports and exports fall, output and the balance of payments are affected. This is shown by the dashed lines leading from the 'Share of imports and exports' dotted block within the 'Market Shares' box. As the current account deficit changes, uncertainty increases and foreigners have fewer dollars to invest in US assets. Both of these factors decrease investment within the 'Output' block.

The elasticity of investment in relation to uncertainty and the interest rate are not easy to calculate. However, in the REMI model, a 1 percent decline in investment leads to a $10 billion decline in GDP. Assuming investment falls by between 5 and 10 percent, GDP would fall additionally between $50 and $100 billion.

Resilience Adjustments

'Resilience' is increasingly used to describe how an economy withstands a major shock (see, for example, Chernick, 2005). Unfortunately, it is rarely defined and at risk of becoming a vacuous buzzword, despite its importance in dampening extreme events like a complete border shutdown. Rose (2004, 2007) has defined economic resilience as the ability to maintain production levels when shocked (static resilience) and to recover quickly (dynamic resilience). Both of these types of resilience are measured in relation to a worst-case scenario for output reduction and recovery time for a given shock.

Resilience applies at the level of the individual firm or household, the market and the regional economy as a whole. Examples at the micro level include conservation of critical inputs, input substitution, use of inventories, business relocation, technological change and rescheduling of lost production. Resilience at the market level emanates from the allocating mechanism of markets and prices, as well as adaptive responses such as information clearing-houses that match customers and suppliers to speed adjustment to the dislocation of contracting arrangements. At the macro level, imports of goods and the overall diversity and strength of the economy are sources of resilience.

Only a few studies have actually measured resilience. Moreover, we know from the recent Hurricane Katrina experience that it can be severely eroded by a truly large shock to the system. The few cases where resilience has been measured relate to economic impacts of water and power system outages due to earthquakes or terrorism. Though limited, some of these are more applicable to a border shutdown case than would be the Hurricane Katrina example, because the utility shutdown involves damage to only one system, but leaves the rest of the economy unscathed. That is, in the case of the utility shutdown, factories are not damaged and can soon begin normal operation. This is also the case when a self-imposed embargo is lifted. Estimates of the business resilience to a water outage by Tierney (1997) following the Northridge earthquake are about 75 percent (that is, the economic impacts are about 75 percent lower than a linear model would predict). Analysis by Rose et al. (2007) of a hypothetical terrorist attack on the Los Angeles power system of a two-week duration found resilience to be in the order of 90 percent. The major factors of business resilience in the Tierney study were substitution and conservation, while in the Rose et al. study the major resilience option was production rescheduling.

In the analysis in this chapter, we have incorporated several aspects of resilience. Foremost is the potential diversion of exports to substitute for lack of imports. This analysis also includes an adjustment for excess capacity to help produce import replacements. Yet another source of resilience was the substitution of domestic vacations for international destinations on the part of American tourists. The export diversion and excess capacity options were by far the most effective, and resulted in dampening the negative shock by several hundred billion dollars.

What remaining source of resilience might have a strong effect on the results? It is unlikely that conservation would be able to reduce the impacts by more than a few percentage points. Labor–capital substitution is modeled in REMI, but we were not able to perform a test of the extent of its effectiveness. Other types of input substitution could not be modeled, but again they are unlikely to be able to reduce the shock by more than a few percentage points. The same is true of the use of inventories. Moreover, business relocation is a very limited option in this case, despite the increasing trend toward offshore production.

Perhaps the largest single source of resilience that we did not formally model is production rescheduling. For short-duration business disruptions, there is no reason that factories cannot work overtime or extra shifts to make up a good deal of lost production (Sheffi, 2006). Production rescheduling is less likely to be effective in service sectors because of a fall-off in demand (for example, entertainment, cleaning), but these are not typically imported goods and are only likely to suffer supply-side constraints if faced with limits on energy use. Overall, it is not unreasonable to estimate that the negative impacts of a complete shutdown could be reduced by 25–50 percent for cases of short duration. Another factor lending weight to this conclusion is the pent-up demand that has stimulated expansion following instances where consumption was restrained for a lengthy period, such as just after World War II. Of course, in the case of a border closure, there is also a decrease in income, so the pent-up demand is not as great.

The final point is how resilience is affected by the duration of the event.

Some resilience options wane with time (for example, inventories, conservation), while others improve over time (for example, input substitution, technological change). It is likely that the potential for production rescheduling will also decrease over time, as customers (in this case, international ones) will find other suppliers, and many of them likely to do so on a permanent basis. Hence, one might expect production rescheduling to decay by 50 percent each three-month period. Thus, for a six-month embargo, the major remaining resilience option not explicitly modeled in this chapter would, as a lower bound, reduce the economic impacts of a complete border shutdown presented in Table 13.8 by little more than 10 percent.[7]

Macro Policy Mitigation

Another reason that impacts of a complete border shutdown might be mitigated stems from counteracting government policies. These would include a combination of fiscal and monetary policies, as well as other forms. Some of the policy adjustments are automatic, as in the case of unemployment benefits. Others, such as interest rate and money supply adjustments, would be deliberate. Past experiences during (and after) the Arab Oil Embargo indicate that such policies might be of only limited success. Other policy responses would include accessing the US Strategic Petroleum Reserve, but the indications are that this is rarely done, because of the priority of using this back-up source of supply for times of military tensions rather than countercyclical economic needs. Yet another set of policies might include government facilitation of market adjustments by matching customers who have lost suppliers with suppliers who have lost customers during the turmoil of a complete border shutdown. Still another set of remedial policies would be easing anti-trust strictures against cooperation among firms.

CONCLUSION

Our simulations of a complete shutdown of the US borders to both trade and people for one year predict a reduction in GDP of as much as $1.4 trillion measured in 2006 dollars, or about 10.5 percent of GDP. Employment losses are predicted to be more than 22 million, or more than 12 percent below base levels. In consideration of several relevant factors, we suggest that these figures can be linearly adjusted for more likely shorter time spans. The two major factors affecting the results are export and import shutdowns. Curtailment of international travel is a far smaller influence but still significant, while a halt in in-migration has negligible effects on the results.

The estimates should be considered upper bounds. We included several aspects of inherent and adaptive resilience, such as input substitution and domestic excess capacity, but we did omit several others. Moreover, we did not include the effects of counteracting government policies to cushion the shock.

Thus, our results do not incorporate all potential shocks and countervailing factors, and the REMI model (as with most models) was not designed to handle such large shocks. Nevertheless, this study should prove useful in that it investigates the major channels through which a border closure would affect the US economy (trade, migration, travel) and offers results from enhancing a well-regarded and widely used model.

Finally, it should be noted that we focused entirely on the cost side of the ledger. A complete assessment of the decision to close the US borders needs to also consider the benefits of that action (avoided losses from a terrorist attack or health emergency), with due consideration of the risk involved (the probability of occurrence of the threat).

Another objective of this chapter was to examine how well the REMI Economic–Demographic Simulation Model performed in a homeland security context. The model did yield reasonable results, but not without a good deal of supplementary data and their refinement, as well as significant modification of the model and how it was run. However, not all homeland security applications would be so demanding.

NOTES

* The research in this chapter was supported by a contract from the US Department of Homeland Security. The authors wish to thank Eric Schneider, George Treyz and Fred Treyz of REMI for their help in developing the scenarios and for running some of the model simulations. We also wish to thank our colleagues Bumsoo Lee, Peter Gordon and Jiyoung Park for helpful suggestions and data. Any views expressed in this chapter are solely those of the authors and do not represent the views of the funding agency or any of the institutions with which the authors are affiliated. Also, any errors or omissions are solely the responsibility of the authors.

1. The lower bound impact was found by increasing oil prices slowly over two years. The upper bound involves a sharp price increase.
2. For example, an initial application of REMI yielded a positive economic impact of reducing US imports to zero, because it held demand relatively constant and automatically simulated making up the shortfall by increasing domestic production and employment by more than 25 percent. It was necessary, therefore, explicitly to incorporate labor force constraints and a cost penalty for higher-cost domestic production (net of transport cost savings) into the analysis. Different refinements were needed for other types of closures, as will be discussed below.
3. If the US shuts down the border in response to an external threat, it is likely that domestic tourism will increase as those who would have traveled outside the country substitute for domestic destinations. However, if the border closure is in response to an outbreak of avian influenza, then this mitigating scenario is less likely. In such a

case, the negative impacts to the economy would be greater than the results presented here.
4. The REMI model is comprised of five main 'modeling blocks'. They are 'Output, Labor and Capital', 'Demographic', 'Wages', 'Prices and Production Costs', and finally 'Market Shares'. Each of these blocks is related mathematically, with this relation represented by the solid arrow. The direction of the arrow denotes causality. For instance, the labor and capital demand block affects output, and output in turn affects the labor and capital demand block. This is represented by the two arrows pointing in opposite directions between the blocks.
5. Further, we assume some of these migrants do not work, and we make additional assumptions on the industrial sectors they work in. (see Appendix 13.C for more detail).
6. For sectors where exports are diverted to replace imports, this is not an expansion of production, but simply a rerouting of existing production. Therefore, these substitution actions will not yield production cost increases.
7. In future research, we plan to utilize a computable general equilibrium (CGE) model to analyze the border closure scenario. This modeling approach is likely to be more facile and comprehensive than the REMI model. For example, it will be able to compute the effects of import substitution and export diversion, including price changes, in a much more straightforward manner, and without any special modeling adjustment. Substitution for international travel and other pent-up demand will be automatic. Moreover, several additional types of resilience can be modeled. This is also true of several types of remedial policies, such as unemployment insurance. The major drawback of the CGE approach is that the adjustments may be too facile, in that they are assumed to be costless and the economy is assumed to readily return to equilibrium. These 'inherent' shortcomings can be rectified to a great extent by using short-run substitution elasticities and by incorporating various types of disequilibria (see, for example, Rose and Liao, 2005; Rose, 2005).

REFERENCES

Abeysinghe, T. (2001), 'Estimation of direct and indirect impact of oil price on growth', *Economic Letters*, **37**, 147–53.
Chernick, H. (ed.) (2005), *Resilient City*, New York: Russell Sage Foundation.
Ciscar, J.C., P. Russ, L. Parousos and N. Stroblos (2004), 'Vulnerability of the EU economy to oil shocks: a general equilibrium analysis with the GEM-E3 model', Paper presented at the 13th annual conference of the European Association of Environmental and Resource Economics, Budapest, Hungary.
Dalsgaard, T., C. Andre and P. Richardson (2001), 'Standard shocks in the OECD interlink model', OECD Economics Department Working Paper 306.
The Economist (2007), 'America's fear of China', 17 May.
Gordon, P., J. Moore, J. Park and H. Richardson (2007), 'Estimating the economic impacts of an attack on the commercial airline industry', *Risk Analysis*, **27** (3), 505–12.
Greene, D., D. Jones and P. Leiby (1998), 'The outlook for US oil dependence', *Energy Policy*, **26** (1), 55–69.
Hunt, B., P. Isard and D. Laxton (2001), 'The macroeconomic effects of higher oil prices', IMW Working Paper 01/14, Washington, DC: Internationaler Wahrungfonds.
Jimenez-Rodriguez, R. and M. Sanchez (2004), 'Oil price shocks and real GDP growth: empirical evidence for some OECD countries', European Central Bank Working Paper 362.

Minnesota IMPLAN Group (MIG) (2006), *Impact Analysis for Planning (IMPLAN) System*, Stillwater, OK: MN.

Passel, J.S. (2006), 'The size and characteristics of the unauthorized migrant population in the US: estimates based on the March 2005 Current Population Survey', Research Report, Pew Hispanic Center, Washington, DC: Pew Charitable Trusts.

Regional Economic Models, Inc. (REMI) (2006), 'The REMI policy analysis and simulation model', Amherst, MA.

Rose, A. (2004), 'Defining and measuring economic resilience to disasters', *Disaster Prevention and Management*, **13**, 307–14.

Rose, A. (2005), 'Analyzing terrorist threats to the economy: a computable general equilibrium approach', in H. Richardson, P. Gordon and J. Moore (eds), *Economic Impacts of Terrorist Attacks*, Cheltenham, UK and Northampton, MA, USA: Edward Elgar, pp. 196–217.

Rose, A. (2007), 'Economic resilience to disasters: multidisciplinary origins and contextual dimensions', *Environmental Hazards*, **7** (4), 383–98.

Rose, A. and S. Liao (2005), 'Modeling regional economic resilience to disasters: a computable general equilibrium analysis of water service disruptions', *Journal of Regional Science*, **45** (1), 75–112.

Rose, A., G. Oladosu and S. Liao (2007), 'Business interruption impacts of a terrorist attack on the electric power system of Los Angeles: customer resilience to a total blackout', *Risk Analysis*, **27** (3), 513–31.

Schneider, M. (2004), 'The impact of oil price changes on growth and inflation', *Monetary Policy and the Economy*, **2**, 27–36.

Sheffi, Y. (2006), *The Resilient Enterprise*, Cambridge, MA: MIT Press.

Tierney, K. (1997), 'Impacts of recent disasters on businesses: the 1993 Midwest floods and the 1994 Northridge Earthquake', in B. Jones (ed.), *Economic Consequences of Earthquakes: Preparing for the Unexpected*, Buffalo, NY: National Center for Earthquake Engineering Research, pp. 189–222.

Travel Industry Association of America (TIAA) (2002), *Expenditure Patterns of Travelers in the United States*, Washington, DC: TIAA.

US Bureau of Economic Analysis (USBEA) (2007), *National Economic Accounts, Table 1.1.5*

US Bureau of Labor Statistics (USBLS) (2006), *Producer Price Index and Consumer Price Index*.

US Census Bureau (2004), *2002 Economic Census*.

US Census Bureau (2005), *Community Survey*.

US Census Bureau (2006a), *US Imports of Merchandise, Statistical Month – December 2005*, Data DVD.

US Census Bureau (2006b), *Current Industrial Reports*.

US Department of Agriculture (USDA) (2007a), *Farm–Retail Price Spreads (Selected Items, US, 2003–2006)*.

US Department of Agriculture (USDA) (2007b), *2005–2006 Statistical Highlights: Crops*.

US Department of Commerce (USDOC), Economics and Statistics Administration (ESA), and US Census Bureau (USCB) (2006), *Manufacturers' Utilization of Plant Capacity: 2005*.

US Department of Transportation (DOT) (2000), 'Bureau of Transportation Statistics, Air Carrier Statistics (Form 41 Traffic), Table T-100 (All Carriers)'.

US Department of Transportation (DOT) (2005), 'Bureau of Transportation Statistics, Air Carrier Statistics (Form 41 Traffic), Table T-100 (All Carriers)'.
US Energy Information Administration (EIA) (2006), *US Petroleum Data on Prices and Imports/Exports*.

APPENDIX 13.A DETAILED DERIVATION OF SECTORAL PRODUCTION COST INCREASE

In our study, we assume that as much of the shortfall of imports as possible would be replaced by the use of domestic excess capacity. Further production expansion is possible under extreme conditions, as evidenced by US experience during World War II, but not without many hardships. For one, expansion of production beyond the use of 20 percent excess capacity would cause significant cost increases in production because domestic substitutes are generally more expensive than imported goods. Moreover, supply curves slope upwards, so that production cost differentials increase with expanded production. In order to estimate the sectoral production cost increase to be used in REMI, we undertook the following calculations: (1) estimate the import replacement gap in each sector; (2) estimate the price differentials between imported goods and their domestic substitutes; (3) calculate production cost increases to serve as inputs in REMI.

Import Replacement Gaps

The import replacement gap for each sector is calculated under two different replacement scenarios. In the first scenario, we only allow the utilization of excess capacity of domestic production at the level of 20 percent to make up the loss in imports. The second scenario is an import–export interactive case, which allows not only the use of excess capacity, but also the full use of exports as substitution of imports.

The calculation of the import replacement gap was undertaken at a disaggregated sectoral level, based on 2004 US 509-sector Input–Output Table. Then we aggregated the results to the sectoral classification of the REMI model. Table 13.A1 presents the import replacement gaps computed under the two replacement scenarios. The table only presents sectors that have a replacement gap. For those sectors that have zero import replacement gap, we assume that there would be no noticeable production cost changes in the sector.

Price Differentials

Shutting down imports from the rest of the world to the US would cause price increases in the domestic market due to the price differentials between imported goods and their domestic substitutes. Given a shortage of imported goods, domestic production needs to be increased to meet the demand of the consumers. Though comparative advantage does not

Table 13.A1 Sectoral import replacement gap

	REMI sector[1]	Scenario I[2]		Scenario II[3]	
		Import replacement gap (million $)	Domestic production level gap (%)	Import replacement gap (million $)	Domestic production level gap (%)
1	Forestry, fishing	7 560	19.19	4 705	11.94
3	Oil & gas extraction	110 907	76.71	108 545	75.08
4	Mining (except oil & gas)	1 233	2.62	944	2.01
8	Wood product mfg	4 693	4.82	1 787	1.84
9	Nonmetallic mineral product mfg	5 674	5.22	5 091	4.68
10	Primary metal mfg	13 545	8.54	8 025	5.06
11	Fabricated metal product mfg	8 559	3.40	5 838	2.32
12	Machinery mfg	19 786	6.76	8 990	3.07
13	Computer & electronic mfg	81 542	15.97	48 498	9.50
14	Electrical equip. & appliance mfg	22 803	19.33	11 157	9.46
15	Motor vehicle mfg	111 719	22.89	84 234	17.26
16	Transportation equip. mfg excl. motor vehicles	4 122	2.03	2 922	1.44
17	Furniture & related product mfg	14 051	17.58	12 406	15.52
18	Miscellaneous mfg	44 430	35.39	34 782	27.70
19	Food mfg	3 559	0.62	2 001	0.35
20	Beverage & tobacco product mfg	4 989	3.38	3 706	2.51
21	Textile mills	3 410	7.38	247	0.53
22	Textile product mills	4 158	11.66	2 931	8.22
23	Apparel mfg	75 567	158.70	71 406	149.96
24	Leather & allied product mfg	23 902	317.51	22 980	305.26
25	Paper mfg	987	0.56	350	0.20
26	Printing & related support activities	637	1.35	475	1.01
28	Chemical mfg	1 413	0.23	1 394	0.22
29	Plastics & rubber products mfg	2 888	1.68	435	0.25

Notes:
1. Those sectors that have zero import replacement gaps are not included.
2. This replacement scenario allows the use of excess capacity at the level of 20%, but no export diversion for imports.
3. This replacement scenario assumes the use of excess capacity at the level of 20% plus full export diversion for imports.

necessarily mean that all imports are cheaper than domestic counterparts, in most sectors domestic substitutes are more expensive. Production cost increases even further as producers move along upward-sloping supply curves.

The data source for the price of imported goods is the Foreign Trade Statistics of the US Census Bureau. Unit prices of imported products are not directly reported in this database, however. In order to estimate the unit price, we accessed the import data at the HTS (Harmonized Tariff Schedule) ten-digit level in terms of both quantity and value. Unit price is computed by dividing the total value (including tariff) of one imported commodity by its total imported quantity. Several sources are used to obtain the price of domestic commodities, which include the US Department of Agriculture, the US Census Bureau and the Energy Information Administration. We used the Current Industrial Reports of the Census Bureau as the major source for manufacturing goods (US Census Bureau 2006b). Again, in many cases, prices are derived from quantity and value data.

Because of data availability and time manageability, it is impossible for us to estimate sectoral price differentials based on every commodity produced by each sector. Instead, we collected data for sample commodities for most sectors that have an import replacement gap, and used the price differentials of the individual commodities to represent the sector. For sectors where more than one commodity's price differential was tabulated, a weighted average level is computed for the sector, using total import values of each commodity as weights. Table 13.A2 presents the price differentials for imports and their domestic substitutes.

Sectoral Production Cost Increase

The final step is to determine the effect of the import substitutes on the sectoral production cost increase, which will be used as input in the REMI model. This cost increase is computed by multiplying the price differential of the sector by the proportion of total import value to the gross output of the sector. Taking the motor vehicle manufacturing sector as an example, the price differential we calculated for this sector is 8.2 percent. Imports equal 53.8 percent of total gross output in this sector. Therefore, the production cost increase is computed as 8.2 percent × 53.8 percent = 4.4 percent. Further, we assume that the production cost increases 50 percent for every additional 20 percent of the import replacement gap (that is, a stepwise supply curve), and use 200 percent as a cap on sectoral production cost increase. For motor vehicle manufacturing, after the use of excess capacity (at a level of 20 percent) and full export diversion, the import replacement gap is 23 percent. Thus, the final production cost increase we used in REMI

Table 13.A2 Price differential of imports and their domestic substitutes

Sector/Commodity	Domestic price		Import			Price Differential (%)
			Value	Price		
Farm (agricultural products)						
Beef	4.09	$/lb	28 110 339	3.74	$/lb	9.48
Tomato	0.91	$/kg	192 156 743	0.85	$/kg	8.03
				weighted avg		7.23
Forestry & logging; Fishing hunting & trapping						
Wood (oak)	143.60	$/m³	2 430 074	157.58	$/m3	−8.87
Oil & gas extraction						
Crude oil	56.64	$/barrel	184 428 952 900	49.9	$/barrel	13.51
Mining (except oil & gas)						
Copper	3.35	$/ckg	460 051	2.07	$/ckg	62.17
Nonmetallic mineral product manufacturing						
Building brick, common brick or facing brick	0.23	$/brick	14 876	0.30	$/brick	−24.94
Clay floor and wall tile	14.00	$/m²	2 257 926	9.21	$/m²	51.99
				weighted avg		51.49

Primary metal manufacturing					
Steel mill products	830.99	$/tonne	34 194 305 000	809.21	$/tonne	2.69
Machinery manufacturing					
Powered lawn and hedge trimmers	86.49	$/unit	200 014 000	70.01	$/unit	23.53
Pneumatic fluid power valves	38.40	$/unit	410 818 000	11.26	$/unit	241.10
				weighted avg		169.86
Computer and electronic product manufacturing					
Computers, digital, analog, hybrid, and other	1 538.67	$/unit	29 089 923 000	720.08	$/unit	113.68
Nonimpact laser printers	182.26	$/unit	3 260 091 000	311.63	$/unit	−41.52
Point-of-sale terminals and funds-transfer devices	1 703.47	$/unit	745 106 000	310.91	$/unit	447.90
				weighted avg		105.92
Electrical equipment, appliance and component manufacturing					
Microwave ovens	269.50	$/unit	1 134 877 000	62.36	$/unit	332.19
Gas ranges, ovens, and surface cooking units	410.89	$/unit	1 312 463 000	208.63	$/unit	96.95
Electric fans (except industrial)	18.44	$/unit	1 043 141 000	37.81	$/unit	−51.24
Air space heaters, portable, fan-forced type	34.47	$/unit	374 819 000	0.02	$/unit	81.50
				weighted avg		124.53

Table 13.A2 (continued)

Sector/Commodity	Domestic price		Value	Import	Price	Price Differential (%)
Motor vehicles						
Motor vehicles (for the transport of persons)	16491	$/per vehicle	128 501 545 296	15071	$/per vehicle	9.42
Motor vehicles (for the transport of goods)	23313	$/per vehicle	17 140 810 674	23569	$/per vehicle	−1.09
Apparel manufacturing				weighted avg		8.19
Gloves and mittens	6.88	$/pair	250 880 000	4.01	$/pair	71.52
	14.15	$/pair	130 081 000	7.48	$/pair	89.23
	12.26	$/pair	53 020 000	7.20	$/pair	70.27
Men's and boys' apparel:						
Suits	159.62	$/unit	742 986 410	54.88	$/unit	190.85
Dress and sport coats	134.85	$/unit	797 625 979	32.04	$/unit	320.82
Other coats, jackets, vests, and ski apparel	40.16	$/unit	3 020 047 293	10.82	$/unit	271.04
Tops	3.61	$/unit	8 013 942 351	4.03	$/unit	−10.54
Bottoms	10.84	$/unit	5 086 446 191	6.21	$/unit	74.60
Swimwear	11.40	$/unit	180 170 763	4.35	$/unit	161.85

Women's and girls' apparel:					
Dresses	26.07	$/unit	2 193 972 715	10.61	$/unit	145.76
Tops	8.74	$/unit	10 665 442 816	4.67	$/unit	86.99
Skirts	11.34	$/unit	2 455 317 826	6.90	$/unit	64.47
Bottoms, except skirts	12.75	$/unit	7 480 456 770	6.27	$/unit	103.41
Suits	30.91	$/unit	728 081 650	8.96	$/unit	245.11
Swimwear	17.44	$/unit	778 062 418	5.76	$/unit	202.78
Foundation garments	7.64	$/unit	2 351 810 753	3.99	$/unit	91.51
				weighted avg		95.81
Textile mills						
Carpet and other textile floor coverings	69.76	$/sq yd	596 636 651	41.18	$/sq yd	58.03
Plastics & rubber products mfg						
Plastics and articles thereof	0.53	$/lb	228 738 589 556	0.66	$/lb	−8.61

Sources: US Census Bureau (2006a, 2006b); USDA (2007a, 2007b); US Census Bureau (2004); USEIA (2006); USBLS (2006); and USBEA (2007).

Appendix Table 13.A3   Sectoral production cost increase

	REMI sector[1]	Scenario I[2] (%)	Scenario II[3] (%)
1	Forestry, fishing	−2.57	−2.29
3	Oil & gas extraction	44.82	44.09
4	Mining (except oil & gas)	5.28	4.81
8	Wood product mfg	11.64	11.04
9	Nonmetallic mineral product mfg	8.41	7.94
10	Primary metal mfg	0.73	0.66
11	Fabricated metal product mfg	0.43	0.40
12	Machinery mfg	70.56	50.74
13	Computer & electronic mfg	59.61	43.42
14	Electrical equip. & appliance mfg	62.39	50.63
15	Motor vehicle mfg	6.60	3.73
16	Transportation equip. mfg. excl. motor vehicles	2.09	1.57
17	Furniture & related product mfg	18.22	17.66
18	Miscellaneous mfg	58.97	48.04
19	Food mfg	3.76	3.56
20	Beverage & tobacco product mfg	5.77	5.58
21	Textile mills	16.98	14.09
22	Textile product mills	17.70	16.63
23	Apparel mfg	200.00	200.00
24	Leather & allied product mfg	200.00	200.00
25	Paper mfg	8.25	7.55
26	Printing & related support activities	2.37	2.29
28	Chemical mfg	−1.97	−1.63
29	Plastics & rubber products mfg	−1.42	−1.28

Notes:
1. Those sectors that have zero import replacement gaps are not included.
2. This replacement scenario allows the use of excess capacity at the level of 20%, but no export diversion for imports.
3. This replacement scenario assumes the use of excess capacity at the level of 20% plus full export diversion for imports.

for this sector is 4.4 percent × (1+50 percent) = 6.6 percent. Table 13.A3 presents the vector of sectoral production cost changes that we used in the REMI model for both of the two import replacement scenarios.

APPENDIX 13.B DETAILED DERIVATION OF INPUT VALUES FOR TOURISM SHUTDOWN SIMULATION

Total Expenditure

The Travel Industry Association of America (TIAA) published an Expenditure Patterns of Travelers in the US for 2002 with the latest data for 2000. In order to relate 2000 data to REMI's latest base year (2005), we use 2005 statistics on international travel.

Number of international passengers in 2000 is 141,288,690 (US Department of Transportation (2000)). We divide by two for round-trip statistics (70,644,345). We compare this with the number of round-trip international passengers in 2005 (74,304,521). Thus taking the ratio between 2005 and 2000 we obtain 74,304,521/70,644,345 = 1.051.

Expenditure of international travelers in the US in 2000 was estimated to be (Travel Industry Association of America) $83.8 billion. Using the multiplier calculated above and adjusting to 2005 dollars we estimate 2005 expenditure to be $97.7 billion.

Further, the above does not include purchases of airline tickets. Assuming two-thirds of tickets are bought from US airlines and 74,304,521 travelers at $1000 per ticket: $49.5 billion.

Adjusting to 2005 dollars (196.8/168.8 * 49.5) yields 57.7 billion. Thus our total estimated expenditure by international travelers is $97.7 + $57.7 = $155.41 billion

Expenditure in Border States

According to the TIAA, the Pacific, South Atlantic, and Middle Atlantic regions of the United States account for 76 percent of total spending of international travelers. If we add New England the total spending for border states would be approximately 79.3 percent and for interior states approximately 20.7 percent.

Expenditure for border states: $155.41* 0.793 = $123.24 billion.

Expenditure in Interior States

$155.41 − $123.34 = $32.07 billion. Finally REMI removes retail sales figures to track production costs directly. This results in about a 17.3 percent reduction in input values.

Table 13.A4 International travel substitution towards domestic travel

Transport mode	Travelers (000s)	Per person expenditure (including transport)	Expenditure ($millions)
Car/Truck/RV	16 434.414	$265	4 355.12
Air	5 430.294	$1 283	6 967.07
Other	2 057.292	$286	588.39
Total			11 910.58

Total expenditure adjusted to 2005 dollars is $13,886.26 million.

Spending Patterns

The TIAA also offers spending patterns for domestic travelers. Domestic tourism expenditure for North East, Middle Atlantic, South Atlantic and Pacific regions totaled 55.90 percent of total domestic tourism expenditure. We applied the 55.90 percent of the $13.886 billion to border states and the rest to interior states.

APPENDIX 13.C DETAILED DERIVATION OF UNAUTHORIZED WORKER SCENARIO

Because undocumented workers generally work for lower wages, we expect that a reduction in the supply of undocumented labor would increase the equilibrium wage. As the wage increases, two effects become apparent. First, there is an income effect, in that as laborers are paid more, they have more to spend. Second, as the wage increases, production cost increases.

To calculate the increase in the wage bill and production costs, we start with the number of undocumented laborers that will not be allowed into the country. According to Passel (2006), from 2000 to 2005 undocumented workers entered the country at a rate of about 850,000 per year. Further, Passel estimates that there were roughly 11 million undocumented workers in the United States as of 2005. In order to calculate the new wage bill, we first compute the total labor supply including undocumented workers. To do this, we multiply quantity of labor in each sector by the undocumented percentage of total labor estimated by Passel (2006) and add this to REMI's labor sector. Then we find the quantity of undocumented labor by multiplying the new updated total quantity of labor by the percentage of undocumented labor (see Table 13.A5 below). Finally, we multiply this number for each sector by the fraction not allowed to enter the country (850,000/11 million). This gives the quantity of undocumented labor that will have to be replaced by documented labor in each sector. However, by basing our calculations on REMI's labor force statistics, we underestimated the quantity of undocumented labor provided by Passel (2006). To bring our numbers in line with Passel (2006) we doubled the estimated quantity of undocumented labor. We then multiply by the difference in wages of an average high school graduate, $609 per week (US Census Bureau, 2005) and a short-term undocumented laborer, $330 per week (Passel, 2006), yielding a cost differential of $279 per week. Finally, we assumed that workers in the hotel and farming industries worked 75 percent and 66.7 percent of the year, respectively. All other sectors work full-time.

To calculate the increase in production cost by sector, we first calculate the total wage bill with no policy change (that is, with undocumented migrants for 2005). Then we calculate the total wage bill where undocumented migrants for the year 2005 are replaced by documented labor. We compute the percent change in wage bill by sector and then multiply by the percent of production cost (value added) that is labor cost. This yields a sectoral increase in production cost associated with cutting off undocumented migration in 2005 (see Table 13.A5 for input values).

Table 13.A5 Undocumented labor sectoring scheme and inputs

REMI sector	Labor cost as a % of total cost[a]	% Undocumented labor of total labor[b]	% Production cost increase
Accommodation	50	10	0.4052
Admin. support	68	11	0.5539
Agriculture	90	13	0.7358
Construction	80	12	0.6489
Food mfg	46	14	0.3767
Food services	64	12	0.5238
Furniture, mfg	66	13	0.5354
Miscellaneous mfg	59	6	0.4773
Private households	100	21	0.8166
Textile mills	76	12	0.6151

Notes:
[a] Labor cost as a percentage of total cost is derived from REMI's Input–Output Table.
[b] From Passel (2006) adapted to fit REMI sectors.

14. Challenges of benefit–cost analyses for terrorism security regulations: observations from regulatory analysis of the Western Hemisphere Travel Initiative

Henry H. Willis and Tom LaTourrette

INTRODUCTION

As the US continues to invest in countermeasures to reduce the risk posed by terrorism, questions have arisen about how to assess the progress of these efforts. One area in which such questions have risen to prominence is the design and implementation of federal regulations focused on improving security against terrorist attacks.

The Implementing the 9/11 Commission Recommendations Act of 2007, passed 9 January 2007, is one example of a statute passed by the US Congress that requires the Department of Homeland Security to regulate terrorism security efforts. Examples of language in this Act related to terrorism security include requirements for enhanced driver's licenses, foreign travel and visa documents, and container scanning and seals. Before major federal regulations can be approved, their benefits and costs must be evaluated to help guide decision-makers in their deliberations (31 USC Section 1111 on Money and Finance: Improving Economic Efficiency; Presidential Executive Orders 12291 and 12866 on economic analysis of regulations).

Accurately estimating the benefits of terrorism security efforts is very difficult, primarily because of the great uncertainty surrounding the risk of terrorism and the lack of data on the effects of security measures on reducing terrorism risks. As a result, benefit analyses of regulations intended to improve terrorism security to date have relied primarily on qualitative assessments and quantitative estimates based on worst-case scenarios. Such approaches are less informative than those used in other regulatory areas, such as environmental protection or occupational safety and health, which have both a longer history and stronger empirical underpinnings.

In an effort to examine some of the challenges involved in estimating benefits of terrorism security regulations, this chapter reviews a break-even analysis (OMB, 2003) recently conducted for a regulation proposed by the US Customs and Border Protection (CBP) Western Hemisphere Travel Initiative in the Land Environment (WHTI-L).

The remainder of this chapter is organized as follows. The next section describes the purpose and proposed implementation of the WHTI-L. The third section provides a review of the break-even analysis conducted for the WHTI-L and identifies challenges to benefit–cost analysis (BCA) of terrorism security regulations that the example reveals. The final section discusses the challenges to assessing benefits of terrorism security regulations for benefit–cost analysis, and approaches that can be used to address each.

THE WESTERN HEMISPHERE TRAVEL INITIATIVE IN THE LAND ENVIRONMENT

Like many recent terrorism security regulations, the impetus for the WHTI-L was the recommendations of the 9/11 Commission. The Commission identified travel document requirements as a source of terrorism vulnerability. Current regulations permit US citizens and non-immigrant aliens from Canada, Bermuda and Mexico to enter the US from certain Western Hemisphere countries without presenting a passport.

In response to the 9/11 Commission findings, the Intelligence Reform and Terrorism Prevention Act of 2004 required that the Secretary of Homeland Security develop a plan for reliably evaluating the identity and citizenship of people entering the US.

The purpose of the Act is to strengthen documentation requirements for people entering the United States through land and sea border crossings. The anticipated effect of the WHTI-L is to make it more difficult for people to enter the US illegally and reduce the illegitimate movement of people, drugs, weapons or other goods into the US.

A regulation addressing this requirement for air borders was approved and went into effect in January 2007. In January 2007 the CBP, jointly with the Department of State, proposed a regulation specifying documentation requirements for people entering the US via land borders from countries in the Western Hemisphere. The proposed regulation would require all US citizens to possess a traditional passport book, a newly proposed passport card, or a CBP trusted traveler card, to enter the US from Canada, Mexico or the Caribbean (Chertoff and Fore, 2007). The WHTI-L (or some other provision satisfying the Act) is required to be in place by June 2009.

BREAK-EVEN ANALYSIS FOR THE WESTERN HEMISPHERE TRAVEL INITIATIVE IN THE LAND ENVIRONMENT

The BCA that was conducted for the WHTI-L used a probabilistic terrorism risk modeling approach in a break-even analysis (Willis and LaTourrette, 2007). Analyses were conducted for different assumptions about the level of terrorism threat and consequences, and using different methods for valuing morbidity and mortality consequences.

As stated above, the effect of the WHTI-L was expected to be a reduction in the illegitimate movement of people and materiel into the US. The BCA represents this effect in terms of the reduction in terrorism risk due to the regulation. A decrease in terrorism risk leads to fewer terrorism losses, so the benefit of the WHTI-L can ultimately be expressed in terms of avoided terrorism losses. The incremental benefit is therefore the difference between the annualized loss from terrorism without and with the regulation in place, and the regulation is efficient if:

$$L_b - L_n \geq C_r \qquad (14.1)$$

where L is the annualized loss from terrorism, the subscripts b and n indicate conditions without the regulation (baseline) and with the regulation (new), respectively, and C_r is the annualized cost of the regulation.[1]

The effect of a new terrorism security regulation is to change the risk, and in so doing change the annualized loss from L_b to L_n. A regulation may change terrorism risk by changing the probability of attack, the consequences, or both. It is generally difficult to ascribe the influence of a terrorism security effort exclusively to reducing probability or exclusively to reducing consequences, because of the dynamic nature of terrorist adaptation (Jackson et al., 2007). A terrorism security measure could deter potential terrorists or protect potential targets so that the probability of attack would decrease. Alternatively, terrorists could adapt by shifting to different attack modes or target types that would change not only the probability of successful attack, but also the expected consequences of attack. Since terrorism risk reflects both probability and consequence, using risk reduction as the measure of benefit in a benefit–cost analysis captures both effects.

To make the focus on risk reduction more explicit, the WHTI analysis defined risk reduction, R, as:

$$R = (L_b - L_n)/L_b. \tag{14.2}$$

R is a dimensionless parameter characterizing the risk-reducing effectiveness of a proposed regulation. For a positive risk reduction (that is, $L_n \leq L_b$), R ranges from 0 (no risk reduction) to 1 (complete mitigation of risk).

Combining (14.1) with (14.2) gives:

$$R_c = C_r/L_b$$

In this equation R_c is the percentage risk reduction required for regulatory benefits to exceed regulatory costs.

Costs of WHTI-L Regulation

Direct costs for the WHTI-L were estimated by Industrial Economics Incorporated (IEc) (IEc, 2007). These cost estimates comprise two components: welfare losses to travelers resulting from the increased cost of access, and the anticipated government implementation expenditure. Welfare losses represent the cost of purchasing the necessary travel documents for those travelers choosing to continue traveling under the WHTI-L plus the consumer surplus lost from trips not taken for those travelers choosing not to purchase the necessary travel documents. Government implementation costs include the costs to install and operate passport card technology at land points of entry, including an increase in secondary inspections resulting from implementation of the regulation. IEc, Inc. examined a number of different cases reflecting different documentation requirements being considered, different estimates of the future rate of cross-border travel, and the rate at which future expenditure is discounted. These costs (Table 14.1) represent the annualized costs for a ten-year planning horizon.

Estimates of Terrorism Losses

As noted above, the benefit of terrorism security regulations is avoided terrorism losses. Economic theory suggests that the benefits that should be included in BCA comprise private and external components. The private component includes factors such as the directly borne costs of medical treatment, lost productivity and decreased quality of life. The external component reflects the value of non-private avoided losses, such as health

Benefit–cost analyses for terrorism security regulations 275

Table 14.1 Estimated total direct costs ($ million) for the WHTI-L

Alternative	Alternative 2: Passport book only		Alternative 3: Passport book, passport card, or trusted traveler card	
Discount rate	3%	7%	3%	7%
No children exemption				
Decreasing cross-border travel rate	$320	$340	$370	$390
Steady-state cross-border travel rate	$380	$400	$420	$450
Increasing cross-border travel rate	$490	$510	$500	$520
Children under 14 exempt				
Decreasing cross-border travel rate	$270	$290	$330	$340
Steady-state cross-border travel rate	$330	$340	$370	$390
Increasing cross-border travel rate	$390	$400	$420	$430
Children under 16 exempt				
Decreasing cross-border travel rate	$260	$280	$320	$340
Steady-state cross-border travel rate	$320	$330	$360	$380
Increasing cross-border travel rate	$370	$380	$400	$420

Source: IEc (2007).

care costs paid by the public sector and productivity losses not borne directly by the victims (OMB, 2003). To compare benefits to costs quantitatively, both need to be expressed in common units, which are typically monetary. To the extent possible, therefore, BCA requires monetization of relevant benefits.

Estimates of the annualized loss from terrorist attacks in the US were derived from the RMS Probabilistic Terrorism Model.[2] The RMS model estimates terrorism losses in terms of property damage and casualties. Model results for the standard risk estimate are shown in Table 14.2. Property damage in the RMS model is monetized by using insurance records and other metrics of property value to convert damage to buildings and contents to monetary values. The RMS model performs this conversion by means of nationwide databases of property characteristics and values. Monetization of casualties is more challenging because there are several ways to estimate the monetary values for casualties and none perfectly capture both the private and external costs. The regulatory analysis estimated causalities using both cost-of-injury and willingness-to-pay approaches. Alternative approaches that were used to estimate the costs of casualties are discussed in more detail below and in Willis and LaTourrette (2007).

Table 14.2   Standard risk estimate from the RMS Probabilistic Terrorism Model

Loss category	Annualized loss
No. casualties – Medical Only or Minor	7120
No. casualties – Temporary Total	710
No. casualties – Permanent Partial – Minor	270
No. casualties – Permanent Partial – Major	170
No. casualties – Permanent Total	80
No. casualties – Fatal	450
Total casualties	8800
Building	$395 000 000
Contents	$231 000 000
Business interruption	$675 000 000
Total property	$1 305 000 000

Source: Willis and LaTourrette (2007).

Notes: Standard risk estimate is the expected (average) annual loss using the standard threat outlook. Losses are annualized over a ten-year planning horizon (see text). Property losses rounded to the nearest million $. Casualty estimates rounded to the nearest 10.

Conclusions of the WHTI BCA Study

Taken together, the uncertainties in the terrorism risk level and casualty costs translate into a wide range in the necessary risk-reduction effectiveness of the WHTI-L (see Table 14.3). For the low risk level estimate and the cost of injury casualty costs, the annualized loss is $1 billion and the critical risk reduction is 35 percent. At the other extreme, the high risk level estimate combined with the casualty costs based on the quality-of-life approach anchored to a $6 million value of a statistical life (VSL) results in an annualized loss of $10 billion, requiring a risk reduction of 3.5 percent. Based on the RMS standard risk estimate and a casualty cost scale anchored to $3 million per fatality, Willis and LaTourrette (2007) estimates for the expected annualized loss from terrorism range from $2.7 billion to $3.2 billion. For this range in annualized loss and the regulatory costs estimated by IEc, the WHTI-L would need to reduce terrorism risk in the US by 13 percent to 11 percent in order for its benefit to equal its cost. Using a casualty cost scale anchored to $6 million per fatality increases the annualized loss estimate and decreases the critical risk reduction for the WHTI-L to about 8 percent. A cost-of-injury casualty cost scale leads to a lower annualized loss and a greater required risk reduction. However,

Table 14.3 Annualized loss and critical risk reduction for different assumptions about terrorism threat and value of casualties

	Annualized Loss ($B)			Critical Risk Reduction (%)		
	Low risk	Standard risk	High risk	Low risk	Standard risk	High risk
Cost of injury	1.0	2.1	4.2	35	17	8.7
Willingness to pay ($3M VSL)	1.4	2.7	5.5	26	13	6.6
Quality of life ($3M VSL)	1.6	3.2	6.5	22	11	5.6
Willingness to pay ($6M VSL)	2.0	4.1	8.2	18	8.8	4.4
Quality of life ($6M VSL)	2.6	5.2	10	14	6.9	3.5

Source: Willis and LaTourrette (2007).

Notes: Results are for preferred regulation cost.

cost-of-injury estimates are generally considered to underestimate the value of casualties greatly because they do not account for the associated private welfare losses (for example, Tolley et al., 1994). Basing results on a lower risk level that results in halving the annualized terrorism loss would double the critical risk reduction, and a higher risk level that results in a doubling of the annualized terrorism loss would cut the critical risk reduction in half.

CHALLENGES OF ESTIMATING BENEFITS OF TERRORISM RULES

While the results from the break-even analysis summarized above are useful for understanding uncertainties or perspectives related to the costs and benefits of a proposed terrorism security regulation, they do not directly inform decisions about whether a particular regulation is justified on a benefit–cost basis. For such an analysis to be prescriptive, regulators must also have a means to estimate the actual benefit, in terms of avoided losses, provided by a terrorism security regulation. Developing approaches to estimate benefits provides a way to connect terrorism risk assessment to terrorism risk management and thus improve the effectiveness of homeland security policies and resource allocation. This analysis discusses three challenges for terrorism regulation BCA: (1) developing approaches for estimating risk reduction; (2) developing estimates of the cost of casualties from terrorism; and (3) understanding how risk reduction affects the distribution of risk.

There exists a substantial literature base to draw upon in addressing these challenges. Ultimately, methods of estimating risk reduction need to be applied to terrorism security if the benefits of terrorism security are to be quantified. Given an understanding of risk reduction, it will then be necessary to develop means of valuing the terrorism casualties avoided by the security rule and comparing this value to the costs of implementing the rule. Finally, it may not be adequate to analyze security regulations using only the calculus of expectations, given the common tendency to perceive and manage catastrophic risks differently than other types of risks. Reviewing the literature related to each of these topics can inform efforts to mature applications of benefit–cost analysis to terrorism security.

Estimating the Benefits of Terrorism Security Measures

The impacts of homeland security regulations and policies are very difficult to recognize and may take a long time to become apparent. A complicating factor is that the impact that is achieved by terrorism security measures is also dependent on whether and how terrorists adapt tactics after the measure is in place. If terrorists are able to circumvent the measure, the impact could erode or be eliminated over time. If terrorists are able to capitalize on new vulnerabilities created by the measure, the impact could even be negative. Thus, estimating the effectiveness of security measures requires an understanding of how adversaries may adapt over time.[3] In general, three types of approaches can be used to estimate the impact of terrorism security measures: program evaluation and assessment, modeling and simulation, and expert judgment.

Program evaluation and assessment is the only one of the three approaches that can provide empirical evidence of risk reduction. The steps of program evaluation and assessment include establishing goals, defining metrics and measures, assessing performance, and analyzing and improving policy based on findings. Examples of such assessment of regulations include studies of the Terrorism Risk Insurance Act (for example, Doherty et al., 2005), the 9/11 Victims' Compensation Fund (Dixon and Stern, 2004), and gun violence prevention programs (Tita et al., 2003). As the Department of Homeland Security (DHS) considers promulgating regulations and implementing new programs, incorporating evaluation into the planning will enable future assessment of program effectiveness.

Modeling and simulation allow a prospective analysis of what benefits alternative regulatory strategies might yield. Approaches for using modeling and simulation to assess the consequences of terrorism or risk management strategies include scenario-based models like the RMS model used to estimate terrorism risk by the insurance industry (Willis et al., 2005; Willis, 2007; Carroll et al., 2005; Dixon et al., 2007), agent-based models (N-ABLE, 2006; Tsvetovat and Carley, 2002), game theory (Kunreuther, 2005; Bier et al., 2005), economic input–output models (Haimes et al., 2005; Gordon et al., 2007), probabilistic risk analysis (Rosoff and von Winterfeldt, 2007) and operations research approaches (Martonosi et al., 2005; Wein, 2006). Each approach provides a unique perspective and requires limiting assumptions. Thus, the use of modeling and simulation to assess the effectiveness of regulations can benefit from approaches that use combinations of models together.

Finally, expert judgment is often used when neither empirical data nor appropriate models adequately describe the performance of a policy or regulation. In general, expert judgment may be called upon when outcomes are difficult to quantify, such as when they span multiple objectives that are difficult to express in common metrics, or when outcomes are difficult to attribute to specific regulatory actions, because of either the complexity of causal relationships or lags in time between implementation and measurement (for example, Morgan and Henrion, 1990). Expert judgment has already been used by the DHS to assess the effectiveness of grant applications, and can be a continued tool to supplement assessment and modeling and simulation.

In continued consideration of the benefits of its initiatives, DHS regulators can draw upon these three approaches to understand better whether a proposed regulation is normatively justified.

Valuing Terrorism-Related Casualties

Monetary estimates of the costs of casualties vary over a considerable range (Tolley et al., 1994) and it is therefore useful to understand different approaches used to estimate these costs. Methods for monetizing health impacts include analysis of direct expenditure and lost productivity, eliciting comparisons of the utility of different health status conditions, estimating wage-premiums demanded for employment at increased risk, and contingent valuation techniques that derive values for morbidity states from the willingness to pay for treatment or risk reduction. In the analysis of the WHTI presented above, Willis and LaTourrette (2007) estimated the costs of injuries using three methods: estimates of health care and productivity costs (cost of injury); willingness-to-pay estimates derived from a meta-analysis of the wage-rate literature (willingness to pay); and comparisons of utilities for different health states (quality of life).

One difficulty in monetizing casualties is that different valuation studies

Table 14.4   Description of MAIS Casualty Categories

MAIS Injury Severity Category	Conditions that would fall into the various categories in both the MAIS and RMS scale
1 Minor Injury	Abrasion, laceration, strains, sprains, contusions: can be treated and released.
2 Moderate Injury	Simple broken bone, loss of consciousness, serious strains and sprains: requires follow-up and several weeks or months to heal, but will heal completely.
3 Serious Injury	Complicated fracture, serious joint injury, concussion, minor crush injury: requires substantial follow-up and some minor disability will result.
4 Severe Injury	Massive organ injury, heart laceration, loss of limb, crushed extremities: hospitalization, substantial temporary disability and moderate long-term disability.
5 Critical Injury	Spinal cord syndrome, crush syndrome with kidney failure, massive head injury: extended hospitalization, significant long-term disability.
6 Immediately Fatal	Death

Source: Willis and LaTourrette (2007).

Note: Examples of injuries provided by Sullivan (2007).

use different injury classification systems. The majority of expected casualties from many types of terrorism attacks are injuries or deaths resulting from physical trauma. Examples of attack modes that cause such consequences include bombs, sabotage attacks and conflagration. Because of this, the most relevant readily available casualty cost estimates are those associated with trauma injuries from automobile crashes. One scale developed to categorize trauma injuries for automobile crashes is the Maximum Abbreviated Injury Scale (MAIS; Association for the Advancement of Automotive Medicine, 2005). The MAIS categorizes injuries into six levels of severity ranging from minor to fatal. Table 14.4 provides examples of injuries associated with each category. Casualty cost estimates from several approaches used in the WHTI analysis are shown in Table 14.5 and discussed below.

Cost-of-injury estimates
The easiest morbidity and mortality costs to measure are the direct costs incurred for the treatment of injury. Adding these costs to estimates of lost labor productivity and effects of lost productivity of others in the household provides a measure of the financial consequences of morbidity and

Table 14.5   Casualty cost estimates

MAIS category	Cost of injury[1]	Willingness to pay ($3M VSL)[2]	Quality of life ($3M VSL)[3]	Willingness to pay ($6M VSL)[2]	Quality of life ($6M VSL)[3]
MAIS 1	$7 000	$0	$0	$0	$0
MAIS 2	$70 000	$79 000	$330 000	$79 000	$660 000
MAIS 3	$202 000	$79 000	$480 000	$79 000	$960 000
MAIS 4	$383 000	$79 000	$210 000	$79 000	$420 000
MAIS 5	$1 222 000	$79 000	$2 430 000	$79 000	$4 860 000
MAIS 6	$1 086 000	$3 000 000	$3 000 000	$6 000 000	$6 000 000

Sources: Willis and LaTourrette (2007) derived from the following sources: [1]Blincoe et al. (2002), [2]Viscusi and Aldy (2003), [3]Graham et al. (1997).

Notes: All values are reported in 2005 US$ using the consumer price index. VSL = value of a statistical life. Casualty costs are rounded to the nearest $1000.

mortality consequences, sometimes referred to as the cost of injury. In contrast to the other approaches used in the WHTI analysis, this method does not formally account for private loss components such as welfare losses associated with persistent reduction in one's quality of life (that is, pain and suffering). In accounting for external loss components but neglecting the much larger private components, cost-of-injury estimates represent lower bounds for the purposes of benefit–cost analyses. While estimates of the external and private components of casualty losses could, in principle, be summed to derive a total casualty loss estimate, few loss estimates are unambiguously restricted to include only private or only external components. Most estimates, including cost-of-injury estimates, contain elements of both. Adding such estimates would therefore overestimate the casualty loss (Tolley et al., 1994).

Willingness-to-pay estimates
The willingness-to-pay literature estimates the value of fatalities and injuries by stated and revealed preference methods. Stated preference methods typically ask respondents to state their willingness to pay to avoid being injured. A common revealed preference method analyzes the relationship between hourly wages and occupational fatality and injury risks. In theory, workers demand higher wages for incurring exposure to such risks. Thus, any risk-related wage premium represents a revealed valuation of injuries.

Viscusi and Aldy (2003) reviewed 40 studies presenting willingness-to-pay estimates of injury risk premiums derived from wage differential analyses. These studies examine non-fatal job risks in terms of the overall injury rate, the rate of injuries severe enough to result in a lost workday, and the rate of total lost workdays. In contrast to the cost-of-injury and quality-of-life based cost estimates, the willingness-to-pay based injury cost estimates do not distinguish costs for injuries of different severities. Across these studies the value of injury ranged from approximately $20,000 to $70,000 (2000 US$).

The WHTI analysis used the high end of the range of injury values from the willingness-to-pay literature and assigned this value for all non-fatal injury categories, with one exception. The analysis excluded injuries in the lowest-severity category because they are very minor and would not be representative of the types of injuries that are associated with the estimated wage premiums. Despite using the high end of the range of injury values, it is likely an underestimate for the value of severe injuries.

For fatal injuries, the WHTI analysis used estimates of willingness to pay to avoid fatal injuries, which is commonly referred to as the value of a statistical life (VSL). VSL estimates of $3 million and $6 million reflect assumptions typically used by the US Department of Transportation and the US Environmental Protection Agency, respectively (Institute of Medicine, 2006).

Quality-of-life estimates
The value of injuries can also be estimated by eliciting people's preferences for different health states and comparing these preferences to estimates for the VSL. The Center on the Evaluation of Value and Risk in Health at Tufts University (2006) maintains a registry of cost-effectiveness and relative preference weights for health states from the published literature. To derive monetized values for casualty estimates that capture welfare costs excluded by the NHTSA analysis, we reviewed this database to identify estimates of preference weights for injuries similar to those associated with the casualties of terrorist events.

As discussed above, injuries associated with terrorist attacks are most similar to trauma injuries due to trauma incidents and automobile accidents. One citation in the Tufts University registry published preference weights[4] for injuries corresponding to the MAIS injury severity categories (Graham et al., 1997). These values were derived from estimates of the utility of different health states following injuries from motor vehicle accidents using the Functional Capacity Index. In deriving these preference weights, Graham et al. adjusted the values to account for the proportion of injuries in different MAIS categories that have non-persistent health effects, based on the work of Segui-Gomez (1996). The resulting preference weights are shown in Table 14.6. The preference weight values do not vary monotonically because of variance in the proportion of non-persistent injuries by

Table 14.6   Preference weights for different injuries

Injury level	Best estimate
MAIS 2	0.89
MAIS 3	0.84
MAIS 4	0.93
MAIS 5	0.19
Fatality	0

Source: Graham et al. (1997).

MAIS category. In particular, estimates that a large proportion of MAIS 4 injuries are non-persistent results in a relatively high preference weight for this category and reduces the relative significance of these injuries.

The WHTI analysis estimated quality-of-life estimates for the value of casualties by multiplying two monetary estimates of the VSL, $3 million and $6 million, by the preference weights described above. Like Graham et al. (1997), the analysis excluded injuries associated with MAIS 1 because they are very minor and the measurement of preference weights for very minor injuries is very unreliable.

Overview of approaches to valuing casualties

Each of the methods discussed in this section has its respective limitations. Approaches that estimate the cost of injury exclude potentially important private costs. Willingness-to-pay literature is thin on injury mechanisms that are analogous to those expected from many types of terrorism, and it is quite possible that fear generated by terrorism may lead people to value injuries and fatalities differently if they are the result of terrorist actions rather than other causes. In addition, this literature generally does not differentiate injuries in terms of severity. Finally, the Institute of Medicine (2006) concluded that methods that monetize quality-of-life metrics combine metrics developed for different purposes and do not have a strong theoretical basis.

Because injuries from terrorist events may occur in numbers comparable or larger than fatalities, the method used to value non-fatal casualties can have a substantial influence on the merits of regulations. But despite a substantial body of work directed at evaluating the costs of injuries, illnesses and fatalities related to environmental and workplace risks (for example, US EPA, 1999, 2000; Viscusi and Aldy, 2003), there is not a generally accepted casualty valuation scale for use in regulatory BCA of terrorism security regulations.

This problem may warrant additional basic research. However, many of the methods used result in casualty valuation estimates of similar orders of magnitude. Thus it is worth considering the value of information for regulatory analysis that would be produced by such research.

Reflecting the Catastrophic Nature of Terrorism in BCA

A significant proportion of terrorism risk estimates are associated with unlikely events that would have catastrophic consequences if they were to occur. Basing risk management of events solely on the expected value of a distribution of consequences like this can be misleading (Haimes, 2004). For example, there may exist opportunities to reduce the maximum consequences of a risk, that is, cap the maximum losses. If the probability associated with consequences above the established cap is sufficiently small, such an option might provide sufficiently little reduction in overall risk that the benefit may not exceed the expected costs of the option. Nevertheless, it may be justifiable to take such an action if the consequences being averted are irreversible and/or catastrophic.[5] To address this issue, it is necessary to understand not just the expected risk reduction associated with policies or programs, but also how they are expected to change the distribution of risk.

If it is appropriate to incorporate measures of extreme consequences into decision-making, there are several approaches that could be used. Subjective expected utility provides an axiomatic method for incorporating preferences to avoid extreme consequences into decision-making (Savage, 1954; Raiffa, 1968; von Winterfeldt and Edwards, 1986). Alternatively, rather than basing decisions on expected values, decisions could be based on an alternative percentile of the consequence distribution (for example, 90th or 95th percentile) or on a partitioned expected value that represents the magnitude of the upper tail of the consequence distribution (Haimes, 2004). Finally, in other contexts, such as flood risk management, decisions are based on the avoidance of consequences associated with events of specified return periods. For example, flood plains are frequently determined based on 50-year and 100-year floods, and the Netherlands has designed its national sea wall system to avoid consequences of a 10,000-year storm.

Each of these approaches has its corresponding advantages and disadvantages. Though some consider subjective expected utility to have a normative basis for decision-making, subjective utility elicitations are only meaningful if those contributing the estimates fully understand the probabilities and consequences comprising the risks being considered. Accurately conveying such information is very difficult for low-probability, high-consequence risks, particularly for those as unfamiliar as terrorist attacks. It may therefore be impractical to elicit stable utility preferences for terrorism risk management. While the partitioned expected value method provides a quantitative approach for incorporating extreme consequences into decision-making, most people do not conceptualize risk in terms of probability distributions and it may be challenging for decision-makers to discuss risk in term of percentiles of a consequence distribution. In contrast, return periods are more familiar to risk management discussions than probability distributions. However, many terrorism security regulations do not work like levees or dams in providing full protection up to a level at which the capacity they provide is exceeded. Thus, the return period analogy may only have limited applicability to terrorism security measures.

Summary

BCA is a method built upon established theories, validated analytic tools, and several decades of application. However, BCA has only been widely used for terrorism security for a few years.

The example of break-even analysis for WHTI that is presented earlier provides a current snapshot of how the methods of BCA are being applied within the DHS. While this example represents significant advances in the maturation of BCA for terrorism security regulations, it also clearly demonstrates the shortcomings of current approaches. With each new proposed regulation for which the DHS conducts a regulatory analysis, there is an opportunity to improve on the approaches used to conduct BCA.

Each of the challenges identified here raises difficult theoretical and methodological problems. As the DHS continues to refine the application of BCA to future terrorism security regulations, new methods and data will need to be developed to address these challenges.

ACKNOWLEDGEMENTS

This research was made possible through support by the US Customs and Border Protection and the Center for Risk and Economic Analysis of Terrorist Events at the University of Southern California funded by the DHS Science and Technology Directorate's University Programs.

NOTES

1. Regulations could result in net savings, in which case C_r would be negative.
2. For further descriptions of the RMS Probabilistic Terrorism Model refer to the RMS

website (http://www.rms.com) or descriptions contained in Willis et al. (2005) or Willis et al. (2007).
3. For a more thorough discussion of terrorist adaptation to security measures see Jackson et al. (2007).
4. Preference weights reflect the relative utility of the quality of life associated with decreased health states compared to perfect health. By convention, perfect health is valued at 1, death at 0, and preference rates can be negative.
5. It is important to be as specific as possible about the term 'catastrophic' when it is used. In this context, the term is used to describe events from which it would be difficult or impossible to return to the state that existed prior to the event. In the context of terrorism, a scenario involving a nuclear detonation in a city could arguably be such a scenario.

REFERENCES

Association for the Advancement of Automotive Medicine (2005), *Abbreviated Injury Scale (AIS) 2005*, Barrington, IL.

Bier, V.M., A. Nagaraj and V. Abhichandani (2005), 'Optimal allocation of resources for defense of simple series and parallel systems from determined adversaries', *Reliability Engineering and System Safety*, **87**, 313–23.

Center on the Evaluation of Value and Risk in Health (2006), *The Cost-Effectiveness Analysis Registry*, Boston, MA: Tufts-New England Medical Center, ICRHPS; http://www.tufts-nemc.org/cearegistry, as of 20 December 2006.

Chertoff, M. and H. Fore (2007), 'Documents required for travelers departing from or arriving in the United States at sea and land ports-of-entry from within the Western Hemisphere; proposed rule', *Federal Register*, **72** (122), 35088–35116; http://www.regulations.gov/fdmspublic/component/main?main=DocketDetail&d=USCBP-2007-0061.

Dixon, L., R. Lempert, T. LaTourrette and R.T. Reville (2007), *The Federal Role in Terrorism Insurance: Evaluating Alternatives in an Uncertain World*. MG-679-CTRMP, RAND Corporation, Santa Monica, CA.

Dixon, L. and R.K. Stern (2004), *Compensation for Losses from the 9/11 Attacks*. MG-264-ICJ, Santa Monica, CA: RAND Corporation.

Doherty, N., E. Goldsmith, S. Harrington, P. Kleindorfer, H. Kunreuther, E. Michel-Kerjan, M. Pauly, I. Rosenthal and P. Schmeidler (2005), *TRIA and Beyond*, Philadelphia, PA: Wharton Risk Management and Decision Process Center, University of Pennsylvania; http://grace.wharton.upenn.edu/risk/downloads/TRIA%20and%20Beyond.pdf, as of 3 October 2005.

Gordon, P., S. Kim, J. Moore, J. Park and H.W. Richardson (2007), 'The economic impacts of a terrorist attack on the US commercial aviation system', *Risk Analysis*, **27**, 505–12.

Graham, J.D., K.M. Thompson and S.J. Goldie (1997), 'The cost-effectiveness of air bags by seating position', *Journal of the American Medical Association*, **278**, 1418–25.

Haimes, Y.Y. (2004), *Risk Modeling, Assessment, and Management*, 2nd edition, Hoboken, NJ: John Wiley & Sons.

Haimes, Y., B. Horowitz, J. Lambert, J. Santos, C. Lian and K. Crowther (2005), 'Inoperability input–output model for interdependent infrastructure sectors. I: Theory and methodology', *Journal of Infrastructure Systems*, **1** (2), 67–79.

Industrial Economics Incorporated (IEc) (2007), 'Regulatory assessment for the notice of proposed rulemaking: documents required for travel within the Western Hemisphere', June 2007, Prepared for the US Customs and Border Protection, Department of Homeland Security, Cambridge, MA; http://www.regulations.gov/fdmspublic/component/main?main=DocketDetail&d=USCBP-2007-0061.

Institute of Medicine (2006), *Valuing Health for Regulatory Cost-Effectiveness Analysis*, Washington, DC: National Academies Press.

Jackson, B.A., P. Chalk, K. Cragin, B. Newsome, J.V. Parachini, W. Rosenau, E.M. Simpson, M. Sisson and D. Temple (2007), *Breaching the Fortress Wall: Understanding Terrorist Efforts to Overcome Defensive Technologies*, Santa Monica, CA: MG-481-DHS, RAND Corporation.

Kunreuther, H. (2005), 'IDS models of airline security', *Journal of Conflict Resolution*, **49**, 201–17.

Martonosi, S.E., D.S. Ortiz and H.H. Willis (2005), 'Evaluating the viability of 100 percent container inspection at America's ports', in H.W. Richardson, P. Gordon and J.E. Moore II (eds), *The Economic Impacts of Terrorist Attacks*, Cheltenham, UK and Northampton, MA, USA: Edward Elgar Publishing, pp. 218–41; also available as RAND RP-1220 at http://www.rand.org/pubs/reprints/RP1220/.

Morgan, M.G. and M. Henrion (1990), *Uncertainty: A Guide to Dealing with Uncertainty in Quantitative Risk and Policy Analysis*, Cambridge: Cambridge University Press.

Raiffa, H. (1968), *Decision Analysis: Introductory Lectures on Choices Under Uncertainty*, New York: Random House.

Rosoff, H. and D. von Winterfeldt (2007), 'A risk and economic analysis of dirty bomb attacks on the Ports of Los Angeles and Long Beach', *Risk Analysis*, **27**, 533–46.

Savage, L. (1954). *The Foundation of Statistics*, New York: John Wiley & Sons.

Segui-Gomez, M. (1996), *Application of the Functional Capacity Index to NASS CDS Data*, Washington, DC: National Highway Traffic Safety Administration.

Tita, G., K.J. Riley, G. Ridgeway, C.A. Grammich, A. Abrahamse and P.W. Greenwood (2003), *Reducing Gun Violence: Results from an Intervention in East Los Angeles*, MR-1742-NIJ, Santa Monica, CA: RAND Corporation.

Tolley, George, Donald Kenkel and Robert Fabian (eds) (1994), *Valuing Health for Policy: An Economic Approach*, Chicago, IL: University of Chicago Press.

US Environmental Protection Agency (EPA) (1999), *The Benefits and Costs of the Clean Air Act 1990 to 2010*, EPA 410-R-99-001, Washington, DC; http://www.epa.gov/air/sect812/1990-2010/fullrept.pdf.

US Environmental Protection Agency (EPA) (2000), *Guidelines for Preparing Economic Analyses*, EPA 240-R-00-003, Washington, DC; http://yosemite.epa.gov/ee/epa/eed.nsf/webpages/Guidelines.html.

US Office of Management and Budget (2003), 'Regulatory analysis', Circular A-4, Washington, DC.

Viscusi, W.K. and J.E. Aldy (2003), 'The value of a statistical life: a critical review of market estimates throughout the world', *Journal of Risk and Uncertainty*, **27**, 5–76.

von Winterfeldt, D. and W. Edwards (1986), *Decision Analysis and Behavioral Research*, New York: Cambridge University Press.

Wein, L.M., A.H. Wilkins, M. Baveja and S.E. Flynn (2006), 'Preventing the importation of illicit nuclear materials in shipping containers', *Risk Analysis*, **26**, 1539–6924.

Willis, H.H. and T. LaTourrette (2007), 'Using probabilistic terrorism risk modeling for regulatory benefit–cost analysis: application to the Western Hemisphere Travel Initiative implemented in the Land Environment', *Risk Analysis*, In Press.

Willis, H.H., T. LaTourrette, T.K. Kelly, S.C. Hickey and S. Neill (2007), *Terrorism Risk Modeling for Intelligence Analysis and Infrastructure Protection*, TR-386-DHS, Santa Monica, CA: RAND Corporation.

Willis, H.H., A.R. Morral, T.K. Kelly and J.J. Medby (2005), *Estimating Terrorism Risk*, MG-388-RC, Santa Monica, CA: RAND Corporation.

Index

Abadie, A. 120, 148
ABN Amro 144
Abu Sayef 140
Accelerated Disaster Response Initiative (ADRI) 51
acceptability, of anti-terrorist policy 109
accidents 25–6
Afghanistan 14
Afghanistan Investment Guarantee Facility 144
African Union (AU) 21
Aguirre, Fernando 138
AIG 80
air travel
   airports 148, 149–50, 155, 158–63, 164
   losses from border closure 202–4, 207, 210–19, 229, 267–8
   9/11 effects analysis 6, 150–64, 165–6
   9/11 effects hypotheses 148–50
   regulation 272
   stock market effects of terrorism 126
   as terrorism target 19
   see also international travel, and border closure
Alaskan earthquake (1964) 50
Aldy, J.E. 281
Alexander, Dean C. 1, 5
al-Qaeda 14, 107, 125
Amadeus (travel booking service) 127, 130
American Nuclear Insurers (ANI) 81
Anthrax and Beyond initiative 62–4
anthrax attacks 45, 62–4, 76, 85–7
antiterrorist organizations 14
Aon Corporation 82
Arab League 21
Argus (Project) 108
Arizona 207

Arthur Andersen & Co 23
Asia-Pacific Economic Cooperation (APEC) 21
Asian Development Bank 192
assessable reciprocal mutual insurance 81
Association of British Insurers (ABI) 97, 112
Association of South-East Asian Nations (ASEAN) 21
Aum Shinrikyo 78–9
Australia 20, 87
Autodefensas Unidas de Colombia (AUC) 137–8
automatic number plate recording cameras (ANPR) 111
avian influenza 7–8, 45, 201–2
Aznar, José María 123, 128

Bae, Chang-Hee Christine 7
Baily, E. 100
Banadex 137, 139–40
Bangladesh 38
banks 52–3
Baumert, Thomas 1, 5
Becker, G.S. 149
Beeler Asay, Garrett R. 6
behaviour, and risk 46–51
Belgium 14
benefit assessment of terrorism security regulations 277–85
Bethune, Gordon 40
Bhopal gas tragedy (1984) 80
Bier, V. 56
bilateral terrorist attacks
   effect on trade 6–7, 169–72, 182–4
   empirical analysis of trade effects 172–82
bilateral trade
   effect of terrorism on 6–7, 169–72, 182–4

empirical analysis of terrorism
    effects 172–82
Bin Laden, Osama 2, 14
biological weapons *see* nuclear,
    biological, chemical and
    radiological (NBCR) attacks
bioterrorism 78
Blomberg, S.B. 172
bomb attacks 76, 93, 94
    see also car bomb attacks
border closure
    air travel losses 202–4, 207, 210–19,
        229, 267–8
    duration 202, 249–50, 253–4
    economic impact of 7–8, 201–2,
        206–8, 228–9, 244–55
    export effects 228, 237–9, 244,
        245–6, 248, 250–51, 253
    financial markets 250–52
    immigration effects (NIEMO model)
        204–6, 207, 222–5, 229
    immigration effects (REMI model)
        234, 241–4, 245–6, 248, 269–70
    import effects 228, 235–7, 244,
        245–6, 248, 250–51, 253, 259–66
    international travel effects 228,
        239–41, 245–6, 248, 253, 267–8
    investment 250–52
    models of 7, 8, 202, 229–35, 255
    and shopping 206, 207, 214, 226–7,
        229
    simultaneous shutdown of all
        activities 201–2, 247–8
    trade losses 204, 205, 207, 220–21
BP 31, 35
break-even analysis of terrorism
    regulations 8–9, 273–85
Britain 14, 20
    see also United Kingdom (UK)
British Airways 126
Bröttcher, Volker 133
Brzezinski, Z. 11
budgets, and risk estimations 48–9
Buesa, M. 121
Bush, George W. (Jnr.) 19, 20
business
    and globalization 13–14
    mutual support 18
    risk assessment 183
    and terrorism 1–2, 191–4, 198–9

trade, and border closure 204, 205,
    207, 220–21
uncertainty 3–4
see also transnational corporations
    (TNCs)
business continuity
    disruption planning 33–9, 40–41,
        99–101
    disruption types 23–30
    emergency management 30–32
    empowerment of individuals 39–40
    priority chart 29
    resilience 2–3, 101–6, 108–11, 244,
        252–4

CAC40 index 126, 128, 130
California 87, 205, 207
Canada 20, 104, 272–3
Canary Wharf 95, 97
capital 231, 232, 233, 234, 235, 243, 251
car bomb attacks 93, 94, 102, 107
    see also bomb attacks
Caribbean 272–3
cars, driving risk 149
Carter, D. 121
casualties 279–84
catastrophic risk
    break-even analysis of terrorism
        regulations 284–5
    and globalization 3
    and individual behaviour 46–51
    losses 42–6
    mitigation 51–4, 57–62
Chamber of Commerce (London) 96,
    110
chemical weapons *see* nuclear,
    biological, chemical and
    radiological (NBCR) attacks
Chen, A.H. 120
Cheng, I.-H. 173, 176
Chernobyl nuclear plant disaster 45
Chicago 148–9
child labor 27
Chile 13
China 7, 44, 190, 192, 194, 197, 250
Chiquita Brands International (CBI)
    5, 136–40
Chiron Inc. 27
Choudhry, T. 121
CIA (Central Intelligence Agency) 125

Citigroup 66
citizens, role of 104
City Property Association 97
Civil Contingencies Act 103
Clemens, Jeffrey 6
closed circuit television (CCTV) 95, 108, 110
CNI (Centro Nacional de Inteligencia) 123, 125
Coaffee, Jon 4
Coast Guard, US 40
Cold War 103
collaboration 37–8, 62–4
Colombia 5, 136–40, 143
Colombo 93
colonial empires 14
Comité Européen de Régulation Postale (European Committee for Postal Regulation) 63–4
communities, role of 104
competition 183–4
consumer expectations 27
Consumer Federation of America 84
CONTEST strategy 105–6
Continental Airlines 40
contingency planning 99–101
cooperation 10, 15–22
coordination 15–16
cost-benefit analysis of security measures 8–9, 273–85
costs
 of casualties 279–84
 individuals' risk estimations 48–9
 REMI model 232, 233, 234, 235
 terrorism regulations 274–7
counter terrorism business 2
Counter Terrorism Security Advisors (UK) 107
Crisis Recovery Plans (CRPs) 100
cross-border shopping 206, 207, 214, 226–7, 229
crowded public places 106–7, 109
 see also density of economic activity; population
Customs and Border Protection (CBP) 272

Dax index 126, 128, 130
debriefing between international organizations 63–4

demand 231, 232, 233
Democratic People's Republic of Korea (DPRK)
 denuclearization of 188–9
 economy 189–91
 investment as antiterrorism strategy 191–4, 198–9
 Kaesong Industrial Complex (KIC) 194–7, 199
 nuclear weapons development 78
 reunification with Republic of Korea (ROK) 7, 189, 193, 194
 and terrorism 187–8
 Tumen River Project 7, 197–8, 199
Denmark 13
density of economic activity 148–9, 159
 see also crowded public places
denuclearization 188–9, 191–2, 199
Department of Homeland Security (DHS) see Homeland Security, Department of (DHS)
derivatives markets 131
Dermisi, S. 148
Des Moines 77
detection, of disruptive events 38–9
Deutsche Bank 32
development stage of countries 177–82, 184
dirty bombs 76
disaster assistance 49–51
disaster plans see evacuation plans
disasters, US Presidential declarations of 50–51
disruption
 emergency management 30–32
 empowerment of individuals 39–40
 planning for 33–9, 40–41, 99–101
 priority chart 29
 types of 23–30
Docklands, London 94, 95, 97, 98
domestic travel (US) 203–4, 215, 239–41, 253, 255, 268
Dow Jones index 126, 128, 130
Drakos, K. 121
driving risk 149
Du Pont 25–6
Dunriding Compant N.V. 143

early warning systems 38–9
earthquakes 10, 24, 44, 46, 80, 253
East-West coast (US) air travel 148, 163–4, 165–6
economic activity 148–9, 159
economic infrastructure, threats to 4–5, 92–3, 106–7
Eldor, R. 121, 122
Ellsberg, D. 79
embassies, as terrorist targets 19
emergency management centers (EMCs) 30–32, 34–5, 40
emergency response testing 104–5
emissions reductions 57
employees 31–2, 35, 39–40
empowerment 39–40
Enron 23
epidemics 201–2
 see also avian influenza; pandemics
Ericsson 18, 23
ETA (Euskadi Ta Askatasuna, 'Basque Homeland and Freedom') 120, 123–6, 140
euro 128
Europe 15
European Union (EU) 20, 28, 192
evacuation plans 5
ex ante business decisions 183
ex post business decisions 183
expert judgement 279
exports, and border closure 228, 237–9, 244, 245–6, 248, 250–51, 253
externalities 45, 57
extortion
 Chiquita Brands International (CBI) 136–40
 effects on host country 144–6
 risk reduction by transnational corporations (TNCs) 141–4
 risks to transnational corporations (TNCs) 140–41
ExxonMobil 13

Federal Emergency Management Administration (FEMA) 39
financial assistance 49–51
financial centres, as terrorism targets 92–3, 106–7
financial institutions 187, 192, 193
financial loss mitigation 33–4

financial markets
 border closure effects 250–52
 Madrid train bombings (2004) 1, 5, 119–20, 122–32
 and terrorism 74, 120–22
fire fighters 16
first responders 17
flexibility 36–7, 64
floods 80, 284
Ford 13
foreign direct investment (FDI) 191–4
Foxmeyer 23
France
 global business 14
 mutual support 20
 nuclear, biological, chemical and radiological (NBCR) risks 87
 postal security 63
 stock market effects of Madrid train bombings 126, 128, 130
 strikes 28
franchising, of global terrorism 14
Fratianni, M. 172
Frist, William 78
FTSE 100 index 126, 128, 130

G8 (Group of Eight) nations 21
Gardeazabal, J. 120
gas 1–2
General Agreement on Tariffs and Trade (GATT) 12
General Motors (GM) 13, 18, 24
Germany
 global business 14
 mutual support 20–21
 nuclear, biological, chemical and radiological (NBCR) risks 87
 postal security 63
 reunification 189
 stock market effects of Madrid train bombings 125, 126, 128, 130
Gigerenzer, G. 149
Gladwell, M. 49
Glaeser, E.L. 148
Glasgow airport attack (2007) 107
Glick, R. 172
global business
 and globalization 13–14
 mutual support 18
 risk assessment 183

and terrorism 1–2, 191–4, 198–9
  trade, and border closure 204, 205, 207, 220–21
  uncertainty 3–4
global integration 183–4
global interdependencies
  Anthrax and Beyond initiative 62–4
  nature of 55–7
  and risk 42–6
  risk mitigation 57–62, 65–9
Global Risk Network 3, 55, 66–9
global risks 54–5, 65–9
  see also risk
global security 15–16
global supply chains 57–62
global terrorism 10, 14–22, 170–71
  see also terrorism
global trade 183–4
  see also trade
globalization
  and catastrophic risk 3
  and global business 13–14
  and global terrorism 10, 14–22
  sources of 11–12
  and terrorism 2–3
Globalization and the Future of Terrorism: Patterns and Predictions (Lia) 15
Gordon, Peter 7, 149, 229
government role 74–6, 97–9, 130–31, 254
government standards 62
Graham, J.D. 282, 283
Great Britain *see* Britain; United Kingdom (UK)
Great Depression 12
Greece 13
Greene, D. 230
greenhouse gas emissions 57
Griffin (Project) 108
guarantees for transnational corporations (TNCs) 143–4
Gum Arabic Co. 2
Guy Carpenter & Co. 87

Heal, G. 81
Heath, C. 49
Helix 37
Hess, G.D. 172
Hewlett-Packard (HP) 37

Hiroshima 78
Hogarth, R. 79
Holguin, Carlos 139
Holland 14, 20, 63
Homeland Security, Department of (DHS)
  creation of 14
  Hurricane Katrina 39–40
  terrorism security regulations assessment 271, 272, 278, 279, 285
  terrorism strategy 19
Hon, M. 121
Hong Kong 56
hospitals 16
hub-and-spoke business model 150
Hughes, C. 198
Hurricane Katrina 31, 32, 39–40, 42, 44, 46, 50
Hurricane Rita 46
Hurricane Wilma 46
hurricanes 42, 44, 46
Hyundai 195

Iberia Airlines 127, 130
Ibex 35 index 122–32
Iguaran, Mario 138
illegal immigration, and border closure 205–6, 207, 224–5, 229, 241–4, 245–6, 248, 269–70
Illinois 205
immigration
  NIEMO model of border closure effects 204–6, 207, 222–5, 229
  REMI model of border closure effects 234, 241–4, 245–6, 248, 269–70
  see also illegal immigration, and border closure; legal immigration, and border closure
IMPLAN model 202
imports
  effects of border closure 228, 235–7, 244, 245–6, 248, 250–51, 253, 259–66
  oil 230
India 38
individuals, role of 39–40, 46–51
Indonesia 13, 14, 38, 56

influenza 12, 27
information 64, 104, 132
infrastructure 4–5, 34–5, 92–3, 106–7, 192, 193, 194–7
initiative, use of 39–40
injury, cost of 280–81
input-output models 202, 229, 247, 279
instability 140–44
institutions 19–21
insurance
   anthrax attacks 85–7
   disruption planning 33–4
   long-term cover 53–4
   long-term loans 52–3
   losses from catastrophic events 42–6, 77, 96, 106–7
   9/11 terrorist attacks 47
   nuclear, biological, chemical and radiological (NBCR) risks 4, 75–80, 87–8
   nuclear reactors 80–81
   political instability risks 142–4
   and risk 53–4, 101
   terrorism insurance 74–5, 96–9
   and Terrorism Risk Insurance Program Reauthorization Act (TRIPRA) 75–6, 81–4, 88
   workers' compensation 84–7
Intel 18, 34, 36
intelligence 17, 18–19
intentional disruptions 27–8
interchangeability 36
interdependencies
   Anthrax and Beyond initiative 62–4
   local 49
   nature of 55–7
   and risk 42–6
   risk mitigation 57–62, 65–9
interest rates 250–52
international cooperation
   global terrorism 15–16
   information protocols 132
   investment as antiterrorism strategy 191–4, 198–9
   Kaesong Industrial Complex (KIC) 194–7
   resilience planning 109–10
   Tumen River Project 197–8, 199
international institutions 19–21

International Longshore and Warehouse Union (ILWU) 27–8
International Monetary Fund (IMF) 20
International Tourism Exchange (ITB) 127
international trade 183–4
   see also trade
international travel, and border closure 228, 239–41, 245–6, 248, 253, 267–8
   see also air travel; tourism; Western Hemisphere Travel Initiative in the Land Environment (WHTI-L)
Intriligator, Michael D. 2, 11
investment 191–4, 198–9, 250–52
Iran 78, 230
Iraq 14, 171, 193
Ireland 14
Irish Republican Army (IRA) 4–5, 93, 94, 98
iron collar 95–6, 101
Islamic Conference 21
Islamic terrorist attacks 14, 107, 123, 125, 127–30
Israel 13, 14, 34, 87, 121, 122, 199
Italy 20–21, 126, 128, 130
Ito, H. 148, 149, 150, 151, 152, 153, 154, 164

Jaffee, Dwight 4, 81
Japan 14, 20, 126, 192, 197–8
JARring actions 57

Kaesong Industrial Complex (KIC) 7, 194–7, 199
Kahneman, D. 78
Kang, H. 172
Katrina, Hurricane 31, 32, 39–40, 42, 44, 46, 50
Kenya 19
Keohane, N. 56
kidnapping 144
Kim Dae Jung 190
Korea 7, 189, 192, 194
   see also Democratic People's Republic of Korea (DPRK); Republic of Korea (ROK)

Korea-United States (KORUS) Free Trade Agreement (FTA) 196–7, 199
Kousky, C. 57
Kunreuther, Howard C. 3, 79, 81

labor 231–4, 235, 243, 251
Lagadec, Patrick 63
Landes, William 19
Landmines Treaty 20
Langewiesche, W. 78
Läpple, Klaus 127, 133
large airport hypothesis 148, 149–50, 158–63, 164
LaTourrette, Tom 8, 275, 276, 279
Lee, D. 148, 149, 150, 151, 152, 153, 154, 164
legal immigration, and border closure 204, 205, 207, 222–3, 229, 241–4, 245–6, 248
Leung, Billy (Rose et al.) 8
Li, Quan 6
Lia, Brynjar 15
liberalization 11–12
Libya 21, 171
Little, R. 108–9
loans 52–3
local interdependencies 49
Lockerbie bombing (1988) 56
London
  CONTEST strategy 105–6
  contingency planning 99–101
  crowded public places 106–7
  as economic target 4–5, 92–3
  financial sector 94
  resilience planning 101–5, 108–11
  risk reduction measures 94–6
  size of financial sector 107
  terrorism insurance 96–9
London bombings (2005) 5, 77, 79, 106–7, 110, 120, 122
London First 104, 110–11
London Resilience Partnership 103–5
long-term insurance 53–4
long-term loans 52–3
Los Angeles 10, 16, 17, 21, 149
losses, insured 42–6, 77, 96, 106–7
  see also border closure
low-cost carriers (LCCs) 149–50, 152

Lower Manhattan Security Initiative 110
Lu, Z. 198

Madrid train bombings (2004)
  choice of target 28, 93
  events of 119
  stock market effects 1, 5, 119–20, 122–32
Major, John 93
Maldives 38
Malta 56
market share 232, 233, 234–5, 243, 251
Marsh & McLennan 66
Maximum Abbreviated Injury Scale (MAIS) 280
McKesson 23
media 122–32
Meliá (hotel chain) 127
Melnick, R. 121, 122
Merrill Lynch 32, 66
Metrovacesa 130
Mexico 272–3
MI6 (Secret Intelligence Service) 125
MIB index 126, 128, 130
Michel-Kerjan, Erwann O. 3, 63
Middle East peace process 20
MIGA (Multilateral Investment Guarantee Agency) 143–4
migration *see* illegal immigration, and border closure; immigration; legal immigration, and border closure
military action 177
Mississippi Power 35
Mitchell, Michael 137
mitigation of risk 51–4, 57–62, 65–9
Mitsubishi 13
modeling terrorism approaches 278–9
  see also NIEMO (National Interstate Economic Model); REMI (Regional Economic Models Inc.) Policy Insight Model
Mongolia 198
Moore, James E., II (Gordon et al.) 7
morbidity 280–81
Morocco 14
mortality 280–81
Moss, D. 84
Mossad (Institute for Intelligence and Special Operations) 125

Motorola 143
Mueller, J. 78
multilateral cooperation
  global terrorism 15–16
  information protocols 132
  investment as antiterrorism strategy 191–4, 198–9
    Kaesong Industrial Complex (KIC) 194–7
    resilience planning 109–10
    Tumen River Project 197–8, 199
multinational corporations 1, 13, 14
mutual support, and global terrorism 10, 16–22
Myanmar 38
myopia 47–8, 51–4

Nagasaki 78
Napoleoni, L. 2
Nasdaq index 126
National Counter Terrorism Security Office (NaCTSO) 107
nations, mutual support of 18–19
natural disasters 24–5, 51–4, 55
natural gas 1–2
natural resources 197
negative externalities 57
negligence 26–7
Netherlands 14, 20, 63
New York 31, 77, 85, 93, 109–10
news 122–32
NH Hoteles 127, 130
NIEMO (National Interstate Economic Model)
  air travel, and border closure 202–4, 207, 210–19, 229
  economic losses from border closure 206–7
  immigration, and border closure 204–6, 207, 222–5, 229
  shopping, and border closure 206, 207, 226–7, 229
  trade, and border closure 204, 205, 207, 220–21, 229
Nigeria 1
Nike 27
Nikkei index 126
9/11 Commission Recommendations Act 271, 272

9/11 terrorist attacks
  air travel effects 6, 150–64, 165–6
  air travel effects hypotheses 148–50
  business continuity 32
  global interdependencies 45
  global terrorism 14
  insurance 47
  international responses 101–2
  losses from 42, 43, 77
  stock market effects 2, 5, 120, 122
Nitsch, V. 172, 176
Nokia 18, 23
non-governmental organizations (NGOs) 19–20
North Korea 7, 78, 189, 193, 194
  see also Democratic People's Republic of Korea (DPRK)
Northern Ireland 96
Northridge earthquake 253
Norway 13, 20
nuclear, biological, chemical and radiological (NBCR) attacks
  anthrax attacks 45, 62–3, 76, 85–7
  insurance coverage 4, 76–80, 87–8
  international action 87
  response to 102, 104
  and Terrorism Risk Insurance Program Reauthorization Act (TRIPRA) 75–6, 81–4, 88
  workers' compensation 84–7
nuclear reactors 45, 76, 80–81
nuclear weapons 76, 78, 188–9, 199

O'Brien, G. 103
OECD (Organisation for Economic Co-operation and Development) 177–82
Office of Emergency Management (New York) 109
oil 1–2, 230, 254
Olympic Games, London (2012) 105
OPIC (Overseas Private Investment Corporation) 142–3
Organization of Petroleum Exporting Countries (OPEC) 230
output 231, 232, 233, 243, 251

Pakistan 13, 14, 27
Palestine 199
Pan America flight 103 crash (1988) 56

pandemics 7–8, 12, 38, 44–5, 201–2
Paris 93
Park, Jiyoung (Gordon et al.) 7
Park Chung Hee 189
Passel, J.S. 242, 269
Payne, J. 48
pharmaceutical industry 27
Philippines 14
Philips Electronics 18, 23
Poland 13, 20
police 16, 109
political instability risk 140–46, 194, 197
Pool Reinsurance (Pool Re) 97–9, 101, 102, 106, 110
population 231, 232, 233, 235, 243
  see also crowded public places
Portugal 20
postal security 62–4
PostEurop 64
prevention 30
Price-Anderson Act 80–81, 83
prices
  and investment 251
  migration effects 243
  REMI model 232, 233, 234, 235, 259–61, 262–5
PricewaterhouseCoopers (PwC) 69
process design 37
process safety management (PSM) 25–6
Procter & Gamble 32
production costs 232, 233, 243, 251, 259–66, 269–70
production rescheduling 253
Project Argus (UK) 108
Project Griffin (UK) 108
Proliferation Security Initiative (PSI) 20–21
protection, assessment of need for 46–51
Provisional Irish Republican Army (PIRA) 4–5, 93, 94, 98
public places 106–7, 109

quality of life 281, 282–3

radiological weapons *see* nuclear, biological, chemical and radiological (NBCR) attacks

RAND Corporation 85, 207
ransom 144
Read, P. 103
recovery 30
  see also resilience
Redfearn, C. 149
redlining, of insurance cover 96
redundant capacity 36
Régie Autonome des Transports Parisiens (RATP) 28
regionalism 198
regionalization 198
regulation 62, 271–2
  see also terrorism security regulations
REMI (Regional Economic Models Inc.) Policy Insight Model
  duration of border closure 249–50, 253–4
  economic impact of border closure 228–9, 244–55
  exports, and border closure 228, 237–9, 244, 245–6, 248, 250–51, 253
  immigration, and border closure 234, 241–4, 245–6, 248, 269–70
  imports, and border closure 235–7, 244, 245–6, 248, 250–51, 253, 259–66
  international travel, and border closure 239–41, 245–6, 248, 253, 267–8
  investment 250–52
  methodology 8, 230–35, 255
  simultaneous shutdown of all activities 247–8
Republic of Korea (ROK)
  and Democratic People's Republic of Korea (DPRK) 187, 192, 193, 194, 199
  economy 189, 190
  Kaesong Industrial Complex (KIC) 194–7, 199
  reunification with Democratic People's Republic of Korea (DPRK) 7, 189, 193, 194
  Tumen River Project 197–8
resilience 2–3, 101–6, 108–11, 244, 252–4
  see also business continuity

Resilient Enterprise, The (Sheffi) 10, 18
responsibility for attacks 122, 132
retail sales, and border closure 206, 207, 214, 226–7, 229, 267–8
Revolutionary Armed Forces of Colombia (FARC) 139
Richardson, Harry W. 7
ricin gas 79
ring of steel (London) 94–5, 101, 107
risk
   break-even analysis of terrorism regulations 8–9, 273–7
   and global interdependencies 42–6
   global risks 54–5, 65–9
   and individual behaviour 46–51
   insurance premiums 53–4
   management 30, 101
   mitigation 51–4, 57–62, 65–9
   from political instability 140–46, 194, 197
   rating urban centres 98
   reduction 94–6, 141–4, 278–9
Risk Management Systems 85
Riyadh 93
Rose, Adam Z. 8
Rose, Andrew 172, 252, 253
Royal and SunAlliance 126
Rubinstein, Y. 149
Russell, Thomas 4, 81
Russia 20, 190, 192, 197

safety 25–6
San Francisco 10, 16, 77
Sandler, T. 56
Santayana, George 12
sarin gas attacks 76, 79, 111
SARS (Severe Acute Respiratory Syndrome) 44
Saudi Arabia 171
scenario analysis 207
Schelling, T. 49, 62
Schkade, D. 48
Schumacher, D. 172, 176
security, cost of 149
security externalities 45
security plans 100
Segui-Gomez, M. 282
September 11, 2001 terrorist attacks *see* 9/11 terrorist attacks
severity of attacks 183

Shapiro, J.M. 148
share dealing *see* stock markets
Sheffi, Yossi 2, 3, 10, 18
shopping, and border closure 206, 207, 214, 226–7, 229, 267–8
Siems, T. 120
Simkins, B. 121
simulation 278–9
   see also NIEMO (National Interstate Economic Model); REMI (Regional Economic Models Inc.) Policy Insight Model
Singapore 20
Slovic, P. 78
Small Business Administration (SBA) 50–51
Soll, J.B. 49
Somalia 38
South Africa 13, 87
South Korea 7, 189, 193, 194
   see also Republic of Korea (ROK)
Southwest Airlines 36
Spain 20, 87, 122–32
speed 36
Sri Lanka 14, 38
stock markets
   Madrid train bombings (2004) 1, 5, 119–20, 122–32
   and terrorism 120–22, 184
   trading by terrorist groups 2
storms 44
strategic emergency plans 104
strategic gaming 207–8
strikes 27–8
Sudan 2, 14
suicide attacks 102
Sullivan, John P. (Lieutenant) 17
sunshine policy 190
Sunstein, S. 78
supply chains 18, 57–62
surveillance 102
Sweden 45
Swiss Re 66
Switzerland 14

Tanzania 19
tariffs 28
technology 11, 14, 21
telecommunications 203–4, 215, 216–17

terrorism
  adaptation of methods 278
  as business 2
  business collaboration with 5, 136–40
  cost-benefit analysis of security measures 8–9, 273–85
  deaths resulting from 78
  Democratic People's Republic of Korea (DPRK) 187–8
  effect on trade 6–7, 169–72, 182–4
  empirical analysis of trade effects 172–82
  and financial markets 74, 120–22
  global 10, 14–22, 170–71
  and global business 1–2, 191–4, 198–9
  global interdependencies 55–7
  and globalization 2–3
  and insurance 74–5, 96–9
  as intentional disruption 28
  meaning of 14, 170
  nuclear, biological, chemical and radiological (NBCR) risks 75–80
  and stock markets 120–22, 184
  targets 19
Terrorism Early Warning (TEW) unit, Los Angeles 17, 21
Terrorism Risk Insurance Act (TRIA) 74, 75, 82, 86, 88
Terrorism Risk Insurance Extension Act (TRIEA) 74, 82, 83
Terrorism Risk Insurance Program Reauthorization Act (TRIPRA) 74–6, 81–4, 88
terrorism security regulations
  benefit assessment 62, 271–2
  benefit estimation 277–85
  break-even analysis 273–7, 284–5
  catastrophic events 284–5
  Western Hemisphere Travel Initiative in the Land Environment (WHTI-L) 272–7
testing emergency responses 104–5
Texas 205, 207
Thailand 38
threats, and business continuity 27–8
Tierney, K. 253
time horizons 47–8, 51–4

tipping point, of loss mitigation 61–2
Tokyo subway gas attack (1995) 79, 93, 111
tornadoes 24–5
tourism
  effects of border closure 239–41, 248, 255, 267–8
  Madrid train bombings (2004) 126–7, 130
  9/11 terrorist attack effects 148, 163–4, 165–6
  see also international travel, and border closure
Toyota 13, 18, 40
trade
  Democratic People's Republic of Korea (DPRK) 196–7, 199
  effect of terrorism on 6–7, 169–72, 182–4
  empirical analysis of terrorism effects 172–82
  extent of 183–4
  liberalization 11–12
  losses from border closure 204, 205, 207, 220–21, 229
  see also exports, and border closure; imports
trade associations 62
transnational corporations (TNCs)
  Chiquita Brands International (CBI) case 136–40
  effects on host country 144–6
  political instability risk 140–44
  see also business
transnational terrorism 10, 14–22, 170–71
travel see air travel; international travel, and border closure; tourism
Tropical Storm Agnes (1972) 50
tsunamis 38
TUI 126
Tumen River Project 7, 197–8, 199
Tversky, A. 78
typhoons 44

uncertainty 3–4, 250–52
uninsurable risks 76–80
Union Carbide 80
Unión Fenosa 130

United Kingdom (UK)
  CONTEST strategy 105–6
  crowded public places 106–7
  as economic target 4–5, 92–3, 106–7
  emergency response testing 104
  global business 14
  influenza vaccine 27
  mutual support 20–21
  nuclear, biological, chemical and radiological (NBCR) risks 87
  postal security 63
  regional threats 108
  stock market effects of Madrid train bombings 126, 128, 130
United Nations (UN) 16, 19–21, 197
United States (US)
  air travel, and border closure 6, 202–4, 207, 210–19, 229, 267–8
  anthrax crisis 62–3
  and China 250
  Chiquita Brands International (CBI) case 137–8
  and Democratic People's Republic of Korea (DPRK) 192, 194, 196–7
  disaster assistance 49–51
  economic impact of border closure 7–8, 201–2, 206–8, 228–9, 244–55
  emergency response testing 104
  exports, and border closure 228, 237–9, 244, 245–6, 248, 250–51, 253
  global business 14
  global terrorism 15, 169, 187–8, 198
  illegal immigration, and border closure 205–6, 207, 224–5, 229, 241–4, 245–6, 248, 269–70
  imports 2, 28
  imports, and border closure 228, 235–7, 244, 245–6, 248, 250–51, 253, 259–66
  individuals' risk estimations 47
  influenza vaccine 27
  international travel, and border closure 228, 239–41, 245–6, 248, 253, 267–8
  legal immigration, and border closure 204, 205, 207, 222–3, 229, 241–4, 245–6, 248

  mutual support 10, 16, 17, 20–21
  nuclear, biological, chemical and radiological (NBCR) risks 4, 74–6, 77, 81–7, 88
  oil price shocks 230
  shopping, and border closure 206, 207, 214, 226–7
  simultaneous shutdown of all activities 201–2, 247–8
  stock market effects of terrorism 126, 128, 130, 184
  strikes 27–8
  trade, and border closure 204, 205, 207, 220–21, 229
  workers' compensation 84–7
Universal Postal Union 63
UPS 18, 38, 40
urban terrorism
  CONTEST strategy 105–6
  economic targets 92–3
  fortification of London 94–6
  resilience planning 99–105
  terrorism insurance 96–9
US Coast Guard 40
US Customs and Border Protection (CBP) 272
US Postal Service 64
USIO model 202

value of a statistical life (VSL) 282
vehicle-borne improvised explosive devices (VBIEDs) 93, 94, 102, 107
victims, number of 122, 132
Viscusi, W.K. 281

wages
  and investment 251
  migration effects 243, 269–70
  REMI model 232, 233, 234, 235
Wall, H.J. 173, 176
Wal-Mart 13, 31, 32, 35
Washington 77
weapons of mass destruction (WMD) 46
  see also nuclear, biological, chemical and radiological (NBCR) attacks
weather early warning systems 38
Wei, Dan (Rose et al.) 8

Western Hemisphere Travel Initiative in the Land Environment (WHTI-L) 272–7, 279, 282, 283, 285
Wharton Risk Management and Decision Processes Center 3, 53, 66
willingness to pay 48, 281–2
Willis, Henry H. 8, 275, 276, 279
workers' compensation 84–7
World Bank 20, 192
World Economic Forum (WEF) 3, 20, 55, 66, 69
World Health Organization (WHO) 38
World Social Forum 20
World Trade Centre terrorist attacks *see* 9/11 terrorist attacks
World Trade Organization (WTO) 12, 20, 28
World War I 12
World War II 12, 15, 253, 259

Yongbyon nuclear reprocessing plant 188

Zeckhauser, R. 56, 57